Our Monthly Newspapers from Year 6
January – December 2017

© 2018 Gabriel Communications, Inc.
All rights reserved
Including the right of reproduction in whole or in part in any form

ISBN: 978-0-9893989-3-0

Published by Gabriel Communications, Inc.
916 Harpeth Valley Place
Nashville, TN 37221

To order more copies:
www.cfrvideos.com
www.larrycountrydiner.com
800-820-5405

CONTENTS

January
Johnny Counterfit serious author — 5
Roast & Toast Larry Black — 18
Auction of the Stars — 20
Gordon Mote Gammy nomination — 23

February
Granddaughter of Jean Shepard murdered — 24
Daily and Vincent Opry Induction — 29
Hee Haw Producer dies at 88 — 37
Jeannie Seely Release Party — 41
Moe Pitney welcomes new baby — 44

March
Crystal Gayle inducted into Opry — 47
20th Anniversary CFR Cruise — 51
Lefty and David Frizzell — 55
Mac Davis — 59
The Bellamy Brothers World Tour — 60

April
Jeanne Pruett — 67
Henry Slaughter 90 sings God's praises — 70
Dottie and Shelly West — 75
Tennessee Ramblers — 80

May
Jimmy Wayne Homeless to Success — 82
Singer/Songwriter Craig Campbell — 90
The Kendall's — 95
LuLu Roman-A changed life — 97

June
Loretta Lynn suffers stroke — 104
Larry's Country Diner in Branson — 107
Mike Snider: Humor and Music — 112
Narvel Felts — 117

July
John Anderson receives spotlight — 121
Moe Bandy's newest CD — 122
Judd's to release Greatest Hits CD — 123
Billy Grammer — 124
Jerry Clower who made us laugh — 125

August
Ray Stevens CabaRay — 136
Bobby Bare 100 Greatest Artists — 140
Mark Chesnutt 2017 Tour Dates — 146
Charley Pride Life Time Achievement — 147
Shane Owens making music — 149

September
Glen Campbell: Talent, Success, Love — 156
Tim Atwood, former Opry piano player — 160
The Maddox Brothers and Rose — 164
Kenny Rogers Farewell Concert — 167

October
Don Williams Dead at 78 — 179
Troy Gentry-Lucky to Have Been Here — 181
Rose Lee and Joe Maphis — 190
Homer and Jethro-"Lives well Writ" — 191

November
Jeannie Seely 50th Opry Anniversary — 202
Jimmy Dean: Country Legends of Past — 207
Larry's Country Diner Shines in Branson — 210
Cousin Jody- More than Just a Funny Face — 216

December
Merle Haggard Museum in Nashville — 224
Crook and Case Past & Present — 226
Bill Anderson's 80th Birthday Celebration — 229
Grandpa Jones Comedic and Musical — 234

JANUARY

Johnny Counterfit proves he is more than a comedian with a new serious novel on Kennedy

When you think of Johnny Counterfit, you think of comedy. But his new book, JFK: Averting the Assassination, is anything but comedy. He has written a serious Sci-Fi book that is not a conspiracy-laden, finger pointing worn out story. Applying historic facts blended with fiction, Counterfit, after decades of research, captures the wit and personality of President Kennedy.

"The initial writing of my book coincided with the 30th anniversary of a moment in history nearly all of us would have wanted to change, November 22, 1963." Counterfit says, "I was careful to steer clear of the conspiracy theories, finger pointing, and vicious claims that have mutated over the years. After writing it, I filed it away and pretty much forgot about it due to my show business career and family responsibilities."

As timing would have it, John F. Kennedy would have turned 100 in 2017, so Counterfit decided to release the book to coincide with that date. In June 2016, as he read his original draft, "I was drawn into the story to such a degree, I resolved to make the story deeper by further developing the characters, and use my decades of research on the Kennedy administration, in an attempt to make readers feel as though I personally knew President and Mrs. Kennedy, by virtue of my conversations with them, in the book; I hope I have accomplished that."

Finishing the rewrite ahead of schedule, "I weighed the pro and con of presenting a book containing just under 15,000 words. Because I've been in show business for nearly 36 years, I reminded myself the importance, to the audience, of keeping a song, a joke, and a story to the point, without extraneous fluff, so I present my book in it's current form I deliberately released my book into the marketplace on November 22, 2016."

The premise of the book is that the author travels back in time to convince President Kennedy not to ride in the motorcade through Dallas, Texas, on November 22, 1963. In addition to the plot in Dealey Plaza, there are two additional plots to murder John F. Kennedy involving Air Force One, and explosive-laden aviate fuel truck, and Kennedy's Lincoln Continental limousine.

This book pierces the fabric of time gone by, and takes the reader back to prevent the most sinister crime in our nation's history.

MORE ABOUT JOHNNY COUNTERFIT ON P16

January 2017

1 Night. 1 Place. 1 Time:
A Heroes & Friends Tribute To Randy Travis

On February 8, 2017, the stars will gather for a tribute to one of country music's finest, Randy Travis. The event, titled 1 Night. 1 Place. 1 Time.: A Heroes & Friends Tribute to Randy Travis, will feature performances from Alabama, Kenny Rogers, Rodney Atkins, Chris Janson, Jamey Johnson, Montgomery Gentry, Michael Ray, Ricky Skaggs, Michael W. Smith, The Randy Travis Band, Tanya Tucker, Josh Turner and more to be announced. Tickets for the highly anticipated event go on sale to the general public Friday, December 9 at 11:00am CST at all Ticketmaster locations and the Bridgestone Arena Box Office.

In October, Randy Travis was officially inducted into The Country Music Hall of Fame. The multi-platinum country giant suffered a massive stroke in 2013 and has made miraculous strides towards recovery since, recently singing "Amazing Grace" at his Country Music Hall of Fame induction ceremony as well as the tagline to his iconic "Forever and Ever, Amen" at the 2016 CMA Awards in November alongside numerous country legends and stars.

A portion of the proceeds will go to the Randy Travis Foundation; a 501(c)3 non-profit that raises money for stroke research and rehabilitation.

"Nashville is coming together on February 8 for one night in one place and at one time to give back to their friend and musical hero, Randy Travis. It's amazing to see the support that Randy has received from the music industry since his stroke. We're thrilled to have all of these artists come out and pay tribute to him," said producer of the event and Travis' manager, Tony Conway of Conway Entertainment Group.

1 Night. 1 Place. 1 Time.: A Heroes & Friends Tribute to Randy Travis is produced by Mary Travis along with Tony Conway of Conway Entertainment Group, Mike Smardak of Outback Concerts of Tennessee, Inc. who is also the promoter of the event and Kirt Webster of Webster and Associates.

CFR News
is published monthly by
Gabriel Communications, Inc.
P.O. Box 210796,
Nashville, TN 37221
615-673-2846

Larry Black, Publisher
Renae Johnson, General Manager
Paula Underwood Winters, Editor

Subscriptions: $29.95 yearly
Renewals: $24.95 yearly
To subscribe or renew:
1-800-820-5405

NEW 5 DVDs

$79.80
+ $6.95 s/h

Hosted by Bill Anderson, we've honored the one and only... MERLE HAGGARD. Including three of his sons, Marty, Noel and Ben. This is the singer songwriter that so many of today's country artists point to as their inspiration. Many of today's country artists sang Merle's songs and told their stories of life on the road and in concert with Merle. Others included in the show were: Mac Wiseman, Ronnie Reno, David Frizzell, Daryle Singletary, John Conlee, Teea Goans, Bobby Bare, Ray Benson, Dallas Wayne, Rhonda Vincent, Vince Gill, Paul Franklin, Mark Wills, Emily Gimble, T. Graham Brown, Mo Pitney, Jeannie Seely, Jim Lauderdale, The Isaacs, Tony Booth, Gene Watson.

1-800-820-5405
www.cfrvideos.com

January 2017

Nadine
The Church Lady

Lord, give me a sense of humor,
Give me the grace to see a joke,
To get some humor out of life,
And to pass it on to other folk.

Funny Hymn Titles

Dentist....
"Crown Him with Many Crowns"

Weatherman...
"There Shall Be Showers of Blessings"

Contractor...
"The Church's One Foundation"

I look forward to reading my Country's Family Reunion paper. Oh, by the way who is Nadine's REAL husband?
Marilyn Payne
Linville, VA

NADINE's husband is Homer. For more information on Nadine see her website at www.nadinenadine.com

Treasures sent to us by fans of the show!

Recipe from Johnny Lee

THIS IS HOW I MAKE CHUNKY CHILI

I get the butcher to cut up in cubes a sirloin steak or I cut it up myself, and I will add, when I have it, a package of venison, same way, cubed. Shake the meat in a sack with flour, garlic powder, salt and pepper. Shake off pieces of meat and sear in a very hot skillet with some, not a log, of olive oil, just to brown it, hot and fast, like my first marriage. Add in chili powder, like Gilley's or any store brand. Add 1/2 package to meat while it is searing, add other 1/2 when you put it in the pot you cook in.

- At least 2 chopped tomatoes
- 1 lg. can Hunt's tomato sauce
- 1 med. can tomato paste
- 4 or 5 cloves chopped garlic
- 1 beer, Bud or Miller lite, have one yourself, it's fun while you make chili
- salt and pepper to taste
- 1 chopped jalapeno pepper, take out the seeds
- 1/4 tsp cayenne pepper
- 1 can any brand you like chili beans, add only if you want.

Cook on low heat a couple of hours, stirring when you need to. On the side, chopped onions and grated cheese for toppers.

Serve on macaroni if you like.

January 2017

Singer Songwriters

By Sasha Kay Dunavant

Marty Robbins

Throughout the history of Country Music, thousands of songs have been written and performed. Many of those songs were written by famous performers. Some were written for a star's own records, while others were created to be sung by another artist. This Singer-Songwriter Series explores some of those talented individuals whose work we know and love.

Maybe it was those tales of the American West that his grandfather told him. Maybe it was just what came naturally to him after he taught himself how to play guitar in the Navy during World War II. Whatever gave Marty Robbins the imagination, skill and giddy-up to write hit after hit made him a legend.

"I'll Go on Alone" was written by Robbins and became his first hit in 1952. Robbins wrote "I Couldn't Keep From Crying" in 1953, and the song reached No. 5 on the Country chart. Later, it was included on Johnny Cash's 1960 album, "Now, There was a Song."

Robbins went on to host his own TV show on KPHO-TV, meeting Little Jimmie Dickens when he made a guest appearance on the show. Dickens introduced Robbins to Columbia Records and the music lovers have benefited since.

"A White Sport Coat (and a Pink Carnation)" was released on March 4, 1957. Robbins wrote the Rock and Roll song in 20 minutes, inspired by looking out the window of a car and seeing all the teenagers getting prepared for prom. The song became Robbins's third No. 1 hit and sold more than a million copies. It was declared Gold and reached No. 1 on Australian charts. "A White Sport Coat (and a Pink Carnation)" became a hit for later recordings released by Terry Dene, The King Brothers, Johnny Desmond and Jimmy Buffet.

"El Paso," written by Robbins was the first track released in September 1959 from "Gunfighter Ballads and Trail Songs." It became a major hit on both Country and Pop charts and also received the Grammy for Best Country & Western Recording in 1961. The Grateful Dead, Michael Martin Murphy, the Mills Brothers, Tom Russell, Max Staling and many others have covered "El Paso."

"Big Iron," a track on "Gunfighter Ballads and Trail Songs," was released in September 1959. Robbins tells a story of a town, Agua Fria, that fears an outlaw named Texas Red will kill their ranger. In the end the ranger kills Texas Red with his gun, which is referred to as "the big iron on his hip." "Big Iron" reached No. 5 on the Billboard Country Chart. Robbins wrote 1961's "The Hands You're Holding Now" for Country Music artist, Skeeter Davis. It reached No. 11 on the Billboard Magazine Hot C & W Sides chart.

"Don't Worry," written by Robbins reached No. 3 on the Hot 100, making it a successful crossover hit. Robbins wrote "I Told The Brook" in 1961. Billy Thorpe later recorded the ballad.

1962's "Devil Woman was the seventh single pinned by Robbins to reach No. 1 on the Country charts.

January 2017

reached and remained No. 1 on Country Charts for two weeks.

Robbins was a prolific writer, penning such memorable songs as "Sugaree," "San Angelo," "Pain and Misery," "Tennessee Toddy," "The Cowboy in the Continental Suit," "Pretty Words," "Old Red," "A Castle in the Sky," "All Around Cowboy" and "Cigarettes and Coffee Blues."

Robbins recorded more than 500 songs and won two Grammy Awards. He was named The Artist of the Decade (1960-1969) by the Academy of Country Music. A personal accomplishment rare in the entertainment business was that he had been married to his wife, Marizona, for 34 years when he died on Dec. 8, 1982.

It peaked at No. 16 on the Pop chart. The song has been translated to several languages, including Spanish and Serbian. Trini Lopez also recorded "Devil Woman" in 1968.

Robbins's tenth No. 1 single, "Begging to You," spent 23 weeks on the charts in 1963. "Tonight Carmen" spent one week at No. 1 and 12 weeks on the charts in 1967. Numerous artists have recorded "You Gave Me a Mountain," which Robbins wrote about personal struggles and setbacks. The passionate and meaningful words reminds listeners to be strong and grateful. 55 year-old Frankie Laine's 1969 version of the song was even more successful than Robbins, reaching No. 24 on the Billboard Hot 100 and remaining on the Top 40 for seven consecutive weeks. Robbins's 1970's hit, "My Woman, My Woman, My Wife," spent a week at No. 1 and won the Grammy for Best Country Song in 1971.

He wrote the 1972's, "Kate" for Johnny Cash. It was the third single from Johnny Cash's album "A Thing Called Love." It reached No. 2 on Billboards Hot Country Singles chart and reached No. 1 on the Canadian Country charts as well.

"El Paso City" was written and released by Robbins in March 1976. The song is a revised, sequel-like version of Robbins's 1959 hit, "El Paso." The hit

Look who's on the Diner this week!

Thursdays at 7 p.m. central Saturdays at 10 p.m. central

RIDERS IN THE SKY
Jan. 5 & 7

DALLAS WAYNE
Jan. 12 & 14

JEANNIE SEELY
Jan. 19 & 21

EXILE
Jan. 26 & 28

January 2017

Dolly's fund will provide monthly assistance to those who lost homes in wildfires

In a video message released November 30, Dolly Parton announced a new effort by The Dollywood Company and The Dollywood Foundation to establish a fund to assist the victims of the Great Smoky Mountain wildfires in Tennessee. The new My People Fund will provide $1000 each month to Sevier County families who lost their homes.

"I've always believed charity begins at home and my home is some place special," Parton explained. "That's why I've asked my Dollywood Companies—including the Dollywood theme park, and DreamMore Resort; my dinner theater attractions including Dixie Stampede and Lumberjack Adventure; and my Dollywood Foundation—to help me establish the My People Fund.

"We want to provide a hand up to those families who have lost everything in the fires. I know it has been a trying time for my people and this assistance will help get them back on their feet."

Anyone who would like to contribute to the My People Fund may visit dollywoodfoundation.org.

A highly-awarded and widely-recognized leader in the amusement industry, The Dollywood Company consists of the 150-acre Dollywood theme park; the 35-acre Dollywood's Splash Country; Dollywood's DreamMore Resort; and Dollywood's Smoky Mountain Cabins. As unique as its namesake and owner Dolly Parton, Dollywood is the 2010 Applause Award winner, the theme park industry's highest accolade; winner of nearly 30 Golden Ticket Awards; and recipient of 25 Brass Ring Awards for Live Entertainment (more than any other theme park in the world). In 2014, Dollywood was named a top three US theme park by USA Today and TripAdvisor recognized Dollywood as a top 20 worldwide theme park in 2015. Dollywood is open nine months a year (late March through early January) and offers rides and attractions, shows, and a dozen crafters authentic to the East Tennessee region. Dollywood's Splash Country, recognized by the Travel Channel as one of the country's most beautiful waterparks and named 2009's Must-See Waterpark by the International Association of Amusement Parks & Attractions, operates from Memorial Day to Labor Day. The 300-room Dollywood's DreamMore Resort provides guests spectacular mountain views and family-friendly amenities next door to Dollywood theme park and Dollywood's Splash Country. Dollywood's Smoky Mountain Cabins offers luxurious cabin accommodations overlooking Dollywood. For more information, call 1-800-DOLLYWOOD or visit dollywood.com. Operating days and hours vary.

January 2017

COUNTRY LEGENDS OF THE PAST & PRESENT
BY TOM WOOD

The Dixie Yodeler was Bashful.

Really.

The year was 1936. Zeke Clements, an Alabama native who over the previous decade had become known to country music fans as the "Dixie Yodeler" for his falsetto vocalizations and colorful cowboy outfits, was in Hollywood auditioning for a role in that was perfectly suited for his talents.

It was a new movie that included eight musical numbers. An actor for the character in question had been hired, but the producer needed a singer who could handle the specific yodeling duties for this character, one of seven singing coal-miners for this particular number.

The song? As the yodeling might suggest, it was aptly titled "The Silly Song."

The producer? Walt Disney himself.

The movie? Yep, the historic, full-length animated feature Snow White and the Seven Dwarfs.

And the yodeling Bashful was in reality Zeke Clements.

Of course, you'll not find his name — none of the actors were listed —among the credits, just their roles, including Snow, Doc, Sneezy, Dopey (my favorite), etc. Not even Disney received a credit as producer — pretty cool, actually, to keep the focus on the movie and not the actors. The movie of course was an instant classic, nominated for the musical score and earning an honorary Oscar for Disney for its ground-breaking animation. The movie cost approximately $2 million in 1937 dollars and earned nearly $22 million in its 1938 release, according to figures at the International Movie DataBase (IMDB). And thanks to re-releases, VHS, DVR and other iterations over the decades, the movie has made nearly $185 million in the U.S. alone, according to IMDB.

Zeke Clements helped make it happen — and he wasn't bashful in letting people know about his role in the film.

Of course, that wasn't the only highlight of his career.

Zeke began his career as one the Oklahoma Cowboys, found success in Nashville with his Bronco Busters as a member of the Grand Ole Opry cast, and then he headed to Hollywood for a stint as a singing cowboy in B-Westerns.

Following the success of Snow White and the Seven Dwarfs, Zeke returned to Nashville, where he spent most of his remaining days until his death in 1994. He formed a new band, the Western Swing Gang, and earned recognition as both a singer and songwriter, though he performed for a while on The Louisiana Hayride and lived in Florida for a time, playing in a Dixieland band.

Zeke's first No. 1 hit as a writer was "Smoke On the Water," co-written with Earl Nunn and recorded by Red Foley in 1945. He followed that in 1948 with "Just a Little Lovin' (Will Go a Long, Long Way)" for Eddy Arnold. One of the best-known songs Zeke wrote and recorded was the popular, up-tempo "Brown's Ferry Boogie" in 1948.

Those writing credits earned Clements membership in the Nashville Songwriters Hall of Fame in 1971, the second year of its existence. He was one of 19 writers inducted that year, along with the likes of Bill Monroe, Tex Ritter, Smiley Burnette, Bradley Kincaid and many other legends.

That's certainly nothing to be bashful about.

Author Tom Wood, who writes thrillers and Westerns, is a regular contributor to Country Family Reunion News. Reach him at tomwoodauthor.com

January 2017

A special Tribute for Jean Shepard at Nashville Palace

The great Connie Smith.

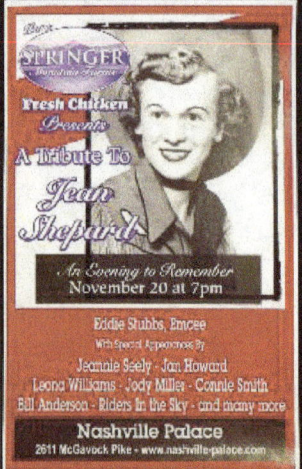

Riders in the Sky opened the show in "The Cowboy Way."

Mandy Barnett sang her heart out.

Below: David Frizzell (second from right) presented Jean's sons, Harold Hawkshaw, Corey and Donnie with a special drawing he did of Jean.

Kim Brown Corwin and Becky Brown.

Husky siblings.

Jeannie Seely, Jan Howard, Jody Miller and Leona Williams performed separately and together.

Photos by Lynn Woodruff Gray and Renae Johnson

Emcee Eddie Stubbs from the Opry kept the show moving.

The wonderful Bill Anderson!

January 2017

It's A Family Tradition

By Sasha Kay Dunavant

Shooter & Terry Jennings – Sons of Waylon Jennings

The legend of Waylon Jennings lives through his creative and motivated sons, Terry and Shooter.

Born when his father was only 19 years old, Terry Jennings has been around music his entire life. Terry Vance Jennings is one of four children with Waylon's first wife, Maxine Lawrence.

Terry was introduced to the music business at an early age through his work as production manager for his father and is respected for his extensive experience at all levels of the business, including management of major label acts since 1972. He's also worked for booking agencies, publishing companies and as a talent scout for major label companies like RCA Records. He is the founder and CEO of Korban Music Group LLC, a full service management, consulting and publishing company.

In 2016 he published his book, Waylon: Tales of My Outlaw Dad, which not only tells the story of his father, it explores Terry's relationship with him. Terry discusses life on the road with Waylon Jennings, their recreational drug use and the day Waylon quit doing drugs cold turkey in 1985. The book addresses myths about his late father and redefines the Outlaw Movement.

"It could be called the Survival Movement instead of the Outlaw Movement because that is all they were trying to do," he told the Nashville Tennessean in an interview.

Terry writes about how much his father loved the Highwaymen – Johnny Cash, Willie Nelson and Kris Kristofferson, and Terry received encouragement from Waylon when he expressed his passion for writing a book about their adventures to his father before Waylon's death in 2002.

Terry's younger half brother, Waylon Albright "Shooter" Jennings, is the only son of Waylon and fourth wife Jessie Colter. Born in 1979, Shooter lived his early years touring with his parents. His love for musical instruments was noted early when he began playing the drums at five years old and the piano at age eight.

January 2017

When Shooter was 14, he began playing guitar and entered a school talent competition with his Industrial Rock Band, KiiRaven. It was the guitar and the love for Southern Rock that inspired the forming of his Los Angeles rock band, Stargunn, in 2001. In 2002 Stargunn was featured on "I've Always Been Crazy: A Tribute to Waylon Jennings."

After eight locally successful years with Stargunn, Shooter eventually returned to his Country Music roots with a new band, the 357s. He debuted with single, "4th of July" from his 2005 album, "Put the O Back in Country." A year later Jennings second album, "Electric Rodeo," was released. The singles, "This Ole' Wheel" and "Walk of Life" were released from his 2007 album, "The Wolf."

A compilation album entitled "Black Magic: The Best of Shooter Jennings and the 357s" was released in 2009. It includes Jennings's version of his father's song, "Lonesome, On'ry and Mean."

Jennings changed the name of the 357s to Hierophant in 2009. Author Steven King plays the voice of futuristic radio DJ, Will O' the Wisp, on the 2010 album, "Black Ribbons." The album tells a story set in the future when the government controls the radio waves and a radio DJ plays the only band that is forbidden.

On Nov. 8, 2016, an updated version of "Black Ribbons" was re-released because of the historic and controversial election.

In 2011 Jennings formed a new back-up band, The Triple Crown, with his childhood friend, Erik Deutsch. Eighteen recorded tracks were divided between two albums. The first album was 2011's "Family Man" with the second entitled "The Other Life." A self-titled film about a travelling musician haunted by a mysterious woman accompanied the album. It won Best Short Film at the 2013 Horror Hound Festival.

Shooter formed a label called Black Country Rock Media. Among its releases was a re-mastered version of Waylon Jennings's album, "Right for the Time" and Jesse Colter's live album, "Live from Cain's Ballroom." Jennings released an EP in tribute to his mentor, George Jones, in August 2014.

In February 2016 the album, "Countach," a tribute to producer, Giorgio Moroder was released. The album opened with Waylon Jennings' 1972 hit, "Ladies Love Outlaws." Shooter teamed up with performers Marilyn Manson, Steve Young, Brandi Carlie and Richard Garriot on a few of the tracks.

Terry and Shooter Jennings continue to tap their background, talent and legacy to defend and represent their family. They persistently change the meaning of the country music "Outlaw" and educate others on what it means to survive, persevere and make monumental creative changes in the sometimes static world of Country Music.

January 2017

Renae Johnson Wins International Book Award for PRECIOUS MEMORIES MEMORIAL

The Beverly Hills International Book Award focuses on excellence in print books. The competition for award contest is judged by experts from all aspects of the book industry, including publishers, writers, editors, book cover designers and professional copywriters. They select award winners based on overall excellence.

Renae Johnson is thrilled to have one of her books recognized by the Beverly Hills Book Awards, but particularly grateful to have won in a category that not only honors country music legends but gives fans the tools and references needed to visit the final resting places of these stars.

Precious Memories Memorial is a journey that takes you from their deaths (when and how) to their celebration of life and who attended. It shares photos of the gravesites and a map that guides you to their exact locations. It's a powerful book that brings honor to these traditional country music legends.

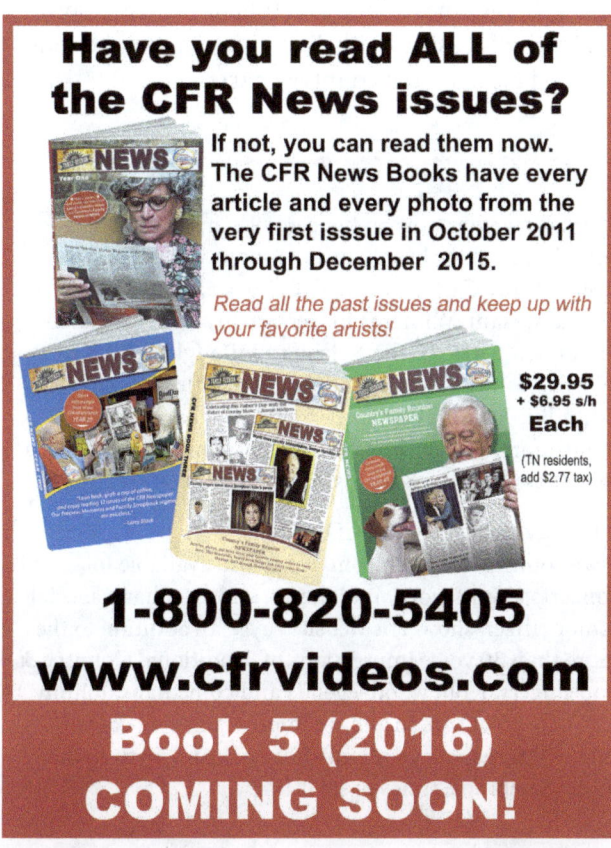

January 2017

Singer, songwriter & former member of Exile, Mark Gray, dies

Country songwriter and recording artist Mark Gray, country songwriter and recording artist, died on December 2 in Lebanon, Tenn. He was 64 years old.

Gray, who was known as a talented songwriter in the music industry, was responsible for a host of Top 10 country songs, including Alabama's "Take Me Down" and "The Closer You Get," Janie Fricke's "It Ain't Easy Being Easy" and Gary Morris' "Second Hand Heart." He also saw great success as a solo artist, and as a member of the country-pop band Exile.

"Yesterday, my bandmates and I lost a brother and a friend, Mark Gray," Sonny LeMaire wrote on Facebook. "I will be forever grateful to him for his generosity as a musician, songwriter, and most importantly, his gift of friendship! …Please extend prayers to his caring wife, Janice, his children and extended family. God and his angels have another soulful face singing in his heavenly choir! Good-bye, my brother … Rest In Peace."

Gray was born on Oct. 24, 1952, in Vicksburg, Miss., and spent much of his childhood involved with music. He began playing the piano when he was 12, and was a regular singer in his church's gospel choir, which led Gray to form his own gospel group in 1972, the Revelations.

Gray's first big break was when the Oak Ridge Boys saw him perform and convinced him to move to Nashville, work for their publishing company and join them on tour as a backup singer. Following his time with them, Gray concentrated into songwriting and recording demos, one of which landed in the hands of Exile producer Mike Chapman, who invited Gray to join the band. He recorded and toured with Exile for three years, from 1979 until 1982.

In 1982, Gray signed to Columbia Records as a solo artist and went on to released three albums and eight Top 40 country hits, five of which landed in the Top 10. His biggest chart success was a cover of Dan Hill's "Sometimes When We Touch," which Gray performed as a duet with Tammy Wynette; the song reached No. 6 on the country charts.

MORE ABOUT JOHNNY COUNTERFIT

Johnny Counterfit was born in Omaha, Nebraska. As a young boy, Johnny would sit in front of the television and absorb every variety, comedy, and music show of the late 1960's and into the 1970's, while imitating as many voices as he heard. Johnny began listening to the LP records his parents played on their stereo console, and decided to teach himself how to sing, while he practiced imitating the voices of each singer, until each voice was just right. This same commitment is carried out with every performance, as Johnny is now the one on television, radio, and live concert stages. Johnny recreates each legendary star with astonishing accuracy. NO MUSIC TRACKS are used during his show! Whether he is accompanied by the Time Travelers Band, or simply with his guitar, the audience is treated to a show they will always remember!

Today he entertains audiences with more than 30 voice impressions in a 90 minute show, voices range from Johnny Cash to Vince Gill, Buck Owens to Dwight Yoakam, Hank Williams to George Strait, Dean Martin to Frank Sinatra, Willie Nelson to Julio Iglesias, John Wayne, Jimmy Stewart, Rodney Dangerfield, Archie & Edith Bunker, Bill Clinton, Ronald Reagan, and many, many more! Watch the television clips on the Home page to witness how accurate his voice impressions really are!

Johnny has DVDs and CDs available on his website, www.johnnycounterfit.com. He is also available for concerts, events, corporate shows, and even has a special senior citizen show. His website says, "In addition to the more than 30 voice impressions of Traditional Country & Pop singers, Hollywood legends and comedians, Johnny will take great care in adding impressions and comedy that will transport your audience back and forth to the most memorable times of their life!"

Salute to the Kornfield
Everything you always wanted to know about the cast
By Claudia Johnson

George Lindsey – Glad He Made You Laugh

George Lindsey had a diverse career in entertainment, appearing in plays, movies, TV dramas and variety shows. It was, however, his seven-year portrayal of mechanic Goober Pyle on "The Andy Griffith Show" and "Mayberry RFD" and a 20-year stint on Hee-Haw that secured his place in comedic history.

The Fairfield, Alabama, native may have played the country goofball, but he earned a bachelor's degree in 1952 in physical education and biology from Florence State College, where he played quarter-back on the football team. After college he enlisted in the United States Air Force and was stationed at Ramey AFB in Puerto Rico. Following his discharge, he taught for a year at Hazel Green High School in Hazel Green, Alabama, while waiting to be accepted by the American Theater Wing in New York City in 1956. With Broadway performances under his acting belt, he headed to Hollywood where he appeared in some of the era's most popular shows, including "Gunsmoke," "The Rifleman," "The Real McCoys," "The Twilight Zone," "Daniel Boone," "Voyage to the Bottom of the Sea" and three episodes of "The Alfred Hitchcock Hour." He played a sailor in the 1964 film "Ensign Pulver," the sequel to "Mister Roberts."

Lindsey sought the role of Gomer Pyle, on "The Andy Griffith Show" but lost to fellow Alabamian Jim Nabors. He was soon cast as Gomer's cousin, Goober, whose crazy Goober Dance and horrible Gary Grant impression helped distinguish him among his fellow Mayberry residents.

His childhood prepared him to some extent for his mechanic role. According to a 2012 Tennessean article, "Lindsey liked to hang around his Aunt Ethel's gas station, where the mechanics wore felt caps to keep the grease and oil from dripping into their hair. Those caps would inspire Lindsey's trademark "beanie" worn by Goober."

Though Goober's role was expanded when "The Andy Griffith Show" transitioned into "Mayberry RFD," Lindsey later expressed that he did not feel the caliber of writing was equal to the original series. CBS cancelled "Mayberry RFD" in 1971, and Lindsey continued appearing in other projects like "M*A*S*H," "Cannonball Run II," "Snowball Express" and "News Radio."

Lindsey's talents were not always used on screen. He even voiced characters in Disney animated movies "The Aristocats," "Robin Hood" and "The Rescuers."

As a regular on "Hee-Haw," Lindsey reprised his role as Goober. He'd suddenly appear in the "PFFT! You Was Gone!" skit with Archie Campbell, pop up in "The Cornfield" delivering a corny joke or join the rest of the cast in asking Grandpa Jones "Hey Grandpa! What's for supper?"

Lindsey's starring segment was "Goober's Garage," where he'd play his classic role of Goober, owner of the local garage. Sometimes a city slicker/con-artist type would try to pull a fast one while Goober emerged as more intelligent.

January 2017

After the death of Archie Campbell, Lindsay often sang the verse in "PFFT! You Was Gone!" He was narrator for Misty Rowe's "Bedtime Stories" segment, and appeared as a leisure suit-clad narrator in Lisa Todd's "Advice to the Lovelorn" sketch.

After Hew-Haw ended, Lindsey remained in Nashville and often portrayed Goober in personal appearances. After "Return to Mayberry," a 1986 made-for-TV movie became a hit, Lindsey's participation at Mayberry reunion events and festivals drew large crowds of fans over the next two decades.

When Lindsey died in 2012 at age 83, much was said of his charitable endeavors.

His "The Andy Griffith Show" co-star Ron Howard, who played Opie Taylor remembered Lindsey as "warm, intelligent and lovable," noting that "He generated lots of laughs and raised a lot of money for Special Olympics."

In fact, Lindsey raised more than $1 million for the Alabama Special Olympics through 17 years of the George Lindsey Celebrity Weekend and Golf Tournament in Montgomery, Alabama, and another $50,000 for the Alabama Association of Retarded Citizens. He also participated as Head Coach-Winter Games in the Minneapolis, Minnesota Special Olympics National Competition.

He was honored by the City of Nashville with Goober Pyle Day in 1990.

He established and perpetuated the George Lindsey Academic Scholarships at his alma mater, University of North Alabama, which bestowed upon him an honorary doctorate in 1992. In 1998, he established the George Lindsey/UNA Film Festival held annually at the university each spring.

In 1995, the same year he published his autobiography, Goober in a Nutshell, he was recognized with the Governor's Achievement Award in the Alabama Music Hall of Fame.

The Minnie Pearl Lifetime Achievement Award was presented to Lindsey in 1997. In 2004, Lindsey shared the TV Land Legend Award with other members of the "Griffith" cast and crew.

He was the 2007 recipient of the first ICON Award presented by the Nashville Associations of Talent Directors.

"George Lindsey was my friend," Andy Griffith said upon Lindsey's death. "I had great respect for his talent and his human spirit. In recent years, we spoke often by telephone. I am happy to say that as we found ourselves in our eighties, we were not afraid to say, 'I love you.' That was the last thing George and I had to say to each other. 'I love you.'"

Lindsey often commented that he was torn about what he wanted his tombstone to say, with the choices being "I told you I was sick" or "I hope I made you laugh." His children settled the matter. The simple tombstone in his vault at Oak Hill Cemetery in Jasper, Alabama, says, "I'm glad I made you laugh."

January 2017

Artists Roast & Toast Larry Black

A very special Roast & Toast was held for Larry Black on December 13. The event was a complete surprise to Larry who thought the last show was only supposed to be a Facebook Live event, but when he entered the studio he found it filled with artists, friends, family and co-workers.

The Roast & Toast aired as an almost two-hour live event on Facebook. It is saved to the Larry's Country Diner facebook page so people can go back and watch it anytime.

Bill Anderson and Keith Bilbrey hosted the event. Some of the artists included: Rhonda Vincent, T. Graham Brown, Johnny Lee, Jimmy Fortune, Ronnie Reno, Rory Feek, T.G. Sheppard, Linda Davis, Gene Watson, Jeannie Seely, John Conlee, Dallas Wayne, Exile, Bradley Walker, Dan Miller, Hawkshaw Hawkins Jr., Teea Goans, and Carl Jackson. Also The Gatlin Brothers, The Oak Ridge Boys, The White and Ricky Skaggs couldn't be there in person, so they sent video clips for everyone to see.

Bill Anderson gets a lot of stories from Larry's wife Luann while Dan Miller waits to sing his song for Larry.

John Conlee gives Larry a pair of rose colored glasses. Jeannie Seely waiting her turn to roast and toast Larry.

Rory Feek smiles as Jimmy Fortune tells stories on Larry.

Rhonda Vincent made trip to roast and toast.

Gene Watson talked about fun times with Larry and the crew.

Johnny Lee couldn't find biscuits so he brought buns instead.

The Diner cast...Renae, Larry, Nadine, Keith and Jimmy have been with Larry through a lot.

T. Graham Brown and wife, Sheila

T. G. Sheppard and Hawkshaw Hawkins Jr.

Dallas Wayne, Jimmy and Michele Capps

January 2017

Auction of stars
by Scot England

Country Music fans and antique collectors turned out for a four day estate sale held at the home of Country Music Hall of Famer Tom T. Hall.

The event took place in November at Hall's famous Fox Hollow estate in Franklin Tennessee.

Michael Taylor Estate and Moving Sales hosted the sale. Taylor says his company handles two to three celebrity estate sales each year.

"We have a strong customer base of about 8,000 people. And this was a very good sale. We were busy all four days. Tom is a great guy. He was great to work with. And he has a lot of fans."

One of those fans was Nashville resident Tami Loving.

"I was always a Tom T. fan. I'm a fan of all of the country music legends.

I met Tom many years ago at Ponderosa Park in Salem Ohio."

Loving says she found numerous bargains as she walked through Hall's home.

"I am already wearing Tom's necklace. And I bought two clocks, a crock pot, a blanket, some drinking glasses and a couple things that he and Dixie made. I also got a framed poem that was on his wall. It's called 'The Songwriter's Prayer.' That's special since Tom T. is one of the all-time great songwriters."

It was Tom T's songwriting that first caught the attention of those in Nashville. Tom's 'Harper Valley PTA' became an instant classic when it was recorded by Jeannie C. Riley.

Hall then started singing his own songs and had major hits with 'Old Dogs, Children and Watermelon Wine,' 'I Love,' 'Country Is,' and 'Faster Horses.'

Some of the more unique items found at the sale included hand crafted furniture that Tom built himself. Hall also signed each piece.

A civil war signal cannon was quickly purchased for $3,000. Hall's antique collection also included a 12 foot column from the first Tennessee Governor's mansion. That had a price tag of $3,800. Tom's grand piano was listed at $12,900.

Hall's love of the outdoors was evident with many taxidermy items for sale. One of those was a rare black swan that was a gift to Hall from Dottie West.

An even more unique gift came from President Jimmy Carter. Two bricks that came from the chimney of Carter's mother Lillian were also offered for sale for $125.

Tom T. was inducted into Country Music Hall of Fame in 2008. He retired in 1998. Hall's wife Dixie

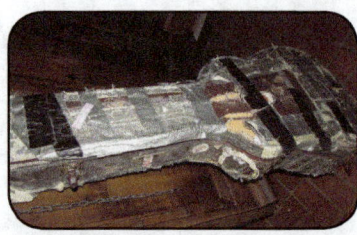

died in 2015. While he is still in good health, now at the age of 80, Hall decided it was a good time to start downsizing.

"Tom and his wife Miss Dixie loved Fox Hollow. And he still loves it." Michael Taylor adds, "While he is selling the house and most of the acreage, he is keeping a small parcel of five acres and he will live there. He has renovated a barn into a really nice home and he likes it there."

January 2017

Q: I have a question for you. I read in George Jones' book that he had two sons (Brian and Jeffery) I believe were their names. Could you tell me anything about what they are doing now? I was wondering if they are in country music. Anything you could tell me, I would appreciate so much. I really, really enjoy your CFR newspaper and look forward to it every month.

Wanda Scholz, Atchison, KS

A: Jones was married four times. First, he married Dorothy Bonvillion in 1950. The union lasted less than a year; they were divorced by the time their daughter Susan was born. In order to make the court-mandated child support payments, George joined the Marine Corps. He didn't see combat, but he obtained some gigs singing on Saturday nights and continued to hone his craft.

George then married Shirley Corley in 1954. Although the marriage lasted fourteen years and produced two sons, the two were not well suited for each other. Shirley showed little interest in George's career and opted to remain in Texas when he moved to Nashville. The couple divorced in 1968.

Bryan (left) Jeff (right) (courtesy of Georgette Jones Lennon)

Both sons with Shirley live in Texas....both are married. Jeff is oldest with 3 kids and Bryan younger with 2 kids. Jeff runs his own business doing flooring and Bryan manages a hardware store. Jeff has two grandchildren and Bryan has one grandson.

Shortly after George's divorce he met Tammy Wynette. They were married from 1969 to 1975. Together they had daughter, Georgette.

His last marriage was to Nancy Sepulvado from 1983 until his death.

Bryan (left) Jeff (right) (courtesy of Georgette Jones Lennon).

If you have questions send them to Paula, CFR News, P.O. Box 210796, Nashville, TN 37221 or email them to paula@gabrielcommunications.com.

Dallas Wayne, international artist and radio host

A very special Roast & Toast was held for Larry Black on December 13. The event was a complete surprise to Larry who thought the last show was only supposed to be a Facebook Live event, but when he entered the studio he found it filled with artists, friends, family and co-workers.

While touring Europe in the early 90s, Dallas forged a deal with Texicalli Records in Finland and was signed to record an album. He went on to record six albums. Later, he moved to Scandinavia, where he became a staff writer for Warner/Chappell Music.

After four years living and touring in Europe, Dallas returned to the U.S. and signed a record deal with HighTone Records. In addition to recording two albums of his own on the HighTone label, Dallas was a part of the honky-tonk supergroup, the TwangBangers.

Dallas got his start in radio in 1989, drawing on his many years as a performer. He solidified his radio career when he joined Outlaw Country on SIRIUS Satellite Radio in 2005. A year later he accepted a position at KHYI 95.3 FM in Dallas, Texas, where he served as Program Director and morning drive-time DJ until the end of 2007. After the merger of SIRIUS and XM in 2008, Dallas became On-Air Personality and Associate Format Manager for the Texas-based honky-tonk channel Willie's Place, which later became Willie's Roadhouse.

Dallas released his most recent album, Songs The Jukebox Taught Me, on the Heart of Texas Records label in May 2016. He currently lives outside Austin, Texas, where he performs with the legendary band Heybale! in addition to his radio career, songwriting and touring.

In addition to his busy schedule on-air in Outlaw Country and Willie's Roadhouse, Dallas currently holds the position of Operations Manager for SiriusXM Satellite Radio's Austin, Texas, studio. He can be heard five days a week on SiriusXM Satellite Radio: Monday through Friday from noon to 6 p.m. Eastern at Willie's Roadhouse (channel 59), and Tuesday through Friday in Outlaw Country (channel 60) from 10 a.m. to noon Eastern.

Dallas can be seen on Larry's Country Diner on January 5 & 7.

January 2017

Legendary Country Group to Hit the Road in 2017 in Celebration of Three Decades of Music

Legendary country group Shenandoah will hit the road in 2017 to commemorate 30 years of their classic sound. Next year marks the bands third decade since originally forming in 1987. Today, a handful of dates were announced for the Shenandoah "30th Anniversary Tour."

The tour kicks off on January 22 in Annapolis, Maryland and will continue throughout the year with many additional live dates scheduled across the country. Shenandoah will also perform two live concerts in Zurich, Switzerland, a first for the band. Additional tour dates will be announced soon.

"After 29 years in the music business, we find ourselves more determined than ever before," says lead singer Marty Raybon. "The past helps us to realize where we've been and sets vision to where we want to be. Our mission in 2017, with new music, is to expand our fanbase while continuing to enjoy the performances and making our 30th year the best ever."

To celebrate the holiday season, Shenandoah released a new Christmas single for country radio. The single, "The First Noel," is included on the group's Christmas Comes Alive EP. The song is now available for radio airplay, as well as digital download Amazon and iTunes.

Concert Schedule for Shenandoah "30th Anniversary Tour"

January 22 - Annapolis, MD
February 25 - LaBelle, FL
March 2 - Zurich Switzerland
March 3 - Zurich Switzerland
March 25 - Weatherford, TX
March 30 - Vienna, GA
March 31 - Hartsellle, Alabama
April 8 - Winchester, Ohio
April 29 - Geneva, Alabama
June 3 - Syria, VA
June 10 - Emmetsburg, IA
June 20 - Clayton, NY
July 29 - Rural Retreat, VA
August 4 - Schulenburg, TX

January 2017

Gordon Mote receives Grammy Award nomination

Gordon Mote's last project, "Gordon Mote Sings Hymns and Songs of Inspiration" is a final nominee in the "Best Roots Gospel Album" category for the 59th Annual Grammy Awards.

"Hymns and Songs of Inspiration" is the second project recorded on the New Haven Records label and is co-produced with Grammy Award winning producers, Wayne Haun and Phil Johnson.

The project consists of nine traditional hymns along with three more contemporary titles that will someday become classics. The thirteenth title is the very timely tune penned by Gordon Mote and friend Lyn Rowell "Only Jesus Can Heal This Hurting World", which has been a huge radio success.

The Grammys' will air on CBS Sunday February 12th.

For more info, go to his website at: www.gordonmote.com.

Bible Word Search:
NAMES AND TITLES OF JESUS

```
U Q O K A I S N S M T K R P M
V L F Z J T Y O A E E O A O R
O M G Y V O N T N Z I C B X K
Y D N Y M O E N U V A N B O A
D L O V F H T C A S I R I X R
E R I G W A R S P D S H E W E
N T O G B M A L I D O V Z N D
F D J L H Q Y V K R T T R Z E
I G Q R R T A E G T H V E P E
P B Y I H D S E K E U C T X M
T S W K F T Y A J I O Q S L E
L I I O N A M F O N O S A H R
V N N Q Z Y K V A D E J M V R
G O J E S U S E M M A N U E L
S V B G G W T Z T P B Q J F E
```

CHRIST	EMMANUEL	JESUS
KING of the Jews	LAMB of God	LIGHT of the World
LORD	MASTER	NAZARENE
RABBI	REDEEMER	SAVIOR
SON OF DAVID	SON OF GOD	SON OF MAN

Ref: Wikipedia

Instructions: Find and circle the words shown in all capital letters. Words may be forward, backward, vertical, or diagonal within the puzzle.

January 2017

FEBRUARY

Tragedy strikes Jean Shepard's family again

Icie Hawkins, 18-year-old granddaughter of the late Jean Shepard and daughter of Don Robin Hawkins, was killed in the early hours of Saturday, December 17. Jean's husband Benny Birchfield was also stabbed in the incident and 21-year-old Travis Sanders, whom police said stabbed both Icie and Benny, died from a gunshot wound.

Sgt. Jim Vaughn of the Hendersonville Police Department said police received a phone call about a stabbing at the home on the 200 block of Elnora Court around 3 a.m. Saturday.

He said when police arrived, a 79-year-old man was in the front yard of the home and wounded. The man, according to police, stated he had been stabbed. Vaughn declined to reveal the name of the man, but records show the address matches the residence of Benny Birchfield, who is 79, and the former residence of Shepard. Benny, a musician, and Shepard had been married since 1968.

Inside the house, where the attacks took place, police found Sanders, who was pronounced dead at the scene. Sanders died from a .38 caliber gunshot wound, Vaughn said. They also found Icie Hawkins, who was transported to a hospital where she was later pronounced dead. Icie was stabbed, police said.

Officers interviewed the man and based on his account, and the conditions at the crime scene, they are satisfied that "the situation was contained at the house," Vaughn said.

"Everybody who was there was identified," he added.

Vaughn said the department does not have a possible motive at this point. Vaughn said Benny underwent surgery for his injuries and that his condition is improving.

It was determined that Benny acted in self-defense when he shot and killed a man inside his Hendersonville home following the fatal stabbing.

After meeting with the Sumner County District Attorney's Office, no charges will be brought against Benny Birchfield for the fatal shooting of 21-year-old Travis Sanders, according to Det. Sgt. Jim Vaughn.

Benny told police he heard a disturbance in the basement and began calling out for his granddaughter, Icie.

"He thought he heard her but he didn't know for sure what she was saying," Vaughn told reporters during a press conference. "He went down to investigate and… that is when he was confronted by Mr. Sanders."

During a struggle, Benny was cut on the neck and head by Sanders with a 10-inch knife that police say had also been used to stab Icie, Benny then shot the 21-year-old five times in self-defense with his .38-caliber pistol.

Sanders was located inside and pronounced dead at the scene. Icie, who had what police described as self-defense wounds and upper body injures caused by the knife, died on the way to the hospital.

Investigators are still unsure what led to the stabbing.

"This is still an active and ongoing investigation," Vaughn said. "It's going to take some time. In order to find a motive we're going to have to interview a lot of friends and family."

"We've got all the answers now except for the why," he added.

Family members said that Icie had been living with her grandparents to help Shepard, who had Parkinson's disease. After Jean died in September, Icie stayed to help Benny with errands and the house, said her mother, Velvet Sloan.

Icie and Sanders started dating earlier this year after a few years of friendship. They broke up after Sanders stole money from her, Sloan said.

February 2017

A handwritten note from Benny, when he was released from the hospital, was read by Vaughn during a press conference.

Neighbors have created a GoFundMe page to help with the family's various recovery costs. As of Wednesday, $150 of the fundraiser's $5,000 goal had been raised.

"I would like to thank the Hendersonville police and fire departments for their quick response and professionalism during this tragic time," he wrote.

"I also want to thank everyone for their thoughts and prayers, and for those who have asked, I am okay and my wounds are slowly healing."

A memorial service was held for Icie on Friday, December 23.

"She was a beautiful sweet girl," said Icies' mother, Velvet Sloan. "She loved so many people."

She was buried next to her biological grandfather, the late country music star Hawkshaw Hawkins, in Goodlettsville.

Icie and her cousin, Rachel, Hawshaw Jr.'s daughter, were seen last year on Larry's Country Diner with their grandmother, Jean.

Reba to have new television show

Reba McEntire is headed back to the small screen, reports The Hollywood Reporter.

Reba, who will release her new gospel album "Sing It Now: Songs of Faith & Hope" on Feb. 3, has partnered with "Desperate Housewives" creator Marc Cherry for a one-hour television drama that was ordered by ABC.

"I play a female sheriff in a small town in the south and it's very dark," McEntire explained. "It's got funny times in it, but it is dark."

According to The Hollywood Reporter, Reba McEntire is heading back to the small screen. Reba's character Ruby Adair is a sheriff in the conservative Oxblood, Ky., whose views are challenged by a young Middle Eastern FBI agent on hand to help her solve a crime.

"I play a female sheriff in a small town in the south and it's very dark," McEntire explained. "It's got funny times in it, but it is dark."

Reba, who will release her new gospel album "Sing It Now: Songs of Faith & Hope" on Feb. 3, has partnered with "Desperate Housewives" creator Marc Cherry for a one-hour television drama that was ordered by ABC.

ABC executives are planning to read the script over the weekend and if they like it, she thought she would be shooting the pilot in March. As a result, McEntire will move from promoting her album immediately into filming her television show.

Cherry will write the script and executive produce the show alongside McEntire.

NEW 5 DVDs

$79.80
+ $6.95 s/h

Hosted by Bill Anderson, we've honored the one and only... MERLE HAGGARD. Including three of his sons, Marty, Noel and Ben. This is the singer songwriter that so many of today's country artists point to as their inspiration. Many of today's country artists sang Merle's songs and told their stories of life on the road and in concert with Merle. Others included in the show were: Mac Wiseman, Ronnie Reno, David Frizzell, Daryle Singletary, John Conlee, Teea Goans, Bobby Bare, Ray Benson, Dallas Wayne, Rhonda Vincent, Vince Gill, Paul Franklin, Mark Wills, Emily Gimble, T. Graham Brown, Mo Pitney, Jeannie Seely, Jim Lauderdale, The Isaacs, Tony Booth, Gene Watson.

1- 800-820-5405
www.cfrvideos.com

February 2017

Recipe from our friend, Jeanne Pruett

Jeanne Pruett's Feein' Friends Cookbook III has many great recipes. Here's one from our friend Jeanne!

Sausage and Wild Rice

1 lb. sausage, fried, drained & crumbled

1 TBSP onion flakes

1 can cream of mushroom soup

1 can cream of chicken soup

1 can milk

1/2 cup blanched almonds

1 box long grain & wild rice cooked as directed

2/3 cup Hi-Ho cracker crumbs

1 TBSP butter

1 can Durkees onion rings

Mix sausage, onion flakes, soup, milk, almonds and rice and pour into casserole dish. Top with cracker crumbs mixed with butter and onion rings. Cook at 350 degrees for 30 minutes.

Refrigerator Slaw

3/4 cup sugar

1 head cabbage, chopped

1 green pepper, chopped

1 onion chopped

1 tsp celery seed

1/2 cup vinegar

1/2 cup oil

1/4 tsp salt

Combine cabbage, pepper, onion, and celery seed. Cover with sugar and let stand 2 hours. Make a solution of vinegar, oil and salt. Bring to a boil and pour over mixture. Keeps well for days in the fridge.

February 2017

Mel Tillis back at his home in Florida, continuing to improve

Country legend Mel Tillis is now recuperating in Florida after being in critical condition following complications from colon surgery. All of last year Mel's health was questionable, but his daughter, Pam, kept country fans at ease with updates about her legendary father.

At times she begged fans for prayers, but later posts reassured us Mel was feeling much better. She even went on to say that he was sitting up, watching TV!

She gave an update in December 2016 saying, *"Dad had a serious diverticulitis attack last January after a busy fall 2015 performance schedule. On the way to the hospital, he became septic and was in the I.C.U. for the better part of a month. Everything he is dealing with now, almost a year later, is a direct result of that crisis. Due to the nature of his illness, his care was best served in several facilities in Nashville up until November. Currently, he is at home in Ocala, Florida receiving full time in-house care. His transition, initially, involved a few more weeks in the hospital there. Now, he's back at home and on track. His vital signs are good and his sense of humor is fully intact!"*

Mel's publicist Don Murray Grubbs issued a statement about his health since he left the care facilities.

"In November, Mel made the trip from Nashville back to his home state of Florida. He is currently at home in Ocala where he is being cared for by nurses as needed and continued physical therapy. His vitals are good and his sense of humor is very much intact. He is trying to get stronger and we are hopeful that will be the case now that he's back at home. He misses all of his loyal fans and is beyond thankful for all the well wishes," the statement reads.

We continue to pray that Mel's health improves and that one day he feels well enough to be back entertaining again.

Ricky Skaggs & Bruce Hornsby Kick Off Six-city Tour

Country and bluegrass legend Ricky Skaggs and renowned pianist and songwriter Bruce Hornsby, fellow friends and GRAMMY® winners, will soon hit the road once again to collaborate with Skaggs' razor-sharp band Kentucky Thunder on brand new tunes and traditional bluegrass classics. The "Ricky Skaggs & Bruce Hornsby with Kentucky Thunder" tour kicks-off on February 26 in Tarrytown, NY with additional New York dates to follow, as well as stops in Pennsylvania, New Jersey, and Delaware.

At times she begged fans for prayers, but later posts reassured us Mel was feeling much better. She even went on to say that he was sitting up, watching TV!

"I always get excited when I know I'm gonna get to tour with my good friend Bruce Hornsby," says Skaggs. "Fireworks always happen!"

Hornsby adds, "The level of virtuosity required to play bluegrass music with the freaks of Ricky Skaggs and Kentucky Thunder requires a good deal of practice; I always have to prepare a good deal, practicing with the metronome at break-neck speed, crazy tempos, to be able to hang with those guys."

February 2017

Without any restrictions, their music is as fascinating and masterful as the two stars that created it. The pair blends songs drawn from deep roots in mountain music, adding piano and Hornsby's inimitable songwriting to Skaggs' instrumental core of mandolin, guitar, bass, fiddle and banjo into a musical feast. Punctuating the show is a vibrantly expansive version of Hornsby's early hit "The Way It Is" and a performance of "White Wheeled Limousine," and to sum up the free-spirited nature of their collaborations, Skaggs and Hornsby joyfully present the vintage fiddle tune "Cluck Ol' Hen." Skaggs and Hornsby promise to kick up a storm with their mix of high-lonesome harmonies, full throttle bluegrass picking, and improvisational piano.

2017 "Ricky Skaggs & Bruce Hornsby with Kentucky Thunder" Tour Dates:

Feb 26 - Tarrytown, NY - Tarrytown Music Hall

Feb 27 - Red Bank, NJ - Count Basie Theatre

March 1 - Brookville, NY - Tilles Center for the Performing Arts

March 3 - Lancaster, PA - American Music Theatre

March 4 - Wilmington, DE - The Grand Opera House, Copeland Hall

March 5 - Verona, NY - Turning Stone Resort & Casino at The Showroom

Earning 12 #1 hit singles, 14 GRAMMY® Awards, 11 IBMA Awards, nine ACM Awards, eight CMA Awards (including Entertainer of the Year), two Dove Awards, the ASCAP Founders Award, three honorary Doctorate degrees, inductions into the Musicians Hall of Fame and GMA Gospel Music Hall of Fame, the 2013 Artist-In-Residence at the Country Music Hall of Fame and Museum, an Americana Music Association Lifetime Achievement Award in the Instrumentalist category along with countless other awards, Ricky Skaggs is truly a pioneer of Bluegrass and Country music. Since he began playing music more than 50 years ago, Skaggs has released more than 30 albums and has performed thousands of live shows. He started his own record label, Skaggs Family Records, in 1997 and has since released 12 consecutive GRAMMY®-nominated albums. His latest release, Hearts Like Ours, with his wife, celebrated artist Sharon White of The Whites features the couple dueting on handpicked country love songs. And the Grand Ole Opry member has released his first-ever autobiography, "Kentucky Traveler." The book details the life and times of Skaggs and provides a descriptive history of Country and Bluegrass music, as told by the master himself. In addition to his regular touring schedule with his band, Kentucky Thunder, he recently performed a string of dates with his better half Sharon White along with guitar legend Ry Cooder on the critically-acclaimed "Cooder-White-Skaggs" tour and from time to time hits the road with versatile singer/songwriter and pianist Bruce Hornsby on another critically-acclaimed tour, "Ricky Skaggs & Bruce Hornsby with Kentucky Thunder."

For more information on Ricky Skaggs, visit www.rickyskaggs.com.

Bruce Hornsby's work displays a creative iconoclasm that's been a constant in the artist's two-and-a-half decade recording career. His commercial stock soared early on, when "The Way It Is"–the title track of his 1986 debut album–became one of the most popular songs on American radio. Despite his early mainstream successes, Hornsby has pursued a more personal, idiosyncratic musical path, focusing on projects that sparked his creative interest, including collaborations with the Grateful Dead, Spike Lee, Ricky Skaggs, Don Henley, Ornette Coleman, Bob Dylan, Bela Fleck, Bonnie Raitt, Pat Metheny, and Robbie Robertson. Hornsby's performance will offer a glimpse of a restless spirit who continues to push forward into new musical terrain.

For more information on Bruce Hornsby, visit www.brucehornsby.com.

Dailey & Vincent Opry Induction Set For March 11, 2017

Marty Stuart surprises Daily & Vincent with the invitation to join the Opry.

Three-time IBMA Entertainers of the Year and multi-Grammy®-nominated super duo Dailey & Vincent have been invited to become official members of the Grand Ole Opry. The pair returned to the Opry at the Ryman Auditorium tonight to celebrate the kick-off of its 10th year as a duo, which began on the Opry at the Ryman stage in 2007. The night also marked the duo's 100th Opry appearance. The duo will be formally inducted into the Opry on Saturday, March 11.

During a special half-hour Dailey & Vincent set, the two were joined by a series of guests including Opry members Marty Stuart and Connie Smith as well as John Carter Cash and his wife Ana Cristina in addition to Dailey's father JB Dailey and Vincent's mother Carolyn Vincent. After a performance with the duo, Stuart gave Jamie Dailey and Darrin Vincent the surprise of their lives, inviting the duo to officially join the Opry. "Country music needs you. Country music loves you. And the Grand Ole Opry welcomes you," Stuart said.

"This is one of the most special things that has ever happened to us," a shocked Dailey said after a few seconds of stunned silence. "We're so thankful."

Before closing out the show along with their guests on the gospel favorite "This Old House," and equally surprised Vincent shared, "I have no words. I'm so honored. The Lord is so faithful to us."

"Dailey & Vincent have thoroughly entertained thousands of fans on the Opry stage over the past decade," said Opry Vice President and General Manager Pete Fisher. Jamie Dailey and Darrin Vincent embody so much about what fans love about the Opry. They have a tremendous respect for tradition, and they're also innovators committed to the future of the music they love. We're excited to welcome them as official members of the family in March."

Crystal Gayle is set to be inducted into the Opry by her sister Loretta Lynn on Saturday, January 21. Other artists scheduled to play the Opry in early 2017 include Brandy Clark, Chris Janson, Ricky Skaggs, and Josh Turner, among many others.

Five-time Grammy award winners individually, three-time Grammy award nominees collectively, four-time DOVE Award winners, and winners of 35 IBMA Awards altogether (including 3-time IBMA Entertainer of the Year Award winners and 3-Time Vocal Group of the Year Award winners), Jamie Dailey and Darrin Vincent, backed by one of the best bands on tour today, are some of the most reputable and elite entertainers in American music; bluegrass, traditional country and gospel music. The concoction of the fantastically instinctive vocal blends of Dailey's tenor and Vincent's reedy harmonies, has gained them well-deserved praise for their own distinctive style and worldwide recognition as American Music gold. Dailey & Vincent has garnered world-wide attention with their first national, top-rated television series, "The Dailey & Vincent Show," on RFD TV and over 500 airings of their PBS special "Dailey & Vincent ALIVE - In Concert." Their most recent CD, Dailey & Vincent ALIVE, debuted at #1 on the Billboard Bluegrass charts and remained at the top position for over 15 weeks.

February 2017

The DeZurik Sisters

Guess I'm on a yodeling kick, so I might as well get it out of my system.

A few months back, I wrote about Elton Britt, the "King of the Cowboy Yodelers," and last month's column focused on Zeke Clements, AKA the "Dixie Yodeler."

This month features My Little Lady Who (that's a yodeling reference/joke; sorry, I got carried away) … actually, it's a look back at a couple of ladies — The DeZurik Sisters, who also performed as The Cackle Sisters for their bird-like warbling on "Arizona Yodeler" (1938) and other classic chirruping's.

The it turns out the dynamic DeZurik duo was actually a threesome during their career which basically spanned 15 years from the mid-1930's to the mid-50's.

But they always performed as a duet, Carolyn and Mary Jane for most of that first decade and youngest sister Lorraine stepping up as needed.

Mary Jane and Carolyn both got married in 1940, and Mary Jane took a year off in 1943 to take care of her in-laws while husband/accordionist Augie Klein was fighting overseas during World War II.

Carolyn's husband Ralph "Rusty" Gill — a guitar player and singer who had his own band, the Prairie Ramblers — was also drafted into the Army, and she spent most of 1943 performing with Sonja Henie's Ice Review while her sister was fulfilling her family obligations.

The sisters reunited in late 1944, and these bluebirds of music happiness hit the road with regular appearances as members of the Grand Ole Opry.

Best year of their careers was undoubtedly 1938, when they appeared as "The Cackle Sisters" with their warbling sound on the Ralston Purina Mills' hit radio show, Checkerboard Time. Purina hired the DeZuricks because the company sold chicken feed among their many products and they thought it would be a good branding. The sisters also appeared as "The Cackle Sisters" in 1940's "Barnyard Follies" movie produced by Republic Pictures.

They also were featured regulars on the WLS-AM radio show National Barn Dance during this period.

Their fine, feathered songs that year included the lilting "Arizona Yodeler," the bouncy "I Left Her Standing There" and "Go To Sleep My Darling Baby" (more like a screaming-alarm, wake-up-sleepy-head song). Those were among six songs they recorded for Vocalion Records, along with "Sweet Hawaiian Chimes," "Guitar Blues" and "Birmingham Jail."

There are some other recordings which can be found on various collections, and some of their 1950's television appearances can be found on YouTube.

Mary Jane was injured in a car accident in 1946 and that's when Lorraine took over full-time until she mostly retired in 1951. Carolyn kept singing and joined her husband's band, and she also sang with a polka band as yodeling's popularity faded.

The girls were raised on a Minnesota farm, and they always credited that early upbringing for helping them develop their unique yodeling style. "We listened to the birds and tried to sing with the birds," Carolyn often told interviewers about their trilling style.

All the sisters are gone now. Mary Jane died in 1981 and would have been 100 on Feb. 1, 2017. Carolyn was born in 1918 and died at age 90 in suburban Chicago on March 16. 2009. Lorraine, who was born in 1927, died less than two months after Carolyn, on May 1, 2009, in Renton, Wash.

The cackles were hushed, but they left a legacy that still lives strong with old-time country music fans.

Author Tom Wood, who writes thrillers and Westerns, is a regular contributor to Country Family Reunion News. Reach him at tomwoodauthor.com

February 2017

Singer Songwriters

By Sasha Kay Dunavant

Brad Paisley

Throughout the history of Country Music, thousands of songs have been written and performed. Many of those songs were written by famous performers. Some were written for a star's own records, while others were created to be sung by another artist. This Singer-Songwriter Series explores some of those talented individuals whose work we know and love.

Brad Paisley believes that singer–songwriters must push themselves to the limit when it comes to writing songs. In a 2014 "Taste of Country" interview the singer suggested, "I'm just saying that we as writers can do better." Growing tired of repetition the star insisted, "There are phrases that are totally cliché that we as songwriters owe it to ourselves to not use again."

During his career, the Glen Dale, West Virginia native, has written countless songs for himself and other singers, and many of them his fans know by heart.

Though he earned a Bachelor of Business Administration degree from Belmont University, he still found time to pursue his passion for songwriting and singing. In his early career, Paisley opened for Ricky Skaggs, George Jones and The Judds.

His debut single, "Who Needs Pictures," earned him an invitation to the Grand Ole Opry stage in 1999. He co-wrote his number one hit, "He Didn't Have To Be," with Kelley Lovelace, who discussed her collaboration experience with Paisley in a 2015 interview with "Song-Writer Universe."

"Brad and I…we've been friends since 1994," she said. "We got to be buddies before we started working together. We have very alike personalities. Whenever he's in the studio, whenever he's writing and recording, I'm pretty much doing that. I'm trying to come up with ideas, feed him ideas and feed him songs and be as much a part of that process as possible. It's a huge blessing to have that kind of relationship with any artist, much less one as successful as Brad has been over the years. That's my first priority when he's recording."

Further songwriting in 2000 resulted in Top 20 hit "Me Neither" and Paisley's second No. 1 single, "We Danced." In 2001 Paisley reached all-star status when his album went platinum and the Country Music Association handed him the Horizon Award. The same year at age 28 he became the youngest member ever to be inducted into the Grand Ole Opry. He was also given the Best New Male Vocalist Trophy from the Academy of Country Music.

Paisley co-wrote several songs with Chely Wright. One of the songs, "Hard To Be A Husband, Hard To Be A Wife," was written for a PBS special that was nominated for the Country Music Association's Vocal Event of the Year award. Paisley continued to co-write, sing and play guitar on Wright's 2001 album, "Never Love You Enough."

In 2002 Paisley won CMA's Video of the Year for, "I'm Gonna Miss Her (The Fishin' Song)." His part two album remained on charts for 70 weeks and produced his co-written Top 10 hits, "Two People Fell In Love," "Wrapped Around" and "I Wish You'd Stay." Paisley's two-time platinum 2003 album, "Mud on The Tires" produced "Whiskey Lullaby," "Celebrity," "Mud on The Tires" and "Little Moments." All three singles made the top three on country charts.

"Whiskey Lullaby," Paisley's duet with country and bluegrass star Allison Krauss, won 2005's Country Music Association Award for Song of The Year. Paisley's 2005 album, "Time Well Wasted,"

February 2017

won the Country Music Association Award for Best Album and was named 2006's Album of Year by the Academy of Country Music. His self-written single, "Alcohol" reached number four on Billboard's Hot Country Songs chart and was nominated for two Grammys.

Paisley continued his songwriting and recording success with his fifth album, "5th Gear." The album produced another four No. 1 singles, including "Ticks," "Letter To Me," "I'm Still a Guy" and "Online."

On Feb. 10, 2008, Paisley won the Grammy for the Best Country Instrumental for his song, "Throttleneck." Paisley wrote "Then" in 2009 for his album, "American Saturday Night." He performed the song on American Idol the same year. Paisley also performed for President and Mrs. Barack Obama at the White House in 2009. His song, "Old Alabama," is from Paisley's tenth album, "This Is Country Music." The number one hit is about a man spending Saturday night with the woman of his dreams.

Paisley co-wrote 2011's "Remind Me" with Kelley Lovelace and Chris DuBois. The song became a hit duet with Country music sweetheart, Carrie Underwood. Paisley joined forces again with Kelley Lovelace and Chris DuBois while writing the 2012-2013 hit singles, "Southern Comfort," "Beat This Summer," "I Can't Change The World" and "Mona Lisa." The star teamed up with Hip-Hop artist, LL Cool J in 2013. Together they wrote "Accidental Racist." The song discusses Southern Pride in a whole new light and discourages racism.

In 2016 Paisley featured pop sensation Demi Lavoto in "Without a Fight." His latest hit, "Today," had 41,000 downloads the week it was released and has sold more than 90,000 copies. Paisley provided original songs for the animated motion picture, "Cars" and "Cars 2."

Paisley has won multiple awards, including three Grammys, 14 CMA Awards, two American Music Awards and 14 Academy of Country Music Awards. He continues writing, singing, playing guitar and touring across America. He married former "Nashville" star Kimberly Williams in 2003 with whom he has two sons, Huck and Jasper.

February 2017

It's A Family Tradition
By Sasha Kay Dunavant

Roseanne Cash

Singer-songwriter Roseanne Cash was began life in the musical river town of Memphis, Tennessee, the daughter of Vivian Liberto and Johnny Cash, a Country singer who was not yet the legend he would become. The Cash family relocated to Los Angeles, California, in 1958 when Roseanne was three. After her parents divorced in 1966, 11-year-old Roseanne moved to Ventura, California, with her mother and siblings, graduating from St. Bonaventure High School in 1973. She soon began traveling with her father, who was a star by that time, first working as his wardrobe assistant and eventually becoming a backup singer and occasional soloist.

Cash's first recorded a Kris Kristofferson's song, "Broken Freedom Song," in 1974 on her father's album, "Junkie and the Juicehead Minus Me." She spent a year in London, England, working for CBS Records, but she returned to Nashville, Tennessee, in hopes of graduating from Vanderbilt University. However, she decided to go back to California to study method acting at Lee Strasberg Institute.

By 1978 had Cash had decided that pursuit of a musical career was more appealing than her acting classes and released a self- titled album. The album was mainly produced in Munich, Germany, but three tracks were recorded in Nashville and produced by talented singer, songwriter and producer Rodney Crowell.

Although, the album was never released in the United States, it caught the attention of Columbia Records. Cash began playing with Crowell's band, "The Cherry Bombs," and the pair fell in love while working together. Cash and Crowell were married in 1979 and soon after she began working on her next album. In 1980 Cash's album, "Right or Wrong" produced the hits, "No Memories Hangin' Around," "Couldn't Do Nothing Right," and "Take Me, Take Me."

In 1981 the couple settled in Nashville, and Cash gave birth to her their child. She was also working on what has become her signature album, "Seven Year Itch." The title track reached No. 1 on the Billboard Country Chart and No. 22 on the Billboard Pop Chart. Cash went on to release a 1982 album, "Somewhere in the Stars."

Her third album, 1985's "Rhythm and Romance" produced the hits, "I Don't Know Why You Don't Want Me," and "Never Be You."

Cash's second gold album, "King's Record Shop," produced Cash's cover of her father's hit, "Tennessee Flat Top Box," and John Stewart's, "Runaway Train." Cash's first compilation album, "Hits 1979-1989" introduced Cash's No. 1 version of the Beatles song "I Don't Want to Spoil the Party" and another hit "Black and White," that earned her a fifth Grammy nomination. Cash produced and co-wrote her 1990 album, "Interiors," which discussed her rocky marriage with Crowell. Although controversial, "Interiors" received a Grammy nomination for Best Contemporary Folk Album.

In 1992 Cash divorced Crowell and in 1995 she remarried songwriter and producer, John Leventhal. Together they co-produced Cash's album, "The Wheel," a memoir of her marriage to Crowell.

Cash has been nominated for 15 Grammy Awards, and she has won four of them. She has released 15 albums and has had 21 top 40 hits. 11 of the top 40 hits were number one singles. Cash is an author of four books and countless essays, some of which have appeared in The Rolling Stone, The New York Times, The Nation and The Oxford American.

February 2017

Cash was awarded with an honorary doctorate from the Memphis College of Art, where she gave a commencement speech for the graduating class of 1997. Cash became pregnant with her fourth child, Jakob, in 1998. She put her career on hold and left her album, "Rules of Travel" undone until it was released in 2003. Cash and her father joined together in the track "September When It Comes," the last recording Johnny made before his death in September 2003.

Cash developed a polyp in her vocal cords and was unable to sing for two years. During her healing process she began writing a children's book, "Penelope Jane: A Fairy's Tale."

In 2006 she released her album, "Black Cadillac." The album commemorated the loss of her father, Johnny Cash, her mother, Vivian Liberto, and her step-mother, June Carter Cash. "Black Cadillac" was nominated for the Grammy Award for Best Contemporary Folk/ Americana Album.

In 2007 Cash was diagnosed with Chiari Malformation, a disease that can cause deafness, paralysis and death. She underwent surgery and was forced to relearn speech patterns, but she was not defeated. In 2008 she returned to the stage and in 2009 she began a project called "The List."

When Cash turned 18, her father gave her a list of what he thought were the 100 most essential American songs. "The List" album had 12 songs and included duets with Bruce Springsteen, Rufus Wainwright, Elvis Costello and Jeff Tweedy. "The List" won the Americana Music Album of the Year. Cash's next album, "The River and The Thread" received three Grammy Awards. In 2010 Cash's childhood memoir, "Composed," became a best seller.

The star is involved with Children Incorporated, an organization that educates needy children. She is a member P.A.X, which prevents gun violence among children. Cash has also worked with Arkansas State University on an initiative to raise money to restore the home of her father in Dyess, Arkansas.

She served as 2015- 2016 Artist-in-Residence at the Country Music Hall of Fame Museum in Nashville, Tennessee, and continues to perform for audiences at home and abroad.

February 2017

Lane Brody – From The Yellow Rose to Walden's Puddle
By Scot England

"The Lord took me where he wanted me to go. And he continues to do that," smiles Lane Brody, as she answers the question of "Where have you been?"

Most country music fans first heard Lane Brody in 1983. That year her song 'Over You' from the film 'Tender Mercies' was nominated for an Oscar. The next year she had a number one duet with Johnny Lee with 'The Yellow Rose.'

"God gave me this gift, my voice, when I was a little girl. I started singing when I was five years old. I started playing guitar when I was ten," says Lane. "I am a singer songwriter. And by the grace of God I got into country music. I got into country music because I have a country soul."

Lane's time atop the U.S. country charts was short. But she later found that her greatest popularity was in other countries.

"I didn't know how popular I was in Europe until the internet came around! Then I started going to Holland and Germany. I did a lot of USO tours. Now I get fan mail from around the world."

In 2010, Lane appeared on Country's Family Reunion.

"I didn't know what to expect. I was surprised at how warm everyone was. They really welcomed me. The Opry ladies really embraced me. I was kind of shocked."

Brody say that Family Reunion taping is a highlight of her career.

"The experience of being with all of that talent, Charley Pride, Mickey Gilley, Johnny Lee, Ronnie McDowell, Jim Ed Brown and Lynn Anderson is something I will never forget. I became friends with Lynn. At first she couldn't figure me out. But as the years went by and she saw my philanthropic work, she embraced me. And she used to say, "I look up to you and respect you." I loved her and respected her very much."

Now, more than 30 years after 'The Yellow Rose,' you can usually find Lane Brody at a place called 'Walden's Puddle.'

"I do my work at 'Walden's Puddle' to give back to the community, and to give back to God. It is important to keep your humility and an easy way to do that is by taking care of the least and those who everyone else has forgotten."

'Walden's Puddle' is a Wildlife Rehabilitation and Education Center that provides care for over 3, 500 animals of 120 different species each year. Set on 14 acres in Joelton Tennessee, 'Walden's Puddle' offers treatment for sick, injured or orphaned wildlife.

"When I took over 'Walden's Puddle' six years ago, it was a complete disaster," says Lane. "The man who was in charge was arrested and went to jail. There were two legal loans on the property. It was in debt $250, 000. Now we are totally solvent. We have money in the bank!"

'Walden's Puddle' relies on donations, and receives no state or federal funding. Under Brody's leadership, 97% of all donations now go directly to the care of the animals.

"I see things every day at 'Walden's Puddle,' astounding miracles, things people wouldn't even believe. I've seen eagle's mates wait six months while we were caring for an eagle. They wait for a half year and the day we take it back out to the wild, its mate will be there to meet it. They fly to meet them!" Brody adds, "I've seen flocks of starlings come to meet one single starling that we've been taking care of."

Brody also devotes her time to Veterans causes.

"I work with Veterans a lot. I've sung at the Vietnam Wall in Washington D.C. several times.

February 2017

I've worked with 'Operation Stand Down' for the homeless vets in Nashville.

When I sang at the Ryman, I dedicated my songs 'Thanks For What You Did' and 'That's Where Love Comes In' to all of the veterans. I got a standing ovation. And Eddie Stubbs told me, "Everyone wants a standing ovation at the Ryman." I just looked up and said, "Glory to God."

Lane has limited her live concerts in recent years, but says she may one day do a one woman show.

"I would like to do a show that will allow me to tell my life story as I sing. I am also working on a new recording project. My husband is producing it. I think he is one of the greatest producers in the world. And my fans can order that at www.lanebrody.com."

For more information on 'Walden's Puddle,' or to make a donation, log onto www.waldenspuddle.org or write to PO Box 641 Joelton TN 37080.

Lane Brody with her husband, legendary session drummer Eddie Bayers

Gordie Tapp Memorial

Hee Haw's Gordie Tapp, died on Dec. 18, 2016, at age 94. A multitalented musician, writer and comedian, Tapp was mourned in his native Canada as well as by American audiences who had been entertained by his memorable Hee Haw characters like Cousin Clem, Samuel B. Sternwheeler, Mr. Gordon the storekeeper and Lavern Nagger.

When he died in Burlington, Ontario, following a lengthy illness, he had been married to his wife, Helen, for 73 years. Daring and fearless, Tapp had given up rollerblading at 83 and stopped riding his Harley and his horses when he turned 85.

Tapp was born in 1922 in London, Ontario, and told an interviewer that he got the comedy bug as a young man when visiting his dying 93-year-old uncle, explaining that the elderly man was in great spirits telling jokes and making people laugh.

During World War II he was Master of Ceremonies for the Canadian Army Show, playing every base in Nova Scotia, New Brunswick and PEI.

After studying at the Lorne Greene Academy of Radio Arts, he founded and hosted a 1950s Canadian radio show called Main Street Jamboree where he created a character he called Gaylord.

At a 2012 press conference he recalled that he preferred jazz over the country music format of the show and considered leaving.

"But they offered me $35 dollars more each week to stay, so I did," he laughed. "That was a lot of money in those days."

He later emceed the CBC television show Country Hoedown between 1956 and 1965, where he conceived of the Cousin Clem character he brought to "Hee Haw." He was host of The Performers, a series of shows featuring up and coming young Canadian talent, which was recorded in major Canadian cities like Montreal, Toronto, Winnipeg and Vancouver. His Canadian show, "What's On Tapp," entertained audiences for five years.

His first American television appearances were on the Perry Como and Jonathan Winters shows.

February 2017

He served as writer for 78 of the 90 "Hee Haw" episodes in which he appeared. Tapp's other acting credits included the 1983 indie movie Sweet Country Music, which he also wrote, and Wild Horse Hank, a 1979 film by director Eric Till that co-starred Linda Blair and Richard Crenna.

Tapp made 27 world tours during his career, and continued to perform into his 90s.

"Seeing the reaction of the audience and how much they enjoy it all is what keeps me going," he told an interviewer in 2012.

He cited three events from his life that were most remarkable to him. In 1967 he played in India and had tea with Indira Gandhi. On a US tour he had dinner with President Gerald Ford in Louisville, Kentucky. He also appeared before Prince Phillip in London for a Command Performance.

His 1980 album, 'Both Sides', featured both his comedic and singing talents. Tapp received the Order of Canada in 1998 and the Order of Ontario in 1999. He is a member of the Canadian Country Music Hall of Fame.

"If laughter is the best medicine, Gordie Tapp cured more country music enthusiasts than anyone else in the history of Canada," said the Canadian Country Music Hall of Fame, adding, "While Gordie Tapp's gift of laughter is uniquely country, his gentle sense of humour is known as being uniquely Canadian."

Sam Lovullo, producer of Hee Haw dies at 88

In other sad Hee Haw news, Sam Lovullo, producer and casting director of the long-running series (1969-1992), died Tuesday, January 3 at his home in Encino, California. He was 88.

Lovullo was born on September 30, 1928, in Buffalo, New York. He moved to Los Angeles when he was 15 years old. His first introduction in the entertainment business was as chief accountant in business affairs for the CBS radio and television network.

He started the production side on The Jonathan Winters Show (1967-1969), moving up to the post of associate producer. It was there Lovullo met the show's writers, John Aylesworth and Frank Peppiatt. The three men noticed that the show's generally stale ratings came to a boil whenever it featured country music stars.

When Winter's show was canceled, the three persuaded CBS to finance and air a country music variety show — shot in Nashville — which they named Hee Haw. It ran on CBS from 1969 to 1971 and in syndication until 1992, with Lovullo steadily at the helm.

In all, he produced 86 episodes of Hee Haw, as well as segments for Nashville Palace and Hee Haw Honeys. The Academy of Country Music presented him its Jim Reeves Memorial Award in 1974, an honor conferred on those who contribute substantially to the acceptance of country music throughout the world.

Valued for his work in Nashville's entertainment community, Lovullo served on both the Country Music Association and Gospel Music Association boards.

He documented his Music City experiences in the 1996 book, Life in the Kornfield: My 25 Years at Hee Haw.

Although residing in California, Lovullo continued to do occasional television work in Nashville after Hee Haw closed down. In 2001, he produced an all-star benefit concert at the Grand Ole Opry for ailing Opry star Johnny Russell.

Lovullo leaves a son, Torey, who was a major league baseball player and coach and now manages the Arizona Diamondbacks.

February 2017

New Gospel CD by Bradley Walker released

Bradley Walker met singers Joey and Rory nearly a decade ago and became close friends. Before Joey died of cancer in March 2016, she expressed wishes for Walker to sing at her funeral. Bradley had no idea that his simple act of love would also lead to his new album, Call Me Old-Fashioned.

Bradley sang the hymn Joey requested, "Leave it There," at her graveside service at the couple's Tennessee Farm. Southern gospel legend Bill Gaither, his wife Gloria and the team from Gaither Music Group were also attending the funeral. They were so impressed with his voice, they signed him to a record deal.

Rory produced Call Me Old-Fashioned and hosted the companion concert DVD, which was filmed in his barn, which occasionally doubles as a live music venue. It will air as a TV special on several networks including RFD-TV, PBS, Gaither TV, TBN, Family Net, and CTN, and will also be available at retail.

Born with muscular dystrophy, Walker has spent his life in a wheelchair, but has never let his physical challenges dim his passion for music. The Oak Ridge Boys invited him to sing on national television when he was only 10 years old. He recalls meeting the legendary Keith Whitley that night and from then on, he knew he wanted to be a country singer. Yet his practical streak led Walker to get an education and take a job as a materials analyst at Browns Ferry Nuclear Plant, where he continues to work when he's not recording and performing.

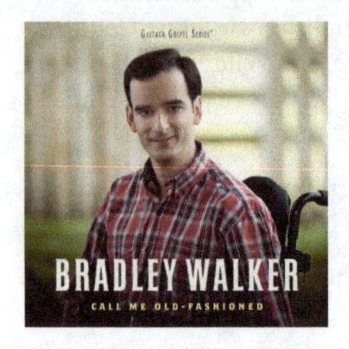

When asked to describe Call Me Old-Fashioned, Walker has unique and fairly unexpected response: "I think of this as a gospel record for people who don't go to church," he says. "I hope this can be an inspiration not only to people who are saved and who are in church —because I believe that's where we all need to be, but I want to reach people also who aren't in church and get them thinking about life. These are songs about real life."

Join us on our new YouTube Channel

Larry Black, producer of the TV shows Country's Family Reunion and Larry's Country Diner announced that they are doing something new and want you to know about it... THE BRAND NEW, FREE, YouTube Channel called Country Road TV. Think of Country Road TV as your one stop shop of all things Country Music including Country's Family Reunion, Larry's Country Diner and so much MORE!

And best of all, it's FREE! The Country Road TV YouTube channel has tons of video clips of some of our favorite performances and moments from all of our shows. It's totally FREE to subscribe? Of course if you don't want to subscribe, you are more than welcome to watch all of the videos at your leisure as many times as you like.

We'll update the channel at least twice every week with new clips featuring rare performances, exclusive behind-the-scenes content, artist interviews and our favorite moments from all of our TV productions. You will definitely want to subscribe to the channel to stay informed whenever we upload new content or simply book mark the page so that you can easily access it!

Well, look-ee there... We're finally getting into the 21st century! It took us a while, didn't it?

February 2017

Pete Fishers leaves Opry for ACM Awards

Big news in the country music community on January 9 as it was announced that Pete Fisher, the long-time Vice President and General Manager of the Grand Ole Opry, had accepted the job as CEO of the Academy of Country Music in Los Angeles. After 32 years in Nashville, Pete Fisher will be moving to California to head the country music's second-biggest awards show. Long-time ACM CEO Bob Romeo left the position in May of 2016, leaving the post vacant ever since. Pete Fisher will only be the 2nd CEO in the ACM's 53-year history.

"As I enter my 30th year in the Country music industry, I am extremely grateful for all of the opportunities I have been given to serve those who both create Country music and those who help connect that great music with fans all over the world," Fisher says. "I want to thank the Officers and Board for giving me this exciting opportunity to lead the ACADEMY into a new era. I look forward to collaborating with them and our passionate and talented staff, charting an exciting course into the future."

There were mixed emotions when it was announced. Pete Fisher is out at the Grand Ole Opry where he's been presiding over everything Opry related for the last 17 years. Some believe that as one of the most powerful, influential in Country Music he did a wonderful job of bringing life into a sometimes less than money making venture and others felt he was one of the most vilified men in all of country music for the same reason because he took the direction of the Grand Ole Opry in a new direction and away from traditional country music. Many were unhappy with how the Opry functioned under the Pete Fisher regime.

While Pete Fisher headed the Grand Ole Opry, it invited more modern pop country entertainers into its ranks of members that ever before—acts such as Blake Shelton, Darius Rucker, Rascall Flatts, and Little Big Town. Also during this time, many of these big names shirked their performance obligations to the Opry like never before with no real consequences. By accepting membership, artists agree to play the Opry stage at least 10 times a year. Out of the new batch of current country stars, Carrie Underwood is the only one who regularly meets her performance obligations.

Apparent ageism took hold at the Opry beginning with Pete's tenure in 1999. On September 29th, 2002, in an article that appeared on the front page of The Tennessean, long-time Opry members Charlie Louvin, Del Reeves and Stonewall Jackson blasted Fisher for cutting back on their performances after years of loyalty to the institution. Stonewall Jackson said Pete Fisher told him he "would work as hard as possible until no gray hair was in the audience or on the stage." Eventually Stonewall Jackson sued the Opry for age discrimination. The case was settled privately.

. Hank Williams III's Reinstate Hank campaign continues to work towards the goal of having the Opry show their final respects to Hank Williams, but Hank3 says Pete Fisher swore to him, "We will never reinstate a dead guy." The 3rd generation performer was hoping the Grand Ole Opry would reinstate him as a symbolic gesture of respect. Hank Williams was fired from the Opry in 1952 for drunkenness and missing rehearsals. The Opry promised to let Hank Williams back if he cleaned up his act, but Hank Williams died before he was reinstated.

After years of trying to get today's country stars to play the Opry by giving them the institution's highest distinction, the Opry obviously had a shift in attitude about how to approach membership when they recently asked Crystal Gayle, the sister of Loretta Lynn and singer of "Don't It Make My Brown Eyes Blue" was asked to become a Grand Ole Opry member by Carrie Underwood in November, 2016. And then on December 30th, bluegrass duo Dailey & Vincent was also asked to join the Opry.

February 2017

Pete Fisher also did some good things. Opry attendance increased dramatically from before his tenure. Fisher also helped when the Grand Ole Opry was devastated by the flooding in Nashville in 2010.

The biggest question for Grand Ole Opry fans is who will be Pete Fisher's replacement, and what direction will the new leadership take the institution? The pendulum seems to be swinging as country music and Nashville seem to be seeing a rise in more traditional leaning music with deeper substance, and the commercial aspects in the Americana music scene are picking up.

Country's Family Reunion has always honored the traditional artists and will continue to do so and it is hoped by many that the Grand Ole Opry will do so going forward with a new leader.

Q: I would like to know if C.W. McCall is kin to Dennis and Darrell or if they are different breeds of cats?

The old "Crawler Hauler"
Al Beaupre, Milton, VT

A: C.W. McCall is not a real person. "C.W. McCall" isn't the name of the group that recorded the music. C.W. McCall is the nom de chanteur of Bill Fries, an advertising man who created the character of C.W. McCall.

In 1972, while working for the Omaha advertising firm of Bozell & Jacobs, Bill Fries created a television campaign for the Old Home Bread brand of the Metz Baking Company. The advertisements told of the adventures of truck driver C.W. McCall, his dog Sloan, and of the truck stop that McCall frequented, The Old Home Café. Bill based the character and his environment on his own upbringing in western Iowa. The commercials were very successful. So successful, that the Des Moines Register published the air times of the commercials in the daily television listings.

From those commercials came the first of the C.W. McCall songs, named after the restaurant: "Old Home Fill-er Up An' Keep On A-Truckin' Café". While Bill provided the lyrics to the song and the voice of C.W. McCall, his collaborator Chip Davis wrote the music. Soon C.W.'s first album, Wolf Creek Pass, was released; its title song was a misadventure of a truck with brake failure.

C.W. McCall's popularity reached its peak in January 1976, when "Convoy" — from his second album, Black Bear Road — reached the number one position on both the pop and country charts of Billboard.

Darrell McCall was born and raised in New Jasper Township, Greene County, Ohio. He was a boyhood friend of fellow future musician Johnny Paycheck. At the age of 15, he landed a job as a disc jockey at a local Ohio radio show on Saturday mornings. During this time, he also performed as a musician at dances and other events. After graduating from high school, McCall joined the military and was stationed in Kentucky.

Q: Dear Paula,

I just finished reading the story where Larry Black was being roasted. When I read this I got the feeling that there isn't going to be any new Larry's Country Diner shows. I hope not! I want for Larry and sit nights just for all those shows. I just feel so relaxed and I do my sewing while listening to this show. Please answer this in the CFR News.

Jean Lilley, Masontown, PA

A: Have no fear. The Roast was simply a way to show Larry the love and to celebrate the 20th anniversary of Country's Family Reunion which is 2017! We are already scheduled to shoot more Larry's Country Diner shows in February. If you'd like to attend a taping (anyone) call Customer Service at 800-820-5405.

If you have questions send them to Paula, CFR News, P.O. Box 210796, Nashville, TN 37221 or email them to paula@gabrielcommunications.com.

February 2017

Jeannie Seely CD Release Party for Written In Song

Jeannie really is glowing during her performance.

Jeannie Seely held a free CD release party at 3rd & Lindsley in Nashville, TN on Tuesday, January 10 to a full house. The new CD. WRITTEN IN SONG, includes 14 tracks all co-written or self-penned by Jeannie.

Special guests include Connie Smith, Marty Stuart, Jessi Colter, Jan Howard, Kenny Sears, and Tess Sears. The CD is $15.00 plus s/h and can be ordered from her website www.jeannieseely.com.

Sponsored by Springer Mountain Farm Chicken's Gus Arrendale who is known for supporting great traditional country music, the show was a rousing success. Donations were accepted at the door to support The Opry Trust Fund, which provides financial assistance in time of extraordinary need, emergency or catastrophe to individuals who are or have been employed full time in a facet of the country music industry (i.e. performer, songwriter, publisher, radio, session musician, etc.).

The audience was filled with fans and friends, including many country music artists and their families.

Jeannie posted on her facebook page, "Thank you Charlie Monk! So this is the first chance I've had to say thank you to all of the wonderful people in my life who went out of their way to make my CD release party last night such a success! It was an event I will relive the rest of my life. I didn't even know some of you were there!! I appreciate the tremendous support of everyone onstage, offstage and backstage!!! The love I felt last night is overwhelming....and I'm so glad you like the new project! Thank you from the bottom of my heart!!"

Jan Howard sings with Jeannie.

Jimmy Capps backs up Jeannie on guitar.

Julie Keech-Harris, Hawkshaw Hawkins Jr. and Charlene Tilton

Jan Howard sings with Jeannie.

February 2017

Jessi Colter releases religious album

Country music luminary Jessi Colter is releasing her second album since husband, Waylon Jennings, died. The Psalms is a labor of love for Jessi and is set to be released March 24 on Legacy Recordings. It is a collaboration with guitarist Lenny Kaye.

Jessi grew up in a Christian Pentecostal home singing holy songs where the sacred defined daily life in the presence of the secular; her mother was a preacher, but her dad built and drove race cars. Kaye grew up loving the minor key of Jewish cantorial music, but also had an uncle who wrote the lyrics to the love theme from The Godfather. Kaye met Colter in the mid-1990s, while co-writing the memoir of her late husband, Waylon Jennings. When they met, he found her devising piano melodies for psalms she'd randomly select from her Bible.

Kaye writes in the liner notes for The Psalms, "It was one of the most beautiful expressions of belief I've ever witnessed."

The Psalms offers listeners the sound of one woman's praise.

Jim Glaser still performing

From the time Jim Glaser left his family's 1200-acre farm in the heart of Nebraska, at age nineteen, to travel the world with famed singer Marty Robbins, he has been at the vanguard of country music's developments and trends. Well-known as a singer and songwriter by country music fans the world over, and well-respected by the most prominent players in the music business today, Jim Glaser is the perfect performer to fill your entertainment needs.

As members of the Grand Ole Opry for fifteen years, Jim Glaser and his two brothers (Tompall and the Glaser Brothers) won nearly every group award country music had to offer.

The Glaser Brothers travelled with the Marty Robbins show for three years, and it's Jim's tenor voice you hear on Marty's classic, "El Paso."

Today, Chuck and his wife, Beverly Ann Zegers Glaser, are the parents of 6 grown children, 4 in-laws, and 12 grandchildren. Jim and his wife, Jane Evens Glaser, are the parents of 4 grown children, 1 daughter-in-law, and 7 grandchildren.

Jim is still performing at a variety of venues but Chuck has retired from the music business.

Tompall died on August 13, 2013, aged 79, leaving behind his widow, June Johnson Glaser.

COUNTRY'S FAMILY REUNION Presents

Sweethearts
Feb. 3 & 4
Feb. 10 & 11

Merle Haggard
Feb. 17 & 18
Feb. 24 & 25

7 p.m. Friday   11 p.m. Saturday
(CENTRAL TIME)

February 2017

Diner Chat
with Renae the Waitress

It's easy...it's FUN!!
You don't want to miss a call.
Listen live by Phone or on the web,
every Thursday at 3:00 p.m. EST.

1-425-440-5100
ID Code: 909005#

Happy Valentines Day!…I hope all of you enjoy our CFR Sweethearts shows on RFD in February. Rhonda Vincent and her husband, Herb is on that series and had so much fun. Herb doesn't like public display of affection so you can see him blush when Rhonda holds his hand. Rhonda joined us on Diner Chat in January and she was such a delight. If you missed the call go to www.larryscountrydiner.com/dinerchat and listen to the recorded call. And check out her cool paper dolls on her website at www.Rhondavincent.com.

NEW SHOWS

We will have new Diner Shows in February and my daughter; Chi joins me again as a Diner Waitress. Both the girls where there for lunch. Rio is 3 ½ and Sedona is 10 months old. Boy do they grow up fast!!

THE PROMISE

And speaking of Rio….you can see her photo in my new book THE PROMISE. If you are a true Diner Fan then you need to order this book. It has over 60 promise scriptures including artist photos and the original airdate. It makes a nice devotional with a ribbon marker in a rich red hardback cover. This book makes a great gift and I will autograph each one ordered. When I thought about a new book I wanted a devotional but not just a book with scripture verses. I think you will agree this book is very special.

CUSTOMER SERVICE

Many of you have asked us to repeat our customer service phone number.

800-820-5405 Customer service hours are M-F 8:30-4:30 Mountain Time zone. Although customer service is located in Price, Utah both Jason and DeAnn are employed by Larry Black. So if you think you are talking to random operators when you call…… that is not the case. In fact some days I may answer Customer Service calls from my Desk in Nashville. We think this is such a benefit to our company to have our very own customer service department. Jason also joins me on DINER CHAT every week and DeAnn runs our HELP DESK onboard our CFR Cruise. They are so good at their job that they actually remember our customers.

DINER TV SHOW TAPINGS

We always hear folks say they would like to attend one of our tapings but think they can't get in. Not TRUE. We tape every other month. So as soon as we have our dates confirmed DeAnn starts booking folks. We tape 4 shows in one day so call DeAnn or Jason for dates and taping times. And the best thing about our tapings is that they are FREE.

1-800-820-5405 February 14 is our current taping date.

If you have a friend that would like our NEWS PAPER then call customer service and we will send out a complimentary issue. Call 1-800-820-5405.

February 2017

"To Joey With Love" DVD now available

Husband-and-wife singing duo Joey+Rory wanted more to life … so they chose less. In preparation for the birth of their child, the couple simplified their lives by putting their music career aside and staying at home, planting roots deep in the soil of their small farm, and the community they loved.

They believed God would give them a great story … and He did.

Experience the incredible true story of Joey and Rory Feek in the poignant new film TO JOEY, WITH LOVE. Intimately filmed by the couple over two and a half years, the movie documents the stirring journey of the 2010 Academy of Country Music Top New Vocal Duo.

TO JOEY, WITH LOVE takes moviegoers from the birth of their daughter Indiana, born with Down Syndrome, through Joey's struggle with and ultimate surrender to cancer—all amidst their never-ending hope in something far greater. God gave Joey+Rory a love story for the ages, one that is sure to inspire hope and faith in all who experience it.

To Joey With Love is now available on DVD. It can be purchased from Rory's website www.tojoeywithlove.com or you can purchase it from Amazon, Walmart, Barnes & Noble, Christianbook.com, Family Christian, liftertoday, Best Buy and Target. You may need to check to see if it is available in the store or if they need to order it for you to pick up later. Depending on the store you choose to purchase the DVD from, the price varies from approximately $11.00 - $20.

For more information or to order by mail, please call "To Joey With Love" 615-476-5276.

Mo Pitney & wife welcome new baby, Evelyne Nadine

Mo Pitney announced the birth of his little girl on Thursday, January 12 by way of Instagram saying, "Well, Evelyne Nadine decided to have her birthday early! Em and I had a number of scares this morning but God intercepted every one of them with His powerful sovereign love.. I couldn't be more thankful to have our baby and my wife safe and loved.."

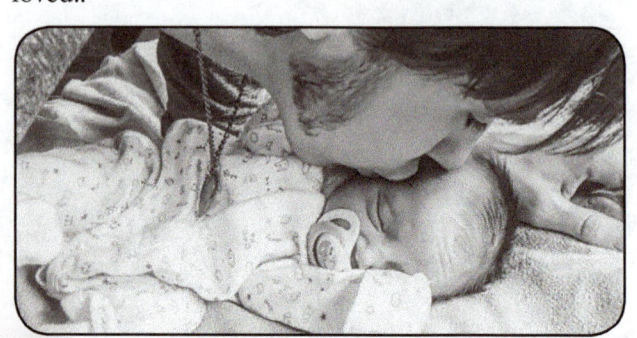

He continued with, "Finding new kinds and depths of love..thankful for His beautiful design."

Baby Evelyne was expected to arrive sometime in February; Pitney and his wife, Emily, revealed their pick for the baby's name, and her sex, in mid-September, after announcing in early August that they were expecting.

Pitney and his now-wife were engaged in September of 2015 and married in early March.

February 2017

MARCH

Tribute evening features special performance of "Amazing Grace" by Randy Travis & All-Star Cast

1 Night. 1 Place. 1 Time: A Heroes and Friends Tribute to Randy Travis was a star-studded event enjoyed by a sold-out crowd. The concert featured performances from over 40 artists including Tanya Tucker singing Travis favorite "I Told You So," The Bellamy Brothers singing "Diggin' Up Bones" and a special rendition of "Forever and Ever, Amen" from Garth Brooks.

Nashville Mayor Megan Berry made a special appearance during the show with a proclamation announcing the day as Randy Travis Day in the city of Nashville.

The Governor of Tennessee, Bill Haslam showed up to wish Randy well and honor the adopted Tennessean by declaring the day Stroke Awareness Day.

Other special performances included a Grand Ole Opry Moment featuring John Conlee, Dailey & Vincent, Rudy Gatlin, Jan Howard, Riders in the Sky and Jeannie Seely. The group came together on stage to perform "I'll Fly Away."

The end of the show featured a performance by Travis himself. With the all-star lineup, Randy Travis sang "Amazing Grace" and "Will The Circle Be Unbroken."

A portion of the proceeds are to go to the Randy Travis Foundation; a 501(c)3 non-profit that provides support for victims of strokes and cardiovascular diseases as well as arts and entertainment education for at-risk children. For more information, visit www.randytravisfoundation.org.

1 Night. 1 Place. 1 Time: A Heroes and Friends Tribute to Randy Travis was produced by Mary Travis along with Tony Conway of Conway Entertainment Group/Ontourage Management, Mike Smardak of Outback Concerts of Tennessee, Inc. who is also the promoter of the event and Kirt Webster of Webster and Associates.

With lifetime sales in excess of 25 million, Randy Travis is one of the biggest country record sellers of all time and the most recent inductee into the Country Music Hall of Fame class of 2016. His honors include seven Grammy Awards, 10 Academy of Country Music statuettes, 10 American Music Awards, two People's Choice awards, seven Music City News awards, eight Dove Awards from the Gospel Music Association and five Country Music Association honors. In addition, three of his performances earned CMA Song of the Year honors, "On the Other Hand" (1986), "Forever and Ever Amen" (1987) and "Three Wooden Crosses" (2003). To date, he has 18 No. 1 singles, 29 top-10 smashes and more than 40 appearances in feature films and television shows to his credit. Ten of his albums are Gold Records. Eight are Platinum. Two have gone Double Platinum. One is Triple Platinum and another is Quintuple Platinum. In 2004, Randy was honored with his own star in the Hollywood Walk of Fame and is honored on the Music City Walk of Fame in Nashville, TN. He has been a member of the cast of the Grand Ole Opry since 1986. Since his near fatal stroke in 2013, with the help of his wife Mary and vigorous physical therapy, Randy continues to make improvements in his speaking, walking, and yes, singing.

March 2017

Nadine
The Church Lady

Lord, give me a sense of humor,
Give me the grace to see a joke,
To get some humor out of life,
And to pass it on to other folk.

Funny Hymn Titles

The Tailor's Hymn....
"Holy, Holy, Holy"

The Golfer's Hymn...
"There's a Green Hill Far Away"

The Politician's Hymn...
"Standing on the Promises"

REAL NAMES OF COUNTRY ARTISTS

Christina Claire
Wynonna Judd

Eileen Regina Edwards
Shania Twain

Donald Eugene Lytle
Johnny Paycheck

Treasures from fans of the show! Stained glass from the Warniments

Recipes from Trisha Yearwood

"Garth likes to cook breakfast. It's wonderful to sleep in and wake up to the smell of bacon cooking. Don't be too jealous, but he always has a fresh pot of coffee already made, too! He created this breakfast bowl because he wanted something really hearty. He's the first person I ever met who puts pasta with eggs and bacon, but it works, and it tastes great! If you're really hungry, all the better if you're going to eat one of these breakfast bowls. Don't worry if you can't finish it; Garth will come along later and "clean up"!"

-Trisha Yearwood

Ingredients

2 tablespoons butter

8 large eggs

1 16-ounce bag frozen hash browns or Tater Tots, thawed

1 pound pork sausage

1 pound bacon

1 9-ounce package cheese and roasted garlic tortellini

10 ounces sharp Cheddar cheese, grated (about 2½ cups)

Cooking Directions

In a large skillet, melt the butter and scramble the eggs.

In a separate large skillet, cook the hash browns according to package directions.

In a third large skillet, break up the sausage with a wooden spoon and cook until browned.

Drain off the excess fat. Transfer the sausage to a bowl. Cook the bacon in the same skillet. Drain on paper towels and set aside.

Cook the tortellini according to the package directions. Layer a large bowl with hash browns, sausage, bacon, tortellini, eggs, and cheese.

Any potato will do. Garth's even been known to use french fries! I sometimes fry an egg sunny side up and pile it on top of Garth's bowl. He likes the way the yolk oozes into the dish.

Serves 4

46 CFR NEWS

March 2017

Crystal Gayle inducted into Grand Ole Opry by sister and Opry legend Loretta Lynn

Grammy®-winning songstress Crystal Gayle was inducted into the Grand Ole Opry® this evening at the Ryman Auditorium by her sister and Opry legend Loretta Lynn. Gayle made her Opry debut 50 years ago on the Ryman stage, singing the country classic "Ribbon of Darkness" at age 16. She had been publicly invited to join the Opry by Opry member Carrie Underwood in November.

"We've been together a long time, honey. And we've never had a fight," Lynn said. "It was the greatest moment of my life when they made me a member of the Grand Ole Opry in 1962. I know she is just as happy as I was then." "Being a member of the Opry is just incredible," Gayle beamed. "It's really hard to comprehend. I have felt like a part of the Opry for all these years. Now, I'm official."

Grammy-nominated duo Dailey & Vincent is set to be formally inducted into the Opry on Saturday, March 11.

Crystal Gayle is an award-winning country music icon whose reign in the music business includes 20 No. 1 country hits, six albums certified Gold by the RIAA and the first female artist in country music history to reach platinum sales with her 1977 album, We Must Believe in Magic. Her 1977 country-pop crossover hit song, "Don't It Make My Brown Eyes Blue," became an iconic staple and solidified her as one of the top female vocalists during the 1970s and 1980s. Her list of platinum and gold was to be matched only by her awards and accolades. CMA's "Female Vocalist of the Year," for two consecutive years, she became a Grammy Award Winner for "Best Female Vocal Performance," thanks to her beloved "Brown Eyes" - a song that she today admits she has never grown tired of singing. Crystal swept the Academy of Country Music Awards for three of their "Top Female Vocalist" statuettes. She is the recipient of three "American Music Awards," voted by the nation as America's "Favorite Female Artist." Perhaps nothing sums up Crystal's career achievements as well as being awarded with a star on the fabled Hollywood Walk of Fame in October 2009. Also famous for her nearly floor-length hair, she was voted one of the 50 most beautiful people in the world by People Magazine in 1983. She is the younger sister (by 19 years) of singer Loretta Lynn, and a distant cousin of singer Patty Loveless. Gayle also has a star on the Hollywood Walk of Fame near Lynn's star. In August 2016, the Academy of Country Music honored Crystal with the Cliffie Stone Pioneer Award during the 10th Annual ACM Honors.™ For more information, visit crystalgayle.com

Look who's on the Diner this week!

ROY CLARK
Thursday, March 2
7 p.m. Central
Saturday, March 4
10 p.m. Central
PREVIOUSLY AIRED

MANDY BARNETT
Thursday, March 9
7 p.m. Central
Saturday, March 11
10 p.m. Central
NEW SHOW

DAN MILLER
Thursday, March 16
7 p.m. Central
Saturday, March 18
10 p.m. Central
NEW SHOW

THE MALPASS BROS.
Thursday, March 23
7 p.m. Central
Saturday, March 25
10 p.m. Central
NEW SHOW

BILLY YATES & MICHAEL PETERSON
Thursday, March 30
7 p.m. Central
Saturday, April 1
10 p.m. Central
NEW SHOW

March 2017

Duo pays tribute to their fathers, Harold & Don Reid of the Statler Brothers

Songs Our Dads Wrote is distributed exclusively by BFD through RED Distribution, with standout songs on the project also including former Statler Brothers hit, "Guilty," originally released in 1983, when it stormed into the Billboard Hot Country Songs top ten. The new version takes on a rootsy feel, with original Statler Brothers member Jimmy Fortune also appearing on vocals.

Wilson Fairchild is a country music duo made up of Wil and Langdon Reid from the beautiful Shenandoah Valley of Virginia. These two men, referred to as "the Reid boys," have been writing, performing and playing music together their whole lives. To sum up their passion and drive for their music and career, a self-penned line from their new title cut, "Country On", says it all: "We love country music and we'll never let it die."

Wil and Langdon are highly acclaimed songwriters. They both have been writing songs since their teenage years, in between baseball and football games and girls, of course. Along with recording their own music, such artists as the Statler Brothers, Ricky Skaggs and Dailey & Vincent have recorded their songs, as well. So yes, that means their songwriting gamut spans through the country, bluegrass, and gospel fields. They learned the craft from the best and know how to put an idea to music and come away with a great storytelling song.

Songs Our Dads Wrote Track Listing:

1. Left Handed Woman
2. I'll Even Love You (Better Than I Did Then)
3. How Are Things in Clay, Kentucky?
4. She's Too Good
5. Second Thoughts
6. Some I Wrote 
7. Guilty
8. A Letter From Shirley Miller
9. He went to the Cross Loving You
10. The Statler Brothers Song

Wilson Fairchild On Tour:

Mar. 25 Waynesboro, Va. – The Wayne Theatre

Jul. 04 Staunton, Va. – America's Birthday Celebration

Jul. 29 Luray, Va. – Duke's Fest

Dec. 09 Waynesboro, Va. – The Wayne Theatre

Fans can learn more at wilsonfairchild.com

Country's Family Reunion Presents

Tribute To Merle Haggard
March 3 & 10

Gettin' Together
March 17, 24 & 31

7 p.m. Friday   11 p.m. Saturday
(CENTRAL TIME)

March 2017

COUNTRY LEGENDS OF THE PAST & PRESENT
BY TOM WOOD

Carl Butler and Pearl

Some artists are lucky to count a crossover hit during their career.

In 1962, Carl Butler and Pearl scored their own "Cross Over" of a sort.

"Don't Let Me Cross Over" was the first single recorded by the husband/wife duo, and was an immediate hit with fans of the newest Grand Ole Opry members. In four short weeks, the song had climbed all the way to No. 1 — where it stayed for 11 weeks total (though it wasn't 11 consecutive weeks).

That in itself is a pretty cool story. "Don't Let Me Cross Over" made its debut at No. 1 on Dec. 29, 1962, then fell out of the top ranking as the calendar page turned to 1963.

Marty Robbins took over the top spot in the new year's first ranking on Jan. 5 with the wonderful "Ruby Ann." But a week later, "Don't Let Me Cross Over" nudged back to No. 1 in the Jan. 12 countdown.

It then got bumped by "The Ballad of Jed Clampett" from Flatt & Scruggs, but roared back to the top spot for the weeks of Jan. 26. Then the Flatt & Scruggs theme song of The Beverly Hillbillies television show regained the top spot and held it and again on Feb. 16, when "Don't Let Me Cross Over" once again took over at No. 1.

In sports terms, think of this as a tag-team wrestling match pitting Carl and Pearl against Flatt & Scruggs over that three-month stretch. It was Whispering Bill Anderson who finally ended Carl and Pearl's reign at No. 1 on April 6, 1963, scoring with "Still" for seven weeks at No. 1.

The strength of that country classic "Don't Let Me Cross Over" was enough to keep the couple in the public spotlight for much of the next two decades.

They had a total of 14 songs make the charts from 1961-69, though only one other cracked the Top 10. That was 1964's "Too Late to Try Again," which peaked that year at No. 9. Some of their other better-known works were "Loving Arms" (1963) and "I'm Hanging Up The Phone" (1964). Both of those hits reached No. 14.

Carl Butler was also a top-notch songwriter in his day, penning the hit "If Teardrops Were Pennies" for Carl Smith—it went to No. 8 in 1951 and was a 1973 top 10 song for Porter Wagoner and Dolly Parton. Carl also co-wrote "Crying My Heart Out Over You" in the early 1960s—which Ricky Skaggs recorded in 1981 and it became his first chart-topper.

Following the success of that Skaggs version, the Butlers pretty much retired to their "Cross Over Acres" home in Franklin, Tennessee. They got married in 1952 and were married for 36 years until Pearl died in 1988. Carl "crossed over" in 1992, joining his wife in eternity.

Author Tom Wood, who writes thrillers and Westerns, is a regular contributor to Country Family Reunion News. Reach him at tomwoodauthor.com

March 2017

Jimmy Fortune Hits the Road in 2017 for North American Tour

Country Music Hall of Fame singer/songwriter Jimmy Fortune is gearing up for his upcoming 2017 North American tour, which includes more than 40 stops. The must-see tour is already underway, with several standout appearances in 20 different states. Fans will also have a chance to catch waves with Fortune later this year, as he appears on the 14th Annual Jimmy Fortune Alaskan Cruise, July 16 - 23

"This is my 14th year as a solo artist and I've been very blessed to have also had a successful career with the Statler Brothers, and now still being able to go to these great places and towns," said Jimmy Fortune. "Being able to say thank you to the fans is what I look forward to the most. Signing autographs and hearing stories from fans after each show is always a highlight."

Since getting his start with the iconic Statler Brothers exactly 35 years ago singing tenor, the chart topper has transitioned from group member to a successful solo artist. As a member of both the Country Music Hall of Fame and Gospel Music Hall of Fame, along with penning No. 1 country hits such as "Elizabeth" and "Too Much On My Heart," Fortune has a history of captivating country and gospel music fans. The award-winning singer looks to build upon that momentum on the blockbuster tour, performing a combination of gospel standards, along with some of the biggest Statler Brothers hits.

Fortune is kicking off the year on a high, after a huge 2016, which saw the singer being awarded the "Cliffie Stone Pioneer Award" by the Academy of Country Music with the Statler Brothers. Fortune was also the recipient of his very first Dove award for "Bluegrass Recorded Song of the Year," along with the Oak Ridge Boys for their song "Life's Railway To Heaven" featured on Fortune's critically acclaimed project Hits & Hymns. The popular TV special, "Jimmy Fortune: Hits & Hymns" also helped to propel Fortune to new heights, being featured on nationwide television throughout the year.

Jimmy Fortune On Tour:

Mar. 10 - Columbia, S.C. - Private
Mar. 24 - Rocky Mount, Va. - Harvester Performance Center
Mar. 25 - Lovingston, Va. - Nelson County HighSchool
Apr. 4 - Leesburg, Fla.- Lake Yale Baptist Conference Center
Apr. 7 - Corsicana, Texas - The Palace Theatre
Apr. 8 - Arlington, Texas - Arlington Music Hall
Apr. 22 - Hegins, Pa. - Tri Valley JR-SR High School
May 2 - Branson, Mo. - Starlite Theatre
May 7 - Elkins, W.Va. - American Mountain Theatre
May 19 and 20 - Scottsburg, Ind. - Ross Country Jamboree
May 26 and 27 - Gatlinburg, Tenn. - Gaither Family Fest
June 10 - Steelville, Mo. - The Meramec Music Theatre
June 25 - Confirmed TBA
July 1 - Hiawassee, Ga. - Anderson Music Hall
July 4 - Radford, Va. - Radford 4th of July Celebration
July 16 through July 23 - Alaska - Jimmy Fortune Alaskan Cruise
July 29 - Benton, Ky. - Kentucky Opry
Aug. 15 - Lewisburg, W.Va. - WV State Fair
Sept. 2 - Lancaster, PA - American Music Theatre
Sept. 4 - Paden City, W.Va. - Paden City Labor Day Celebration
Sept. 9 - McLeansboro, Ill. - McLeansboro Fall Festival
Sept. 14 - Bremen, GA - Mill Town Music Hall
Sep. 18 - Lawrenceville, Ga. - Gwinnett County Fair
Sept. 21 - Branson, Mo. - Starlite Theatre
Sept. 23 - Prairie du Sac, Wisc. - River Arts Center
Oct. 6 - South Boston, Va. - Halifax County Fair
Oct. 7 - Manteo, N.C. - Outer Banks Bluegrass Festival
Oct. 15 - Pigeon Forge, Tenn. - Country Tonite Theatre
Oct. 17 and 18 - Branson, Mo. - Starlite Theatre
Nov. 11 and 12 - Branson, Mo. - Starlite Theatre
Dec. 2 - York, Pa. - York Expo Center
Dec. 3 - Lebanon, Pa. - Lebanon Expo Center
Dec. 7 - Weyers Cave, VA - Weyers Cave Community Center
Dec. 8 - Amherst, Va. - Clifford Baptist Church
Dec. 9 - Liberty, N.C. - The Liberty Showcase Theater

March 2017

20th Anniversary of CFR celebrated on cruise

Daryl Singletary and Rhonda Vincent duet.

Teea Goans kept it country

Leroy Van Dyke sings his hit "The Auctioneer"

Bill Anderson opened the first Country's Family Reunion show aboard the ship.

The Malpass Brothers were a big hit!

March 2017

The Larry's Country Diner show had the multiple personalities of Johnny Counterfit as well as Mark Wells and the Malpass Brothers. Together they kept everyone laughing and entertained.

'Chicken Man' Gus Arrendale was speechless when Jeannie Seely and husband Gene Ward came on stage as 'Gus' and his chicken. Everyone was in stitches!aboard the ship.

Watching the leg, listening to the song of the Malpass Brothers.

The autograph sessions are always a hit. Seated: Larry Black, Gene Watson, Michele Capps. Standing: Leroy Van Dyke, Taylor Malpass, Rhonda Vincent, Daryl Singletary, Jeannie Seely, Johnny Counterfit, Jimmy Capps, Bill Anderson, Mark Wills, Keith Bilbrey, Teea Goans, Chris Malpass, Nadine and Renae the Waitress.aboard the ship.

March 2017

Show two of Country's Family Reunion onboard the ship.

Johnny Counterfit and his many voices.

Our favorite bluegrass performer, Rhonda Vincent.

The always popular Gene Watson.

Bill Anderson entertains the crowd.

Mark Wills has become a cruise favorite.

March 2017

53 CFR NEWS

Donnie Winters, son of Don Winters who sang with Marty Robbins performed a yodeling song in tribute to his dad and all the cowboy singers.

Jimmy picked and Michele sang as a special treat to open Nadine's show.

Nadine always keeps everyone laughing with her wit and wisdom on aging.

Dancing at Rhonda's Jam Session with Rhonda and Daryl.

Sisters sing Elvira and have everyone singing along along in the Jam.

The show's finale has everyone on their feet, singing along with the artists!

54
CFR NEWS

March 2017

It's A Family Tradition

By Sasha Kay Dunavant

Lefty & David Frizzell

The role of the family is an integral theme of Country Music. Some of County's greatest songs have captured memories from family life. Family acts, including sibling duos, have long been a staple on the Country stage. Some families have produced numerous talented members, both performers and songwriters, who separately made their impact on the genre. In other families, each generation has expanded the legacy of the one before it. This series celebrates Country Music's family connections.

Lefty Frizzell, who was born in Corsicana, Texas, in 1928, counted among his earliest influences Jimmie Rodgers, Ernest Tubb and Ted Daffan. As a teenager, Lefty began singing on a KELD El Dorado radio station and continued singing on radio, in nightclubs, for dances and in talent competitions throughout the Southern states into young adulthood.

His career was interrupted when the 19-year-old was jailed for the statutory rape of an underage fan. His guilt-ridden separation from his young wife inspired him to write poetry and songs, some of which later would become hits. Upon his release from jail, Lefty worked as an oilman with his father but soon missed his passion for performing.

He collected a dedicated fan base in 1950 while performing at the Texas nightclub, Ace of Clubs. The owner of the Ace of Clubs, Jim Beck had musical connections and encouraged Lefty to record a demo in April of 1950. The demo included Lefty's own songs such as, "If You've Got the Money (I've Got the Time)." Even though Little Jimmie Dickens passed on the offer to record the song, Columbia Records producer, Don Law was impressed by it. "If You've Got the Money (I've Got the Time)" and "I Love You A Thousand Ways" launched Lefty into stardom. His drawn out syllables and softer singing style smoothed down the toughness of Honky Tonk and became the sought after way of singing country music. Lefty performed on The Louisiana Hayride and The Grand Ole Opry multiple times during the height of his career in the mid 1950s.

Hank Williams and Lefty Frizzell are considered to be two of the major influences on Country Music singers for generations. In a 1973 homage to the pair, Stoney Edwards recorded the top 40 hit, "Hank and Lefty Raised My Country Soul." Lefty became frustrated with Columbia Records for not releasing the material he thought they should and began touring and working with Jim Denny at Nashville's Cerdarwood Publishing Company in 1959. His last major hit was 1964's "Saginaw, Michigan," which was nominated for a Grammy.

Lefty has influenced Country Music legends, such as Willie Nelson, Merle Haggard, George Jones, Roy Orbison and The Everly Brothers. "If You've Got the Money (I've Got the Time)" earned Lefty a Grammy Hall of Fame Award. In 1972 he was inducted into Nashville's Songwriters Hall of Fame. Lefty suffered from alcoholism and died of a massive stroke on July 19, 1975. He was 47 years old. In 1982 Lefty was inducted into the Country Music Hall of Fame.

Many would say that Lefty's little brother, David, is the mirror image of his older brother. David was born in 1941 in El Dorado, Arkansas. At 12 years of age, he hitchhiked to California and began touring with Lefty in the 1950s. David recorded Rockabilly albums for Columbia records when

March 2017

he was 18 years old. However, his music career was put on hold while he served a four-year stint in the U.S. Air Force during the Vietnam War. Immediately after leaving the military, he re-signed with Columbia Records in 1970.

David's debut single, "Just Can't Help Believing," made the top 40. He soon moved to Nashville and began appearing on Buck Owens' "All American TV Show" in 1973. After signing with Capital Records, David recorded the hits, "Words Don't Come Easy" and "Take Me One More Ride." He began touring with his younger brother, Allen Frizzell, and his wife, Shelley West. West and David quickly entered a contract with Warner Brothers.

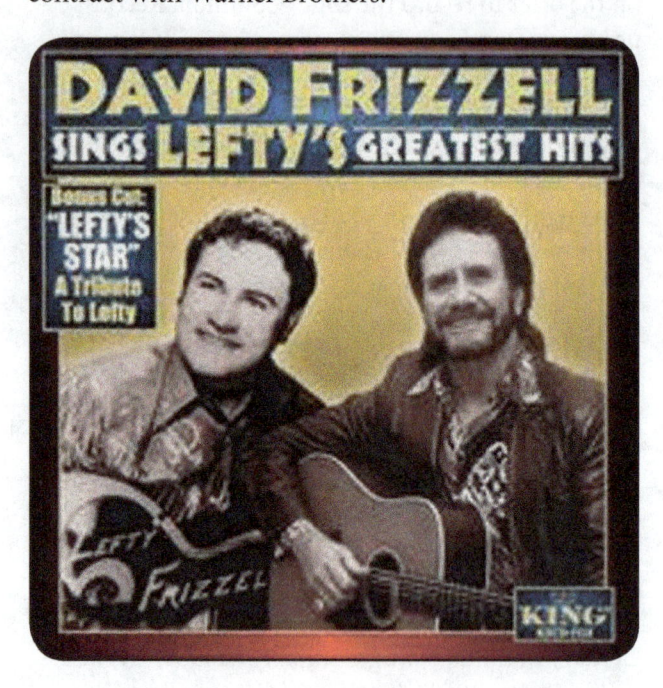

In 1981 David's duet with Shelley West, "You're the Reason God Made Oklahoma" became a number one hit. It also became Song of the Year, Vocal Duet of the Year and was featured in the Clint Eastwood movie, "Any Which Way You Can." David and West won the Academy of Country Music Award for the Vocal Duo of the Year in 1981 and 1982.

The two recorded top ten hits, "Another Honky Tonk Night on Broadway" and "I Just Came Here to Dance." They continued winning duo awards throughout their career together. David hit number one with his 1982 solo, "I'm Gonna Hire a Wino to Decorate Our Home." The song was later nominated for a Grammy. His solo success continued in 1982 – 1983 with songs such as "Lost My Baby Blues" and "Where are You Spending your Nights These Days." In 1984 he teamed up with West again and produced hits, such as "Silent Partners" and "It's a be Together Night. They performed and recorded together until 1986.

In addition to the previously mentioned awards, the duo received the Music City News Award for Duet of the Year twice and Song of the Year. David's solo career earned him many trophies and awards, including three Grammy Nominations. David is currently the producer of his Nashville America Records label, "Frizzell and Friends." His projects have provided him the opportunity of working with Country Recording artists such as Crystal Gayle, Bobby Bare, Merle Haggard, Johnny Lee, Gene Watson, Lacy J. Dalton, Jimmy Fortune of the Statler Brothers and many more.

In 2011 David released a tribute to his late brother, I Love You A Thousand Ways: The Lefty Frizzell Story. The book features a forward by Merle Haggard and was named one of Country Music Television's Best Books of The Year. David continues writing, producing, performing and touring.

Salute to the KoRNFieLD
Everything you always wanted to know about the cast
By Claudia Johnson

Hager Twins – Double the Talent

The Hager Brothers, Jim and Jon, may have been born in Chicago, Illinois, in 1941, but fans of Hee Haw accepted the twins as pure Country.

Their adoptive father, Jack Hager, was a Methodist minister, while adoptive mother, Frances, was a schoolteacher. The Hagers were very active in their church choir and performed on local television stations in their youth. After graduating high school, they joined the United States Military. The identical twins performed at Officer's Clubs and NCO Clubs in the United States and Europe. Their talent followed them wherever they went, and they confidentially decided to move to California when their time in the service ended.

The Hagers landed a job at Ledbetter's Night Club in Los Angeles, California, that boasted a lineup of performers that later became beloved stars such as The New Christy Minstrels, The Carpenters, Steve Martin, John Denver and Kenny Rodgers.

Country tycoon Buck Owens spotted the Hagers working at Disneyland and immediately signed them. They began opening for Country music acts including Billie Jo Spears, Lefty Frizzell, Tex Ritter and Wynn Stewart. The twins signed a contract with Capitol Records in 1969 and released the chart-topping hit, "Gotta Get To Oklahoma (Cause California's Getting' To Me)." They went on to record several more albums with Barnaby Records and Elektra-Asylum.

The singing twins were guitarists and drummers and initially arrived on the set as original members of "Hee Haw" in 1969 for the musical segments. As the show progressed the two were eventually worked in as comedy acts.

"People laughed at themselves," Jim Hager said in a 1988 Associated Press interview about 'Hee Haw.' They liked the chemistry on the show and the fast pace… (the jokes) were not all platinum. The writers count on the person delivering the line to pull it off. It was cornball, no denying it."

In addition to performing on Hee Haw, the brothers appeared on television series such as "The Bionic Woman," "Country Kitchen" and "Sanctuary Earth." They were in television commercials and also starred next to Lillian Gish in a made for TV movie, "Twin Detectives." In 1973 the handsome twins appeared in the pages of "Playgirl" magazine.

"They had a fun personality," recalled Hee Haw producer Sam Lovullo. "They were also the answer to the Hee-Haw Honeys. We were always looking for the other side of the gender – for good-looking hunks. They fit the bill very nicely."

The Hagers continued to perform long after their days at "Hee Haw" came to a close in 1986. Both brothers were very active in charitable events.

"They were always contributing their talents to whatever was needed, not for money but just so they could help out," Lovullo said. "They did a lot of fund raisers and were supportive of young people who were ill."

The pair told a media source in 1988 that they had always been together with the exception of three and a half years in the 1960s when Jon moved to Nashville and Jim remained in Los Angles before he, too, relocated to Nashville.

In May 2008 Jim Hager was found dead in the parking lot of the Nashville coffeehouse, The Frothy Monkey. A Vanderbilt University Medical Center spokesman said he had died of a heart attack.

"Jim was a delightful, funny, loyal friend," Hee Haw cast mate Lulu Roman told the Associated Press. "He will be missed greatly as one of my true

March 2017

friends. He and Jon were a dynamic and extremely talented duo. I pray for his family."

Eight months after the untimely death of his brother, Jon Hager died in his sleep from poor health exacerbated by deep depression. Friends reported that Jim's death had consumed Jon.

The Hagers are remembered for their All-American good looks, charismatic personalities and true musical talent that made them stars of Hee Haw and beyond.

Country Music Questions & Answers

Q: What was the crime that sent Meryl Haggard to prison and how long did he serve. A grandson gave my husband one of the CDs and we really enjoy it.

Anne Moore

A: Haggard did his first stint in jail at age 11, when his mother turned him over to the juvenile authorities as "incorrigible."

But what sent him to prison was when he attempted to rob a restaurant along with two other burglars; the three were drunk at the time. Believing it was three o'clock in the morning, the trio tried to open up the back door of the restaurant. However, it was 10:30 and the establishment was still open. Although the trio fled the scene, Haggard was arrested that day. The following day, he escaped from prison in order to make peace with his wife and family; later that day, he was recaptured. Haggard was sentenced to a 15-year term and sent to San Quentin prison where he served 2 years before being released on parole. Governor Ronald Reagan later pardoned him.

Johnny Cash played his first-ever prison concert on January 1, 1958—a concert that helped set Merle Haggard, then a 20-year-old San Quentin inmate, on the path toward becoming a country music legend.

Q: We have enjoyed watching the Family Reunion tribute to Merle Haggard which he sadly missed. Would like to know Mr. Haggard's wives and his son's mothers.

Linda Partin, Somerset, KY

A: Merle was married to Leona Hobbs in 1956, with whom he four children: Dana, Marty, Kelli and Noel. They were married until 1964. Haggard married Bonnie Owens in 1965. She was the ex-wife of Buck Owens, and was also Merle's singing partner They divorced in 1978. Leona Williams was the next wife from 1968-1983 followed by Debbie Parrett from 1985-1991. His last wife, Thereasa Ann Lane is the mother of his last two children, Ben and Jenessa. He was married to her from 1995 until his death.

If you have questions send them to Paula, CFR News, P.O. Box 210796, Nashville, TN 37221 or email them to paula@gabrielcommunications.com.

Merle and Leona with children, Dana, Marty, Kelli and Noel

Merle with Jenessa and Ben

March 2017

Singer Songwriters
By Sasha Kay Dunavant

Mac Davis

Throughout the history of Country Music, thousands of songs have been written and performed. Many of those songs were written by famous performers. Some were written for a star's own records, while others were created to be sung by another artist. This Singer-Songwriter Series explores some of those talented individuals whose work we know and love.

Some of the 1970's and 1980's catchiest tunes – the kinds of songs that got stuck in your head and heart – were penned by Mac Davis.

Growing up in Lubbock, Texas, Davis lived in an ultra-religious home. After recording a couple of singles with his Rock and Roll band, Zots, Davis began working for the Vee Jay Record company. He later worked for Liberty Records and began exercising his talent for songwriting. Davis worked for Nancy Sinatra's company, Boots Enterprises, Inc. The company helped publish Davis's later recorded hits, such as "Friend, Lover, Woman, Wife," "Home" and "It's Such a Lonely Time of Year."

His first big break was in 1968, when he was only 26 years old, when Elvis Presley recorded Davis's song, "A Little Less Conversation." Davis wrote the song in one night while staying at artist Billy Strange's house in Los Angeles, California. Presley requested more material from Davis after the success of the song. Davis wrote "In The Ghetto," which was originally suggested for Sammy Davis Jr. but became a huge Presley hit. Presley also recorded Davis's songs "Memories" and "Don't Cry Daddy." "A Little Less Conversation" was re-released in 2002 and became number one in 26 countries.

Davis signed his own recording contract in 1970 and released his first single, "Whoever Finds This, I Love You." The same year Kenny Rogers recorded Davis's song, "Something's Burning," which became a worldwide Top 40 hit. In 1971 Bobby Goldsboro recorded Davis's contemporary song, "Watching Scotty Grow." The song soared to No. 1.

In 1971 Davis recorded his own songs, "Daddy's Little Man," "Closest I Ever Came," "Once You Get Used to It" and "Yesterday and You." In 1972 Davis reached No. 1 with his pop song, "Baby, Don't Get Hooked on Me." The song had crossover success, reaching the Top 20 on Country charts. The self-titled album produced songs such as "Dream Me Home " and "Everybody Loves A Love Song."

Davis also wrote songs for The Rascal Flatts, O.C. Smith and Vikki Carr. He recorded his signature song, "I Believe in Music" in 1971. Davis wrote the song in a hotel room while using Bee Gees artist, Maurice Gibb's guitar. Unfortunately the song didn't do well on Pop charts for Davis. The music group, Gallery, covered "I Believe in Music" in 1972 and had international success. "I Believe in Music" has been covered by artists, such as Helen Reddy, B.J. Thomas, Louis Jordan, Perry Como, Liza Minnelli, Marian Love and Lee Towers.

Davis continued his success through the 1970s and 1980s with hits such as "Stop and Smell the Roses," "Burnin' Thing," "Forever Lovers," "It's Hard To Be Humble" and, "Texas In My Rearview Mirror." His biggest Country hit was 1980's "Hooked on Music." Davis's last self-recorded hit was 1985's "I Never made Love (Till I Made Love With You)." The same year Davis performed "God Bless The USA" at Ronald Reagan's inaugural gala. In 1990 Davis wrote Dolly Parton's hit, "White Limozeen." Davis also hosted a musical variety show, "The Mac Davis Show," on NBC television in the late 1970s. He was listed as one of the 12 most promising actors of 1979 for his performance in football film "North Dallas Forty." In 1981 he performed in a comedy film "Cheaper To Keep Her." He also appeared in a 1983 Robert Redford movie "The Sting 2."

Davis took to the stage as Will Rogers in the Broadway production of "The Will Rogers Follies." He has appeared or narrated in television shows, such as "The Muppet Show," "Oswald," "King of The Hill," "8 Simple Rules" and " Rodney." Davis was inducted into the Nashville Songwriters Hall of Fame in 2000. He also has a star on Hollywood's Walk of Fame. Mac Davis is a major contributor to all genres of music and one of the most successful crossover artists and writers of all time. He continues to do charity work, perform and write songs.

March 2017

The Bellamy Brothers 2017 World Tour

Iconic duo and international sensation, the Bellamy Brothers, will embark on their 2017 World Tour in Dubai, Singapore, Switzerland, Ireland and Faroe Islands. David and Howard Bellamy leave this week to criss-cross the globe and celebrate their 25th Anniversary of their own record label, Bellamy Brothers Records, which licenses products in more than 30 countries.

The duo's upcoming performance in Singapore also resulted in another licensing deal with EQ Music and Media for their 40 Years: The Album, a compilation of past hits and new songs that encompasses "Let Your Love Flow," "Redneck Girl" and "If I Said You Have a Beautiful Body (Would You Hold It Against Me)" and 20 new songs.

The Bellamy Brothers wrapped up 2016 with television, radio, print and online features, including performances and appearances on "Fox & Friends," "PBS Metro Focus," SiriusXM's Prime Country, "Celebrity Page," "Good Day New York," Fox News Radio, as well as features on DoYouRemember.com and a 4-page spread in Closer Weekly.

Howard and David Bellamy have created one of the most successful careers in the history of country music with 27 Top 10 and 14 No. 1 singles among a catalog that includes "Let Your Love Flow," "If I Said You Had A Beautiful Body (Would You Hold It Against Me)," "Redneck Girl," "Old Hippie," and "Kids Of The Baby Boom."

But, that only tells a mere fraction of the story of The Bellamy Brothers. A close look at their concert schedules over the past two decades reveals one of the most global careers in the history of country music. The duo has taken their music to a wide variety of countries across the world over the years – including stops in Germany, Norway, and Sweden.

The Bellamy Brothers performed a sold-out string of shows with Swiss superstar Gola – adding his name to a list of collaborators over the years that has included Neil Diamond, Dolly Parton, George Jones and Blake Shelton. In Switzerland, their crowds numbered into the 70,000 range, as well – demonstrating their international appeal.

In addition, the Bellamy Brothers have taken their music to places where no other country act has ever performed, such as Qatar, Sri Lanka, New Caledonia and even India. In fact, one of their classic hits there made an impact on the audience unlike any the duo has ever seen in the states.

In a 2014 interview with Billboard, David recalled that on one of their India visits that "People came up to us and asked 'Are you going to do the 'first dance' song? We weren't sure what they were talking about, but it was 'Beautiful Body' because they use it as the first dance song at weddings. You never know how someone will interpret a song, I guess," he said. Of course, the song that he is referring to is their first No. 1 country hit, 1979's "If I Said You Had A Beautiful Body (Would You Hold It Against Me)."

And, as The Bellamy Brothers gear up for their next forty years, they are keeping their close ties with their fans abroad. Howard and David take a lot of pride in pleasing the audience – regardless of which continent their feet are planted on.

"We have been very blessed to have taken our music to a lot of venues and destinations that have always surprised us," said Howard Bellamy. "Regardless of where we might be, what makes each night special is that relationship with the fans, and getting to hear them sing along. After all," he reasons, 'Redneck Girls' are everywhere.

BELLAMY BROTHERS ON TOUR:

March 2 World Champion BBQ Cookoff - Houston, Texas
March 4 Orange Blossom Opry - Weirsdale, Fla.
March 6 The Strawberry Festival - Plant City, Fla.
March 10 Wilkes Community College - Wilkesboro, N.C.
March 11 Mill Town Music Hall - Bremen, Ga.
March 17 Renfro Valley Entertainment Center/New Barn Theater - Mt Vernon, Ky.
March 18 Red Barn Convention Center - Winchester, Ohio
March 24 Medina Ballroom - Hamel, Minn.
March 30 Cherokee Casino/Lee Creek Tavern - Roland, Okla.
March 31 Heritage Hall - Paris, Texas

For the rest of their tour, see their website at www.bellamybrothers.com.

March 2017

YOU CAN NOW PRE-ORDER OUR BRAND NEW DVD SERIES, KICKIN' BACK!

CHECK OUT THIS VERY SPECIAL OFFER!!!

Among the artists attending our taping on March 22, 2017 will be: Bill Anderson, T. Graham Brown, Rhonda Vincent, Mark Wills, David Ball, Jeannie Seely, Larry Gatlin, Gene Watson
PLUS SURPRISE GUESTS!

Pre-order and you'll also get the FREE Unedited DVDs to watch until the show is edited and finished.

The new "Kickin' Back" series is only $79.80 plus S/H for a total of $86.75

But, we want to sweeten the pot a bit...

Your choice of ONE of the following series for 1/2 PRICE

"God Bless America Again"
"Old Time Gospel"
"Sweethearts"
"Gettin' Together"
"Bill Anderson's 50th Anniversary Celebration"

If you want the new Kickin' Back series AND another series of your choice select one from those listed above. This second option is just $119.80 plus s/h, for a total of $136.75

1-800-820-5405
www.cfrvideos.com

March 2017

APRIL

Touring and spreading God's word, Dove Award winners The Isaacs

The Isaacs, a multi-award-winning family group who began singing 35 years ago are based out of Hendersonville, TN. The vocalists are mother Lily Isaacs and siblings Ben Isaacs, Sonya Isaacs Yeary and Rebecca Isaacs Bowman. Playing their own acoustic instruments and joined by other band members, The Isaacs have a unique style that blends tight family harmony with contemporary acoustic instrumentation that appeals to a variety of audiences. Their musical style has been influenced by many genres of music including bluegrass, rhythm and blues, folk, and country, contemporary, acoustic and southern gospel.

They perform frequently at the Grand Ole Opry, are active members on the Gaither Homecoming Videos and Concert Series, and travel internationally throughout the year to perform to welcoming fans in countries such as South Africa, Norway, Holland, Scotland, Ireland, Israel, Canada and many more. Concert venues include civic centers, auditoriums, arenas, fair grounds, parks, churches and other locations. They have been nominated at and performed on the Dove Awards, IBMA (International Bluegrass Music Association) and NQC (National Quartet Convention) Awards, the ICMA Awards (Inspirational Christian Country). Other notable performances include CMA Fan Fest (Country Music Fan Fest), Carnegie Hall, and many professional sporting events, including a Cincinnati Bengal's football game, Nashville Predators Hockey games, and an Astros/ Braves baseball game.

The Isaacs have won over 7 Doves in various categories and have had several Grammy nominations in their career. They feel blessed to be able to travel and spread the message of hope and grace through song and story.

Lily Isaacs is a vocalist and matriarch of the group. She was born in Germany after World War II to two Polish Jewish Holocaust survivors and moved to the United States when she was 2 years old. She grew up in the Bronx, NY studying theatre and performing on Off Broadway and in 1968 recorded a folk album on Columbia Records with her friend as "Lily and Maria." She became a Christian in 1971 when a death in the family brought her and patriarch Joe Isaacs to church for the first time.

Soon after, they began singing Christian music and laid the foundation upon which the Isaacs ministry has been built. Also, a 30-year breast cancer survivor, she was the inspiration for a hit country song called I'm Gonna Love You Through It, co-written by Sonya and Jimmy Yeary, recorded by Martina McBride. Lily's testimony has been an inspiration to people around the world, so much that she has written an autobiography about her life's story. Her love for Jesus has brought her through every chapter of her life and she loves to sing and share about His love.

Ben Isaacs is the bass player and vocalist for the Isaacs. He and his wife Mindy have three children: Jacob, Kyra and Cameron. He spends much of his time off the road in the studio producing not only The Isaacs, but also many well-known artists including, The Gaither Vocal Band, The Oak Ridge Boys, Karen Peck, and Cherryholmes to name a few. He has been nominated for over six Grammys and has been voted Producer of the Year several times in the Absolutely Gospel Awards. He also has produced several Dove award winning albums. He has played

April 2017

bass and sang on numerous artists projects including Don Williams, George Jones, Merle Haggard, Trace Adkins, Doyle Lawson, JD Crowe and Paul Williams. He has been voted Male Vocalist of the Year and Musician of the Year in several prominent award shows. Ben accepted Christ as a young boy and has always had a heart for ministry and helping people.

Becky Isaacs Bowman is the guitar player and vocalist for the Isaacs. She is married to singer/musician/minister John Bowman. They have two children Levi and Jakobi. Becky started writing songs as a teenager and has written songs that many artists have recorded. Her first number one song was Stand Still and she has since had charting songs recorded by many artists. Some other songs you may recognize written by Sonya and Becky are Heroes, winning Bluegrass Song of the Year from the Dove Awards, and Waiting in the Water, Your Cries Have Awoken The Master, and a Miracle Today. She has sang background vocals on a variety of artists projects including, Paul Simon, Alabama, Dolly Parton, Don Williams, Merle Haggard, Trace Adkins, Russ Taff, and Jason Crabb, to name a few. She has been nominated and awarded Female Vocalist and Songwriter of the Year in several awards programs. Becky has a passion for the Lord and loves to minister through song and testimony.

Sonya Isaacs Yeary is the mandolin player and vocalist for the Isaacs. She is married to singer/songwriter Jimmy Yeary and they have two sons, Ayden & Gatlyn. After her solo adventure with country label Lyric Street Records, she began writing songs professionally and has had songs recorded by Trisha Yearwood, Leann Rimes, Martina McBride, Vince Gill and many more. Many gospel artists have also recorded songs she and Becky have written. , and she has won several Doves for her songs. She also enjoys singing background vocals for such artists as, Reba, Brad Paisley, Dierks Bentley, Trisha Yearwood, Vince Gill to name a few. Many kids will recognize her as a background singer for Miley Cyrus in the Hannah Montana movie and on soundtrack performances on Disney Films Geppetto and My Neighbor Totoro. IBMA, SGMA, CCMA have nominated Sonya for Female Vocalist many years running, and she has won various awards in all these genres. Sonya accepted Christ at 6 years old. She has dedicated her life to spreading the gospel and shining God's light wherever she goes. Levi Bowman is the son of John and Rebecca Isaacs Bowman. He is the latest member to join The Isaacs playing guitar and singing. He just released a new solo album titled "Find Yourself". Levi has traveled on the bus with his family assisting in various positions. He has a heart to serve the Lord and has recently announced his calling to preach the Gospel.

The above information is provided by The Isaacs website: www.theisaacs.com.

Look who's on the Diner this week!

Thursdays at 7 p.m. central Saturdays at 10 p.m. central

PREVIOUSLY AIRED
DALLAS WAYNE
April 6 & 8

PREVIOUSLY AIRED
JEANNIE SEELY
April 13 & 15

PREVIIOUSLY AIRED
EXILE
April 20 & 22

PREVIOUSLY AIRED
BRADLEY WALKER
April 27 & 29

63
CFR NEWS

April 2017

Nadine
The Church Lady

Lord, give me a sense of humor,
Give me the grace to see a joke,
To get some humor out of life,
And to pass it on to other folk.

Funny Hymn Titles

The Tailor's Hymn....
"Holy, Holy, Holy"

The Golfer's Hymn...
"There's a Green Hill Far Away"

The Politician's Hymn...
"Standing on the Promises"

REAL NAMES OF COUNTRY ARTISTS

Kitty Wells
Ellen Muriel Deason

Roy Rogers
Leonard Franklin Slye

Brenda Lee
Brenda Mae Tarpley

NOTICE

ALL CFR NEWS SUBSCRIBERS

We are pleased to announce all subscribers will be placed on auto renew if you have a credit card or debit card on file. We have been flooded with calls from customers who do not want their newspaper subscription to lapse but forget or do not know when to renew.

SO... we are making it easy. Your renewal month will not change. If you prefer to pay your renewal by check this will not apply to you.

If you do not want to be placed on auto renewal, we need to hear from you by Jan 1st.

1-800-823-5405

Stuffed Crescent Roll Carrots

Ingredients

8 (12x4-inch) sheets of foil
1 can (8 oz) Pillsbury™ refrigerated crescent dinner rolls or 1 can (8 oz) Pillsbury™ refrigerated crescent dough sheet
1 8 oz cream cheese, softened
1/4 cup chopped fresh parsley
1/4 cup chopped fresh chives
1 teaspoon grated lemon peel
1/4 teaspoon salt
16 small sprigs fresh parsley

1. Heat oven to 400°F. Roll sheets of foil from shorter ends into coneshaped molds. Unroll dough on work surface; if using crescent rolls, press seams to seal. Use pizza cutter or knife to cut dough lengthwise into 8 (1-inch) strips.

2. Wrap 1 strip around each foil mold to create carrot shape. Place 1 inch apart on ungreased cookie sheet.

3. Bake 7 to 9 minutes or until golden brown. Transfer to cooling rack; cool completely before removing foil molds. Gently twist foil molds for easier removal from crescents.

4. In medium bowl, beat cream cheese, parsley, chives, lemon peel and salt with electric mixer on medium speed until smooth and combined. Pipe or spoon cream cheese mixture into cavity of each crescent. Top with 2 sprigs parsley for carrot top.

Swap cream cheese mixture with your own favorite filling, such as egg salad or chicken salad or even peanut butter and jelly! Prep 35 min Total 40 min

Ingredients 8 Servings 8

April 2017

2018 CFR / LCD Cruise leaving from Galveston

It's time to make your reservations for the 2018 Country's Family Reunion & Larry's Country Diner Cruise! Customer Service is booking cabins now!

Leaving out of Galveston, the 7- Night Western Caribbean Cruise goes to Roatan, Honduras, Puerto Costa Maya, Mexico and Cozumel, Mexico.

The lineup for 2018 is GREAT! Bill Anderson hosts the Country's Family Reunion show with Rhonda Vincent, Gene Watson, Mark Wills, Linda Davis, Teea Goans, the Malpass Brothers, Moe Bandy and another Mo....Mo Pitney! Also this year the Dan Miller Cowboy Revue will perform a preshow for Nadine!

Seats in the theatre are assigned based upon the time of the reservation, so the earlier you book, the better your seats! Of course, all the seats are great....

Interior cabins start as low as $1195 per person. Promenade cabins (interior room with window overlooking the Promenade) start at $1620, Ocean View start at $1640, Deluxe Ocean View with balcony start at $1870, Superior Ocean View with balcony start at $1950, Junior Suites start at $2600, Grand Suite $3200, and Owner's Suite $3800. All prices are per person based on double occupancy.

The CFR Cruise 2018 Package Includes:
3 Country's Family Reunion Shows
1 Larry's Country Diner Show with Larry, Renae The Waitress, The Sheriff, Keith and Nadine!
1 Nadine Comedy Show with Pre-show featuring the Dan Miller Cowboy Revue
Exclusive Chance to Meet the Stars Autograph and Photo Signings Exclusive Jam Sessions!

Cruisers have great things to say about the CFR/LCD Cruise: My husband and I had the mostwonderful time on our cruise with CFR. We would highly recommend going on this cruise. We can't wait for the next one! - Barbara Walters

This cruise was on our bucket list and we saved up and went on it last year. The cruise exceeded our expectations. From the friendly staff to the amazing shows we couldn't have been more happy with our decision. - Myron Jones

Best cruise ever!!! When is the next one? - Charles Stanley

Call Customer Service today at 800-820-5405 to book your cruise!

7 Night Western Caribbean Cruise - Jan. 28th - Feb. 4th, 2018

April 2017

650 AM WSM / Springer Mountain Farms 5K Run

The 9th Annual 650 AM WSM / Springer Mountain Farms 5K event took place on Saturday, March 18 around the Grand Ole Opry Complex. Participants received a race t-shirt, a commemorative wooden Opry circle medal, and a special post-race photo on the stage of the world-famous Grand Ole Opry!

A portion of the race proceeds will benefit Tennessee Voices for Children and Kiwanis Club Foundation. Sponsors were Springer Mountain Farms, The Ledger, Nova Copy, Premier Parking, Good Guys Moving and Delivery, Chef's Market, and the Grand Ole Opry.

April Birthdays
APRIL 1 Hillary Scott, Jim Ed Brown, Billy Dean
APRIL 2 Emmylou Harris
APRIL 4 Steve Gatlin
APRIL 5 Jack Clement
APRIL 6 Merle Haggard
APRIL 7 Bobby Bare
APRIL 9 Hal Ketchum, Carl Perkins
APRIL 11 Jim Lauderdale
APRIL 12 Vince Gill
APRIL 14 Loretta Lynn
APRIL 15 Roy Clark
APRIL 20 Wade Hayes
APRIL 22 Glen Campbell
APRIL 24 Richard Sterban
APRIL 25 Rory Feek
APRIL 29 Willie Nelson

Do you recognize them?
These two lovely ladies are Jean Shepard (left) and Marvis Thompson Husky (right).

April 2017

Jeanne Pruett

BY TOM WOOD

Google "satin sheets," and your screen will be filled with colorful phrases such as luxurious, silky smooth, plush, lush, decadent, opulent, lovely, slippery, sultry, sexy and lustrous. Many of those same descriptions apply to the 1973 smash hit "Satin Sheets" by Jeanne Pruett — along with sad, mournful heartache and other classic country themes.

Within weeks of its release, the song became Jeanne's signature song, the only one to skyrocket to No. 1.

And the crossover hit (it reached No. 28 on the Billboard Hot 100 charts) was powerful enough to propel her into membership of the world's most exclusive country club — The Grand Ole Opry — where she remained an active performer until her official retirement in 2006.

Country music has a long history of songs that tap into the livin' and lovin' issues of everyday life that so many of us must cope with. But "Satin Sheets" took it up a notch and struck a chord with unhappy housewives who sought love outside a loveless marriage. And the pink bedroom satin outfit Jeanne wore for the cover shot didn't hurt album sales; it also zoomed to No. 1.

Back in 1973, I didn't know the first thing about "Satin Sheets." I was a high school senior that year that spring, and country wasn't cool with the group I ran with. But my father was a big Grand Ole Opry fan, and I remember him talking about this great new song out of Nashville.

As an adult, I've grown to enjoy the old-school country sounds and have come to embrace songs like "Satin Sheets" as one of those songs you hate to love. The pain that comes through Jeanne's powerful intonations is something we've all been able to identify with at some stage in our lives.

The hit earned Jeanne several major CMA Awards nominations in 1973, but Loretta Lynn was named Female Vocalist of the Year over Jeanne, Donna Fargo, Tanya Tucker and Tammy Wynette. The song, written by John Volinkaty, was also nudged out for the Single, Song an Album of the Year categories.

Jeanne had four other Top 10 singles in "Temporarily Yours" (No. 5 in 1980), "Back to Back" (No. 6 in 1979), "I'm Your Woman" (No. 8 in 1973) and "It's Too Late" (No. 9 in 1980). In all, she placed 25 songs in the Country Top 100.

Not a bad career at all. And it all started with "Satin Sheets," which opened the door for many other opportunities, including soap opera appearances on One Life to Live, a series of music-themed cookbooks an hosting a cooking show on The Nashville Network (TNN).

And if you have a really good memory, you may remember eating at her Feedin' Friends (named for her cookbook series) Opryland restaurant. Since she retired in 2006, Jeanne has stayed busy behind the music scenes, and recently celebrated her 80th birthday.

Author Tom Wood, who writes thrillers and Westerns, is a regular contributor to Country Family Reunion News. Reach him at tomwoodauthor.com

---

Generations & SECOND GENERATIONS Combo

First gathered in 1999, then again in 2011, this is a gathering of country music legends and the children of country music legends such as Marty Robbins, Conway Twitty, Faron Young, Tammy Wynette, George Jones, Roger Miller, Johnny Russell, Hank Williams, and Dottie West sharing stories and the songs their parents made famous.

GET BOTH FOR ONLY $79.80
plus $6.95 s/h

Robyn Young, Bill Anderson, Karen Wheeler, Michael Twitty, Jean Shepard, Donnie Hawkins, Charlie Rich Jr., Phil Campbell

George Hamilton V, George Hamilton IV, Hawkshaw Hawkins Jr, Melissa Luman, Chrystie Wooley, Georgette Jones

Jett Williams, Dean Smith, Jan Howard, Will Reid, Langdon Reid, Bill Mack, Dean Miller, Ronny Robbins, Shelly West, Jim Ed Brown

Roy Clark, Bill Anderson, Dean Miller, Michael Twitty, Ronny Robbins, Johnny Russell, Billy Walker, Bobby Lord

Georgette Jones, Jan Howard, Robyn Young, Rex Allen Jr., Jett Williams, Merle Kilgore, Hawkshaw Hawkins Jr., Del Reeves

1-800-820-5405
www.cfrvideos.com

April 2017

What exactly IS the YouTube channel Country Road TV

Did you know that we are the owners of a YouTube channel called "Country Road TV?" Yep, we started the YouTube channel about 3 months ago as a place to show clips from Country's Family Reunion, Larry's Country Diner, and several other series we have access to. It's a FREE way to let our fans watch fun moments from random series throughout the 20 years we've been in business.

This is our invitation to YOU to check out our Country Road TV YouTube page. Here's how you do it: On your computer, type www.youtube.com into your computer's web browser bar at the top of the screen.

Once you get to the YouTube website, look for the search icon (might look like a magnifying class) and type in Country Road TV. After you've typed in Country Road TV, you should be taken to a web page that has a list of items that contain the words "Country" and "Road" and "TV." You SHOULD see a channel called "Country Road TV."

Click on that... and you'll be taken to our specific Country Road TV YouTube Page where you can watch tons of fun clips from all the shows we produce. These are not FULL episodes, but we do include full songs and moments you can enjoy.

On our main Country Road TV YouTube web page, there should be a button you can click on that says

"Subscribe." It's a completely FREE subscription, but you'll be notified first when we have uploaded new content to watch and enjoy.

Some of the videos include: Gene Watson singing "It's Not Love But It's Not Bad", T. Graham Brown singing "Forever Changed", Ronny Robbins sings El Paso, Vince Gill sings "Go Rest High On That Mountain", Joey and Rory sing "That's Important to Me". More videos are added daily, so subscribe and watch these country artists performing some of your favorite songs.

Hopefully, it will be a simple thing to do-- We will be posting all kinds of fun stuff every week... from actual clips from our shows to fun things that happen around our office. Who knows? Maybe Nadine will start to put together some fun clips for y'all to watch.

It's our way of moving into the digital age. If you have a computer, please join the fun at our YouTube page, Country Road TV. Plus, it's a wonderful way for folks who don't get our shows on their television cable or satellites to watch great country music!

Type www.youtube.com in the webbrowser as shown above.

Once on the YouTube site, type Country Road TV in the search bar as shown above.

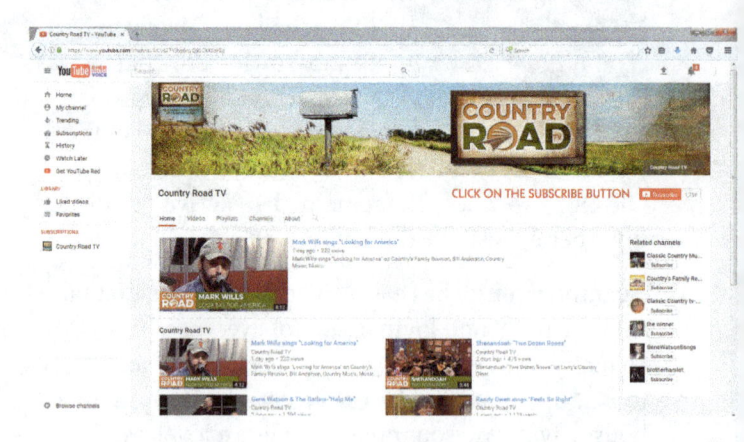

When you are on the Country Road TV page, click on the SUBSCRIBE button on the right, as shown above.

April 2017

Easter traditions and where they come from

You won't find them in the Bible, but many cherished Easter traditions have been around for centuries. The most prominent secular symbol of the Christian holiday, the Easter bunny reportedly was introduced to America by the German immigrants who brought over their stories of an egg-laying hare. The decoration of eggs is believed to date back to at least the 13th century, while the rite of the Easter parade has even older roots.

Other traditions, such as the consumption of Easter candy, are among the modern additions to the celebration of this early springtime holiday.

EASTER BUNNY

The Bible makes no mention of a long-eared, short-tailed creature who delivers decorated eggs to well-behaved children on Easter Sunday; nevertheless, the Easter bunny has become a prominent symbol of Christianity's most important holiday. The exact origins of this mythical mammal are unclear, but rabbits, known to be prolific procreators, are an ancient symbol of fertility and new life. According to some sources, the Easter bunny first arrived in America in the 1700s with German immigrants who settled in Pennsylvania and transported their tradition of an egg-laying hare called "Osterhase" or "Oschter Haws." Their children made nests in which this creature could lay its colored eggs. Eventually, the custom spread across the U.S. and the fabled rabbit's Easter morning deliveries expanded to include chocolate and other types of candy and gifts, while decorated baskets replaced nests.

Additionally, children often left out carrots for the bunny in case he got hungry from all his hopping.

EASTER EGGS

Easter is a religious holiday, but some of its customs, such as Easter eggs, are likely linked to pagan traditions.

The egg, an ancient symbol of new life, has been associated with pagan festivals celebrating spring. From a Christian perspective, Easter eggs are said to represent Jesus' emergence from the tomb and resurrection. Decorating eggs for Easter is a tradition that dates back to at least the 13th century, according to some sources. One explanation for this custom is that eggs were formerly a forbidden food during the Lenten season, so people would paint and decorate them to mark the end of the period of penance and fasting, then eat them on Easter as a celebration. Easter egg hunts and egg rolling are two popular egg-related traditions.

In the U.S., the White House Easter Egg Roll, a race in which children push decorated, hard-boiled eggs across the White House lawn, is an annual event held the Monday after Easter. The first official White House egg roll occurred in 1878, when Rutherford B. Hayes was president. The event has no religious significance, although some people have considered egg rolling symbolic of the stone blocking Jesus' tomb being rolled away, leading to his resurrection.

EASTER CANDY

Easter is the second best-selling candy holiday in America, after Halloween. Among the most popular sweet treats associated with this day are chocolate eggs, which date back to early 19th century Europe. Eggs have long been associated with Easter as a symbol of new life and Jesus' resurrection. Another egg-shaped candy, the jelly bean, became associated with Easter in the 1930s (although the jelly bean's origins reportedly date all the way back to a Biblical-era concoction called a Turkish Delight). According to the National Confectioners Association, over 16 billion jelly beans are made in the U.S. each year for Easter, enough to fill a giant egg measuring 89 feet high and 60 feet wide. For the past decade, the top-selling non-chocolate Easter candy has been the marshmallow Peep, a sugary, pastel-colored confection. Bethlehem, Pennsylvania-based candy manufacturer Just Born (founded by Russian immigrant Sam Born in 1923) began selling Peeps in the 1950s. The original Peeps were handmade, marshmallow- flavored yellow chicks, but other

April 2017

shapes and flavors were later introduced, including chocolate mousse bunnies.

EASTER PARADES

In New York City, the Easter Parade tradition dates back to the mid-1800s, when the upper crust of societywould attend Easter services at various Fifth Avenue churches then stroll outside afterward, showing off their new spring outfits and hats. Average citizens started showing up along Fifth Avenue to check out the action. The tradition reached its peak by the mid-20th century, and in 1948, the popular film Easter Parade was released, starring Fred Astaire and Judy Garland and featuring the music of Irving Berlin. The title song includes the lyrics: "In your Easter bonnet, with all the frills upon it/You'll be the grandest lady in theEaster parade."

The Easter Parade tradition lives on in Manhattan, with Fifth Avenue from 49th Street to 57th Street being shut down during the day to traffic. Participants often sport elaborately decorated bonnets and hats. The event has no religious significance, but sources note that Easter processions have been a part of Christianity since its earliest days. Today, other cities across America also have their own parades.

At 90 Henry Slaughter still sings God's praises

Henry Thaxton Slaughter was born January 9, 1927, on a tobacco farm near Roxboro, North Carolina, to parents Moses "Chummie" and Lila Slaughter. At the age of seven Slaughter was able to take piano lessons.

Until then, he had health issues, including a heart murmur and scarlet fever. After graduating from high school with honors, he attended the Stamps-Baxter School of Music in Chattanooga, Tennessee. After a few months there, he was called to join the Army in World War II.

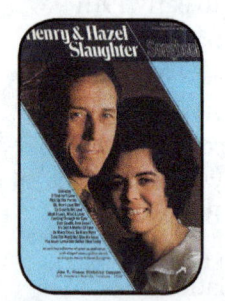

In the 1940s, soon after being released from the Army, he was asked to join the Ozark Quartet as a singer. Six months later, he became the piano player for the group.

Slaughter married Hazel Myers in Laurel, Mississippi on December 22, 1952. Today, he and Hazel live in Tennessee. He continues to write his internationally acclaimed "I Remember" column for MyBestYears.com, featuring precious memories of the people and places during the past seven decades on the road as one of Gospel music's premier keyboard artists.

Along the way, he wrote numerous songs that are considered gospel classics, including "What a Precious Friend is He," "Lonely Mile," "If The Lord Wasn't Walking By My Side" (recorded by Elvis Presley, on How Great Thou Art), and "I've Never Loved Him Better Than Today." In 1965, the Imperials released a full album of his songs, called Slaughter Writes - Imperials Sing.

Since the 1940s Slaughter has been with such memorable groups as the Stamps-Ozark Quartet, The Weatherford Quartet (1958–61), The Imperials (1964–66), and since the 1970s as Henry and Hazel Slaughter, including numerous appearances with Bill Gaither, the Gaither Praise Gatherings, and the Gaither Homecoming series.

Henry Slaughter has won five Dove Awards and is a cousin of Enos Slaughter, St. Louis Cardinals baseball player and member of MLB Hall Of Fame.

His autobiography, In Search of the Pearl of Great Price, written with Darryl Hicks, was published in 1980.

Most recently Henry Slaughter was part of the Country's Family Reunion Wednesday Night Prayer Meeting DVD series.

Henry and Linda Davis at the taping of Wednesday Night Prayer Meeting

April 2017

Country's Family Reunion brings the Gospel to your television

Larry Black loves country gospel music. "I grew up in Missouri and Alabama...two very different parts of our country," Larry says, "but the one common thread was those Tuesday and Thursday nights at prayer meeting. (It wasn't until much later that Wednesday night service became the norm.) But on Tuesday and Thursday nights especially, everybody that could play an instrument brought it along."

After filming the original Country's Family Reunion show in 1997 and Country's Family Reunion 2 in 1998 Larry decided to go back to his roots and in 1999 he filmed Country's Family Reunion Gospel.

Included in this series are: Bill Anderson Gathering Flowers for the Master's Bouquet, Bill Carlisle Gone Home, Billy Walker Where Could I go But To The Lord, Bobby Lord Family Bible, Carol Lee Cooper Hide Me O Blessed Rock of Ages, Charlie Louvin Whispering Now, Charlie Walker I'll Fly Away, Freddie Hart Where He Leads Me, George Hamilton IV Life's Railway to Heaven and Amazing Grace, Hank Locklin The Glory Land Way, Jack Greene Do Lord, Jan Howard The Unclouded Day and Just A Little Talk With Jesus, Jean Shepard What A Friend We Have In Jesus, Jeanne Pruett Jesus Loves Me, Jim Ed Brown Church in the Wildwood, Jimmy C. Newman Farther Along, Johnny Russell Just A Closer Walk With Thee, Kitty Wells Precious Memories, Leroy Van Dyke He'll Understand and Say Well Done, Margo Smith Precious Lord, Martha Carson Satisfied, Skeeter Davis If We Never Meet Again, Stonewall Jackson Kneel A The Cross, Stu Phillips Supper Time, The Whites Mansion Over the Hilltop and He Took Your Place, and Wanda Jackson I Can't Feel At Home in This World.

By 2009 Country's Family Reunion had many shows that were sprinkled with gospel music, so Larry put together a series called Gospel Classics which pulls together all the gospel songs from all the different series.

With 55 songs from Country's Family Reunion, Country's Family Reunion 2, Country's Family Reunion Celebration, Country's Family Reunion Gospel and Grassroots to Bluegrass, this 3 disc series also includes the songbook with the words to these great songs so you can sing along with the artists.

This set has the songs from the original Gospel series but also features: Ashamed To Own The Blessed Savior, Baptism of Jesse Taylor, Drinking form my Saucer, Duston the Bible, Give Me That Old Time Religion, Give Me The Roses While I Live, Hallelujah Side, He Is My Everything, He Will Set Your Fields On Fire, I'd Rather Live By The Side of the Road, In The Garden, I Saw the Light, Jesus Is Whispering Now, Jesus Walks In, Just Over in the Gloryland, Old Violin, Peace in the Valley, Rock of Ages, The Family Who Prays, The Farmer and the Lord, The Old Country Church, The Old Rugged Cross, The Touch of the Master's Hand, thirty Pieces of Silver, Victory in Jesus, Wait a Little Longer Please Jesus, and Will The Circle Be Unbroken.

By 2011, Larry was ready for some more gospel and he filmed Old Time Gospel. With many of the artists who performed on the earlier series gone on to glory, this series is a mixture of newer artists and a few of the elders mixed in amongst them.

This series has Barbara Fairchild Follow Me, Bill Anderson Suppertime, Con Hunley Hollow Man, Dailey & Vincent Mansion Over the Hilltop, Dallas Fraizer The Baptism of Jesse Taylor and Ain't Gonna Blow My House Down, Duane Allen with Norah Lee Allen and Jamie Allen Martin Keep Our World Safe, Ed Bruce The Family's Growing, Gary Morris Love Lifted Me, Gene Watson Before the Hammer Could Ring, George Hamilton IV How Can I Refuse Him Now, Gordon Mote Hold Me

April 2017

Up, Jan Howard Lord, I Hope This Day Is Good, Jean Shepard Where No One Stands Alone, Jeannie Seely Me and Jesus, Jim Ed Brown Life's Railway to Heaven, Jimmy Fortune How Great Thou Art, Jimmy Fortune with Dailey & Vincent I Believe, Joey + Rory Leave It There, John Conlee Clinging To A Saving Hand, Larry Black Christian Cowboy, Larry Gatlin & the Gatlin Brothers Help Me, There's Room at the Cross, Alleluia, Linda Davis with Cheryl and Sharon White Do You Know My Jesus, Phil Johnson The Day He Wore My Crown, T. Graham Brown Softly and Tenderly and The Whites I Know Who Holds Tomorrow.

The newest of the gospel series is a throwback to the more relaxed setting of the Wednesday Night Prayer Meeting, and that's just what it's called. Sharing stories, testimonies and songs, both cheerfully and tearfully are: Bill Anderson Standing On The Promises, The Whites Where the Roses Never Fade, Gene Watson Where No One Stands Alone, The Isaacs I'm Gonna Love You Through It and It Is Well With My Soul, Con Hunley Amazing Grace, Jimmy Fortune Victory in Jesus and Rock of Ages, Linda Davis with Lang Scott and Rylee Scott Love Remains, The Oak Ridge Boys I Love to Tell The Story and Time Has Made A Change In Me, Rhonda Vincent Where We'll Never Grow Old, Kristin Gatlin Spencer with the Gatlin Brothers and Henry Slaughter What A Precious Friend He Is, T. Graham Brown Beulah Land and In The Garden, Doyle Dykes How Great Thou Art, John Conlee He Touched Me, Linda Davis with Lang Scott and Henry Slaughter There's A Sweet, Sweet Sprit in This Place, Gordon Mote Power in the Blood, Phil Johnson with Gordon Mote Give Them All To Jesus, Barbara Fairchild If I Could Hear My Mother Pray Again, John Berry Blessed Assurance, Ricky Skaggs with the Whites Wings of a Dove, Gene Watson with The Gatlins Help Me, The Martin Family Circus Mary Don't You Weep and I Know, Teea Goans I Know The Lord Will Stand By Me, and the CFR Choir and everyone at the taping close with Just As I Am.

If you love gospel music, not just a the special holidays, but all year round, you'll want to own these series! Call Customer Service at 800- 920-5405, www.cfrvideos.com or see the ad on page 6 for details.

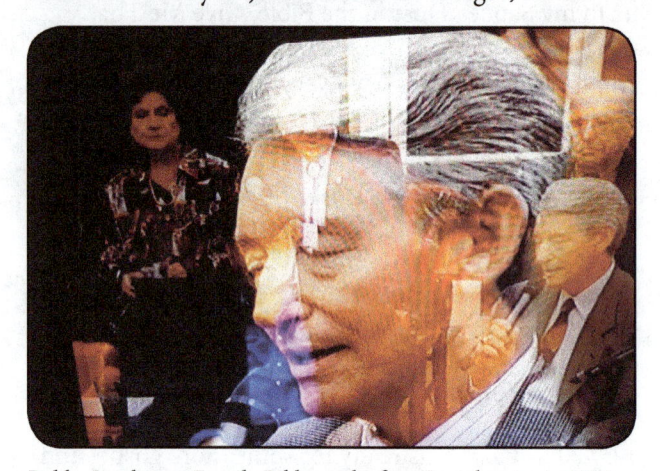

Bobby Lord sings Family Bible on the first Gospel series in 1999.

The Oak Ridge Boys singing during Wednesday Night Prayer Meeting.

April 2017

Easter Sunrise Service at "God's Acre" in North Carolina

Many churches in the American South still hold traditional sunrise services in cemeteries as a sign of recognition that Jesus no longer lay in the tomb on Easter morning. The service starts early in the morning and is timed so that the attendants can see the sun rise when the service is going. Services usually loosely follow the format of the church's normal service and can include music (hymns or praise band), dramatic scenes and the Easter message.

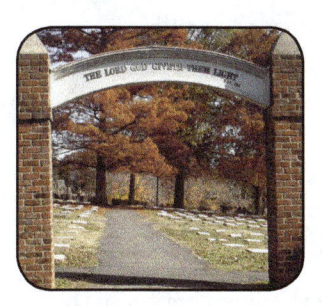

Entrance to "God's Acre".

After the service, the church may serve a breakfast for the attendees. One of the oldest Sunrise Services in the United States is probably that of the Salem Congregation in what is now Winston-Salem, NC, held annually since 1772. More than six thousand worshipers gather before dawn in front of the church to proclaim the Resurrection. The worshipers then move in procession to the historic graveyard, or "God's Acre". Brass choirs from twelve congregations, totaling over five hundred members, play hymns antiphonally during the procession. The service concludes with a proclamation of faith and hymns of hope.

The Sunrise Service of the Moravians in Winston-Salem is an old service, rich in deep spiritual significance. It originated in Herrnhut, Saxony, a village which had been established in 1722 on the estate of Count Nicholas von Zinzendorf by a band of religious refugees, descendants of the Ancient Unitas Fratrum. On Easter Sunday in 1732, before dawn, a group of earnest young men met by special appointment on "God's Acre" to sing appropriate hymns and to meditate upon the great fact of Christ's death and resurrection.

To these young men, as they stood among the simply marked graves, singing their songs of hope and faith, watching the rising sun drive darkness from the hills and valleys, there came a deeper appreciation of the resurrection truth than they had ever before experienced. With this simple beginning, the holding of a sunrise service on Easter morning became an annual feature in the worship services of the Moravian Church wherever it has established itself. In Winston-Salem, this service, with little variation from the traditional and liturgical form, has been held since 1772 under the auspices of the Salem Congregation Churches. It is in no sense one of spectacular appeal or pageantry, but is held as a service of true worship, centering attention on the great underlying fact of the Christian Faith, THE RESURRECTION OF JESUS CHRIST, through which God placed a seal of approval on Jesus' atoning sacrifice and established the truth of the claims of our religion.

The service offers each one who attends an opportunity to renew a faith in the Risen Christ, in "the communion of saints," in "the forgiveness of sins," and in "the life everlasting."

Since 1930 the Easter Sunrise Service of The Moravian Church has been broadcast yearly by WSJS, Winston-Salem, North Carolina, and is now available over the internet at WSJS.com. The Moravian Church expresses appreciation to WSJS for making possible an extensive witness to the Resurrection of Jesus Christ. Comments from persons attending the service or listening to it by radio will be appreciated.

The site for the graveyard was selected April 21, 1766; the avenue bordering the graveyard was laid out in the year 1770; and the first body, that of John Birkhead, one of the eight men who first came to the settlement, was interred June 7, 1771.

The Moravians still call their graveyard by that significant and ancient name used by their ancestors – "God's Acre". It is a "field" in which the bodies of loved ones are sown in faith as "physical bodies," in due time to be raised as "spiritual bodies." One of the physical bodies 'resting' in "God's Acre" is country music legend George Hamilton IV who passed away September 17, 2014.

April 2017

Tucumcari Rawhide Days to feature some of Next Generation

Tucumcari Rawhide Days will be held in Tucumcari, New Mexico May 5-6, 2017. It is a celebration of the Old West & the filming of the Rawhide TV series. For anyone coming a day early the Thursday Kickoff Opening Ceremony Services are at the Tucumcari Historical Museum!! All Day, 9-5 with local Churches, Music, Food & Fellowship. There is a Free Showing of Rawhide at the Historic Odeon Theatre…Thursday, Friday & Saturday from 1:30 - 4:30.

Friday night's concert will feature some of the Next Generation: Sons & Daughters of Country Legends which includes Chrystie Wooley's (Sheb Wooley's daughter), Jett Williams (Hank Williams daughter), Dean Miller (Roger Miller's son) and Donnie Winters (Don Winters son) and special guest Michael Smotherman.

There will also be Special Guest Appearances by Clint Eastwood's Daughter, Kimber Eastwood Midkiff and Paul Brinegar's Son, Mark Brinegar. They played Rowdy Yates and Wishbone in the TV series.

The Saturday Night Performance will be Singer Song Writer "Mikki Daniel". And Dancing to Great Country Music by Eleven Hundred Springs.

There will be a Parade, Live Music, Demonstrations, Wagon rides, Gunfights, Chuckwagons, Food, Longhorn photo shoot, Blacksmith Competition, Gun Historian, Vendors, Games, Entertainment and Family Fun.

This festival is held at the Tucumcari Convention Center and is a free event with the exception of the concerts. To purchase concert tickets, go to www.tucumcarirawhidedays.com.

Last year's show featured Robyn Young, Chrystie Wooley and Jett Williams

April 2017

It's A Family Tradition

By Sasha Kay Dunavant

Dottie & Shelly West

The role of the family is an integral theme of Country Music. Some of County's greatest songs have captured memories from family life. Family acts, including sibling duos, have long been a staple on the Country stage. Some families have produced numerous talented members, both performers and songwriters, who separately made their impact on the genre. In other families, each generation has expanded the legacy of the one before it. This series celebrates Country Music's family connections.

Like many of Country Music's greatest star families, Dottie and Shelly West had lives filled with struggles, accolades, tragedies and successes. Dottie, born in 1932 as Dorothy Marie Marsh, near McMinnville, Tennessee, expressed love for music early on and began singing on the local radio station at age 13.

However, her home life was dominated by her father, William Hollis Marsh, a violent alcoholic who beat his family and sexually abused Dorothy. After testifying against her father in court, William Marsh was sentenced to 40 years in prison where he died in 1967.

Dorothy's mother, Pelina, opened a small café to support her 10 children and narrowly escape poverty. Dorothy sang and played guitar for her high-school band, "The Cookskins." Her hard work paid off and by 1951 she had received a music scholarship to Tennessee Technology University in Cookeville, Tennessee.

She met and married steel guitarist, Bill West in 1953. The couple and their children moved to Cleveland, Ohio, where Dorothy earned her stage name, Dottie West. She sang in a country-pop duo with Kathy Dee called the "Kay-Dots" on a local television program, Landmark Jamboree. In 1959 Bill and Dottie West auditioned for producer Don Pierce and were immediately signed to Starday, but their time at Starday proved to be unsuccessful.

After many trips to Nashville, Tennessee, the couple moved there in 1961. They soon became friends with singer – songwriters, Willie Nelson, Roger Miller, Hank Cochran, Harlan Howard and Pasty Cline. Cline taught West all she knew about music and performing. The advice was well received, and West's first Top 40 hit was 1963's "Let Me Off at the Corner." Jim Reeves and West's duet, "Love is No Excuse," climbed the Top Ten in 1964. The same year Chet Atkins produced West's single "Here Come My Baby." The hit reached Billboard Magazine's Top 10 and made West the first female country artist to win a Grammy Award for Best Female Country Vocal Performance. West was also invited to sing at the Grand Ole Opry. In 1965 "Would You Hold it Against Me" turned out to be West's biggest hit. In 1967 West and Atkins worked on three separate albums, "With All My Heart and Soul," "Dottie West Sings Sacred Ballads" and "I'll Help You Forget Her."

During the 1970s West and Kenny Rogers had a string of successful duets, including "All I Ever Need Is You" and "Every Time Two Fools Collide." West also had a couple of solo hits in 1979, including, "A Lesson In Leavin'" and "Are You Happy Baby." In the 1980s West was thought of as a sex symbol after she recorded her cross over hit, "Country Sunshine." The song became a commercial for Coca-Cola. She remarried for a third time to soundman, Al Winters, who was 23 years her junior. West also did a revealing photo spread for OUI Magazine and toured with the Broadway version of "Best Little Whore House in Texas." Her last hit was "We Know Better Now." West died in 1991 due to complications from a car wreck. Daughter Shelly, who was born in 1958, began singing and touring with her mother when she was 17 years old. Shelly soon fell in love with her mother's guitarist, Allen Frizzell. They married and moved to California where they began touring the Southwest with the band of Allen's older

April 2017

brothers, Lefty and David Frizzell. Shelly and David sent a demo of their duet, "Lovin' on Borrowed Time," to record producer, Snuff Garret. He was impressed by their work, and after an unsuccessful try in Nashville, Garret sent a demo of their song, "You're The Reason God Made Oklahoma" to actor, Clint Eastwood. Eastwood recently had bought his own record label and decided to put the song in his new movie, "Any Which Way You Can." Frizzell and West had other hits, such as "A Texas State of Mind," "Husbands and Wives," "Another Honky-Tonk Night on Broadway" and "I Just Came Here to Dance."

The pair worked together until 1985 when West and Allen Frizzell separated. Shelly made her solo debut in 1983 with "Jose Cuervo." The song netted big bucks for tequila companies around the nation and also hit number one on Country Charts.

Her song "Flight 309 to Tennessee" made the top five. West remarried to Gary Hood and had twin boys. In 1984 – 1986 her solo career soared with hits such as "Now I Lay Me Down To Cheat," "Somebody Buy This Cowgirl A Beer" and "Love Don't Come Any Better Than This."

Although West and Frizzell reunited for a short time, West's career virtually ended when her mother, Dottie West died in 1991. Country Music Television honored Shelly West and David Frizzell in 2005 by voting them into the sixth spot on their 100 Greatest Duets Special. In recent years she has made appearances in Branson, Missouri, theatres.

Country Music Questions & Answers

Q: I wonder, does Bill Anderson have a wife? I don't see her with him at any of his shows.

Carol Carpenter, Bay City, MI
Also from Tommy Nelson
Crawfordsville, OR

A: Anderson's first wife was Betty to whom he was married from 1959- 1969. The divorce inspired him to write the song "A Death in the Family," which was later recorded by country artist Little Jimmy Dickens and released as the B-side of Dicken's single "Times Are Gonna Get Better," Anderson's second wife was Becky. The date of their marriage id unknown but they divorced in 1997.

Q: Was Marty Stuart married to Johnny Cash's daughter? And did they have any children?

Margie

A: Marty Stuart was married to Cindy Cash from 1983 - 1988. They had no children. Cindy, daughter of Johnny Cash and Vivian Liberto Cash, was born July 29, 1959.

Q: First off I love the paper and second for no good reason I would like to know if Wilson Fairchild is related to Barbara Fairchild.

Kenneth Blakeslee, Grand Junction, CO

A: The duo, Wilson Fairchild, are sons of Statler brothers Harold and Don Reid. There names are Wil (Wilson) and Langdon Reid. The name Wilson Fairchild comes from their middle names. In the March issue of the CFR News there was an article about their new CD dedicated to their fathers.

Q: I'd like to know if Ralph Sloan is still living. If not, when he passed. I really like watching him and the dancer.

Wanda McDonald, Coffeyville, KS

A: On July 5, 1952, Ralph Sloan and his Tennessee Travelers tapped their feet on the boards of old Ryman Auditorium, a gig Ralph would not relinquish until years later. "Ralph's last performance was a taping for the Hee Haw TV show. He got up from the hospital and went and performed with the team and did an excellent job. A few days after that the cancer ate into his back and he collapsed and was not able to stand," said Melvin Sloan. "But he did get to see his final act on Hee Haw. Ralph died March 12, 1980 "The square dance is now the state dance of Tennessee because of Ralph," noted Melvin, who, along with his late brother was inducted into America's Clogging Hall of Fame in 1997.

If you have questions send them to Paula, CFR News, P.O. Box 210796, Nashville, TN 37221 or email them to paula@gabrielcommunications.com.

April 2017

Salute to the Kornfield
Everything you always wanted to know about the cast
By Claudia Johnson

Gailard Sartain – Creative Artist and Talented Entertainer

Guest Writer Danny Nichols

From Tulsa to Kornfield Kounty, Gailard Sartain has seen or done it all. Affectionately remembered for his roles as Maynard in "The General Store," Orville in "Lulu's Truck Stop," Officer Bull Moose or the trucker in the CB Radio Spot on "Hee Haw," Sartain has become an accomplished and successful actor, comedian, painter and illustrator, graphic artist, radio program host, and entertainer.

Sartain's journey to stardom began in Tulsa, Oklahoma, where he graduated from Will Rogers High School in 1963. He earned a Bachelor of Fine Arts degree from the University of Tulsa and struck out to New York City in 1968, working as an illustrator for a year and spending another year as an artist for Hallmark. To earn his fame and fortune, it would be his hometown of Tulsa that offered that opportunity. Upon returning to Tulsa from New York, Sartain obtained a position as cameraman for local television station KOTV in 1971. It was there an opportunity arose that launched his career in entertainment, although at the time, it seemed merely a means of adding a few extra dollars to his weekly income. It would be from this new position that Sartain would create a late-night comedy program, "The Uncanny Film Festival and Camp Meeting," featuring himself in the role of Dr. Mazeppa Pompazoidi. His improvised skits included guest stars Gary Busey and Jim "Buck" Millaway. His comedy and improvisational skills were soon noticed by agent Jim Halsey, who was also the agent for Roy Clark on the already popular "Hee Haw" television program.

"Hee Haw" debuted on June 15, 1969, finding instant success, but by 1971 CBS had decided to drop all their rural comedies, which included, "The Beverly Hillbillies," "Green Acres," "Mayberry RFD" and "Hee Haw" as the station pursued a different demographic audience. As if destiny had intervened, the producers of "Hee Haw" found another outlet for their successful program – syndication. By moving the program into the non network area, "Hee Haw" found a larger audience in 1972 and continued to remain popular for the next 20 years. It was during this relaunch that Sartain joined the crew of "Hee Haw" and would ride the wave of popularity into viewers' hearts and into the history books.

Sartain, son of a Tulsa fire chief, aspired early on to become an artist. "Ever since I was a kid I wanted to be an artist" he told Tulsa Magazine in 1986. He is remembered today for his accomplished work as a painter and illustrator. He designed the cover for fellow Rogers' Hall of Fame member Leon Russell's "Will o' the Wisp "as well as developing special pieces of art for various charity events in Tulsa and Oklahoma. In speaking about his role in the entertainment industry, Sartain told Tulsa Magazine, "It's a fun way to make a living. I enjoy it a whole lot more than picking cotton or digging a ditch. It sends the kids to school and pays the bills."

Entertainment seems to have set well with Sartain. In addition to making America laugh through his characters portrayed on "Hee Haw" for two decades, he has found time also to appear in more than 50 movies including "The Buddy Holly Story," "The Chase," "Mississippi Burning," "The Outsiders," " The Hollywood Knights," "Fried Green Tomatoes," "The Replacements," "The Big Easy," "The Grifters," "The Patriot" and "Elizabethtown." Sartain also appeared as the character Chuck in the Ernest P. Worrell films starring Jim Varney and the "Hey Vern, It's Ernest" television series. "Doing something funny and doing it right is the hardest thing in the world to do," Sartain admitted. But then the old saying about finding a job you love and you'll never have to work again seems somehow to apply to a man who has kept America entertained for more than 45 years, and at age 70, it sure beats picking cotton!

Appearing with Chuck Norris in Walker Texas Ranger.

April 2017

Singer Songwriters
By Sasha Kay Dunavant

Ted Daffan

Throughout the history of Country Music, thousands of songs have been written and performed. Many of those songs were written by famous performers. Some were written for a star's own records, while others were created to be sung by another artist. This Singer-Songwriter Series explores some of those talented individuals whose work we know and love.

The inspiration was a roadside diner and a few truckers. Theron Eugene "Ted" Daffan noticed that truckers would put a nickel in the jukebox before ordering their food at the café, and he was determined that one day truckers would play the songs that he had written. Daffan is credited with writing the first truck driving song, a subject that remains a popular theme in country music event today. Western Swing artist Cliff Bruner recorded Daffan's first song, "Truck Driver's Blues."

Much to Daffan's surprise, the song sold more than 100,000 copies making it the best-selling record of 1939. Several artists, including Webb Pierce, Lawton Williams, Johnny Gimble and the Texas Swing Pioneers, Rosie Flores, Asleep at the Wheel and Leon Rausch featuring Willie Nelson and Merle Haggard, have all covered "Truck Driver's Blues."

Daffan was born in Beauregard Parish, Louisiana, in 1912, and developed a fascination with electronics as a youth. After his graduation from high school in Houston, Texas, he opened an electric musical instrument and radio repair shop. According to the Texas State Historical Association, Daffan pioneered the electrification of instruments and was also an active figure in the Houston area country dance band scene of the 1930s. He is also lauded as one of the first pioneers of Texas Honky Tonk. His steel guitar often took the place of a fiddle and produced a mixture of blues and swing.

Playing Hawaiian guitar, he first performed on the radio with the group, Blue Islanders, in 1933. In 1934 Daffan closed his repair shop and joined the Blue Ridge Playboys. After playing with several bands for the next six years, he formed his own band, the Texans, with whom he achieved recording and performing success during the 1940s. Among their hits penned by Daffan were "Those Blue Eyes Are Not Shining Anymore," "No Letter Today," "She Goes The Other Way," "Worried Mind" and "I've Got Five Dollars and It's Saturday Night." "Worried Mind," his first hit, sold a reported 350,000 records. Its flip side, "Blue Steel Blues," became a perennially popular country instrumental.

He led other bands in California and Texas, but his recording career slowed down after World War II, and he concentrated on songwriting and other aspects of the music industry. From 1955 to 1971 he ran his own record label, Daffan Records, in Texas.

Undeniably, his most lasting contribution to country music was his songwriting. He was a prolific songwriter, penning almost all the material he ever recorded as well as hundreds of songs for other artists. "Born to Lose" was inspired by a phrase that Daffan overheard while playing poker. Coining a phrase, the song's memorable lyrics stated, "Born to lose, it seems so hard to bear. How I long to always have you near. You've grown tired and now you say we're through. Born to lose, and now I'm losing you." More than 120 different artists, such as Ray Charles, Dean Martin, Rosemary Clooney, Ella Fitzgerald, Fats Domino and Elton John, have recorded

April 2017

"Born to Lose." Both sides of the 1942 single release of "Born to Lose" backed with "No Letter Today" became pop hits in 1943, and the record became one of country music's early million sellers, earning him a gold disk. Ray Charles received a platinum disk for his version of the song in 1982. "Born to Lose" received a BMI "one million air play" award in 1992.

Another major hit, "I'm A Fool To Care," was recorded by Ray Charles, Ringo Starr, Joe Barry, Boz Scaggs and Les Paul and Mary Ford. The timeless song was featured in a Southern Comfort liquor commercial in 2013. Jim Reeves later covered Daffan's 1946 hit recording of "Beyond The Shadow of a Doubt," making it a hit of his own. Tim McNamara, Faron Young, George Jones and George and Gene all rerecorded Daffan's 1950 hit "I've Got Five Dollars and it's Saturday Night."

Teaming up with songwriter Robert Halcomb, Daffan wrote "The Last Drive" for country legend, Hank Snow. When 1950 Daffan and the Texans finally went their separate ways in 1950, Daffan and Hank Snow remained close. The friends and collaborators opened a publishing house in Nashville in the 1958. When Daffan returned in 1961 to Houston, he formed his own music-publishing business and continued to live and work in the music industry there until his death in 1996.

In 1970 Daffan was inducted into the Nashville Songwriters Hall of Fame as a charter member. The Western Swing Society Hall of Fame inducted Daffan in 1994. He was also honored by the Academy of Country Music Hall of Fame, the Texas Steel Guitar Association and the State of Louisiana. In 1981 the Smithsonian Institute included Daffan's music in an anthology of 50 years of American Country Music.

Larry's Country Diner at The Starlite Theatre
Branson   Missouri

- T. Graham Brown — Mon., May 1 - 2:00 p.m.
- Jimmy Fortune — Tues., May 2 - 7:30 p.m.
- Gene Watson — Wed., May 3 - 2:00 p.m.
- Mo & Holly Pitney and the Malpass Brothers — Thurs., May 4 - 2:00 p.m.
- Mark Wills — Fri., May 5 - 2:00 p.m.

417-337-9333   www.starlitetheatre.com

April 2017

Tennessee Ramblers with Cecil Campbell and Harry Blair

Dick Hartman organized the Tennessee Ramblers in the late 1920s, transferred to Charlotte from Rochester, New York in 1934 under the sponsorship of Crazy Water Crystals. At that time, the band featured Hartman, "Horse Thief Harry" Blair, Kenneth "Pappy" Wolfe, Jack Gillette and native North Carolinian Cecil Campbell. They established themselves as WBT radio's most popular string band, receiving over one hundred thousand pieces of fan mail by the end of their first seven months of broadcasting here.

After about a year at WBT, the Ramblers moved to Atlanta to work at stations WSB and WGST. They returned to Charlotte the following year to perform again on WBT for the Southern Radio Corporation.

In the late 1930s and early 1940s, the Ramblers were in and out of Charlotte, visiting Pittsburgh, Cincinatti, and Louisville for radio work. (Dick Hartman left the band in 1937.) Also during this period the group went to Hollywood to make several successful western films with cowboy singing stars such as Gene Autry and Tex Ritter. Titles included Ride Ranger Ride, Ridin' the Cherokee Trail, Swing Your Partner, with Dale Evans and Oh My Darling Clementine, featuring a young Roy Acuff.

In the mid-1940s, Cecil Campbell took the control of the band and led various organizations of the Tennessee Ramblers up into the 1970s. Campbell, born in 1911, was raised on a tobacco farm in Stokes County, North Carolina near Belews Creek and took an early interest in the folk music he grew up hearing. He learned hundreds of songs and became a skillful player of several stringed instruments.

As a young man he determined that he would try to make a living as a country musician and songwriter.

He was given his first opportunity to perform on radio by station WSJS in Winston-Salem, North Carolina. Wanting to expand his horizons, Campbell hitchhiked in 1932 to Pittsburgh where he lived with his brother. He soon auditioned for Dick Hartman who was looking for a guitar player to join his Crazy Tennessee Ramblers. Campbell was given the job and followed the band to Rochester and then back home to North Carolina where he remained.

Campbell stayed close to home for the next thirty years or so, but became an active composer and performer. He was a prolific songwriter with dozens of published songs to his credit. He also recorded a number of albums, several of which feature him on Hawaiian steel guitar.

Every year, Campbell, along with other veterans of the old western films including Claude Casey, performed a favorite number or two at the popular western film festivals held in Charlotte and Raleigh.

William Blair who came to be known as "Horse Thief Harry" is another original Tennessee Rambler participating in The Charlotte Country Music Story. Like Cecil Campbell, Blair joined the group in Pittsburgh in the early 1930s.

Blair was born in August of 1912 in New Martinsville, West Virginia. He went to work for Wierton Steel as a young teenager and picked up guitar from an uncle who also worked in the plant. Around the beginning of the Great Depression, he travelled to Pittsburgh to audition for Hartman's band. He wasn't offered a job and returned to West Virginia. But soon thereafter, he heard Hartman dedicate a song to him on the radio and then announce that he wanted the young musician to come back to Pittsburgh to join the band! Blair recalls with mixed emotions the countless dances

April 2017

the group played for in depressed coal mining towns. "We were lucky to earn seventy-five cents to a dollar for our services back then," he remembers.

Blair remained with the Ramblers until 1943 when he entered the service. He returned to the group following his discharge in 1945 and performed often with Tex Martin (Martin Shope), Cecil Campbell, Jack Gillette, and Claude Casey. Also during the 1940s, he toured with the Grand Ole Opry Tent Show with some of Nashville's biggest stars. At the end of the decade he worked for a time as a solo act in Newport News, Virginia and Nashville, Tennessee.

In 1949, Blair married and moved to Columbus, Ohio. Here the couple gave birth to a son and Blair decided to quit the road to raise his family. Eventually he returned to work at Wierton Steel where he stayed until 1968. Blair and his wife then retired to Murrell's Inlet, near Myrtle Beach, South Carolina.

Cecil Campbell died June 18, 1989, but many of the Tennessee Ramblers' records are now in print again on CD. The early band, as heard in Pittsburgh and on Charlotte's WBT, is the subject of Dick Hartman's Washboard Wonders / Tennessee Ramblers issued on the "British Archive of Country Music" label. The CD is mostly comprised of tracks from the band's June and October 1936 Charlotte sessions. Fiddler Elmer Warren — later rechristened Fiddlin' Hank when he joined the WBT Briarhoppers — contributes some of the first jazz-inspired "takeoff" solos heard in any Charlotte recordings. After Hartman departed the band, they made a few last recordings in Rock Hill, SC, before leaving the area, heard on the BACM CD Tennessee Ramblers, Vol. 2, The Jack Gillette Years 1939 – 46. Hartman's accordion player Cecil Campbell stayed in Charlotte and kept another unit of the Tennessee Ramblers going there for decades, featured on the German CD label Bronco Buster/Binge Discs: Cecil Campbell and His Tennessee Ramblers, and Jasmine records CD Cecil Campbell and His Tennessee Ramblers, Steel Guitar Swing.

Generations of Real Country!

Singer, songwriter, Donnie Winters is 3rd generation entertainer. His grandfather performed as Pop Winters and the Southern Strollers, his father Don Winters, sang with Marty Robbins for over 20 years. Marty recorded many songs written by Donnie and his brother and now Donnie has released his own country CD filled with songs written by himself, other family members & country idols.

Includes "Rosita" - sung on the Larry's Country Diner show on the 2017 Cruise.

16 songs - $15.00

www.donniewintersmusic.com

Donnie Winters, 7558 Buffalo Rd., Nashville TN 37221

April 2017

MAY

Jimmy Wayne: from Foster Kid to Homeless to Success

Many people talk the talk, but singer/songwriter/author Jimmy Wayne walks the walk.

In a private ceremony in Kennebunkport, Maine in September 2016, country artist and New York Times bestselling author, Jimmy Wayne, was honored with the prestigious Points of Light Award for his tireless work raising awareness for youth in Foster care.

Jimmy is a former foster kid turned country music singer/songwriter whose songs, story, and walk halfway across America in 2010 continue to help bring awareness to kids who age out of the foster system and become homeless.

Jimmy said, "No one should receive an award for helping kids; it's what we're all supposed to do and not expect anything in return. But what do you do with an award that's been given to you? Use it to raise awareness for more foster youth."

Prior to receiving this honor —presented to him by Neil Bush— Jimmy met with President George H. W. Bush, the founder of Points of Light, at the Bush family home at Walker's Point in Kennebunkport.

Jimmy told the President about his personal "points of light" — Bea and Russell Costner, the elderly couple who took him in at age 16 and changed his life by giving him a home and a chance to finish high school, go to college and pursue and catch his dream as a recording artist. He then delivered a soul stirring version of "How Great Thou Art," as the President sang along.

"It was an honor for me to meet the President of the United States, and to do that in his living room made it even more special," says Jimmy. "The shoreline leading to his driveway and his home were indeed beautiful, but what impressed me most was how humble he was."

Jimmy's hits include "Stay Gone," "Paper Angels," "Do You Believe Me Now" — which earned BMI's prestigious Million-Air Award for receiving one million radio spins in America — and "I Love You This Much." In 2009, Jimmy toured with Brad Paisley and recorded "Sara Smile" with rock 'n roll Hall of Fame duo Daryl Hall and John Oates.

In 2011, Jimmy released the novel Paper Angels which became a made-for-tv movie of the same title. In 2012, Jimmy helped get legislative bills passed extending the age of foster care to 21 in both California and Tennessee, and in 2015, he did the same in his home state of North Carolina. In 2014, he released Walk to Beautiful, a three-time New York Times Bestselling memoir. In June of this year, it crossed the 100,000 print sales milestone.

Jimmy lives in Nashville and continues to raise awareness for abused and neglected children through performing, writing, speaking and by establishing Project Meet Me Halfway, a resource to those wanting to volunteer as mentors, become foster parents. His ultimate goal is to build transitional homes for youth who age out of foster care without a place to go.

Jimmy can be seen in the new Country's Family Reunion Kickin' Back series.

A 6th Grade Teacher Changed This Country Singer's Tune (and Life)

By: Jimmy Wayne

It was summer of 1989, the same year the Berlin Wall fell. My wall wasn't about to come down anytime soon. I was a long-haired, homeless kid scouring the neighborhood looking for odd jobs so I could earn money to buy food.

I spied an open door to a woodshop where an old man stood at a bandsaw. I approached him and asked if he had any work I could do.

May 2017

Jimmy Wayne (middle row, second from left) in Ms. Crystal Friday (top row, second from left)'s 6th grade class in Bessemer City, N.C., 1985-1986.

"Ask the boss," he said, nodding his head toward a white-haired lady in the back of the woodshop manhandling a radial arm saw. The old lady turned off the saw and walked toward me.

"Do you cut grass?" she asked. "Come back at five."

I showed up on time and began cutting their grass. I noticed the 75-year-old, white-haired lady walking out the front door of her home toward the fence carrying a Coca-Cola. She motioned for me. Bea handed me the ice cold Coca-Cola and doughnut, then started talking about the weather and the job I was doing. She hired me that day to be their lawn-boy for the remainder of the summer. Each week, she gave me a Coca-Cola when I cut their grass.

The Costners eventually allowed me to move into their home, and they single-handedly changed every cell in my body. They gave me the opportunity to attend high school and college, and pursue my dream of writing and performing music professionally.

My love for writing started years earlier, in Ms. Crystal Friday's class. She was my six grade teacher (twice), when my mother was serving time in maximum-security prison. I was living with my granddad—an old bootlegger. He didn't care what I did. I had the run of the trailer park and was always getting into trouble and skipping school. I was a lost, angry 12-year-old boy. But Ms. Friday didn't tolerate any excuses.

Her brother Rufus once said, "During the Civil Rights era, the Fridays' house was the recipient of a fire bomb that was thrown on their front porch by the Ku Klux Klan because Crystal's oldest sister was the first black to integrate the town's high school cheerleading team.

Her father, Mr. Lorenzo Friday, sent all the kids to the back of the house and rushed to put out the fire himself... an image burned into Crystal's memory.

Ms. Friday attended segregated Highland School in her early years and later went to integrated Hunter Huss High School, where she graduated in 1975. She attended and graduated from Livingstone College in Salisburn, N.C., a historic black school, with a degree in education.

Ms. Friday knew that education was important so, she encouraged me to write in a journal every day. Writing journal entries evolved into writing poems, songs, and books including my New York Times bestseller, Walk To Beautiful.

I am indebted to Ms. Friday. I would not be where I'm at today had it not been for her discipline, love and direction. I lost contact with her when I was 13 years old after my mom was released from prison and we went on the run from the law with my new stepdad. After being abandoned at a bus station in Pensacola, Florida, I was picked up by the police and spent the next three years in the foster care system and homeless.

Nearly 20 years later, I moved to Nashville, got my first record deal and released a song I had written called "Stay Gone." It became a hit and sold nearly half a million CDs. I was standing at a "meet and greet" table at Walmart in Gastonia, N.C., signing CDs and taking photos with fans. There was a four-hour line stretched around the building with fans waiting to get a signature and photo.

About two-and-a-half hours later, I noticed two hands slide a CD across the table toward me. I looked up and saw it was Ms. Friday. I immediately yelled out her name, "Ms. Friday!" I hugged her and told her I was sorry for all the hurtful words I said to her in the sixth grade. I thanked her and showed her the report card inside my CD cover that she had signed when I was in her class. It said, "Jimmy needs to improve in writing."

To this day, Ms. Friday comes to every event I perform near my hometown. No matter how hot, humid or cramped the venue is, Ms. Friday is there supporting me.

May 2017

Nadine
The Church Lady

Lord, give me a sense of humor,
Give me the grace to see a joke,
To get some humor out of life,
And to pass it on to other folk.

If you still have your Mom around, call her, give her a hug, take her out to dinner. I miss my Mom. When I was younger, I would have never thought I would say that! My Mom was strict, Ohhhh, she was strict! My Dad died when I was 12, so I guess she knew when she looked at me she had a job on her hands and it wasn't gonna be easy. My two brothers had already left home so it was just me and Mom. That was the problem, she only had me to deal with, so I couldn't get away with a lot. I was one of those kids who would sneak around behind her back and with Daddy for a preacher, I had learned it well. Problem was, all those people who were at church were around town and if they saw you doing something, they were on the phone (that old dial phone) calling Mama to see if I was supposed to be where I was.

I had to be there for supper and it was just her and me and sometimes I felt like I was under one of those big ole lamps with the FBI breathing down my back! If I did something that was wrong, she would send me outside to cut a switch and it better be a good one too. Matter of fact, that's how I learned to dance! She would switch and I'd dance in a circle around her. Lord, I wish I could have a video of that today. Course, today, she would be in a prison somewhere, eating bologna sandwiches. Maybe the switches need to come back and teach some respect to some of these hoodlums. I am not speaking of my grandchildren, of course, they are perfect!

I remember as a teenager coming home from a date, I'd walk in and there was Mom in her bedroom on her knees praying for me! Lord knows I needed it. Thank God for Mama's that will pray for their kids. No nation has ever had a better friend than the mother that teachers her children how to pray. I thank God I had a mama like that. I know that's why I am where I am today, with a Christian man and two grown kids that love the Lord and are praying for their children daily. I owe that to my Mom.

Love on Mom today and if she's already gone, say a prayer of thanks for that lady who taught you respect and discipline in your life. She loved you or she wouldn't have cared whether you were respectful or not. I can tell you right now, I'm pretty respectful, I got a switchin' every week whether I needed it or not. And you know me, I really didn't need that switchin', right?

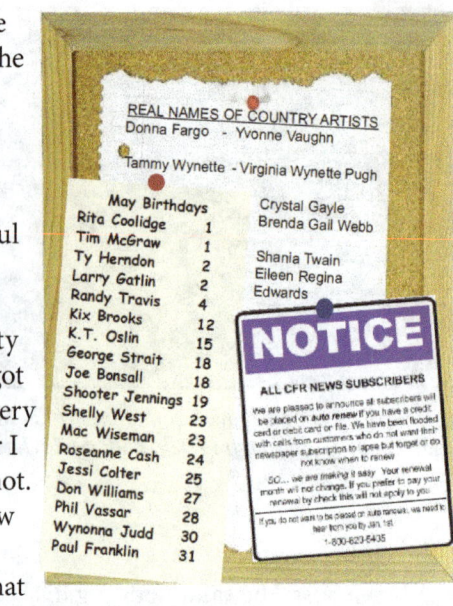

REAL NAMES OF COUNTRY ARTISTS
Donna Fargo – Yvonne Vaughn
Tammy Wynette – Virginia Wynette Pugh
Crystal Gayle – Brenda Gail Webb
Shania Twain – Eileen Regina Edwards

May Birthdays
Artist	Day
Rita Coolidge	1
Tim McGraw	1
Ty Herndon	2
Larry Gatlin	2
Randy Travis	4
Kix Brooks	12
K.T. Oslin	15
George Strait	18
Joe Bonsall	18
Shooter Jennings	19
Shelly West	23
Mac Wiseman	23
Roseanne Cash	24
Jessi Colter	25
Don Williams	27
Phil Vassar	28
Wynonna Judd	30
Paul Franklin	31

NOTICE — ALL CFR NEWS SUBSCRIBERS

We are pleased to announce all subscribers will be placed on auto renew if you have a credit card or debit card on file. We have been flooded with calls from customers who do not want their newspaper subscription to lapse but forget or do not know when to renew.

SO... we are making it easy. Your renewal month will not change. If you prefer to say your renewal by check this will not apply to you.

If you do not want to be placed on auto renewal, we need to hear from you by Jan. 1st.
1-800-823-5435

Look who's on the Diner this week!
Larry's Country Diner
Thursdays at 7 p.m. central Saturdays at 10 p.m. central

NEW SHOW
CRAIG CAMPBELL
May 4 & 6

NEW SHOW
DEAN MILLER
May 11 & 13

NEW SHOW
THE STEELDRIVERS
May 18 & 20

NEW SHOW
BAILLIE & THE BOYS
May 25 & 27

May 2017

Great books by some great country singers

Renowned songwriter, singer, and wife of Waylon Jennings writes an intimate, enormously entertaining memoir of American music, of life with Waylon and the Outlaws, and of faith lost and found.

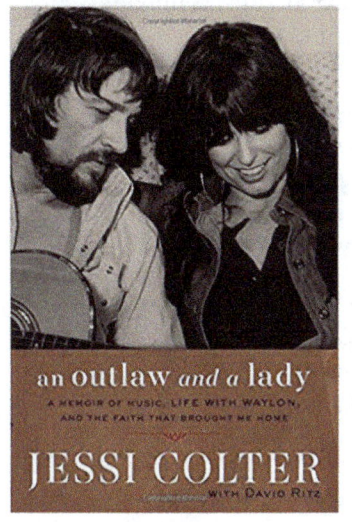

The daughter of a Pentecostal evangelist and a race-car driver, Jessi Colter played piano and sang in church before leaving Arizona to tour with rock-n-roll pioneer Duane Eddy, whom she married. Colter became a successful recording artist, appearing on American Bandstand and befriending stars such as the Everly Brothers and Chet Atkins, while her songs were recorded by Nancy Sinatra, Dottie West, and others. Her marriage to Eddy didn't last, however, and in 1969 she married the electrifying Waylon Jennings. Together, they made their home in Nashville which, in the 1970s, was ground zero for roots music, drawing Bob Dylan, Johnny Cash, Willie Nelson, Kris Kristofferson, Shel Silverstein, and others to the Nashville Sound. And Jessi was at the center of it all, the only woman on the landmark Wanted: The Outlaws album, the record that launched the Outlaw Country genre and was the first country album to go platinum. She also tasted personal commercial success with the #1-single "I'm Not Lisa."

But offstage, life was a challenge, as Waylon pursued his addictions and battled his demons. Having drifted from the church as a young woman, Jessi returned to her faith and found in it a source of strength in the turmoil of living with Waylon. In the 1980s, Waylon helped launch the super group The Highwaymen with Willie Nelson, Johnny Cash, and Kris Kristofferson, and the hits kept rolling, as did Waylon's reckless living. Amid it all, Jessi faithfully prayed for her husband until finally, at Thanksgiving 2001, Waylon found Jesus, just months before he died.

An Outlaw and a Lady is a powerful story of American music, of love in the midst of heartache, and of faith that sustains.

Imagine yourself a thirteen-year-old hundreds of miles away from home, in a strange city, and your mom leaves you at a bus station parking lot and drives off into the night with her lover.

That's the real life story of country music star Jimmy Wayne. It's a miracle that Jimmy survived being hungry and homeless, bouncing in and out of the foster care system, and sleeping in the streets. But he didn't just overcome great adversity in his life; he now uses his country music platform to help children everywhere, especially teenagers in foster care who are about to age out of the system.

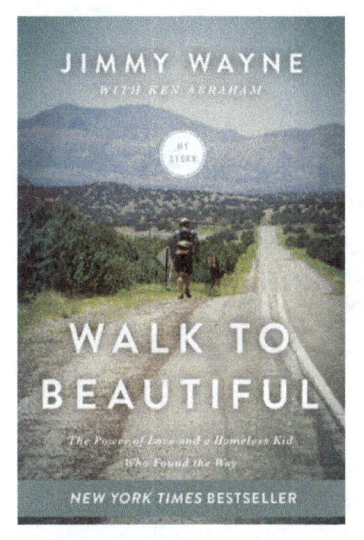

Walk to Beautiful is the powerfully emotive account of Jimmy's horrendous childhood and the love shown him by Russell and Bea Costner, the elderly couple who gave him a stable home and provided the chance to complete his education. Jimmy says of Bea, "She changed every cell in my body."

It also chronicles Jimmy's rise to fame in the music industry and his Meet Me Halfway campaign: his walk halfway across America, 1,700 miles from Nashville to Phoenix, to raise awareness for foster kids.

Join Jimmy on his walk to beautiful and see how one person really can make a difference.

Honkytonk Angels describes the inside workings of both the country music world, and the presence of God's hand upon some of the biggest songs in country music's history. With a birds eye view Bernie Nelson shares rare glimpse of the creation and journeys of these songs. Being a 30 plus year respected veteran of the famous Music Row, Bernie has gained the trust of many of Nashvilles biggest names so as to tell the stories like many of them have never been shared before.

May 2017

Honkytonk Angels shows the undeniable workings of God deeply rooted into the streets of Music City USA. Having been a close participant in many of these stories due to his relationship with the writers, producers, songpluggers and artists himself, the stories bring you closer then ever to their rich history.

Other stories involving God's angels moving about there were told and entrusted to Bernie by those closest to the stories directly to Bernie himself. The book is intriguing, humorous historical and majorly insightful. Most of all it shows the truly amazing grace that is required to take a song from the legal pad or whiskey stained bar napkin in some cases to the Country Music Hall of Fame itself.

God loves music. He is constantly proving that .Through these beautiful stories brought together by the crafted writer that Bernie is ,readers will feel a closeness to the songs like never before.

Take a ride along to a songwriting session with Bernie.Read what it was like the day the song was started. Many of those songs took crazy paths to reach the status that they are today.

Honkytonk Angels will both enlighten you to the inside history of the songs but also deepen the belief that without Gods helping hand they would not have had a snowballs chance in . . . well . . . heck you'll just have to read the book to see how they turned out.

Starting May 5 on RFD-TV
Fridays...7 p.m. central
Saturdays...11 p.m central

May 2017

Marty Robbins' Gunfighter Ballads in National Recording Registry

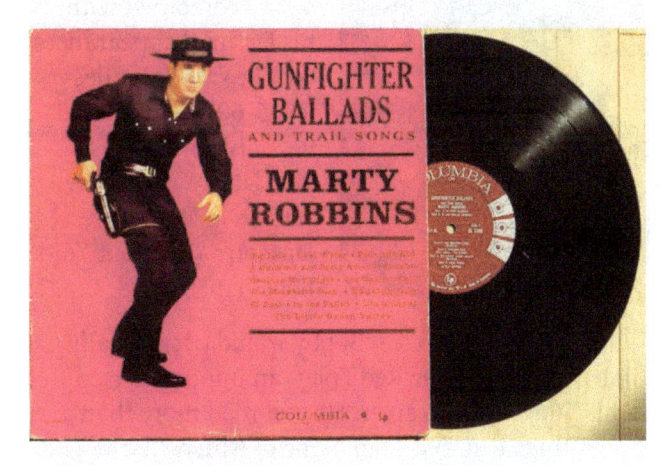

Marty Robbins' quintessential Country and Western album, "Gunfighter Ballads and Trail Songs," was among the recordings added to the National Recording Registry on Wednesday.

"This year's exciting list gives us a full range of sound experiences," said Carla Hayden, Librarian of Congress, in a statement. "These sounds of the past enrich our understanding of the nation's cultural history and our history in general."

The librarian with advice from the Library's National Recording Preservation Board, annually selects 25 titles that are "culturally, historically, or aesthetically significant" and at least 10 years old to be added to the registry.

Big Mama Thornton's "Hound Dog," Country gospel group the Chuck Wagon Gang's 1948 recording of "I'll Fly Away," Wilson Pickett's "In the Midnight Hour" and Judy Garland's classic rendition of "Over the Rainbow" were also among the latest additions. Non-musical selections added to the registry on Wednesday include the Brooklyn Dodgers and New York Giants' last game at the Polo Grounds, a game that was announced by the legendary Vin Scully in 1957.

National Recording Registry additions

1. The 1888 London cylinder recordings of Col. George Gouraud (1888)

2. "Lift Every Voice and Sing" (singles), Manhattan Harmony Four (1923); Melba Moore and Friends (1990)

3. "Puttin' on the Ritz" (single), Harry Richman (1929)

4. "Over the Rainbow" (single), Judy Garland (1939)

5. "I'll Fly Away" (single), The Chuck Wagon Gang (1948)

6. "Hound Dog" (single), Big Mama Thornton (1953)

7. "Saxophone Colossus," Sonny Rollins (1956)

8. The Brooklyn Dodgers and the New York Giants at the Polo Grounds, announced by Vin Scully (September 8, 1957)

9. "Gunfighter Ballads and Trail Songs," Marty Robbins (1959)

10. "The Incredible Jazz Guitar of Wes Montgomery," Wes Montgomery (1960)

11. "People" (single), Barbra Streisand (1964)

12. "In the Midnight Hour" (single), Wilson Pickett (1965)

13. "Amazing Grace" (single), Judy Collins (1970)

14. "American Pie" (single), Don McLean (1971)

15. "All Things Considered," first broadcast (May 3, 1971)

16. "The Rise and Fall of Ziggy Stardust and the Spiders from Mars," David Bowie (1972)

17. "The Wiz," original cast album (1975)

18. "Their Greatest Hits (1971–1975)," Eagles (1976)

19. "Scott Joplin's Treemonisha," Gunter Schuller, arr. (1976)

20. "Wanted: Live in Concert," Richard Pryor (1978)

21. "We Are Family" (single), Sister Sledge (1979)

22. "Remain in Light," Talking Heads (1980)

23. "Straight Outta Compton," N.W.A (1988)

24. "Rachmaninoff's Vespers (All-Night Vigil)," Robert Shaw Festival Singers (1990)

25. "Signatures," Renée Fleming (1997)

May 2017

Bobby Lord

How to describe the entertainment career of Grand Ole Opry star Bobby Lord … that's a hard one. I guess I would call him an underappreciated crossover artist who enjoyed above-average success as both a singer and television host.

In 1962, Carl Butler and Pearl scored their own "Cross Over" of a sort.

As a mostly retired sports writer, I might better be able to frame Bobby's career in baseball terms. On the diamond, he might have been a utility infielder. You know, able to play every position well enough to get the job done, but not probably good enough to be an everyday starter. A dependable, likeable team player who would enjoy a long career as a backup player. One who would come up with some big plays and big hits, but not on a consistent basis to earn a spot in the starting lineup.

That's probably a fair assessment of the career for the personable and fabulously entertaining Lord, who spent more than a decade on the active Opry lineup but never quite reached the level of stardom he deserved.

The Florida native — born in 1934 — made his first splash as a teen-ager in the early 1950s, singing on The Bobby Lord Homefolks Show in St. Petersburg. He garnered national attention in 1952 by winning a TV Guide-sponsored talent competition that led to his appearance on Paul Whiteman's TV Teen Club in Philadelphia, a precursor to American Bandstand.

Good-looking Bobby married his high school sweetheart, Mozelle, at age 20 and watched his career take off over the next few years. Growing momentum gained from those appearances led to a juke-bopping, pedal-to-the-metal rockabilly style that was reflected in his debut record "No More, No More, No More!" (1955).

That one didn't chart but — combined with his featured appearances on The Ozark Jubilee (1955-60) — gave Lord his only Top 10 hit a year later, a rockabilly version of Wanda Jackson's "Without Your Love" (1956).

On The Ozark Jubilee, Bobby would occasionally fill in as host for star Red Foley, an important step in his budding TV career. He recorded more than a dozen singles in that span, none of which charted, and both his and the show's popularity began to wane. When that show was canceled in 1960, Bobby moved his growing family to Nashville to launch the next stage of his career.

Almost immediately upon his arrival in Music City, he was added to the Grand Ole Opry lineup, where he regularly performed until the mid-1970s. He also began hosting Opry Almanac on WSM-TV as well as the syndicated Bobby Lord Show from 1963-68.

During that span, Bobby had cracked the Top 75 eight more times, and reached No. 15 with "You and Me Against The World" (1970).

When that namesake show ended, he briefly stepped from show biz to return to Florida and concentrate on family business interests, including vacation real-estate development. But he had kept a foot in entertainment and staged a comeback in the 1980s to host TNN's Country Sportsman (later renamed Celebrity Outdoors) until 1989.

Except for a few appearances in the early 2000s, Bobby retired and resettled in Florida, where he died of a stroke on Feb. 26, 2008.

You can find many of his appearances on YouTube, both as a young man and in country classic appearances with other stars of his generation. And of course, on CFR!

He might not have been the household name or enjoyed the success that some of his peers achieved, but Bobby Lord made the team.

Author Tom Wood, who writes thrillers and Westerns, is a regular contributor to Country Family Reunion News. Reach him at tomwoodauthor.com

Country Music Hall of Fame Inductees Announced

The Country Music Hall of Fame revealed its Class of 2017 inductees on Wednesday, April 5.

The new members will be inducted into three different categories: Veterans Era Artist, Modern Era Artist and Songwriter. A Veterans Era and Modern Era artist are both inducted into the Hall of Fame each year, while the Songwriter category rotates with the Recording and/or Touring Musician Active Prior to 1980 and Non-Performer categories. The Class of 2017 will be the 57th group of country music artists to be inducted into the Hall of Fame.

The three-member class includes Alan Jackson in the Modern Era category. The late Jerry Reed was inducted in the Veterans category and Songwriter Don Schlitz was also named as part of the Hall's newest class in the Songwriter category. Schlitz's many hits include "The Gambler" for Kenny Rogers, "Forever and Ever, Amen" for Randy Travis and "When You Say Nothing at All" for Keith Whitley.

The Country Music Association created the Country Music Hall of Fame in 1961 to honor artists who have significantly impacted country music. Currently there are 130 members on the Hall of Fame roster, including icons such as Johnny Cash, Garth Brooks, George Jones, Dolly Parton and Reba McEntire. The official induction ceremony for the new members will take place later this year. 2007 HOF inductee Vince Gill was the host, mixing personal stories and jokes in between the speeches.

Jerry Reed

b. Atlanta, GA, March 20, 1937

d. September 1, 2006

Jerry Reed made indelible marks on country music as a recording artist, a songwriter, and a virtuoso guitarist.

Reed's guitar work was marked by syncopation and complexity, while his songwriting and stage persona conveyed strutting wit and backwoods intelligence. Raised in Georgia, he moved to Nashville in 1962, taking jobs as a session guitarist and writing songs for country heavies including Porter Wagoner.

Encouraged by guitar great Chet Atkins, Reed developed an instantly recognizable and idiosyncratic guitar style that suited humor-filled compositions including "Guitar Man" and "Amos Moses." He and Atkins won a 1970 Grammy for instrumental album Me and Jerry, and Reed followed that a year later with a Grammy for country male vocal performance on "When You're Hot, You're Hot." A third Grammy, this one for country instrumental performance, came in 1993 for another duo effort with Atkins.

Other major Reed hits include "Lord, Mr. Ford," "East Bound and Down," and "She Got the Goldmine (I Got the Shaft)." He also won positive notice for his acting roles in films including W.W. and the Dixie Dance Kings, and Smokey and the Bandit.

"Every move he made was to entertain, and make the world more fun," said Reed devotee Brad Paisley. "Because he was such a great, colorful personality with his acting and songs and entertaining, sometimes people didn't even notice that he was just about the best guitarist you'll ever hear."

Alan Jackson

b. Newnan, GA, October 17, 1958

As a songwriter, recording artist, and performer, Alan Jackson brought tradition-drenched country music into the new century.

A member of the Nashville Songwriters Hall of Fame, Jackson has sold more than sixty million albums and notched twenty-six Billboard #1 country singles. His often-autobiographical songs are marked by humility, humor, and eloquent simplicity. He is a three-time CMA Entertainer of the Year, and his plainspoken "Where Were You (When the World Stopped Turning)" won a Best Country Song Grammy.

Jackson revived songs recorded by Country Music Hall of Fame members Tom T. Hall, George Jones, and Don Williams, and he wrote gems including "Chasin' That Neon Rainbow," "Drive (For Daddy Gene)," "Livin' on Love," and "Remember

May 2017

When," all of which mined personal experience in communicating communal truth. In a recording career that began in 1989, he has lived by a simple edict: "Keep it country."

Don Schlitz

b. Durham, NC, August 29, 1952

Don Schlitz is among the most impactful and eloquent songwriters in country music history.

For Don's story, see the Singer/Songwriters article on page 99.

The many sides of singer/songwriter Craig Campbell

Growing up in a strong Southern Baptist home, Craig Campbell fell in love early with the sounds of Country radio, and built a foundation not just as a singer and performer, but as a songwriter. It was a conversation with Luke Bryan, for whom he once played keyboard, that really helped him set his priorities clear. "He said, 'man you need to be writing songs, and you need to be writing with different people, twice a day,'" recalls Campbell. "That's where you can define yourself as an artist, with people writing songs that tell your story. And nobody is going to sing them better than you.'"

That dedication to the craft made him not only understand the importance of crafting songs like the fan-favorite "Tomorrow Tonight" with trusted collaborators, but also to keep writing, constantly. It's an ethos that recently led to Garth Brooks himself cutting his track "All American Kid" for Man Against the Machine. "That was such a huge, huge honor," said Campbell. "I didn't believe it was happening, even when he was recording it."

Campbell kept pushing even through the difficult times, back when his original record label folded. "It was very deflating," he admits, but he kept persevering. His sophomore LP, Never Regret, earned him comparisons to Alan Jackson, Travis Tritt and Clint Black, and "Keep Them Kisses Comin'" climbed into the Top Ten of Country radio. It wasn't long after the shuttering of his former label Bigger Picture that his current home, BBR Music Group's RED BOW, snatched him up nearly instantly. RED BOW recognized that it was crucial to keep that classic-country-bred, smooth-as-molasses voice singing. The innately gifted songwriter additionally signed to BBR Music Group's Magic Mustang Music for publishing.

Campbell has had five consecutive charted hits and over a half million downloads. Those bumps along the way for the Georgia-born artist, on his path from the small town of Lyons to Nashville's Music Row. But through hits like "Keep Them Kisses Comin'," "Fish" and "Family Man," and countless shows, he's kept his eyes on his mission – to bring his fans true country music with a spin all his own, through timeless songs that tell his life story. And with his forthcoming debut project on RED BOW Records – flag-shipped by the earnest "Outskirts of Heaven," which was co-written by Campbell – he is ready to share the next chapter: where that timelessness meets the here and now.

"There are a lot of sides to me that people haven't yet seen," he says, currently at work on his third and most versatile record. "You can expect some great music with a little more energy, and a lot more fire."

He'll certainly show these other sides on his forthcoming LP, which signals a whole new era for Campbell – new label, new songwriters, new producer (Mickey Jack Cones, known for his many successes with Dustin Lynch, Joe Nichols and more) and a new outlook that lets him explore all the facets of his unique niche in the Country landscape. And the timing is perfect. While the genre shoots off in directions left and right, Campbell's a singer capable of melding both the old and the new into something purely special, purely his own.

May 2017

SteelDrivers...combination of soul, country & bluegrass

SteelDrivers, left to right are: Richard Bailey, Brent Truitt, Tammy Rogers, Mike Fleming and Gary Nichols.

"I think that's what moves people when they come to see us: the realness and rawness and edge," says Tammy Rogers, who formed the SteelDrivers in 2005 with Richard Bailey, Mike Fleming, multi-instrumentalist Mike Henderson, and soulful singer (and now-acclaimed contemporary country artist) Chris Stapleton. That version of the SteelDrivers received three GRAMMY® nominations and won an audience that was surprised and initially saddened by the 2010 and 2011 departures of Stapleton and Henderson. But the entries of Gary Nichols and virtuoso mandolin talent Brent Truitt have created a SteelDrivers band that carries the gutbucket ethic of the original combo, but pleases in different ways.

Richard Bailey's banjo plays funky, little Kentucky-goes-to-Memphis rolls. Tammy Rogers' fiddle soars. Brent Truitt's mandolin chops time, and Mike Fleming's bass pounds the downbeat, while Gary Nichols vocals howl with a hurt and anger that reaches into your soul.

"That made me dizzy for a second," Nichols says, remembering the moment he sang the line. "Really, I almost passed out. There are certain lines in SteelDrivers songs that require a little bit of Wilson Pickett."

Nichols is from Muscle Shoals. He grew up as a guitar slinger and a soul shouter, which should not be any help in fronting one of bluegrass music's most engaging outfits. But part of the reason the SteelDrivers are such an engaging band is the seemingly incongruous blend of soul and slink, blues and country, mountain coal and red dirt.

Richard Bailey

BANJO

Grammy nominated banjo player, Richard Bailey has recorded with such diverse artists as Al Green and George Jones. Featured in the book Masters of the 5-String Banjo, Bailey has performed with Bill Monroe, Roland White, Vassar Clements, Loretta Lynn, Chet Akins, Larry Cordle, Laurie Lewis, Dale Ann Bradley, and countless others. He has also recorded with Kenny Rogers, Michael Martin Murphy, Johnny Cash, Tammy Wynette, and Ronnie Milsap and has played at Carnegie Hall and on Austin City Limits.

Mike Fleming

BASS/VOCALS

A versatile veteran, Mike Fleming lays down the firm foundation and sings the baritone harmony that rounds out the SteelDrivers' sound. A self-confessed ``recovering banjo player,'' Mike has recorded with Holly Dunn, Joy Lynn White, and with groundbreaking singer/songwriter David Olney. In addition to traveling the world during stints with Dunn and Kevin Welch, Mike has appeared on Austin City Limits, Nashville Now, Crook and Chase, and too many Grand Ole Opry shows and festivals to count.

Tammy Rogers

FIDDLE/VOCALS

Growing up in a family bluegrass band that also included banjo great Scott Vestal, Tammy brings a lifetime of instrumental and vocal experience to the SteelDrivers. She was also in the legendary pre-Union Station bluegrass band Dusty Miller with Barry Bales, Tim Stafford, Adam Steffey, and Brian Fesler. No stranger to the studio, she has recorded with Neil Diamond, Wynonna, Rodney Crowell, Radney Foster, Bill Anderson, Iris Dement, Randy Scruggs, Patty Loveless, Buddy and Julie Miller, Jim Lauderdale, and many more. She has toured the world with Trisha Yearwood, Reba McEntire, Patty Loveless, Maria McKee, and the Dead Reckoners. Her songs have been recorded by Terri Clarke and Frances Black.

May 2017

Gary Nichols

GUITAR/VOCALS

From Muscle Shoals to Music Row, the talk is always the same, "It's Gary Nichols' gritty and soulful story telling that sets him apart from the rest, he is the real deal!''. For the past half-century, Muscle Shoals, Alabama has produced some of the finest musicians, singers, songwriters and record producers of our day. From W.C. Handy and Percy Sledge to Sam Phillips, Rick Hall and the immortal Muscle Shoals Rhythm Section otherwise known as " The Swampers" or " The FAME Gang". Muscle Shoals has always been a hotbed of talent. Gary Nichols is in the ranks with all the great songwriters, musicians, producers and performers of the Muscle Shoals past and present. In 2002, Gary helped create the first ``FAME Tuesday Music Club'', which consisted of bringing in young talent to develop their recording, performing and songwriting talents in the confines of historic FAME Studios. Gary took advantage of this opportunity to impress everyone at FAME with his work ethic and raw talent. In February of 2004, Gary signed a publishing deal with FAME Publishing Company and a major label deal with Mercury Records, Nashville. After releasing his first top 40 single, Unbroken Ground, his name has spread like wildfire through writing circles and record labels of Nashville and beyond. Now, this singer/guitar-slinger writes, produces, records and tours with the Ameri-Grass super group, The SteelDrivers. When he's not in the studio, on the road with the band or teaching in the Florence High-School Fine Arts program, you can find Gary helping in his community through philanthropic works or spending time with his family.

Brent Truitt

MANDOLIN

Raised in the backwoods of Pure Air, Missouri, Brent Truitt comes from a long line of musicians. At age twelve, he picked up a mandolin and started playing along with his parents and grandfather at local festivals and went on to tour the mid-west extensively. In 1984, Truitt made the move to Nashville and has been fortunate enough to record and tour with legends like Alison Krauss, Dolly Parton, and The Dixie Chicks. Along with being a proud new SteelDriver, Truitt is also an in-demand record producer and Grammy winning engineer, garnering two awards for The Riders in the Sky's "Monsters Inc." and "Woody's Round Up Toy Story II". In total Brent Truitt has recorded over 250 records with plenty more to come.

'Raiding the Country Vault' Drawing Crowds to Starlite Theatre

By Scot England

In 1997, Michael Peterson was enjoying chart topping country hits like 'From Here to Eternity' and "Drink, Swear, Steal and Lie.' Twenty years later, Peterson is now headlining one of the most talked about shows in Branson Missouri.

"I had moved from Nashville to Las Vegas four years ago. I was semi-retired. I was doing a lot of volunteer work in Las Vegas," says Peterson. "My wife and I went to see a show called 'Raiding the Rock Vault.' And we fell in love with the show. Halfway through it, I said, "I have a strange feeling that there is going to be a country version of this show and we are going to be a part of it."

A year and a half later, Peterson met the show producer. The next day that producer called to ask him to be the musical director for 'Raiding the Country Vault.'

"It really is an event. It is more than just a concert," says Peterson. "We have huge video screens behind us that tell the story of the songs we're singing. We have movie and photo clips that help us tell the story of Dolly, Kenny Rogers, Johnny Cash and all of the great, iconic stars. "

Peterson headlines the show with Billy Yates, known for writing the George Jones hits 'Choices' and "I Don't Need Your Rockin' Chair'.

"I sing 'I Don't Need Your Rocking Chair' in the show," says Yates. "The show includes about 25 of the most iconic songs in country music history. I was honored that they chose 'I Don't Need Your Rocking Chair" before they even knew that I was going to be in the show."

'Raiding the Country Vault' debuted in Branson last year at the Mansion Theater. And while the show had a very humble start, it quickly became one of the hottest shows of 2016.

"We started the season late. We didn't have any bus tours booked. And it is not easy to do a show there unless you have some of the tour bus companies bringing in people." Billy Yates explains, "We had to build it from the ground up. The Mansion Theater has 3, 000 seats. And for some of those first shows, we only had 10 to 15 people in the audience. But we gave those 15 people everything we had! And they went home and told their friends and the crowds started growing each night. And after six months, we were playing to 500 to 600 people every night. We believed in what we were doing."

And that belief paid off in a big way. With 158 different shows for ticket buyers to choose from in Branson, by the end of 2016, 'Raiding the Country Vault' was ranked as the Number 3 Most Popular show by Trip Advisor.

"Most of the cast are from Nashville." Yates continues, "Everyone in the show has been very successful in some way in the country music world. Every person in the cast is a true professional."

That cast will showcase their talents in a new home for the show as 'Raiding the Country Vault' moves to the Starlite Theatre.

"We are excited about the move to the Starlite Theatre," says Yates. "Last year when Larry's Country Diner came to the Starlite, I always went to hang out with everyone. So I knew it was a beautiful place."

'Raiding the Country Vault' will run for almost 200 shows from March through December. To reserve your ticket, call the Starlite Theatre at (417) 337-9333 or (866) 991-8445, or log onto www. StarliteTheatre.com

May 2017

Alabama member Jeff Cook reveals he has Parkinsons

Jeff Cook, Randy Owen and Teddy Gentry of Alabama.

Alabama is an American country, Southern rock and bluegrass band formed in Fort Payne, Alabama in 1969. The band was founded by Randy Owen (lead vocals, rhythm guitar) and his cousin Teddy Gentry (bass guitar, background vocals). They were soon joined by their other cousin, Jeff Cook (lead guitar, fiddle, and keyboards). First operating under the name Wildcountry, the group toured the Southeast bar circuit in the early 1970s, and began writing original songs. They changed their name to Alabama in 1977 and following the chart success of two singles, were approached by RCA Records for a record deal.

Jeff Cook revealed recently in a Tennessean (newspaper) interview, that he has been diagnosed with Parkinson's disease. According to the Mayo Clinic, Parkinson's "is a progressive disorder of the nervous system that affects movement."

Jeff first learned of his diagnosis four years ago, but he and his Alabama bandmates decided to keep the news private. He chose to reveal it now because the disease has progressed to the point that it is having a major impact on his body. As a result, Jeff will no longer be touring with Alabama starting on April 29.

He revealed why he is making the decision to take a step back for the time being saying, "This disease robs you of your coordination, your balance, and causes tremors. For me, this has made it extremely frustrating to try and play guitar, fiddle or sing. I've tried not to burden anyone with the details of my condition because I do not want the music to stop or the party to end, and that won't change no matter what. Let me say, I'm not calling it quits but sometimes our bodies dictate what we have to do, and mine is telling me it's time to take a break and heal."

When Jeff received his test results that confirmed his Parkinson's diagnosis, he told Randy Owen and Teddy Gentry right away. They considered no longer performing, but Jeff encouraged them to continue.

"He wants us to go on," Randy said. "We want the music to go on."

Whether Jeff is able to perform or not, Randy and Teddy said they will always leave his microphone up on stage.

"We could hire 10 people, but we can't replace Jeff Cook in the group Alabama," said Teddy Gentry.

Everyone remains hopeful that Jeff may be able to regularly join them on tour again in the future. As of right now, he still intends to perform with the rest of the group at a May 27 concert in Orange Beach, Alabama and at a fan event in June.

"If I'm healed overnight, I'll be at the next show," Jeff said. "I do believe in prayer and I'm not giving up."

Alabama's biggest success came in the 1980s, where the band had over 27 number one hits, seven multi-platinum albums and received numerous awards. Alabama's first single on RCA Records, "Tennessee River", began a streak of 21 number one singles, including "Love in the First Degree" (1981), "Mountain Music" (1982), "Dixieland Delight" (1983), "If You're Gonna Play in Texas (You Gotta Have a Fiddle in the Band)" (1984) and "Song of the South" (1987). The band's popularity waned slightly in the 1990s although they continued to produce hit singles and multi-platinum album sales. Alabama disbanded in 2006 following a farewell tour and two albums of inspirational music but reunited in 2010 and have continued to record and tour worldwide.

May 2017

It's A Family Tradition

By Claudia Johnson

The Kendalls

The role of the family is an integral theme of Country Music. Some of County's greatest songs have captured memories from family life. Family acts, including sibling duos, have long been a staple on the Country stage. Some families have produced numerous talented members, both performers and songwriters, who separately made their impact on the genre. In other families, each generation has expanded the legacy of the one before it. This series celebrates Country Music's family connections.

The flip side of a Country single catapulted Country Music's most famous father-daughter duo to a career that spanned two decades and saw more than 30 of their hits reach the Top 40.

The Kendalls, Royce and daughter Jeannie, may have recorded "Heaven's Just a Sin Away" 40 years ago, but the snappy title has doubtless been "sung" a million times by fans of the song.

"We'd only played the thing once, and we remembered it," Royce, who died in 1998 at the age of 62 from a stroke recalled in an interview. "That's a good sign . . . that's the reason we cut it."

The song was originally the B-side to 1977's "Live and Let Live," but deejays began playing "Heaven's Just a Sin Away" instead, sending it to the top of the country charts for a month and netting awards from both the Country Music Association and the Academy of Country Music as well as a Grammy in 1978.

The Kendalls heavy radio play and burst of commercial success lasted from 1977-1985. Their biggest hits of the late '70s included "It Don't Feel Like Sinnin' to Me," "Pittsburgh Stealers," the number one "Sweet Desire" and "I Had a Lovely Time." In the '80s they had more hits with songs like "You'd Make an Angel Wanna Cheat," "Teach Me to Cheat" and a third number one, "Thank God for the Radio."

Both Jeannie and her father were born in St. Louis, Missouri, but Royce had moved his family to Los Angles, California, in the late '50s to pursue a musical career with his brother, Floyce, who performed as The Austin Brothers, a guitar-mandolin duo. Without finding the success he had hoped, Royce returned to St. Louis and opened a barber shop, but he did not stop singing.

"I was born and pretty much raised there," Jeannie said in a 2003 interview with Jon Weisberger. "We lived in California for a little while when I was really young, but otherwise that was it. Daddy used to sing with his brother, and when I was a little bitty teeny thing, they had a duet called the Austin Brothers. They sang some bluegrass songs, and Louvin Brothers style music, and he would do the harmony, and then he'd switch off and sing the lead. But he never did like singing lead that much, so he started me right out doing that, and then he'd sing harmony to me."

May 2017

When Jeannie was only 15 years old, she teamed up with her father with Jeannie typically singing lead and Royce double tracking his light baritone harmony vocals behind her. They sold a demo tape by mail order and even signed to a small record label, where they recorded a 1970 cover of "Leaving on a Jet Plane" that just missed the country Top 50.

Their sound was perfect for the Country music recording scene in Nashville during the late '70s with its mix of traditional country, country gospel, honky tonk and blue grass. But Country Music changed, and the Kendalls' commercial success did not last. The duo kept recording, relocated from their home in Hendersonville, Tennessee, to Branson, Missouri and switched their focus to bluegrass. Jeannie, a songwriter who had penned several of their recordings, continued writing songs. She and her father had been working on an album when Royce died in 1998 on his way to a performance.

"Daddy sang on two songs on the album - in fact, right before we left, we were working on songs, and that's why we had them done," Jeannie explained to Weisberger. "And then we went out on the road, and that's when he passed away."

Jeannie said it took a couple of years to determine what to do with the album, finally deciding to invite guest artists to help.

"So, we sat down and made a list of different singers and artists we'd like to have on the album. We wanted Alison Krauss and Ricky Skaggs and Rhonda Vincent and, of course, big on the top of the list was Alan Jackson," she said. "I'm thankful that we pretty much got everybody that we were looking for."

Jeannie completed the album in 2003 with the gracious help of musicians who had admired her and her father and those she herself respected.

STORIES & MEMORIES FROM SOME OF THE KIDS OF COUNTRY MUSIC LEGENDS

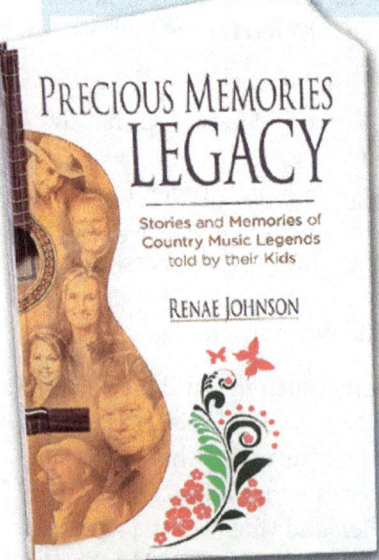

What is your favorite Roger Miller song?

"Can I say two things? 'King of the Road' because it paid for my existence, and 'Old Toy Trains', because it was written for and about me. To this day, I hear it at Christmas time, and it's like my dad putting his arms around me and saying hello, and telling me that he loves me."

-- Dean Miller, son of Roger Miller

$17.95
+$6.95 s/h

Send payment to Renae Johnson, P.O. Box 210796, Nashville, TN 37221
Customer Service at 800-820-5405
www.renaethewaitress.com
www.amazon.com

May 2017

Salute to the KORNFIELD
Everything you always wanted to know about the cast
By Sasha Kay Dunavant

Lulu Roman – A Changed Life

Abandoned by her mother, Lulu Roman's life began in Buckner Orphan Home in Dallas, Texas. Coming into the world as Bertha Louise Hable on May 6, 1946, she was years away from the day she would become the beloved Hee-Haw comic and gospel singer Lulu Roman.

Emotional turmoil surrounded her youth, primarily due to an early diagnosis thyroid issue that caused her to remain heavy throughout her childhood and most of her adulthood. Roman has stated that sugar "became her friend" because it would not hurt her and cause her pain. Other children were cruel, persistently taunting her. Developing a thick skin and sense of humor was her only hope through the tears. At age 23 her life made an amazing turn for the better when she met Buck Owens, a creator of Hee Haw.

In a 2009 article from The Leader Online Roman described an early conversation with Owens, saying, "He told me I was the funniest thing he'd ever seen and that one day I'd be a big star, and he'd have something to do with it."

Lulu was cast at age 23 as a funny overweight girl when Hee Haw premiered in 1969. Roman's weight, which has soared to more than 380 pounds at times, was often the brunt of the joke throughout the 75 episodes in which she appeared over the years. She's best remembered for her parts in the recurring skits "The Culhanes," "In the Kornfield" and "Lulu's Truck Stop."

"I…didn't know anything about country music," she told the Leader. "Remember I was a hippie through and through. I had no idea who Minnie Pearl or Roy Acuff were."

Despite the opportunity offered by inclusion on a hit TV show, the former go-go dancer was unable to control her involvement with drugs, including a powerful addiction to LSD. Though she played homespun characters, Roman's lifestyle was drug-centered, and her career was nearly destroyed when she was arrested twice in the early 1970s. At one of her lowest points she faced more than 20 years in prison if convicted and at age 26 delivered a baby son, Damon, who was born an addict.

During this difficult time, a friend from her orphanage days invited her to church, and by 1973 Roman was determined to abandon her "hippie" nature and place her life in the hands of God. After a powerful conviction Roman accepted Christ as her Lord and Savior.

Roman returned to Hee Haw, and because she knew that the Lord had worked wonders in her life, she longed for others to know that she had found true peace in Jesus. Though she had never had a voice lesson and did not read music, she suggested that the show's writers allow her to sing a Gospel song at the end of each show.

When the Hee Haw television show ended, Roman performed on "Hee Haw Live" from 1992-1995. She's a Dove award winner who was inducted into the Country Music Gospel Hall of Fame in 1999 and into the Christian Music Hall of Fame in 2008.

Among her 23 albums are "Orphan Girl," an acknowledgement of her beginnings, and her 2010 album "Seven Times," which reached No. 2 on the Cash Box Chart. An album of musical standards titled "At Last" was released in 2013 that features duets with Dolly Parton, T. Graham Brown, Linda Davis, and George Jones.

During Roman's Gospel Music career, her increasing weight became a burden that she felt prevented her from effectively spreading the Gospel. Having lost more than 200 pounds after lap band surgery, she continues to keep her weight in check with trust in the Lord and a healthy lifestyle.

"You can allow the blood of Jesus to define who you are," she said in an interview with CBN.

May 2017

"In that is freedom. That gives you the peace of mind that nothing can give you but the blood of Jesus."

A long-time resident of Mt. Juliet, Tennessee, she continues to perform as a comedian and singer, maintains many of the friendships she made while taping Hee Haw and dedicates herself to church and mission work. Her son, Damon, is now 42 and living in Bellingham, Washington. Her younger child, Justin, 39, lives in Nashville.

"I realize God has given me the desires of my heart," she said in interview with the Knoxville News Sentinel. "All I ever wanted to be was somewhat normal."

CFR News Book 5: 2016 now available

The CFR News book is all 12 montly issues of the newspaper printed in an 8 1/2 x 11 color book. If you've missed issues or even past years, this is a great way of catching up on all the news about your favorite artists.

Some of the regular features include Country Legends Past and Present, Singer Songerwriters, Family Tradition, Salute to the Kornfield and Nadine. We've got a Question and Answer section where we've answered readers quesions.

The book lets you know when one of the artists passes away, but it also keeps you up to date on the ones who are still with us.

Each month, the paper lets you know who will be featured on Larry's Country Diner and what shows are airing on Country's Family Reunion.

It is filled with family photos of the stars that you won't see anywhere else, as well as articles about the 'Nashville Brat Pack: Kids of Country Stars."

It's a great piece of history to have and it's only $29.95 plus $6.95 shipping and handling for each book. Call 800-820-5405 to order, or go to www.cfrvideos.com.

Q: How can I get the lyrics to That's How The Yodel Was Born?

A: That's How The Yodel Was Born was written by Ranger Doug Green of Riders In The Sky. It can be found on YouTube and on their Weeds and Water album from 1983. It goes like this:

When you hear a cowboy yodeling a song of open range
Your heart leaps up to hear his stirring tale
But did you ever wonder, at the end of his refrain
Why his voice leaps in a mournful way?
Well, the story as it was told to me
Was handed down through history
Of a singing cowboy brave enough to try
To ride the meanest ol' Cayuse
And bucked him off right at the chute
And left him spinning way up in the sky
The bronco jumped up and the cowboy came down
They met at the old saddlehorn
It made a deep impression, you could say it changed his life
And that's how the yodel was born
 Show 'em, Too-Slim
Hang in there, Slim
Go, Woody
Ride, ranger, ride

Written by Douglas B. Green • Copyright © Songs Of The Sage

If you have questions send them to Paula, CFR News, P.O. Box 210796, Nashville, TN 37221 or email them to paula@gabrielcommunications.com.

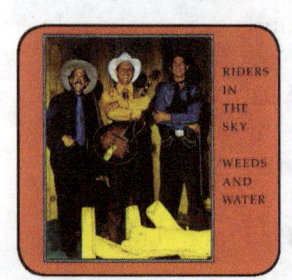

May 2017

Singer Songwriters
By Claudia Johnson

Don Schlitz: Capturing Emotions, Telling Stories

Some of the late 20th century's most beloved songs have come from the pen of one man whose name most Country Music fans may have never even heard.

Don Schlitz was only 20 when he relocated to Nashville from his native Durham, North Carolina, to pursue his love of music.

"In the end, there is only one engulfing reason to be a songwriter… the love of music, the joy of creating," Schlitz states in his website biography. "You do it for the sake of the song. And that is the best possible reason."

Schlitz's love of songwriting has not only kept him employed, it's given generations of music lovers the perfect quotes for experiences both mundane and momentous.

Ever said, "You've got to know when to hold 'em, know when to fold 'em?" Well, those are lines from Schlitz's first hit song, "The Gambler," made an eternal favorite by Kenny Rogers.

Schlitz writes the kinds of songs that take listeners to a place they've been before and sometimes to a place they don't know they are heading – until they hear the song, that is.

How many wedding vows have been exchanged because of Randy Travis' recording of a Schlitz's reassuring, "As long as old men sit and talk about the weather, as long as old women sit and talk about old men…I'm gonna love you forever and ever, forever and ever, amen?"

Then there's another Schlitz classic in which the triumph of commitment over desire is summed up with "On one hand I could stay and be your loving man, but the reason I must go is on the other hand."

The late Keith Whitley and later Alison Kraus recorded Schlitz's "When You Say Nothing at All," a song that captures with these words how two hearts can communicate, "There's a truth in your eyes saying you'll never leave me, a touch of your hand says you'll catch me if ever I fall. Now, you say it best when you say nothing at all."

With dozens of songs written by Schlitz and taken to the top of the charts by some of country's royalty like Garth Brooks, The Judds, Reba McEntire, George Straight, Alabama, The Oak Ridge Boys, John Conlee, Lorrie Morgan, Tanya Tucker and many others, it's no wonder Schlitz has garnered a long list of awards.

In 1979 "The Gambler" earned him a Grammy for Country Song of the Year and the Country Music Association Song of the Year award. In 1986 "On the Other Hand" was named the Nashville Songwriters Association International Song of the Year and the Academy of Country Music Song of the Year.

"Forever and Ever" was named the 1988 Grammy Country Song of the Year and had already been presented in 1987 the Academy of Country Music Song of the Year award and named the Country Music Association Song of the Year.

An answer Schlitz gave about his songwriting to Ali Tonn, Director of Education and Public Programs at the Country Music Hall of Fame and Museum, gives insight into how he's crafted what seems to be the perfect song for the perfect artist over and over again.

"I want to write a song that I'd be willing to sing," he explained. "I can't expect anyone to sing anything that I'm not willing to stand up at the Bluebird Cafe and sing in front of my fellow songwriters. I've tried…but it's never turned out well."

May 2017

Every year from 1988-91 Schlitz was named ASCAP Country Songwriter of the Year. In 1993 he was inducted into Nashville Songwriters Hall of Fame. He was honored in 2007 with ASCAP Artistic Achievement Award, and in 2010 received the Academy of Country Music's Poet's Award for lifetime achievement in songwriting.

His native state of North Carolina honored him with a 1999 induction into North Carolina Music and Entertainment Hall of Fame and a 2010 induction into the North Carolina Music Hall of Fame.

In 2012 he was inducted into Songwriters Hall of Fame in New York City, a city that took notice of the multitalented Schlitz when he wrote the music and lyrics for "Adventures of Tom Sawyer," which opened in Broadway in 2001. During his induction ceremony, Kenny Rogers noted, "Don doesn't just write songs. He writes careers."

As proven by his song, "The Greatest," recorded by Rogers, Schlitz can tell a story and teach a lesson in a few simple lines. Listeners could "see" the boy trying to hit a baseball, believing he was in the tense moments of a ballgame before a stadium crowd. Not until the end is it revealed that he's just practicing alone and imagining himself as the greatest, and recognizing his inability to actually hit the balls he's tossing into the air, he congratulates himself on his pitching prowess

Tanya Tucker recorded "Strong Enough to Bend," in which Schlitz compares an old tree to a solid marital relationship by stating, "Our love will last forever if we're strong enough to bend." Schlitz uses storytelling to express an unsuccessful relationship in "He Thinks He'll Keep Her" recorded by Mary Chapin Carpenter, which describes the perfect wife in every way except that she does not love the husband she serves so faithfully. As for Schlitz himself, he has long been married to wife Stacey, a Nashville attorney, with whom he lives in Franklin, Tennessee.

After decades in Nashville, Schlitz still performs frequently at famed songwriter venues like The Bluebird Café and Puckett's Grocery and continues to write songs, perhaps having perfected the process he described to Ali Tonn.

"I start with an idea," he told Tonn. "I tilt my head sideways and find my unique point of view…then I write what I see and hear. Even if I don't think I'm one of the characters, I'm really all of them. Even if I don't think it's anything I would ever say, it always is, and even if I don't think I can write a song about it, I do."

On Wednesday, April 5, 2017, it was announced that Don was to be inducted into the Country Music Hall of Fame in the Songwriter division. Official induction is in October.

Larry's Country Diner at The Starlite Theatre
Branson   Missouri

T. Graham Brown
Mon., Sept. 18

Rhonda Vincent
Tues., Sept. 19

Gene Watson
Wed., Sept. 20

Jimmy Fortune
Tues., Sept. 21

The Isaacs
Fri., Sept. 22

For tickets
417-337-9333
www.starlitetheatre.com

May 2017

Diner Construction:

Although we cannot confirm any updates in this month's issue of the CFR News concerning our Diner Construction, we do see a ray of sunshine coming our way. The buzzards have quit circling. So keep the faith and keep praying for Larry's Country Diner to be a reality.

Happy Birthday Sedona

Sedona turned "One" on April 25th and is walking like a drunken sailor. She barely crawled before she started walking. But now you can't keep her down. She is nosey and loves the piano. It's the first thing that she goes to when she comes to NaeNae's house.

Her hair is still coming in so the poor thing always has a headband or bow stuck on her head. But she is a beauty and so different than Rio. It's so fun having grandkids!!

Diner CHAT

If you have missed any of our calls, the recordings are now back on our website. Billy Dean, Mike Johnson and Daryle Singletary are a few of guests who have joined us recently. Remember …all you have to do is call on your phone and listen in. Join us every Thursday at 2:00 central time.

Cruise

We are selling cabins for our 2018 Cruise. Your kids don't need your money so join us for a week of pure fun and entertainment. And remember you have to book with DeAnn or Jason in OUR CUSTOMER Service or on our website to be a part of our group. Other cruise passengers do no attend out shows. 800-820-5405

"The Promise"

If you have NOT purchased my latest book "The Promise" then you are not a true Larry's Country Diner fan. Reading the Promise is one of the most important things we do on our shows. In the book are "promises" read on the show with a photo of the artists and original airdate. Yes….Larry did find the one typo in the whole book and I was horrified!!! So order this first edition before it is corrected and I will autograph it. It will someday be a collectors edition. You can find it on Amazon or my website at www.Renaethewaitress.com.

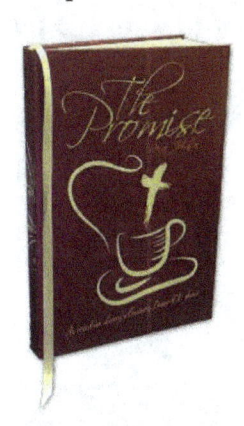

Mother's Day
Second Sunday of May

```
G T O A N O I T A I C E R P P A
D E T O V E D C W G A E R A H S
E N E A M L O A E U S T F I G T
T D A O O M R N I I O C W I S E
H E M V F M O S I D H O S U T P
E R E O S H B R E A K F A S T R
B E R R P R T I R N O U P M E O
E T Y E G R E M A C H E O L T T
S E L R C N I W M E R E U M R E
T E E A E N I A O F O F S O E C
T N N R G L T V U L I T E T T T
E D A R U E E M I T F O S H H I
Y E A V R T E W U G E Y S E G V
E E Y N R I R A E W R G I R U E
M O A E O T E U E J U O K C A T
J L A G R B I I N H U O F E L N
```

APPRECIATION GUIDANCE NURTURE
BEAUTIFUL HUGS PERFUME
BREAKFAST JEWELERY PROTECTIVE
CANDY JOY SHARE
CHARMING KISSES TELEPHONE
COMFORT LAUGHTER TENDER
DEVOTED LOVE THE BEST
FLOWERS MATERNAL WARM
FORGIVING MOM WISE

May 2017

JUNE

New Larry's Country Diner panel truck a hit with Branson audience

Keith, Nadine, Larry, Jimmy and Renae standing in front of the newly restored Larry's Country Diner panel truck they took to Branson.

By Larry Black

Branson…..ah Branson. The StarLite theater smack dab in the middle of Hwy 76 in the heart of the Theaters was a marvelous place to be in May. The Larry's Country Diner Panel Truck was in the Atrium with Max and Margaret giving all the information of this '53 GMC truck that Max saved from the Junk Yard. It looks nothing like a cast-away now with its new coat of paint, Corvette Motor, automatic transmission, air conditioning and new upholstery. Of course, the hit of the day was the license plate on the back that had a picture of Nadine with her hands out in front saying "Back-Off".

And that was just for openers. On Monday when you get in the theater with the rest of the sold-out crowd for the T. Graham Brown Larry's Country Diner Show, you soon discovered you were part of something larger than life. T was entertaining as usual, but he was assisted by Mickey Gilley, Johnny Lee, Billy Yates and Michael Peterson. They all stopped in to sit on the stage and carry on with T. Imagine T. Graham singing "I Tell It Like It Used to Be" and Mickey Gilley stepping up behind him with a mic in his hands and saying "T, I sang it like this".

And that was just the first night. Tuesday night Jimmy Fortune took the stage for another sold out crowd and had Billy Yates in tow. Billy is part of the new show at the StarLite, "The Country Vault" Billy added a couple of hits he wrote for George Jones.

Gene Watson, always a sellout favorite entertained the crowd while we had security watching for Moe Bandy, in case he was trying to sneak in.

And that left just two nights to wrap up a great week. The Malpass Brothers came to conquer Branson and that would have been enough but Johnny Lee showed up once again to add his humor and music to yet another night of fun and what better way to wrap up the night than with Mo Pitney and hit sister Holly. But wait…..that left one more night and climbing down Jacobs Ladder was Mark Wills. Great shows and long autograph lines.

One thing I've got to add, there is a great Bar B Q café called Gettin' Basted in the Atrium of the StarLite. I ate there once because I didn't have time to get anywhere else, but the second and third time was because I didn't want to be anywhere else. Truly GREAT Bar B Q.

Looks like The Sheriff caught up with Gene Watson in panel truck…speeding or did he try to steal it?

Nadine noticed the special license tag telling folks to "Back Off"

102
CFR NEWS

June 2017

HAPPY FATHER'S DAY

A FATHER'S EYES

Jonathan's mother died when he was very young and his father brought him up. Both of them shared a very special relationship. Jonathan loved to play football and his father made sure that he was always there to cheer his son at every match, even if Jonathan wasn't a part of the playing team. Jonathan being small sized, wasn't allowed to play in the main team. Nevertheless, he continued with his practice with full determination. Everyone thought that Jonathan would never be able to make it into the team, though somehow, his determination carried him through. The coach seeing his diligence and dedication decided to keep him on the roster.

One day during practice, the coach met him with a telegram. Jonathan was shocked to read the message contained in it. Swallowing hard, he mumbled to the coach, "My father died this morning. Will it be all right if I miss practice today?" The coach gently put his arm around his shoulder and said, "Take the rest of the week off, son, and don't even plan to come to the game on Saturday." On the day of the game, Jonathan's college team was losing badly to the rival team. The coach and the players had all lost hope when they saw Jonathan coming towards them. Jonathan ran up to the coach and pleaded him to allow him to play this match. At first, the coach wouldn't allow him to play. However after a lot of persuasion, the coach gave in. No sooner Jonathan joined the team in the field, their scores started to improve before both the teams were on a tie.

However, the real cheer came during the crucial closing seconds when he intercepted a pass and ran all the way for the winning touchdown. His team members were ecstatic. The crowd came running towards him to celebrate the win. After the match, the coach went up to Jonathan, who was seated alone in the corner of the locker room and asked, "Kid, I can't believe it. You were fantastic! Tell me what got into you? How did you do it?" He looked at the coach, with tears in his eyes, and said, "Well, you knew my dad died, but did you know that my dad was blind?" The young man swallowed hard and forced a smile, "Dad came to all my games, but today was the first time he could see me play, and I wanted to show him I could do it!"

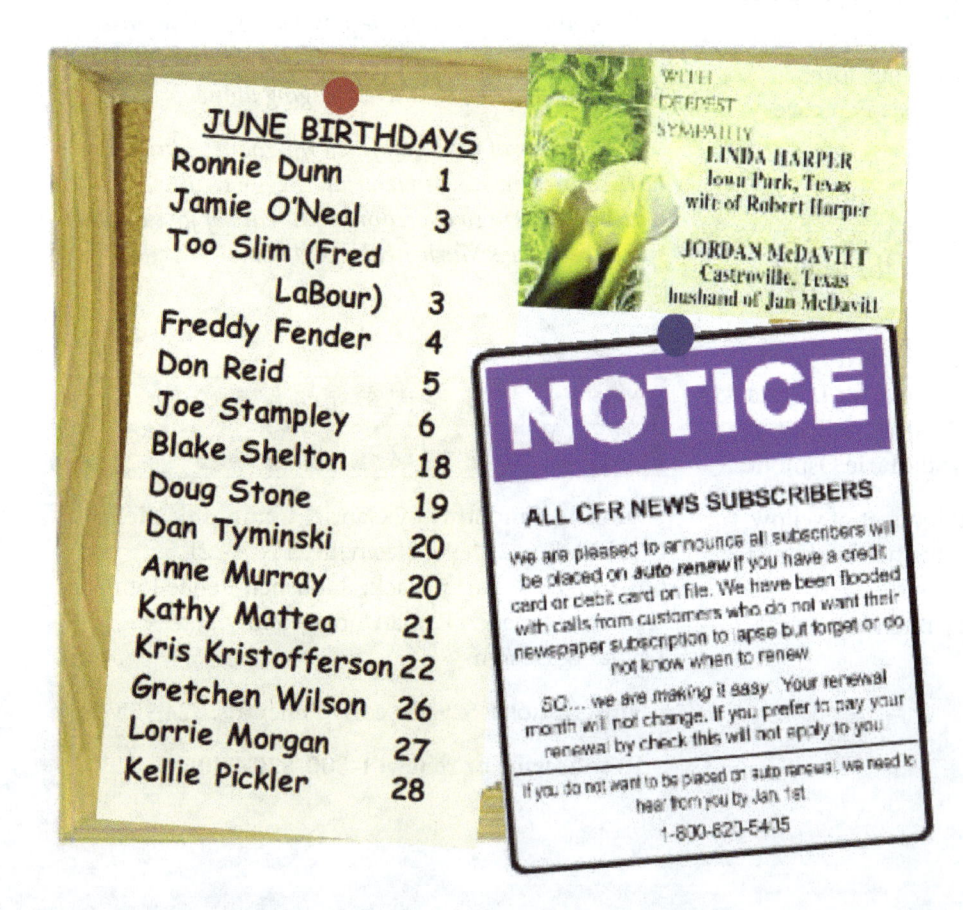

JUNE BIRTHDAYS

Name	Day
Ronnie Dunn	1
Jamie O'Neal	3
Too Slim (Fred LaBour)	3
Freddy Fender	4
Don Reid	5
Joe Stampley	6
Blake Shelton	18
Doug Stone	19
Dan Tyminski	20
Anne Murray	20
Kathy Mattea	21
Kris Kristofferson	22
Gretchen Wilson	26
Lorrie Morgan	27
Kellie Pickler	28

WITH DEEPEST SYMPATHY

LINDA HARPER
Iowa Park, Texas
wife of Robert Harper

JORDAN McDAVITT
Castroville, Texas
husband of Jan McDavitt

NOTICE

ALL CFR NEWS SUBSCRIBERS

We are pleased to announce all subscribers will be placed on auto renew if you have a credit card or debit card on file. We have been flooded with calls from customers who do not want their newspaper subscription to lapse but forget or do not know when to renew.

SO... we are making it easy. Your renewal month will not change. If you prefer to pay your renewal by check this will not apply to you.

If you do not want to be placed on auto renewal, we need to hear from you by Jan. 1st

1-800-620-5435

June 2017

Loretta Lynn suffers stroke but recovering

Loretta Lynn was hospitalized following a stroke on Thursday, May 4, and now fans are being given an update on Lynn's condition.

It was first confirmed on Lynn's official website that she had suffered a stroke while at home in Hurricane Mills and was rushed to a nearby hospital in Nashville, as her team posted a message to fans that revealed Loretta "is currently under medical care and is responsive and expected to make a full recovery."

The message also confirmed that Lynn would be canceling any and all upcoming shows as a result of her stroke and subsequent hospitalization because that the 85-year-old country music legend had been advised by her doctors "to stay off the road while she is recuperating."

"Regrettably, upcoming scheduled shows will be postponed," the statement said.

"Many of you have heard that my sister, Loretta Lynn, had a stroke," Loretta's sister, Crystal Gayle tweeted "Our family appreciates all your love, prayers and support. We hope for a speedy recovery!"

Loretta's fans and friends have also been spreading a lot of love for the star ever since it was announced that she had suffered a stroke with messages of support and love coming from all over the world for the country music legend.

A number of Loretta Lynn's fellow celebrities and country stars have tweeted out their love for Loretta since the news broke, including Martina McBride, Jennifer Nettles, Roseanne Barr, and Marie Osmond.

McBride presented Lynn with a bouquet of yellow roses during a show while celebrating her birthday in April, while the singer and the crowd then launched into a rousing rendition of "Happy Birthday" in celebration of Loretta's big day.

The star then performed two of her biggest hits, "You Ain't Woman Enough (To Take My Man)" and "I Saw the Light" after Martina described Loretta Lynn as being her "closest friend in country music."

According to Lynn's daughter, granddaughter and assistant have said that the country legend is doing "better each day." She is also now able to sit up in her recliner, and is laughing and talking with friends and family.

Loretta's daughter, Peggy, also wrote an emotional Facebook post about a kind woman who visited her mother. This post was shared by Peggy's niece and Loretta's granddaughter, Tayla, and has touched the hearts of all who love Loretta.

As Peggy wrote, she and Tayla were with Loretta when a Kentucky woman stopped by to visit her. She described the woman's kindness in beautiful words:

"She came into the room exchanged hello and hugs with us...then turned her full and sole attention to my mom..so tenderly..with such intimacy she laid her hands on mom..gently stroking my mom's cheek.. whispering to her..so softly..like a mother to a child would..with such focus and devotion that I almost felt as if I was intruding by watching them."

Then, the woman started playing some bluegrass music for Loretta, and Peggy and Tayla's eyes filled with tears as Loretta started singing along.

"The power of God had filled the room...so real and full...so present it was vizierial," Peggy wrote. *"Tayla and I both were so overcome with tears of joys and of spirit. because...Music heals..God heals."*

Published monthly by Gabriel Communications, Inc. P.O. Box 210796, Nashville, TN 37221 615-673-2846 Larry Black, Publisher, Renae Johnson, General Manager, Paula Underwood Winters, Layout & Design

Subscriptions: $29.95 yearly Renewals: $24.95 yearly

To subscribe or renew: 1-800-820-5405

COUNTRY LEGENDS OF THE PAST & PRESENT
BY TOM WOOD

McGee Brothers

It was 1974, and one of Nashville's premier string bands helped tie the knot between the Grand Ole Opry's fabled past and its star-studded future.

On March 15-16 of that year, the world's most exclusive country club cut one cord by playing its last Friday show at the faded but historic Ryman Auditorium before a sellout crowd of 3,000 that featured the biggest stars of the Opry lineup.

The following night, the fabric of country music displayed its shiny new threads at the Grand Ole Opry House at Opryland USA before an invitation-only crowd that included President Richard M. Nixon (playing piano) and his wife Pat.

One of the many acts helping the Opry make that smooth transition was the McGee Brothers — the subject of this column.

Senior Opry members Sam and Kirk McGee wowed the crowd that notable night with their old-timey acoustic set, and Sam singing "San Antonio Rose."

Journalist Garrison Keillor, who went on to produce his popular Prairie Home Companion radio show, was assigned to cover the Opry House event for The New Yorker, but chose instead to listen to the show on a radio at his motel room rather than attend.

He described the McGee Brothers' Opry performance that night in The New Yorker as "the accoustic moment when the skies cleared and the weeping steels were silent and out of the clear blue came a little ole guitar duet."

Wow. That kind of review is one artists live for, and well-deserved.

You can hear clips of the McGee Brothers perform on YouTube or one of several collections, and if you do, watch how fast their fingers fly. Or catch them being interviewed and singing on classic country videos.

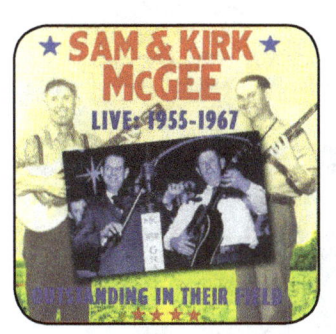

The brothers were born in Franklin, Tennessee in the late 1890s. Sam died in 1975 and Kirk in 1983, but their sweet sounds live on continue to make impressions on Americana aficionados. While both were gifted performers on various strings instruments, Kirk usually had a fiddle or banjo in his hands while Sam dazzled fans with his guitar licks.

They made their Grand Ole Opry debut in 1926 and hooked up with Uncle Dave Macon and his Fruit Jar Drinkers. The 1930s saw them affiliate with Fiddlin' Arthur Smith as the Dixieliners. The 1940s saw them hook up with Bill Monroe and His Bluegrass Boys and appear with many other acts.

Folk music festivals of the 1950s and '60s put them back in the public spotlight, though they never left the Opry lineup over those decades.

Among some of their biggest recordings were Old Master's Runaway" and "Chevrolet Car," and Sam's guitar solos were featured on several recordings by Uncle Dave Macon.

Probably their best-known recording was "Brown's Ferry Blues" (1934), a peppy, fast-paced ditty that features Sam on vocals.

Sources for this article include Wikipedia, the Fayfare's Opry Blog by nationally recognized independent Grand Ole Opry historian Byron Fay, and the The New Yorker magazine.

Author Tom Wood, who writes thrillers and Westerns, is a regular contributor to Country Family Reunion News. Reach him at tomwoodauthor.com

June 2017

Look Who Is Performing At CMA MUSIC FESTIVAL
JUNE 9-12 2016 NASHVILLE
CMAFEST.COM

Larry Gatlin & the Gatlin Brothers
Friday, June 9,
2:45pm - 3:15pm
Budweiser Forever Country Park Stage

Exile
Sunday, June 11,
12:30pm - 1:00pm
Budweiser Forever Country Park Stage

Tracy Lawrence
Thursday, June 8,
12:30pm - 1:45pm
Forever Country Park Stage
Sunday, June 11,
8:00pm - 8:30pm
Nissan Stadium

Daryle Singletary
Thursday, June 8,
2:00pm - 2:30pm
Budweiser Forever Country Park Stage

Bellamy Brothers
Thursday, June 8,
3:30-4:00 pm
Budweiser Forever Country Park Stage

Lari White
Friday, June 9, 11:00am - 11:30am
Budweiser Forever Country Park Stage

Mo Pitney
Friday, June 9,
12:30pm - 12:55pm
Chevrolet Park Stage

Darryl Worley
Friday, June 9, 1:15pm - 1:45pm
Budweiser Forever Country Park Stage

Neal McCoy
Friday, June 9, 4:45pm - 5:15pm
Chevrolet Riverfront Stage

John Berry
Saturday, June 10,
11:45am - 12:15pm
Budweiser Forever Country Park Stage

Doug Supernaw
Saturday, June 10,
1:15pm - 1:45pm
Budweiser Forever Country Park Stage

Mark Chesnutt
Saturday, June 10,
4:15pm - 4:45pm
Budweiser Forever Country Park Stage

John Anderson
Saturday, June 10,
8:00pm - 8:30pm
Nissan Stadium

Collin Raye
Sunday, June 11,
10:30-11:00 pm
Budweiser Forever Country Park Stage

106 CFR NEWS

June 2017

Larry's Country Diner Entertains in Branson

T. Graham Browned opened the week of shows at the Starlite Theatre

Artists played to sell out crowds at the Starlite Theatre in Brason, MO May 1-5. Depsite the rain, everyone had a great time

Nadine loves to watch and listen to Jimmy Fortune

And the cast of the Diner alway keep the audience laughing

Gene Watson always WOWS the crowd

He and Nadine make the audience HOWL

And Jimmy Fortune make them swoon!

107 CFR NEWS

June 2017

The singin is great with Mo Pitney and sister Holly

The Malpass Brothers are entertaining with singing and their wit

You never know who will drop by...Moe Bandy showed up to see Mark Wills and Johnny Lee and Mickey Gilley came by for coffee, pie and laughs

Michael Peterson and Billy Yates stopped in to sing a few songs and Mark Wills closed out a great week in Branson!

June 2017

Tucumcari Rawhide Days with some of the Brat Pack!

For the second year, Tucumcari, New Mexico was host to the Rawhide Days festival to celebrate the Rawhide TV show and the cowboy way.

Chrystie Wooley, daughter of the TV show's Sheb Wooley, along with other Brat Packers Jett Williams, Dean Miller and Donnie Winters, performed for the audience at the Friday night show.

Rawhide Days is the first weekend in May, and is well worth the trip! Keep up with them through www.tucumcarirawhidedays.com!

Dean Miller, Chrystie Wooley, Donnie Winters and Jett Williams entertained the audience.

Chrystie Wooley sings "Are You Satisfied"

Dean Miller rides during the parade down Route 66 in Tucumcari, while Donnie Winters opts for a ride in the back of the wagon.

Jett (not pictured) decided to watch the parade from the motel!

Chrystie enjoyed getting back in the saddle in western gear including a six-gun!

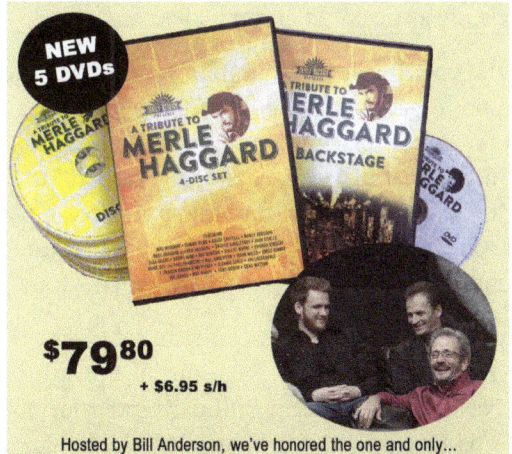

NEW 5 DVDs

A TRIBUTE TO MERLE HAGGARD 4-DISC SET

$79.80 + $6.95 s/h

Hosted by Bill Anderson, we've honored the one and only... MERLE HAGGARD. Including three of his sons, Marty, Noel and Ben. This is the singer songwriter that so many of today's country artists point to as their inspiration. Many of today's country artists sang Merle's songs and told their stories of life on the road and in concert with Merle. Others included in the show were: Mac Wiseman, Ronnie Reno, David Frizzell, Daryle Singletary, John Conlee, Teea Goans, Bobby Bare, Ray Benson, Dallas Wayne, Rhonda Vincent, Vince Gill, Paul Franklin, Mark Wills, Emily Gimble, T. Graham Brown, Mo Pitney, Jeannie Seely, Jim Lauderdale, The Isaacs, Tony Booth, Gene Watson.

1- 800-820-5405
www.cfrvideos.com

June 2017

It's A Family Tradition

By Claudia Johnson

The Overstreets – Paul, Nash & Chord

Paul Overstreet with sons, Nash and Chord

For music lovers from multiple generations and interests, the name Overstreet has meaning. At 64, Paul Overstreet is a legendary country songwriter and performer.

Millennial TV-viewers know gorgeous, award-winning actor and singer Chord Overstreet, 28, as "Glee's" Sam Evans who could belt out a rock ballad as effortlessly as he could croon a love song.

Once the opening act for a rapper, Nash Overstreet, 30, went on to become lead guitarist and backing vocalist for double platinum pop band Hot Chelle Rae, winning an American Music Award in 2011. A songwriter as well as a musician and producer, he has penned songs for Britney Spears, Meghan Trainor and Rachel Platten.

"If my music can speak to people, and it gives them something to identify with… that means everything to me," Nash said in a recent Billboard interview to promote "U Don't Get 2 Do That," his solo debut EP. "Even something as simple as someone falling in love with a beat I've made or the sound of my voice… that's why I do what I do."

He could easily have been speaking for his father or brother. Last fall Chord dropped his single, "Homeland," in homage to his hometown of Nashville where he, Nash and sisters Summer, Harmony, Skye and Charity grew up and where his parents still live nearby. Chord said in an interview with Huffington Post that "Homeland" took him 15 minutes to write.

"It just kind of fell out of the sky and into my lap," he recalled, adding, "My stuff's not country, but it's storytelling, which I think is the root of country music…I think people want to hear stories."

As an actor Chord was nominated for numerous awards for "Glee" including a cast Grammy and individual honors by the Screen Actors Guild, Hollywood Teen TV Awards and Teen Choice, which he won for Male Scene Stealer in 2013. He has worked as a model for many high-profile brands, but at heart he's a musician. He started playing multiple instruments at a young age, including mandolin, drums, flute, piano and guitar.

"I want to be part of great music," Chord said, and he certainly is.

Though both young men have nurtured their own songwriting voices and musical delivery style, in interviews each have expressed appreciation for their parents and admiration of their father's accomplishments.

After moving to Nashville in 1973, Paul "lived" in his '68 Ford Fairlane, doing manual labor jobs while trying to penetrate the music industry. In 1982 his "Same Ole Me" had been taken to number five by George Jones, and Overstreet had his own first charting single with "Beautiful Baby." But he was fighting demons.

"Alcohol and drugs crippled me and really kept me from progressing," he admitted during an interview when he finally began achieving consistent success as a songwriter and soloist.

Paul met cosmetologist and makeup artist, Julie Miller, a Christian, whose influence moved Paul toward the kind of family life he had known growing up as the son of a minister in his hometown of Newton, Mississippi. He gave up his vices, and

June 2017

after marrying Julie in 1985, became one of Country Music's most successful songwriters.

Paul's lyrics are known for their affirmation of married love and the value of family.

The Forrester Sisters soon took his co-written "I Fell in Love Again Last Night" to number one. Later in 1985, Randy Travis had hits with two Overstreet songs, "On the Other Hand" (co-written with Don Schlitz) and Travis' first number one hit, "Diggin' Up Bones." The same year Tanya Tucker, Marie Osmond and Paul Davis had success with his compositions.

In 1986 he teamed up with other artists to form SKO and had a number one hit with "Baby's Got a New Baby." One of his biggest songwriting hits came in 1987 when Travis recorded the Grammy-winning "Forever and Ever, Amen" for which Paul won both CMA and ACM Song of the Year awards. Songwriting success continued over the decades including a hit by both Keith Whitley and Alison Krauss, "When You Say Nothing At All," The Judds' Grammy-winning "Love Can Build a Bridge," "My Arms Stay Open All Night" released by Tanya Tucker, and Kenny Chesney's classic "She Thinks My Tractor's Sexy."

Not only has he written 27 top ten songs, his hits have been recorded by enduring artists like Blake Shelton, Brad Paisley, Carrie Underwood, Glen Campbell, Pam Tillis, Mel Tillis, Travis Tritt, Michael Martin Murphey and many others.

BMI honored Overstreet as Songwriter of the Year for five consecutive years from 1987-1991, a record breaker. He also won CMA and ACM Song of the Year in 1987 and 1988. In 2003, Paul was inducted into the Nashville Songwriters Hall of Fame. Paul's songwriting repertoire has amassed more than 52 million U.S. broadcast performances, which if played back-to-back would total nearly three centuries of continuous play.

The five singles released from Overstreet's first solo project, "Sowin' Love," became top ten hits, including the title cut, "Sowin' Love," "All The Fun" and his first number one solo hit, "Seein' My Father in Me." "Heroes," his second solo album, included the number one hit "Daddy's Come Around" and songs like "If I Could Bottle This Up," "Heroes" and "Billy Can't Read" that was selected as the theme song for CMA/CMT Project Literacy. Paul's first number one song on the Christian charts was "Love is Strong," which earned him one of his three Dove Awards.

Overstreet has been awarded the TNN Christian Country Artist Viewer's Choice Award and received the Christian Country Music Association Award for Mainstream Artist-of the Year as well. He's also been recognized with an historical marker on the Mississippi Country Music Trail.

"It's amazing to realize that the reality is greater than the dreams that started the whole adventure," says Paul, who like his sons, continue to write, sing, play and follow their dreams.

Salute to the Kornfield
Everything you always wanted to know about the cast
By Sasha Kay Dunavant

Mike Snider: Hometown Humor and Timeless Music

Like a handful of Hee Haw's stars, Mike Snider is a member of the Grand Ole Opry. Unlike Grandpa Jones, Minnie Pearl, Roy Clark, String Bean and others, Snider was inducted into the elite membership after he'd risen to popularity with his humor and music on Hee Haw.

Playing banjo since age 16, Snider, who was inspired originally by a Flatt & Scruggs album, became the Tennessee State Bluegrass Banjo Champion, then won the Mid-South Banjo Playing Contest. At age 23 he became the National Bluegrass Banjo Champion.

His resume reads like a history book for late 20th century Country Music entertainment. He made hundreds of appearances on TNN's Nashville Now with beloved host Ralph Emery. He and his band entertained crowds for seven years at Nashville's now closed Opryland USA. In 1987 he joined Hee Haw for a seven-year run that showcased his natural ability to entertain and engage viewers.

Snider carries on the tradition of Minnie Pearl, Jerry Clower and a host of other comedians who turned their ability to laugh at themselves and the people and places they loved into entertainment.

One place Snider, 56, loves is Gleason, Tennessee, his hometown and residence. It is from his rural beginnings and his long marriage to Sabrina, known to his audiences as Sweetie, that he has gleaned his material, delivered with irreverent wit in his country accent.

In 2005 he told McKenzie (TN) Banner reporter Deborah Turner about his first experience at the Grand Ole Opry and how his friends and neighbors shared the moment. Snider became friends with neighbor Gordon Stoker, a member of the Jordannaires quartet, who helped Snider secure an invitation to perform. Not only was Mike invited, the town received an invitation and 1,500 free tickets for the evening. Local media and elected officials helped him distribute them, and when they ran out, 500 more tickets were bought so that some 2,000 members of the audience were people from his small community there to support him when he took the stage on Jan. 21, 1984. When he became a member of the Opry in 1990, Hee Haw and Grand Old Opry comedian Minnie Pearl inducted him.

After 26 years of perfecting the three-finger style of banjo playing, Snider switched more than a decade ago to the clawhammer style in keeping with his interest in old-time mountain music – a style introduced to him by Grandpa Jones. In addition to award-winning banjo playing, Snider has mastered the mandolin and harmonica, which he plays alongside fiddlers and guitar pickers.

Opry announcer and 650 WSM Radio DJ Eddie Stubbs once deemed his group, The Mike Snider String Band, "The best string band in the nation." The band consists of fiddlers Matt Combs and Shad Cobb, bass fiddler Todd Cook and guitarist and banjo player Tony Wray. The Opry website observes that together, these men play "the kind of tight, seamless and timeless old-time mountain music that lays the groundwork for today's bluegrass."

"The string band has a distinctly great sound that comes from playing traditional tunes from across the nation with fresh, engaging arrangements," Snider says on his website, which offers visitors a chance to obtain copies of the recordings.

He is not only respected by the Bluegrass community, he is a crowd favorite.

"It don't seem like I've been at the Grand Ole Opry no 20 years in one way, and then it seems like I've been here my whole life," Mike said in a 2010 interview. "I remember the first night I walked out on the stage, I felt like I was at home."

With more than 30 years performing on the Opry stage, his appeal his not waned.

"When Mike and the boys take the stage, audiences know they'll laugh, tap their toes and hear perhaps the best string band in existence, the Opry's website states. "They will be well entertained, and for Mike Snider, that makes for a good night at the Opry."

June 2017

Country Music Questions & Answers

Mack, Dolly and Porter

Q: What can you tell me about the guy that was the fiddle player of the Wagon Masters on the Porter Wagoner show?

Ruth Carey, Dover, DE

A: Mack Magaha, was the fiddler best known as a former member of Porter Wagoner's band, the Wagonmasters. Magaha spent nine years working with the pioneering bluegrass act Reno & Smiley but came to national prominence after joining Wagoner's band in 1964. A fixture on Wagoner's syndicated television show, Magaha offered an additional degree of showmanship by dancing while he played behind Wagoner and other soloists on the show, including Dolly Parton.

During the '70s and '80s, Magaha regularly performed at the Opryland theme park. Magaha, 74, died Friday, Aug. 15, 2003 at Nashville's Veterans Hospital where he was being treated for pneumonia.

Mack, Dolly and Porter

Q: Has Porter Wagoner ever been married? How much do his beautiful suits cost?

Glennis Trahem, Grapevine, TX

A: Porter Wagoner (1927-2007) was married twice, to Velma Johnson for less than a year in 1943; and then to Ruth Olive Williams from 1946 to 1986, though they separated 20 years before the divorce. He was survived by his three children, Richard, Denise and Debra.

In 2006, Porter Wagoner said he had accumulated 52 Nudie Suits, costing between $11,000 and $18,000 each, since receiving his first free outfit in 1962.

If you have questions send them to Paula, CFR News, P.O. Box 210796, Nashville, TN 37221 or email them to paula@gabrielcommunications.com.

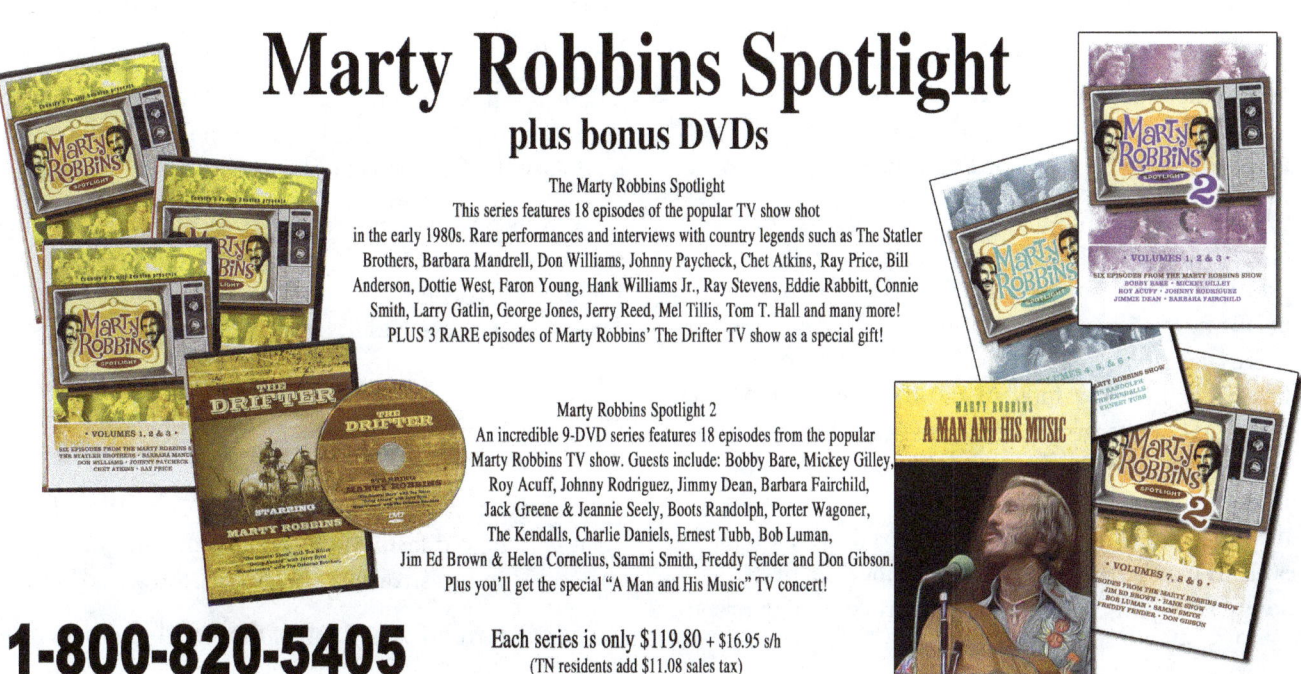

Marty Robbins Spotlight
plus bonus DVDs

The Marty Robbins Spotlight
This series features 18 episodes of the popular TV show shot in the early 1980s. Rare performances and interviews with country legends such as The Statler Brothers, Barbara Mandrell, Don Williams, Johnny Paycheck, Chet Atkins, Ray Price, Bill Anderson, Dottie West, Faron Young, Hank Williams Jr., Ray Stevens, Eddie Rabbitt, Connie Smith, Larry Gatlin, George Jones, Jerry Reed, Mel Tillis, Tom T. Hall and many more! PLUS 3 RARE episodes of Marty Robbins' The Drifter TV show as a special gift!

Marty Robbins Spotlight 2
An incredible 9-DVD series features 18 episodes from the popular Marty Robbins TV show. Guests include: Bobby Bare, Mickey Gilley, Roy Acuff, Johnny Rodriguez, Jimmy Dean, Barbara Fairchild, Jack Greene & Jeannie Seely, Boots Randolph, Porter Wagoner, The Kendalls, Charlie Daniels, Ernest Tubb, Bob Luman, Jim Ed Brown & Helen Cornelius, Sammi Smith, Freddy Fender and Don Gibson. Plus you'll get the special "A Man and His Music" TV concert!

1-800-820-5405

Each series is only $119.80 + $16.95 s/h
(TN residents add $11.08 sales tax)

June 2017

Singer Songwriters
By Claudia Johnson

Whisperin' Bill: Living Out Loud

There's nothing quiet about Whisperin' Bill Anderson. He has lived his life out loud during his long and diverse career.

A member of the Grand Ole Opry since 1961 and current host of Country Family Reunion, he charted seven number one songs as a performer with 29 singles reaching the top 10.

He's released more than 40 studio albums, hosted his own musical television show and two game shows. He's been a television producer, soap opera star, TV talk show guest, radio program host and restaurant spokesman.

He's been honored as Male Vocalist Of The Year, half of the Duet Of The Year with both Jan Howard and Mary Lou Turner and has seen his band, The Po' Folks Band, voted Band Of The Year.

If this wasn't enough to have amplified Anderson's voice, he's quietly spoken volumes through his prolific songwriting for himself and for dozens of performers across six generations who have released more than 400 of his written or co-written songs. In fact, when he was saluted in 2002 by Broadcast Music Inc. (BMI) as its first country music ICON, it was his "unique and indelible influence on generations of music makers" that was cited. Anderson has written nearly 50 charting singles and received more than 50 BMI Country and Pop Awards since his first songwriting hit, "City Lights," recorded by Ray Price in 1958.

"They paint a pretty picture, but my arms can't hold them tight," he penned as a 19-year-old working in broadcast media in Georgia. "And I just can't say I love you to a street of city lights."

The lights of the city have shown favorably on Anderson, who moved to Nashville in the 1950s. He's been voted Songwriter Of The Year six times and in 1975 was voted into the Nashville Songwriters Hall of Fame. The State of Georgia honored him in 1985 by choosing him as only the 7th living performer inducted into the Georgia Music Hall of Fame.

In 1993, he was made a member of the Georgia Broadcasters' Hall of Fame. In 1994, South Carolina inducted him into their Music and Entertainment Hall of Fame, and in 2001 he was honored with membership in Nashville's prestigious Country Music Hall of Fame.

His compositions have been recorded by such diverse musical talents as Porter Wagoner, James Brown, Debbie Reynolds, Ivory Joe Hunter, Kitty Wells, Faron Young, Lawrence Welk, Dean Martin, Jerry Lee Lewis, Aretha Franklin, Walter Brennan, Kenny Chesney, Lynn Anderson, Jim Reeves and many others.

He wrote many of country singer Connie Smith's biggest hits in the 1960s.

"The only time I wish you weren't gone is once a day, every day, all day long," she sang in "Once a Day," a number one hit for eight record-breaking weeks in 1964.

One of Anderson's hits, "Po Folks," which he recorded in 1961, was the inspiration for a restaurant chain and the namesake of his band.

"We was po' folks livin' in a rich folks world we sure was a hungry bunch," Anderson wrote in the venerable favorite. "If the wolf had ever come to our front door he'd've had to brought a picnic lunch."

His song, "Too Country," recorded by Brad Paisley along with Anderson, Buck Owens and George Jones, won CMA Vocal Event Of The Year honors for 2001.

"Too country, what's that?" the lyrics questioned. "Is it just too old fashioned, is it just too antique? Is the question too strong or the answer too weak?"

Anderson won CMA Song of the Year honors for his co-written ballad, "Whiskey Lullaby," recorded by Brad Paisley and Alison Krauss, which also was recognized with awards for Video of the Year and Vocal Collaboration of the Year in 2004.

June 2017

"He put that bottle to his head and pulled the trigger and finally drank away her memory," say the haunting lyrics. "Life is short, but this time it was bigger than the strength he had to get up off his knees."

Anderson writes gospel as easily as country.

"They were solid as a rock and stubborn as a stone…the Good Book says their lot in life was not a bed of roses for Jonah, Job and Moses," sang the Oak Ridge Boys in his co-written "Jonah, Job, and Moses," which won the Dove Award for Country/Gospel Recorded Song of the Year.

George Straight's recording of "Give It Away" gave Anderson his first ACM Song of the Year Award in 2006 for the collaboration that went on to win CMA Song of the Year.

"I've got a furnished house, a diamond ring and a lonely, broken heart full of love," the Grammy-nominated lyrics say, "and I can't even give it away."

In another Grammy-nominated Anderson tune, "Two Teardrops," Steve Wariner sang, "Oh the ocean's a little bit bigger tonight, two more teardrops somebody cried; One of them happy and one of them bluer than blue."

Anderson's autobiography, An Unprecedented Life In Country Music, was one of the best-selling books released by UGA Press and ranked by Forbes as "One of the Best Autobiographies" of 2016.

"It's a great read for country fans and non-country fans alike," said Forbes, calling it "the unlikely tale of a true innovator who succeeded against all odds…and then did it again."

Larry's Country Diner at The Starlite Theatre
Branson Missouri

T. Graham Brown
Mon., Sept. 18

Rhonda Vincent
Tues., Sept. 19

Gene Watson
Wed., Sept. 20

Jimmy Fortune
Tues., Sept. 21

The Isaacs
Fri., Sept. 22

**For tickets
417-337-9333
www.starlitetheatre.com**

115 CFR NEWS

June 2017

Teea Goans helping keep traditional country music alive

Teea Goans grew up in rural Missouri near the Kansas border. "We listened to an AM radio station that played classic country music," she recalls. Although she was singing in church by the time she was three, it wasn't until she turned eight that she got her big break and joined the Truman Lake Opry. She continued to perform there every week until she was 17, frequently opening for such Grand Ole Opry stars as Bill Anderson, Little Jimmy Dickens and Grandpa Jones.

"We listened to an AM radio station that only played classic country music. When I started to school in the 80s, I didn't even know who Michael Jackson and Madonna were," she says.

After high school, Goans earned her associate degree at Longview Community College in Kansas City and remained there after graduation. Teea Goans' primary musical influence during those early years was her maternal grandmother - the late Della Lee Faulkner. A locally popular singer in the 1960s, Faulkner might have pursued a career in Nashville but had to take care of seven children.

In 2002, she crossed her fingers and moved to Nashville. In September 2002, she says, "I remember the day vividly, it just hit me like a ton of bricks that it was time for me to go to Nashville. I moved into my apartment on Halloween night. I didn't know a soul in town."

Three months later she was engaged to high her school sweetheart Brandon, they married shortly afterwards in 2003. Goans started working a variety of jobs, including selling cell phones. Her husband urged her to concentrate on her music and heeding his advice to follow a musical career she started writing songs and singing demos for other writers and played gigs. The first thing Goans worked on was the Ray Price show at the Ryman Auditorium in 2006, this through radio station WSM, who later asked her to book and run talent for The Opry warm-up show. Along with these duties, Goans continued to write and demo songs. At the Station Inn, Nashville's foremost bluegrass club she sang with The Time Jumpers and met her now producer Terry Choate.

Teea's mission is a vital one, she has taken on preserving traditional country music for future generations. Her CDs and live performances are filled with music that makes you remember why you love country music.

One frozen day in early January of 2010, Goans got a call from the Opry. Some of the scheduled performers were snowed in. Could she possibly come in and sing on the 7 o'clock show? Goans rushed to the Ryman and stood at the side of stage until Opry matriarch Jean Shepard called her name. She sang "Walk Out Backwards" and "I'm Still Not Over You," and the crowd loved her.

Since then Teea has been featured on Country's Family Reunion shows, Larry's Country Diner and the CFR Cruises. She is one of the younger generation who is trying to keep traditional country music alive and doing a great job!

"Teea Goans is the whole package...good looks, great voice and a style that is steeped in tradition and yet as fresh as this morning's sunrise. And did I mention she's country with a capital "C?" says Bill Anderson.

Teea currently has three CDs available and is working on her fourth. She can also be found on CFR's Home for Christmas, Ray Price Tribute, Merle Haggard Tribute, and Wednesday Night Prayer Meeting.

Dean Miller's calling as The Dog Whisperer

Most people know Dean Miller as an entertainer and son of entertainer Roger Miller, but there's an entirely different side to him that most people don't know. He trains dogs! He's known by many as a "Dog Whisperer."

Dean Miller has a lifetime of experience with dogs. "From the time I can remember I have had a house full of pets," Dean says. He began studying dog training and animal behavior with his very first dog. Over the last 15 years, he has moved on to a more serious development of a unique training style and the ability to work with owners and their pets.

"I was always the person my friends called when they needed help with their animals," Dean says."After a while, I realized this was my calling." Dean began training privatelywith dog owners in their homes, as well as teaching classes and leading seminars on dog behavior. "I have always felt that knowing the environment that a dog lives in is a huge part of understanding their behavior," Dean said. "Training the owner to understand their dog is just as important as training the dog."

Working with positive rewards and loving motivation, Dean helps hisstudents learn to please their owners because they want to, not because they are forced to.

Dean has studied extensively, taught classes and seminars, expanded his education over many years and lives his life teaching dogs. "But nobody was quite doing it the way I thought it should be done," Dean said. That's when he started developing his own expanded method of dog training and motivation. "I wanted to pass on the things I've learned through my years and years spent living with dogs," Dean says. "I also wanted to expand and refine my knowledge in a way that would be helpful to other people. I wanted to improve people's relationships with their dogs and provide tools for a happy, healthy environment for both owners and their pets."

"I don't just teach dogs, I change lives." Dean has developed a powerful and revolutionary new approach to dog training. His teaching methods begin to show results in the first few minutes. In fact, in one hour, most dog owners find they have changed their relationship with their dog for the better.

"First, I like to speak with the owner and get an idea of their dog's individual situation," Dean says. "That way, I can get a better idea of the circumstances and sometimes even 'translate' for the owner what their dog is trying to tell them."

Clients include: Kenny Chesney, Alan Jackson, Emmylou Harris, George Jones, Clint Black, Matt Hasselbeck (TN Titans), K.T. Oslin and many more.

He is the Official Trainer for the SPCA of Tennessee and was Voted Best Trainer by the readers of Nashville Paw Magazine.

June 2017

JULY

Country artists sing National Anthem at the Stanley Cup in support of Nashville Predators

Carrie Underwood was the first to sing at the playoffs. Her husband is the captain of the Nashville Predators.

The Nashville Predators didn't win the Stanley Cup, but Nashville and country music were big winners! On the last night of the Country Music Festival on June 11, the Nashville Predators lost to the Pittsburgh Penguins in Nashville, but the Nashville Predators hockey team made it to the Stanley Cup playoffs with the help of some major country music artists. During the playoff games and the finals, artists sang the National Anthem before the games. Carrie Underwood's husband, Mike Fisher is the Predators team captain and she asked if she could sing at the first game.

Keith Urban and wife Nicole Kidman are huge Nashville Predators fans and he was thrilled to sing the National Anthem for his adopted country.

Following in her lead were Luke Bryan, Vince Gill and daughters, Trisha Yearwood, Lady Antebellum, Keith Urban and others.

Others who performed the National Anthem at the playoffs were: Trish Yearwood, Little Big Town, Lady Antebellum and Vince Gill and his daughters.

118 CFR NEWS

July 2017

Nashville was well represented throughout the playoff and final games.

"The reaction from our fans in Bridgestone Arena as well as from around the country to seeing and hearing world class performers such as Carrie Underwood, Luke Bryan, Vince Gill and his daughters, Little Big Town and Lady Antebellum during the 2017 Stanley Cup Playoffs has been overwhelmingly positive, bringing national and international exposure to our community while continuing to set our game experience and atmosphere apart from others in professional sports."

Another tradition was carried out throughout the games as well as several folks threw catfish onto the rink. During the first game of the finals against Pittsburgh, Nolensville (near Nashville) resident Jake Waddell, was able to smuggle in a catfish and throw it onto the ice in the second period of play.

He was apprehended and initially charged with disorderly conduct, possessing an instrument of crime and disrupting a meeting. Charges were later dropped.

The tradition of tossing catfish onto the ice in Nashville began in 2003. It's a Nashville take on a Detroit Red Wings tradition of tossing octopus onto the ice in Michigan. At the time, it took eight wins to claim the cup (octopus have eight tentacles).

During game 3 of the first round of the Stanley Cup playoffs against the Chicago Blackhawks, numerous catfish were thrown onto the ice after Carrie Underwood finished singing the National Anthem.

"It's probably better than an octopus," Mike Fisher said.

Alan Jackson played a free concert on Saturday, June 3, in advance of the Nashville Preds first home game of the Stanley Cup Final and Faith Hill performed the final National Anthem at the June 11 game which ended the Predators run for the Stanley Cup….at least for this year!

Nadine The Church Lady

*Lord, give me a sense of humor,
Give me the grace to see a joke,
To get some humor out of life,
And to pass it on to other folk.*

My daughter-in-law was telling me about the new Survivor show. She said six men are dropped on an island with one van and four kids each for six weeks. There is no fast food, kids have to be involved in two sports each and the dad has to take care of his kids, keep his assigned house clean, correct all homework, complete science projects, cook and do laundry. The men only have access to TV when the kids are asleep and all chores are done. The men have to wear makeup daily which they must apply themselves while driving or while making four lunches. They have to attend PTS meeting, clean up after their sick kids at 3:00 a.m., make an Indian hut model with six toothpicks, a tortilla and one marker and get a four-year-old to eat a serving of peas.

The kids vote them off based on performance and the winner gets to go back to his job.

I told her Homer wouldn't last being dropped on an island by himself unless he was at a hotel with room service!

CHURCH SIGN

A smooth sea never made a skilled sailor

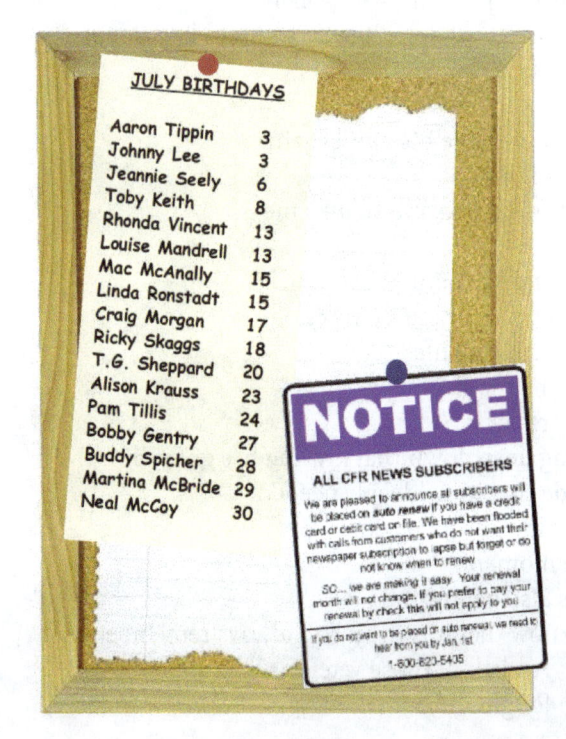

JULY BIRTHDAYS

Name	Day
Aaron Tippin	3
Johnny Lee	3
Jeannie Seely	6
Toby Keith	8
Rhonda Vincent	13
Louise Mandrell	13
Mac McAnally	15
Linda Ronstadt	15
Craig Morgan	17
Ricky Skaggs	18
T.G. Sheppard	20
Alison Krauss	23
Pam Tillis	24
Bobby Gentry	27
Buddy Spicher	28
Martina McBride	29
Neal McCoy	30

NOTICE
ALL CFR NEWS SUBSCRIBERS

We are pleased to announce all subscribers will be placed on auto renew if you have a credit card or debit card on file. We have been flooded with calls from customers who do not want their newspaper subscription to lapse but forget or do not know when to renew.

SO… we are making it easy. Your renewal month will not change. If you prefer to say your renewal by check this will not apply to you.

If you do not want to be placed on auto renewal, we need to hear from you by Jan. 1st.

1-800-823-5435

July 2017

Remember those who fought on this Independence Day!

The Vietnam War Memorial

By Alyssa Ehler, age 13

At the Vietnam War Memorial
I see a veteran
As he looks around at the Wall of Tears
He looks proud of what he has done
He sees me
I walk up to him
We talk and talk
He helps me understand why he fought for our country
He talks about our freedom:
Freedom of speech
Freedom of the press
Freedom to assemble, and
Freedom of religion
I shake his hand and walk away but
I feel
My job is still not done
I walk back up to him with a grin
He tells me how happy it makes him to know that young kids
Appriate what he did
I attempt to shake his hand again
He turns it down
He gives me a hug and thanks me
ME!
Why would he thank me?
I did not fight for our country
I did not risk my life
And yet he thanks me
I now turn away
Knowing deep down that my hug has given him the gratitude that he so deeply needed
Now I know my job is done
For the moment
But it is also beginning
I now know that it is my job to always remember him
And all of those veterans who so bravely fought for our country

120 CFR NEWS

July 2017

Look who's on the Diner this week!
ON RFD-TV
All shows subject to change

Thursdays at 7 p.m. central   Saturdays at 10 p.m. central

DARYLE SINGLETARY & RHONDA VINCENT
July 6 & 8

SHANE OWEN
July 13 & 15

MOE BANDY
July 20 & 22

ASHLEY CAMPBELL
July 27 & 29

FAMILY-REUNION presents....

KICKIN' BACK
July 7 & 8

A Grand Ole Time
July 14 & 5, 21 & 22 and 28 & 29
Fridays...7 p.m. central
Saturdays...11 p.m central

John Anderson receives spotlight exhibit at Country Music Hall of Fame & Museum

When you look back at the history of Country Music, you will find many singers – but few stylists. One thing is for certain about the career of John Anderson. He falls in the latter category. The veteran Country performer, who has influenced countless artists since making his chart debut forty years ago, will be the subject of a new spotlight exhibit at the Country Music Hall of Fame® and Museum, which opened June 16.

A native of Apopka, Florida, John Anderson is one artist who can definitely attest that he worked on the Grand Ole Opry – in more ways than one. In addition to playing the WSM Radio show many times as a performer, Anderson was part of the construction crew that helped build the Opry's current home – which opened in 1974.

"I am very grateful and flattered that the folks at the Country Music Hall of Fame would consider me for an exhibit. This is something that most artists only dream about and for me it's becoming a reality. Love and thanks to the fans who have supported us through the years as well as the folks at the Hall Of Fame," Anderson said.

However, it's his musical talents that helped make him a favorite among fans of traditional Country Music. Signing with Warner Bros. Records in 1977, the singer hit the charts with "I've Got A Feelin' (Somebody's Stealin)." It was the first of many trips up the Billboard Country Singles chart for Anderson, which would go on to include, "She Just Started Liking Cheatin' Songs," "Let Somebody Else Drive," and the CMA Award-winning "Swingin," which is celebrating its' thirty-fifth anniversary this summer. He commemorated the occasion with a performance at the 2017 CMA Music Festival on June 10.

Anderson made a huge comeback to the charts beginning in 1991 with another string of hits that include, "Straight Tequila Night," "Money In The Bank," and "Mississippi Moon." His classic country stylings have made him a favorite of critics, fans, and his fellow artists, such as Merle Haggard, George Jones, and Loretta Lynn.

The new spotlight exhibit will include such items as:

•An early stage costume from Anderson's wardrobe embroidered patterns and rhinestones designed by western designer Manuel.

•A Manuel-designed wool and leather jacket with Native American motifs worn by Anderson on the cover of his Seminole Wind and in the video for "Straight Tequila Night."

•Anderson's 1968 Fender Telecaster that the singer played in the video for "Straight Tequila Night."

•A tooled leather guitar strap with Anderson's initials.

•A stuffed alligator owned by Anderson.

•Anderson's two CMA Awards from 1983 – Horizon Award and Single of the Year ("Swingin")

Photos of Anderson with a wide variety of his heroes and friends, such as Country Music Hall of Fame members Porter Wagoner and Merle Haggard – whom he collaborated with on a cover of Lefty Frizzell's "Long Black Veil" on the 1982 album Wild & Blue. Anderson also recorded "Magic Mama," one of Haggard's last compositions, on the 2015 album Goldmine.

Spotlight exhibits supplement themes of the museum's core exhibition, Sing Me Back Home: A Journey Through Country Music. These short-term, informal displays provide a closer look at a particular person or special anniversaries. Rotated often, spotlight exhibits also offer a glimpse into the museum's unique collection of over 2.5 million artifacts, which includes recorded discs; historical photographs; films and videotapes; thousands of posters; books; songbooks; periodicals and sheet music; personal artifacts such as performers' instruments, costumes and accessories; and more. Recent spotlight exhibits have featured Bob Moore and Keith Whitley.

July 2017

John Anderson On Tour:

July 7 Hinckley, Minn. – Grand Casino Hinckley
July 14 Shawnee, Okla. – The Grand Events Center
July 15 Salado, Texas – Johnny's BBQ
July 17 Kirksville, Mo. – Nemo Fair
Aug. 12 Point Pleasant, W.Va. – Mason County Fair
Aug. 25 Mahnomen, Minn. – Shooting Star Casino
Sept. 3 Caldwell, Texas – Burleson County Fair
Sept. 21 Dade City, Fla. – Dan Cannon Auditorium
Oct. 24 Eau Claire, Wisc. – State Theater
Oct. 25 Madison, Wisc. – Barrymore Theater
Oct. 26 Green Bay, Wisc. – Meyer Theater
Oct. 27 Fairfield, Iowa – Sondheim Center for the Performing Arts
Oct. 28 Steelville, Mo. – Meramec Music Theatre

Learn more at johnanderson.com

Moe Bandy's newest CD: 'Lucky Me' on sale now

By Scot England

How would Moe Bandy sum up his life and career? The name of his newest album provides the answer.

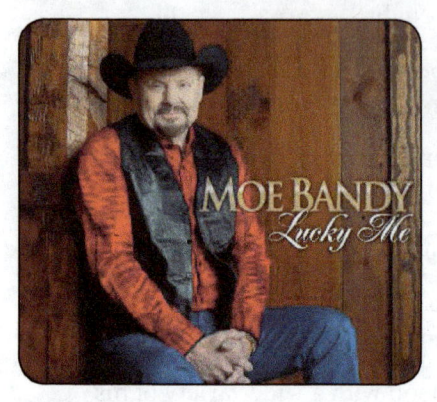

"Lucky Me. Yes, I feel very lucky…and very blessed to be where I am right now," says Bandy. "We are busier than ever. We are doing as many concerts as we possibly can as we try to keep up with all the requests we are getting. I think people have missed that real traditional country music."

Real traditional country music is exactly what Moe's fans will find when they listen to his CD 'Lucky Me.'

"Jimmy Capps produced the album. Jimmy played on almost every hit I had." Bandy continues, "I asked him to get some of the same musicians who played on my earlier albums. We got Pig Robbins, Charlie McCoy and Jimmy also plays three or four different guitars on the album. And Curtis Young and Michele Capps sang harmony."

The album also features a few more of Bandy's country music friends. "I've got The Oak Ridge Boys singing with me on two songs. The Oaks sing "Hell Stays Open," and "Just a Place to Hang My Hat." They are the best. We had a great time. I do a song called "Rarest Flower." Ricky Skaggs was so nice to come in and play mandolin and sing harmony with me. What a thrill that was. And we do a tribute to the cowboys on "Long Line of Cowboys." The Riders in the Sky sing it with me."

The CD also includes a song written by Country Music Hall of Famer Bill Anderson. "'I've Done Everything Hank Williams Did but Die' has got a lot of lines from Hank Williams' songs, so I like to say that Hank Williams and Bill Anderson wrote the song," says Bandy.

To celebrate the album, Moe had a CD release party at the Nashville Palace. Audience members included Jeannie Seely, TG Sheppard, Kelly Lang, Riders in the Sky and Duane Allen of The Oak Ridge Boys.

Moe was also joined on stage by Pig Robbins, and Jimmy and Michele Capps. Hawkshaw Hawkins Jr. opened the show.

"I haven't had a CD release party in many years," says Bandy. "I sang every song from the new album and then I sang most of my older hits. It was great fun." Bandy also had fun with his country pal Gene Watson during the recent "Moe and Gene Show." That special one hour show aired on RFD TV.

"We got such a huge response from the show and it turned out so great," says Bandy. "Everywhere Gene and I go, people ask us if we are going to do everything now, but we are definitely going to be doing similar shows. And it will be very soon, so stay tuned! Moe's tour dates and 'Lucky Me' CD ordering information can be found at www.moebandy.com. He can be seen on Larry's Country Diner on July 20 and 22.

Purchase at www.moebandy.com

July 2017

The Judds to release new Greatest Hits CD

Together, Country Music icons Wynonna and Naomi Judd made musical history throughout their career receiving eight Gold and eight Platinum records, selling over 20 million albums and scoring twenty Top 10 hits between 1984-1990. Now, Curb Records is excited to bring fans the ultimate collection of those years together. The Judds – All-Time Greatest Hits will be released on Friday, June 30 – and will feature each of the classic hits that helped to make them a household name on Country Radio in the 1980s and 1990s.

"Some things continue to get better with time, like fine wine and the Judds music," says Naomi Judd. "I'm so proud that our music has stood the test of time. It makes my heart smile when I turn on Country Radio and I can sing along with our hits."

The twenty-one song set will feature each of the duo's top ten hits, as well as "You Can't Go Home Again (Flies On The Butter)," a recording from 2011. Beginning with the classic #1 hit "Mama, He's Crazy" in 1984, and continuing through 1991's "One Hundred and Two," the duo established a career that will stand with one of the top duets in Country Music history.

Fourteen times the duo topped the Billboard Country Singles chart, and each of their five studio albums were certified Gold or Platinum.

Track Listing:

1. Mama He's Crazy
2. Why Not Me
3. Girls Night Out
4. Love Is Alive
5. Have Mercy
6. Grandpa (Tell Me 'Bout The Good Old Days)
7. Rockin' with the Rhythm of the Rain
8. Cry Myself To Sleep
9. Don't Be Cruel
10. I Know Where I'm Going
11. Maybe Your Baby's Got The Blues
12. Turn It Loose
13. Give A Little Love
14. Change Of Heart
15. Young Love
16. Let Me Tell You About Love
17. One Man Woman
18. Born To Be Blue
19. Love Can Build A Bridge
20. One Hundred And Two
21. Flies On The Butter (You Can't Go Home Again)

Larry's Country Diner at The Starlite Theatre
Branson   Missouri

T. Graham Brown
Mon., Sept. 18

Rhonda Vincent
Tues., Sept. 19

Gene Watson
Wed., Sept. 20

Jimmy Fortune
Tues., Sept. 21

The Isaacs
Fri., Sept. 22

For tickets
417-337-9333
www.starlitetheatre.com

July 2017

COUNTRY LEGENDS OF THE PAST & PRESENT
BY TOM WOOD

Billy Grammer

We moved to Nashville for the first time in 1960, and I can remember riding in the back seat of our blue-and-white Ford Fairlane, listening to my dad singing along with the radio.

I've laid around and played around this old town too long

Summer's almost gone, yes winter's coming on

I've laid around and played around this old town too long. And I feel like I gotta travel on.

Those lyrics by David Lazar, Larry Ehrlich, Paul Clayton and Tom Six didn't make much sense to a five-year-old, but I remember liking the booming, melodic country voice that my dad tried his best to imitate.

The voice belonged to Billy Grammer, and his 1959 version of "Gotta Travel On" sold more than a million singles and peaked at No. 5 on the U.S. country charts and No. 4 on pop charts.

That signature hit earned the Illinois native an invite to join the Grand Ole Opry.

He also had seven other songs in the Top 100, the highest among those being "I Wanna Go Home" (1963) at No. 18. You may recall that song as its better-known name "Detroit City" and made famous by Bobby Bare. His last hit was in 1969, but that was far from the greatness or highlight of his musical career.

Billy's off-stage accomplishments and presence at key events in history tell a remarkable story about both the man and his music.

The son of an accomplished musician (violin, trumpet), Billy achieved far greater fame than his father or 12 siblings ever imagined. The young Grammer learned to play the guitar with such proficiency that he founded his own acoustic guitar company.

The Grammer Guitar quickly became the go-to guitar for many country stars and earned a place in the Country Music Hall of Fame in 1969. Grammer owned the company from 1965-68, then sold it after a fire destroyed the factory. The new owner stopped making Grammer Guitars in 1970, and they are considered collector's items today, selling for thousands.

Billy's most famous song "Gotta Travel On" provided the base-name for his band, the Travel On Boys. It was recorded by numerous artists, including Buddy Holley, who opened his 1959 shows with the song until his death in a plane crash that February.

On May 15, 1972, Billy and the band were performing at a George Wallace rally in Maryland when the Alabama governor was running for president. Following Wallace's speech, he was shot and paralyzed by Arthur Bremmer in an attack that stunned the nation. Billy wept that day.

Other career highlights for Billy include delivering the invocation at the glittering opening of the Grand Ole Opry House on March 16, 1974, and his 1990 induction into the Illinois Country Music Hall of Fame. Others honorees that day were Tex Williams, Patsy Montana and Lulu Belle and Scotty.

Finally, in 2009 the Grand Ole Opry paid tribute to Billy for recognition of his 50 years of membership in the world's most exclusive country club, where only the cream of the crop of artists are invited to join.

Billy — who had gone blind from a degenerative eye disease — died two years later on Aug. 10, 2011, just 18 days before what would have been his 86th birthday. He suffered a heart attack seven months prior to his death.

Sources: Wikipedia, www.grammer guitar.net

Author Tom Wood, who writes thrillers and Westerns, is a regular contributor to Country Family Reunion News. Reach him at tomwoodauthor.com

The People Who Make Us Laugh

Jerry Clower, was a Mississippi Baptist layman who was a fertilizer salesman in his 40s when he "backed into" a career as a country comedian.

Clower, known for his clean humor, was the best-selling country comedian of all time, recording 31 albums, with sales stretching beyond 8 million, all with MCA/Decca records in Nashville, Tennessee.

He was inducted into the Grand Ole Opry in 1973, three years after the release of his first album, "Jerry Clower from Yazoo, Mississippi, Talkin'." That album and two others, "Jerry Clower's Greatest Hits" and "Jerry Clower, Mouth Of Mississippi," reached gold status, each topping 500,000 in sales. He was named country comic of the year by various publications from 1973-81.

He also wrote "Ain't God Good!" and three other books. He did up to 200 performances a year, regularly concluding with a testimony of his faith in Christ. When he fell ill August 4, 1998 at the Georgia Mountain State Fair in Hiwassee it was the first show he missed in 32 years.

Clower, of Liberty, Mississippi, was a member of East Fork Baptist Church, a 100-member congregation in the Amite County, Miss., community of Smithdale -- the church where he trusted Christ at age 13 during a July 1939 revival meeting and was baptized -- the same day as his future wife, Homerline.

They were married for 51 years and raised a son and three daughters. "If God gave me the ingredients and told me to make a woman, I'd make her just like my wife," Clower told Georgia Baptists' Christian Index newsjournal before a show at Brewton-Parker College.

Before returning to his boyhood community in 1988; Clower was an active member of First Baptist Church, Yazoo City, MS, for 34 years.

He was the longtime co-host of "Country Crossroads," a Christian-country program heard weekly on 750 radio stations. Now produced by the Southern Baptist North American Mission Board, the program was begun in 1969 by the SBC's former Radio and Television Commission. Clower joined the broadcast in the mid-1970s.

Clower relayed his humor at Southern Baptist Convention annual meetings in 1975 and 1979, and he remained a popular speaker in Baptist meetings over the years -- spanning boys' Royal Ambassador groups to senior adults -- as well as in local churches.

In 1970, he was one of three incorporators of Agricultural Missions Foundation, now based in Jackson, MS, a nonprofit organization supporting a range of overseas agricultural missionaries and projects.

"I am convinced that there is only one place where there is no laughter, and that's hell," Clower once said. "I have made arrangements to miss hell. Praise God, I won't ever have to be anywhere that there ain't no laughter."

"I love what I do. What I do is biblical," Clower said in a 1993 interview with Music Row

July 2017

magazine in Nashville. "The wisest man that ever lived, King Solomon, said, 'A merry heart doeth good like a medicine.'"

"I've never made an album you couldn't play in church," he told The Christian Index, while telling Music Row that his success proves "that families want to laugh and share together. A lot of talkers today have to hide their records from the children. My tapes can be played for the whole family."

Clower called himself "a forerunner, an introducer and supporter" for Jesus Christ in a 1997 book of notables' favorite Scripture verses, "Lamp Unto My Feet."

Quoting John the Baptist's words from John 3:30, "He must increase, but I must decrease," Clower wrote: "In show business you have advance people who make all the plans and preparation. John the Baptist was such a person. His main objective was to point people to the Lamb of God. In all things if you conduct yourself to make sure Jesus increases and you decrease, you will always be doing what will honor God."

"I realize I'm in the fourth quarter of my life," Clower told The Christian Index. "But I am not a long-range planner. I live one day at a time. … First thing I do every morning is pray. … Worry is a sin."

While being a top-selling artist in truck stops across the country, Clower also was the country artist who held that spot among African Americans, and a number of black radio stations were playing his humor, the newspaper reported.

"It makes sense," Clower said. "If you grew up in the South, you remember hog-killin' time whether you're white or black."

Clower got his start in the entertainment business by tapping his knack for humorous storytelling to keep people awake during sales talks on agricultural chemicals. A friend taped one of his talks in Lubbock, Texas, and sent it MCA, and Clower soon had a recording contract.

Clower's trademark "Whooooooooooooh!" exclamation was described by a writer in The Tennessean as "uttered with tent-revival fervor in a falsetto tone that falls somewhere between a broken locomotive whistle and a championship hog call."

While his stories regularly featured the fictional Ledbetters of Mississippi in such settings as church revivals, county fairs, crappie fishing or cotton farming, Clower maintained that "just about all of my stuff is all almost true," Music Row quoted him as saying. As long as he continues traveling and meeting people, he said he will always have material for new recordings. "It's not things that creative minds sit down and write. The only ability I have is the talent to remember and the talent to tell it" -- and "embellish" it just a bit at times.

"We were standing on a street corner in Liberty, MS, the other day," he told The Tennessean, "and a funeral came by. Everyone in front of the Liberty Drug Store got reverent. They pass by. And this one ol' boy leans over to his buddy and says, 'Who died?' He said, 'The one in the first car.'

"Now you can't think that up," Clower said.

Reared in a single-parent home with few material blessings after his father deserted the family, Clower shared chores with an older brother and credited his Christian mother, Mable, for being a pivotal influence in his life. "I thank God for my mamma who taught me high moral standards, right from wrong and that you gave a hard day's work for a full day's pay," he told a Baptist conference for 2,000 senior adults in Arkansas in 1996. "I am afraid in today's society our moral standards are so low that animals care more for their young'uns than the human race does."

Joining the Navy at age 16 in World War II, Clower served aboard the USS Bennington, earning three battle stars and a presidential citation. "I love this country because I know what it took to keep it free," he told the Arkansas seniors. It was in the war that "I learned about God's provision of guardian angels for those who love and serve him."

Following his military service, Clower determined he would gain a college education and work as a 4-H Club leader because of the influence a 4-H leader had on his life while growing up. He first attended a junior college in Summit, Miss., then transferred to Mississippi State University in Starkville. Although he had never played football before, he became the team's left tackle and gained a football scholarship. Following his graduation with a degree in agriculture, Clower worked for two years as an assistant county agent with 4-H clubs before Cooper recruited him for Mississippi Chemical Corporation.

"He lived his life strictly according to Christian principles," Tandy Rice, Clower's only manager, who worked with the comic on only a handshake for nearly 30 years, told The Tennessean.

Underscoring gratitude for his religious heritage, Clower told the Arkansas seniors that he researched the history of East Fork Baptist Church for the 150th anniversary of its founding in 1810 and had learned "about my forefathers being posted as guards to keep the Indians from interrupting services. This is the background that allowed me to hear the gospel of Jesus Christ."

"I am an heir to a mansion, a robe and a crown and you are, too," Clower told the seniors. "There are enough of you in this auditorium to turn the state of Arkansas upside down for him if you will only tell others of his saving grace."

Urging Christians to quit worrying and to lean on God, Clower said, "I am so appreciative of what God has done for me that wherever I am I let the blood of Calvary speak for me. You, too, should let his blood speak for you rather than tarnishing your witness with personal worries."

Clower died in August 1998 following heart bypass surgery; he was 71 years old

A look at Tammy Wynette's elegant Nashville home

One year before Tammy Wynette and George Jones divorced and went their seperate ways, Jones purchased an elegant estate for them in Nashville, Tennessee. Wynette held on to the home after the couple divorced, and used it as her primary residence until 1992. Other former owners were legendary banjo player Earl Scruggs and drummer Scott Underwood, known for his work in the band Train.

Now, someone else can have the chance to live in Wynette's former home, which is called First Lady Acres. The nine-bedroom, nine-bathroom house recently went on the market with a listing price of $5.5 million.

First Lady Acres was constructed in 1970, and features a 10,000-square-foot home and over eight acres of land. Outside, residents can soak up the Tennessee sun while relaxing at the pool or cabana. While you're at it, you could fix yourself a tasty meal at the convenient outdoor kitchen.

Avid golf players can practice their favorite sport without ever leaving the comfort of their own home. That's right, First Lady Acres comes along with a putting green.

The property is also ideal for those who travel or would like to welcome guests from out of state. There's a helicopter landing pad located at the estate, a feature that you won't find at many homes!

Inside, the home features an open floor plan throughout. Some of the special rooms include a home gym, a complete chef's kitchen, a butler's pantry, and a steam room.

Whoever ends up purchasing First Lady Acres should consider themselves lucky. It's a lovely home with so much history behind it!

Although Jones and Wynette divorced after they bought they home, they remained friends until Wynette's death in 1998. The two collaborated many times over the years, and actually released a single with the word "house" in it. That single was "Two Story House," which was released in 1980.

Above: the pool out back. Below: the front of the house.

July 2017

Larry's Country Diner visits RFD booth at CMA Fest

Renae the Waitress, Nadine and Keith hang out and signed autographs at the RFD-TV booth at CMA Fest.

Renae and Nadine take a break in the cornfield!

Renae, Nadine and Keith had fun playing with all the Springer Mountain Farms props.

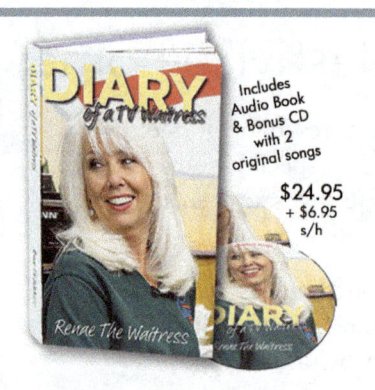

DIARY of a TV Waitress
Everything you alwaysy wanted to know about behind the scenes at Larry's Country Diner!

Includes Audio Book & Bonus CD with 2 original songs
$24.95 + $6.95 s/h

Precious Memories MEMORIAL
A journey of Country Music greats, their celebration of life and sacred resting places

BEVERLY HILLS BOOK AWARDS WINNER
$24.95 + $6.95 s/h

Precious Memories LEGACY
Stories and memories from the children of some of Country Music's Legends

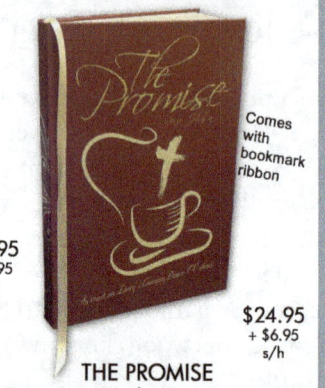

$16.95 + $6.95 s/h

THE PROMISE
Promises as read on Larry's Country Diner TV show, the artists who were on the show and the original air date

Comes with bookmark ribbon
$24.95 + $6.95 s/h

All are available NOW at www.larryscountrydiner.com or www.renaethewaitress.com
Or mail check or money order to: Gabriel, P.O. Box 210709, Nashville, TN 37221

Celebrate America this July 4

This DVD series is devoted to songs that make us proud to be Americans and songs that allow us to enjoy our spiritual roots. Songs you sang in church and songs that recall a time in America when we were free to openly express our faith without fear of ridicule. Bill Anderson will host this first reunion that we're calling

GOD BLESS AMERICA Again

Artists include: Bill Anderson, Lee Greenwood, Bobby Bare, Jimmy Fortune, Aaron Tippin, Ed Bruce, Daryle Singletary, Jan Howard, Larry Gatlin and The Gatlin Brothers, Linda Davis, Jim Ed Brown, David Ball, John Conlee, Joey + Rory, Gene Watson, Ray Stevens, Teea Goans, Con Hunley, Marty Raybon, Jeannie Seely, Rhonda Vincent, Dailey & Vincent, Mark Wills, and Jean Shepard.

800-820-5405
www.cfrvideos.com

$79.80 + $6.95 sh

July 2017

It's A Family Tradition

By Claudia Johnson

Jim and Dan Seals: Return to Country Roots After Pop Success

Two of the most beautiful voices of the 1970s were those of brothers who had grown up in rural West Texas. Each of the brothers gained initial fame as pop singers in separate duos, but one returned to his country roots to achieve further success.

As youth Dan Seals and Jim Seals played country music in The Seals Family Band with their father, an amateur guitarist who had performed with Bob Wills and Ernest Tubb but made his living as a pipefitter in the oil fields.

Jim, born in 1941, won a state fiddle championship when he was nine years old. After high school he toured with The Champs, known for their 1958 hit "Tequila." In 1963, Jim, Dash Crofts, Glen Campbell and Jerry Cole left The Champs to form a band named Glen Campbell and the GCs. The band only lasted a couple of years before the members went their separate ways.

A versatile musician, Jim played rhythm guitar for Buck Owens and saxophone for The Monkees' second album, toured with Eddie Cochran's band and was a member of The Dawnbreakers.

It was Jim's collaboration with his longtime friend and fellow Texan Dash Crofts that secured his place in music history. As the duo Seals and Crofts, the pair wrote and recorded dozens of songs, with "We May Never Pass This Way (Again)," "Diamond Girl," "I'll Play for You," "Get Closer," "You're the Love," "Summer Breeze" and "Hummingbird" all making it to the Top 10. Between 1969 and 2004 they released 17 albums and continued to play together, though the duo originally disbanded in the 1980s to pursue other interests and raise their families. After living in various locations, Jim moved with his family to Tennessee. Their daughters, Juliet Seals and Amelia Crofts, along with Genevieve Dozier, daughter of Seals & Crofts engineer Joey Bogan, formed a musical trio called The Humming Birds.

In 2002 Jim played some of his Seals and Crofts original hits at the Grand Ole Opry alongside his younger brother, Dan Seals, who was a star in his own right.

Dan, born in 1948, recalled standing on an apple crate to play stand-up bass in his father's family band by the time he was four.

"I've loved to play and sing from the moment I knew what it was," he told The Associated Press in 1992.

Performing with high school garage bands, he met John Coley, with whom he formed a country-folk duo in 1969 called England Dan and John Ford Coley. "I'd Really Love to See You Tonight" was released in 1976, and became a No. 1 hit. They released 11 albums and nine singles, including five additional Top 40 singles like "Love Is the Answer," "Nights Are Forever Without You," "It's Sad to Belong" and "We'll Never Have to Say Goodbye Again."

The nickname "England Dan" was bestowed upon the singer by brother Jim after Dan became obsessed with The Beatles in the 1960s and had, for a time, affected an English accent in admiration. Jim, a fan of his brother's who publically praised his singing and songwriting skills, suggested Dan use the youthful moniker professionally.

After the Seals-Coley duo disbanded, Dan returned to his country roots and his given name, ultimately releasing 16 studio albums and charting more than 20 singles on the Country Music charts. Eleven of his singles reached No. 1, including, "Meet Me in Montana" with Marie Osmond, "Bop," which also became a pop hit, "Everything That Glitters (Is Not Gold)," "You Still Move Me," "I Will Be There," "Three Time Loser," "One Friend," "Addicted," "Big Wheels in the Moonlight," "Love on Arrival" and "Good Times," Five more of his singles also reached Top Ten on the Country charts.

People magazine praised Dan in a 1985 article, noting that he "came naturally to his loose, intimate country sound."

By the 1990s Dan had become primarily a touring artist, often in the years before his 2009 death from mantle cell lymphoma, paring with Jim to perform and record.

"We played 'Summer Breeze' and 'Diamond Girl,'" Dan said of their 2002 Opry performance, recalling, "When it was over, the audience stood up and . . . just kept clapping."

This inspired the brothers to launch a long-held dream of forming their own duo, so Seals and Seals was born.

"Working with my brother, Jim, it's almost like a dream," Dan said in a promotional video for the new duo.

They toured extensively for the next several years; performing hits from both their past duo careers as well as numerous original compositions. Jimmy's son Sutherland played lead guitar and son Joshua played bass. However, Dan's battle with cancer drained him of energy necessary for touring, and the brothers turned attentions toward producing a studio album, completing eight songs before Dan died in hospice care at his daughter's Nashville home, surrounded by those he loved.

"There's a side of me that dreams and hopes for a better world," Dan once said in an expression of his profound faith. "I think with my heart. I believe that the people of our planet are all one family."

Country Music Questions & Answers

Q: Gene Watson is my favorite singer and I would like to know more about him. Where was he raised, does he have a family, what is his favorite song that he sings, etc. I have been a fan for years and my favorite song is "Farewell Party". I have it on cd's (which I keep in the car) and every time I hear it on the radio I stop what I'm doing and listen. Will look forward to hearing about Gene. Thank you and please edit this note anyway you would like.

Dee Slay, West Virginia

A: Gene Watson was born in Palestine, Texas, in 1943. He began his music career in the 1960s, performing in local clubs at night while working in a Houston auto body shop during the day.

He said "I'd get off the school bus at this place and work til late, finding hubcaps and car bumpers. I always thought my life's work would revolve around cars somehow. Then along about my early teen years, my brother and I were asked to perform for a local show. We got paid some minimum amount but we got a standing ovation and I was hooked on the notion I could get paid for doing a little singing to help pay for a car."

In 1964, the Grand Ole Opry duo, The Wilburn Brothers, took Gene on the road briefly and itt was The Wilburn Brothers who brought Gene to Nashville for the very first time and allowed him to sing on the stage of the Grand Ole Opry.

In the 1970s and 1980s he released the #1 singles "Fourteen Carat Mind" and "Paper Rosie" He has had six #1 singles, as well as more than 80 charting singles over the course of his career.

He married Mattie Louise Bivins in 1961; the couple has two children named Terry Lynn and Gary Wayne.

Gene Watson quit drinking in 1980 and quit smoking not long after that. He underwent surgery and survived colon cancer in 2000-01. Through it all, he continues to record one critically applauded collection after another.

If you have questions send them to Paula, CFR News, P.O. Box 210796, Nashville, TN 37221 or email them to paula@gabrielcommunications.com.

July 2017

Salute to the Kornfield
Everything you always wanted to know about the cast
By Sasha Kay Dunavant

Roni Stoneman: Banjo Royalty and Comedy Queen

A member of one of early Country Music's most famous families has balanced an equally successful dual career across eight decades. Born in 1938, Veronica Loretta "Roni" Stoneman, the youngest daughter of the legendary Stoneman family, is a well-rounded entertainer with the ability to play her banjo seriously or shower an audience with humor.

Roni began performing and traveling at an early age with her family when her father realized that he could make his Appalachian up-bringing profitable by translating the storytelling quality of traditional folk songs into enjoyable updated music for commercial consumption. Earnest "Pop" Stoneman, the father of 17 children, proved he was right when his genre's mega hit, "The Sinking of The Titanic," became a million-seller in 1925. He later became a permanent chapter in country lore with his induction into "The Country Music Hall Of Fame"

Pop retired from his own music career in 1934, eventually moving his family to Washington D.C. where he worked as a carpenter. Soon the musical children formed their own group that was originally called the "Blue Grass Champs," with six of the Stoneman children displaying their specific talent in the band. Scotty, Van, Patsy, Jimmie, Roni and Donna rallied up a local following and won first place at the "Arthur Godfrey Talent Scouts" show in 1956. The group, which became The Stonemans, would play as much as six nights a week, having little to no time for childish things. They debuted at The Grand Ole Opry in the early 1960s and consistently performed there throughout the decade, having honed their professionalism on the stages throughout Maryland, Pennsylvania and Washington D.C.

The Stonemans had their first major Top 40 hit, "Tupelo County Jail," in 1966. The next year brought The Stonemans even greater success when their hit, "Five Little Johnson Girls," landed in the Top 30 on Country charts. The Academy of Country Music honored The Stonemans with the Vocal Group of the Year Award in 1967 as well.

The group also hosted their own syndicated television show that aired in all 50 states. Two somber events occurred in 1968 – the death of their father and the release of their final hit, "Christopher Robin," which made it to the Top 50. Gradually each of them retired or pursued their own musical interests.

It wasn't until her father's death that Roni began to reach for the stars in the Bluegrass world herself. Roni was the first female artist to use the three-finger Scruggs banjo picking style. Her brother Scotty encouraged Roni to play the banjo like a man. He demanded that she hold her banjo sturdy and play vigorously with the bow. That is exactly what she did, and that advice earned her unmatched accolades in the Country and Bluegrass genres. She has become known as the "First Lady of the Banjo."

July 2017

Roni was known to country audiences when she joined Hee Haw in 1973. She was cast as an unhappy housewife named Ida Lee Nagger. The name rang true to the character, since Ida Lee "nagged" her weary spouse. The gap between her front teeth was real and not a tooth blacked out by a makeup artist. She wore a housecoat and curlers, dragging the iron and harassing Lavern played by Gordie Tapp, her long-suffering husband, who did his own share of nagging right back. She became so recognizable as Ida Lee that she did other Hee Haw skits as the character, including "Pfft! You were Gone!" Her character evolved into a man-crazy flirt where she could be seen sometimes in the Hee Haw Honky Tonk chasing men with a net.

After Hee Haw ended Roni continued with her banjo career, and has not stopped. In a 2009 interview with LA Record, she explained how it feels to be a performer…a feeling she first experienced as a child with her family's band.

"When you're so poor and you got homemade instruments and your shoes are all worn—you're wearing your brothers' shoes—but you're playing good music, and they come up to you and you think they're educated and smart and ain't they wonderful?" she observed. "They taught us from the very beginning, the audience. It sounds corny but it's the truth. They taught us the music was important to them."

ALL THE NEWS FROM THE LAST 5 YEARS!!!

All the articles, photos, jokes, stories and more, all in these 8 1/2 x 11, full color books

What a great way to have all the back issues in one place!

$29.95 each
+ $6.95 s/h

800-820-5405
www.cfrvideos.com

July 2017

Singer Songwriters
By Claudia Johnson

John D. Loudermilk

Nashville Songwriter's Hall of Famer John D. Loudermilk Jr. began his songwriting journey at a very young age when his mother taught him how to play a ukulele his father made from a cigar box.

Perhaps one of the songs North Carolina native Loudermilk is best known for is his tale of his poor upbringing, "Tobacco Road." The song became a Top 10 hit for a British based group called the Nashville Teens in 1964. In America the song reached the Top 20.

Loudermilk spoke of the song at the 2007 "Poets and Prophets" interview at the Country Music Hall of Fame and Museum.

"I didn't even know my family didn't have any money," he recalled. "I always had a place to play, had a camp under the house or a tree house to play in. And I had a bicycle, a pair of shorts and no shoes, and you could go all over Durham with that, but you had to be back by dark."

The emotional and turmoil-ridden lyrics of "Tobacco Road" such as, "I was born in a bunk. Mama died and my daddy got drunk. Left me here to die alone. In the middle of Tobacco Road," have attracted many stars to record their own renditions of the song. Those artists have included Shawn Colvin, Bobbie Gentry, David Lee Roth, Edgar Winter, Steve Earle and Eric Burdon.

A poem Loudermilk wrote in high school called "A Rose and a Baby Ruth" became a song that reached No. 6 on Billboard's Magazine Pop chart when George Hamilton IV heard Loudermilk perform it on a local television station and decided to record what became a well known a cappella version in 1956. Eddie Fontaine recorded a competing version the day Hamilton recorded it, and it was covered several times over the years by artists including Johnny Maestro & The Crests and Al Kooper. Rocker Marilyn Manson included it in 1999 as a bonus studio track on his limited edition version of The Last Tour On Earth live album.

Another song on which Loudermilk was a co-writer and Hamilton was the artist was 1963's "Abilene," an ode to Abilene, Kansas, and as the women who, as the song says, "don't treat you mean," which went to No. 15 on the pop music charts and remains a country music favorite.

In 1959 Loudermilk wrote the country hit, "Amigo's Guitar" with Kitty Wells.

"The moon is lonely tomorrow I'll wonder where you are," Wells sang. "Manana, morning, my darling I'll be blue as Amigo's guitar."

The song was honored with a Broadcast Music, Inc. (BMI) award.

Loudermilk could write songs for every genre of music. His songs could also be arranged for different voices and different tempos.

Through the 1960s and 1970s Loudermilk Created Pop and Country hits for many beloved singers, such as Johnny Cash, The Everly Brothers, Marianne Faithful, Chet Atkins, Johnny Tillotson, Sue Thompson, Stonewall Jackson, himself and many others.

Some of his compositions did better on the charts when recorded by others. Eddie Cochran charted with Loudermilk's tune, "Sittin' in the Balcony," in 1957, while Loudermilk's own recording failed to make a showing. Loudermilk wrote and recorded the first version of "Thou Shalt Not Steal" in 1962 without finding commercial success, but a 1964 recording by Dick and Dee Dee climbed to number 13 on the Billboard chart. Several artists, including Glenda Collins, The Pleazers and The Newbeats have since recorded the song. In 1963 both country singer Ernest Ashforth and pop artist Johnny Tillotson climbed the charts with Loudermilk's song, "Talk Back Trembling Lips."

"This Little Bird" became a No. 6 hit in the U.K. for Marianne Faithfull in 1965. Eddy Arnold made a No. 1 Country Music hit out of "Then You Can Tell Me Goodbye" in 1968. A year before the song reached the Top 10 for The Casinos.

July 2017

Loudermilk's "Ebony Eyes" recorded in 1961 by The Everly Brothers told the story of the loss of a young man's fiancée in a plane crash in dark, stormy weather conditions, conditions that remind him of her ebony eyes. The song, which reached No. 8 on the Billboard Charts, was initially banned from airplay in the United Kingdom because its lyrics were deemed too disturbing.

He was born in 1934 in Durham, North Carolina, and he died in Christiana, Tennessee, on Sept. 21, 2016. Loudermilk was also a cousin to Ira and Charlie Loudermilk, better known as the Louvin Brothers. Loudermilk has first performed as an artist under the stage name "Johnny Dee," recording his early works with a North Carolina-based label called Colonial Records. In 2011 Loudermilk was inducted into the North Carolina Music Hall of Fame. In his later years Loudermilk enjoyed chasing hurricanes and sailing with his wife, Susan, and sons Mike, Rick and John.

The legacy he leaves upon American culture is his song, "Indian Reservation," which was recorded by several artists but made a hit by Paul Revere and the Raiders. Loudermilk explained in an interview on the Viva! NashVegas radio show that he wrote the song after being taken in by the Cherokee when his car was trapped in a blizzard. He claimed that Chief Bloody Bear Tooth asked him to make a song about his people's plight surrounding the Trail of Tears. Loudermilk, after being awarded the first medal of the Cherokee nation for this, was asked to read an old ledger book kept during The Trail of Tears. As he read through the names, he discovered his great grandparents, at the age of 91, were marched 1,600 miles during the deadly relocation from North Carolina to Oklahoma.

"They took the whole Cherokee nation, put us on this reservation," the song recalls, and with hope, adds, "But maybe someday when they learn, Cherokee nation will return, will return."

Bill Monroe's Name & Likeness, Uncle Pen's Cabin offered for sale

Fans of the "Father of Bluegrass Music" have a unique opportunity to own the rights to the name and likeness to Bill Monroe. Regarded as the man who started the format, Monroe joined the WSM Grand Ole Opry in 1939, and was a member for almost six decades – until his passing in September 1996. One of the few members of both the Country Music Hall of Fame and The Rock and Roll Hall of Fame, Monroe's musical legacy included legendary stints on Columbia Records and MCA / Decca, with whom he was associated for forty years. Monroe cast a shadow over music by influencing a wide variety of musical artists.

"I'd still rather listen to Bill and Charlie Monroe than any current record. That's what America is all about, to me." / Bob Dylan

"In all of history, he's the biggest single influence in Country Music. And, he didn't just influence Country Music, he influenced music in general."

Offering the name, image, and likeness of such an American icon is something that is both an honor and a privilege. "While at Buddy Lee Attractions, I was the agent for Bill Monroe for over ten years. I thought of Mr. Monroe as a national treasure. He was like a grandfather to me. We were good friends," says Tony Conway. The ownership also includes rights to the name "Blue Grass Boys," which was the name of Bill's band – a who's who of greats that over the years has included Flatt & Scruggs, Gordon Terry, Mac Wiseman, Del McCoury, and Stringbean (David Akeman).

In addition to the name and likeness offering – also available are the rights to the BillMonroe.com website, fans can also own several exciting parts of the Bill Monroe legacy – beginning with the historic Uncle Pen's Cabin in his hometown of Rosine, Kentucky. A home that has special significance in the history of Bluegrass Music, it's where young Bill went to live with his Uncle after the passing of both parents in 1927. As the only child among his siblings who went to live with Pendleton Vandiver, Monroe received an education about the music of the area from his Uncle through the historic fiddle tunes he would learn – a musical legend that he would eventually take to stages around the world. Bill left the home in 1929, but the music he was exposed to would take hold. Monroe crafted the iconic "Uncle Pen" as a tribute. Over the years, the song was covered by artists such as Hank Williams, Jr., Buck Owens, and Ricky Skaggs – who made it the first Bluegrass song to top the charts in over two decades in 1984. The song received a BMI Award for over one million plays. The home has been in the Monroe family since Bill's son James bought it in 1973, building the cabin with the original logs. Over the years, many of Bill's contemporaries have visited the site, including Don Reno, Jimmy Martin, and Lester Flatt, and thousands of Bill's fans from around the world.

Also being offered in one separate bundle is Bill Monroe memorabilia and personal items, the likes of which has never been available – and will never be available to the public again. Included among the items are over 1,800 personal and business checks – including some written to Earl Scruggs, Ralph Stanley, and Johnny Paycheck; two knives and three wrist watches owned by Monroe, his back brace, social security card, ATM Card and Gas Cards, Christmas Cards, thousands of his personal papers and collectibles, suits, coats, shoes, ties, and even his Last Will and Testament. The collection also includes his own personal record collection, and one of his fiddles – which he kept for sixty-seven years (and has his initials inscribed inside of it!) and an extensive merchandise collection that includes T-Shirts and CD's of Bill's, son James's, caps, 8 by 10 pictures, commemorative plates – and even his own mailing list, with over 10,000 addresses!

But, there's even more. There are well over 250 live recordings from Bill's Bean Blossom Bluegrass Festival that will be offered in one exclusive package. Monroe started the festival in 1967, and it thrives to this day – fifty years after its' inception. Over the years, performers who have played Bean Blossom include Blue Highway, Chris Hillman, J.D. Crowe & The New South, John Hartford, Patty Loveless, and Rhonda Vincent.

And, then....there's parts of the famous Gibson 1923 Lloyd Loar that is on display at the Country Music Hall of Fame. An extra set of tuning keys and a bridge that was replaced. These items from the most famous mandolin in the world are priceless!

It goes without saying that this is going to be a private opportunity of historic proportions, and there will be interest from buyers around the world. Interested parties should contact Tony Conway, Conway Entertainment Group, the exclusive agent for the Bill Monroe Estate, at 615-724-1818 for more information.

Photo Credit: Courtesy of Monroe Enterprises

July 2017

Traditional country music still has a place in

MONDAY - COUNTRY FOR A CAUSE

Hawkshaw Hawkins Jr. and Melissa Luman at the *Country for a Cause* benefit on Monday, June 5 at the Nashville Palace.

Left: Victoria Hallman (from Hee Haw).
Above: T.G. Sheppard and Ronnie McDowell sing with the benefit recipient

The Tennessee Mafia Jug Band entertained everyone!

Sylvia and Jan Howard

Melissa Luman, Kelly Lang and Martie Singleton.

Hawkshaw Hawkins Jr.

Doug Supernaw

Jody Miller

TUESDAY - R.O.P.E. LUNCHEON

Bobby Marquez, Rex Allen Jr. and Tim Atwood strike their "Riders in the Sky Cowboy Way" pose!

Mandy Barnett

WEDNESDAY - FAN CLUB PARTIES
CHARLIE DANIELS & MOORE & MOORE

Above: Charlie Daniels held his Fan Club Party in Mt. Juliet, TN.

Right: Debbie Moore, Barbra Fairchild, Julie Keech-Harris Dianne Sherrill, Carrie Moore at the Moore & Moore Fan Club Party at Nashville Palace

Thanks to photographers, Jerry Overcast, Lynn Woodruff Gray, James Pillow and Paul H. Rubin

July 2017

CMA Week (otherwise known as Fan Fair!)

THURSDAY - NEXT GENERATION: SONS & DAUGHTERS OF COUNTRY LEGENDS

Pictured are Donnie Winters, Leona Williams, Jennifer, Marvis & Terry Husky, Hawkshaw Hawkins Jr., Michael Twitty, Chrystie Wooly, Kathy Louvin, Lorrie Davis Bennett (Carter), Sharon Wilburn, Corey & Ryman Frizzell, Aubry & Johnny Rodriguez, Karen Wheeler, Melissa Luman and many other Next Generationers as well as the band The Loaded Dogs.

George Hamilton V

Donnie Winters

Leona Williams joined her son Ron on stage for a song.

Melissa Luman and Hawkshaw Hawkins Jr. presented Gus Arrandale with a special thanks.

Sharon Wilburn & Mom

Julie & Jennifer Husky with emcee Jennifer Herron (center)

Signing autographs after the show: Dean Miller, Karen Wheeler, Sharon Wilburn, Terry Husky & Lorrie Davis (Carter).

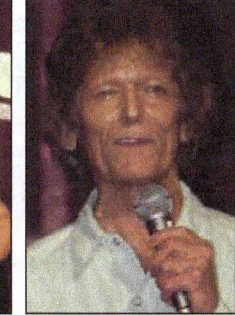

Karen Wheeler

Aubry Rodriguez   and dad,   Johnny Rodriguez

SATURDAY - COUNTRY WITH HEART

Clockwise from left: Bobby Marquez, Ryman Frizzell, David Frizzell and Cheris Lee

SUNDAY - LEGENDS OF COUNTRY

Clockwise from above: Ronnie McDowell, Barbara Fairchild with the Tennessee River Boys and Chris Golden with Jennifer Herron

July 2017

137 CFR NEWS

AUGUST

Life is a cabaret for Ray Stevens, come to his CabaRay in Nashville

Ray Stevens showing the plans for his new CabaRay theatre.

Bellevue's first major entertainment venue expected to open in October

By Tom Wood

Nashville has never seen anything quite like the Ray Stevens CabaRay Showroom that is launching in Music City this fall. That's the promise from the two-time Grammy Award winner, who has been entertaining fans in Nashville for 55 years and counting.

"It's something I've wanted to do for a long time," Stevens, 78, said in a

recent interview. "I've just always loved what I do. I love this business, I love the music business, I love recording and I've been here since 1962 I came up (from Georgia) to be a musician on recording sessions and I've been on a lot of them. And I always enjoyed it. Nashville has always been a good place for me."

His visionary Ray Stevens Cabaray Showroom — a 27,000 square foot, 700-seat, Las Vegas-style entertainment complex that can be used for television tapings and live streaming — will be the crowning achievement of a multi-platform career that has seen him excel as singer, songwriter, producer and a businessman.

When Stevens isn't on the stage — plans call for him to entertain fans three nights a week (Thursday-Saturday and possibly Sundays) — the mammoth facility will serve as production studio for his Ray Stevens CabaRay Nashville television show on Public Broadcasting System stations across the country — and possibly serve as home to other entertainment shows and productions.

"This is sort of the crowning jewel in his career, you know? This is just something he's wanted to do and he was like, 'If not now, when?' " said songwriter Buddy Kalb, Stevens' longtime collaborator and writer of the CabaRay Nashville TV show (tapings which fans will be able to attend).

The show is a light-hearted, nostalgic mash-up of Stevens' music and comedy along mixed in with interviews and performances by big-name Music City guests. His season one guests included the likes of Steve Wariner, Larry Gatlin, Bobby Bare, Tanya Tucker and Don Schlitz, among others.

"Ray's ability to cross — more than anybody else — generational and musical boundaries is what makes the show work so well," said CabaRay Nashville announcer Bill Cody, who is better known as WSM Radio's Disc Jockey Hall of Fame morning personality. "Ray has known and worked with a variety of artists in a career in that spans decades. And he brings that to the show."

August 2017

Indeed, those decades have been quite a ride for Stevens. He has sold millions of records, tapes, books, CDs and music videos over the decades— notably his signature "Everything Is Beautiful" and "Misty" (the two Grammy winners) as well as a string of comedic hits such as "Gitarzan" and "Ahab The Arab."

He also opened a similar concept theater in Branson, Mo., in the late 1990s, but says this new Nashville venture is a "more personal" project. "I'm more hands-on with this than I was at the Branson theater … but this is different. More personal, I guess. It's smaller and more intimate and something I want to do for a long time," Stevens said. "I'm not going to be having any fun when I'm pushing up daisies, so … But truthfully, the main reason I'm doing this is for fun," Stevens joked. Don't worry about Ray "pushing up daisies" anytime soon. He's fit as a fiddle — or fiddle player — and looks like he has many years of entertaining ahead of him. "I don't know. I mean, I'm 78. I could drop dead tomorrow. I don't think I will. I hope I don't. But we'll see."

And he hopes to see you at the Ray Stevens CabaRay Showroom when it opens (hopefully) in October 2017.

Ray Stevens CabaRay Showroom

What is it? A 27,000-square-foot "Las Vegas-style" dinner theater

Address: 5724 River Road, just off Charlotte Pike and I-40, exit 201 in west Nashville

Opens: Likely in October 2017, exact date TBA

Features: A 720-seat showroom for live performances, including 213 seats in the balcony

• Full-service kitchen with a choice of four catered meals available for guests on the floor and lower level

• A state-of-the-art recording studio

• Video production area to tape his TV show CabaRay Nashville, music videos, DVDs, etc., and livestream other events

• Bose sound system will ensure quality throughout the Showroom

• A full bar area

• Gift and memorabilia shop

• Lobby area will include art work by entertainer Bobby Goldsboro

• Ticket office plus offices and headquarters for Stevens' various business operations

• Plenty of parking for both cars and tour buses

Schedule: Ray Stevens will perform Thursday-Saturday evenings; a gospel matinee is likely for Sunday performances; it will be available to other artists Monday-Wednesday nights

Ticket prices: To be announced; lower level seating will include full dinner service; balcony seating will be for the show only, with refreshments available for purchase.

Information: Go to www.raystevens.com and Ray Stevens CabaRay on Facebook; no telephone number yet.

August 4 & 6

August
11 & 13, 18 & 20 and 25 & 27
Fridays…7 p.m. central
Saturdays…11 p.m central

August 2017

Nadine
The Church Lady

*Lord, give me a sense of humor,
Give me the grace to see a joke,
To get some humor out of life,
And to pass it on to other folk.*

When the kids were little we went out west and took one of them helicopter rides to see the sights. While they were up there, the engine lost power and they did an emergency landing in the water. The pilot told them to remain seated and keep the doors closed because the helicopter was designed to stay afloat for 30 minutes, giving the rescuers time to get to them.

Homer just couldn't stand it and got up and ran over and was trying to open the door.

I screamed at him and said, "Didn't you hear what the pilot said?" and Homer hollered back and said, "Yeah, I heard him, but this thing is designed to fly and look how good THAT worked out!!"

Here's what I'm putting on the church sign this week:

Stop letting people who do so little for you control so much of your mind, feelings and emotions.

AUGUST BIRTHDAYS

- 5 - Mark O'Connor
- 5 - Terri Clark
- 5 - Bobby Braddock
- 7 - Rodney Crowell
- 8 - Mark Wills
- 8 - Mel Tillis
- 11 - John Conlee
- 14 - Connie Smith
- 16 - Billy Joe Shaver
- 19 - Clay Walker
- 19 - Donnie Winters
- 19 - Lee Ann Womack
- 19 - Eddy Raven
- 20 - Rudy Gatlin
- 21 - Harold Reid
- 21 - Kenny Rogers
- 22 - Collin Raye
- 23 - Woody Paul
- 25 - Jo Dee Messina
- 25 - Billy Ray Cyrus
- 25 - Henry Paul
- 27 - Jeff Cook
- 28 - Lee Ann Rimes
- 28 - Shania Twain
- 29 - Don Schlitz

NOTICE
ALL CFR NEWS SUBSCRIBERS

We are pleased to announce all subscribers will be placed on auto renew if you have a credit card or debit card on file. We have been flooded with calls from customers who do not want their newspaper subscription to lapse but forget or do not know when to renew.

SO... we are making it easy. Your renewal month will not change. If you prefer to pay your renewal by check this will not apply to you.

If you do not want to be placed on auto renewal, we need to hear from you by Jan 1st.

1-800-820-5435

Jeannie Kendall is touring with a new show!

Jeannie Kendall is back at Carl Acuff Jr. & his stellar Band open the show with their own variety of music and comedy. Carl has had 5 Independent Country Hits in the US and abroad and been nominated for and won many prestigious awards like his 2003 Grammy Submission, 2011 ORAE Entertainer of the Year and 2011 ORAE Male Vocalist of the Year. The Carl Acuff Jr. show has been entertaining audiences in 47 of the continental United States since 1992 and the show is a high energy variety of music, comedy, audience participation and impersonations sure to have your audience on their feet.

The Second Half is the lovely and talented Ms. Jeannie Kendall of "The Kendall's" whose hits include "Thank God For The Radio" and "Heaven's Just A Sin Away". Jeannie is the ultimate entertainer and makes any audience feel at home the minute she hits the stage. Jeannie will take you through the course of her career with all of your favorite Kendall's hits and tunes that she's recorded with other Country Music Artists like her duet with Alan Jackson "Timeless and True Love". You can bring kids of all ages to this show and have a night of clean fun entertainment that your crowd will be talking about for years to come!

August 5, 2017 - Twin Rivers CB Jamboree Addison, NY 607-962-7563

October 14, 2017 - Ohnward Fine Arts Center Maquoketa, IA 563-652-9815

August 2017

T.G. Sheppard extends summer tour dates

T.G. Sheppard added additional dates to his blockbuster "Party Time Tour." The 21-time chart topper is hitting the road in celebration of the 35th anniversary of "Party Time," the song which topped the Billboard Hot Country Songs survey. Audiences will be taken on a walk down memory lane, with a combination of singalong ballads and upbeat tracks.

Rolling Stone Country agrees, while recapping Sheppard's recent "nostalgic" performance at CMA Music Festival as one of the "26 Best

Things We Saw."

"I'm excited to say that this is one of my most successful tours in years," said Sheppard. "It's great to look out and see crowds of all ages who are coming back and gravitating to classic country music of my era." In addition to "Party Time," the country trendsetter will perform a set list full of No. 1 hits. Standards like "I Loved 'Em Every One," "Do You Wanna Go the Heaven" and "Last Cheater's Waltz" will remind fans of the music that they once fell in love with, while creating new ones along the way. In an effort to show that traditional country music is back and more popular than ever, Sheppard will bring a lively, energetic show that will have all of the fans on their feet.

Sheppard's "Party Time Tour" includes stops throughout the United States, along with dates in Canada. One highlight this summer is Sheppard's return home to Memphis for a show with songstress Kelly Lang. The dynamic pair will perform at The Guest House at Graceland Theater on July 1, presented by Springer Mountain Farms®.

Sheppard was a close personal friend of Elvis, with the "Jailhouse Rock" singer gifting Sheppard his first tour bus in 1976 as a token of their friendship.

Additional dates for the "Party Time Tour" will be added weekly at tgsheppard.com.

"Party Time Tour" Dates:

June 23 Pigeon Forge, Tenn. - Country Tonite Theater

June 25 Jefferson, Iowa - Wild Rose Casino

July 1 Memphis, Tenn. - Graceland

July 5 Branson, Mo. – American Bandstand Theater

July 7 Danbury, Wisc. - St. Croix Casino

July 8 Brainerd, Minn. - Iconic Fest

July 9 Menomonie, Wisc. – Mabel Tainter Theater

July 13 Rhinelander, Wisc. – Hodag Festival

July 15 Colby, Kan. - KXXX Radio Show

July 17 Grand Rapids, Mich. - Private

July 20 Jackpot, Nev. - Cactus Pete's Casino

July 21 Jackpot, Nev. - Cactus Pete's Casino

Aug. 10 The Woodlands, Texas - Dosey Doe

Aug. 11 Victoria, Texas - The Welder Center

Aug. 12 Carthage, Texas - TX Country Music Hall of Fame

Aug. 17-23 London, England/ Paris, France

Aug. 25 Watertown, S.D. – Dakota Sioux Casino

Aug. 27 Sauk Rapids, Minn. – Rollies

Sept. 06 Nashville, Tenn. – Charity Concert

Sept. 9 Marmora, ON – Marmora Jamboree

Sept. 10 Spencerville, ON - Spencerville Fair

Sept. 15 Russellville, Ark. – Pope County Fair

Sept. 16 Arlington, Texas Arlington Music Hall

Sept. 23 Weirsdale, Fla. – Orange Blossom Opry

Sept. 30 Red Rock, Okla. - 7 Clans Paradise Casino

Oct. 12 Memphis, Tenn. - Private

Oct. 28 Baytown, Texas - The Chute

Nov. 4 Granbury, Texas – Granbury Live

August 2017

Bobby Bare celebrated as one of '100 Greatest Country Artists Of All Time' by Rolling Stone

Influencers and critics agree, "Bobby Bare's Outlaw Spirit Remains Undiminished" (Tim Ghianni, CMT.com) with the release of his newest album, Things Change. This past weekend saw a Bare takeover on Sirius XM with a subscriber-special airing numerous times on both Willie's Roadhouse and Outlaw Country featuring performances by the legend and hosted by the Country Music Hall of Fame's Peter Cooper from the SiriusXM Music City Theatre. Streaming giant Spotify added album cut "Ain't No Sure Thing" to the popular New Traditions - Country Heroes playlist. Fans can hear the new music and add it to their own playlists on Bare's Spotify page.

Rolling Stone honored Bobby Bare as one of the '100 Greatest Country Artists of All Time' recently. The Country Music Hall of Famer and GRAMMY® winner was ranked number 43 on the list which also included many friends and collaborators including Waylon Jennings and Willie Nelson.

Things Change features 10 tracks written by Bare and a slew of talented songwriters including Hoyt Axton, Mary Gauthier, Guy Clark and the producer of the project, hit singer/songwriter Max T. Barnes. The album features a collaboration on Bare's iconic hit, "Detroit City," with Chris Stapleton. The song was written by Mel Tillis and Danny Dill and originally released by Bare in 1963 highly requested songs at live shows to this day. "Detroit City" won a GRAMMY® in 1964 for Best Country/Western Recording and is one of many Grammy nods for the country legend. Things Change can be purchased at digital retailers and on BobbyBare.com.

"In a career that has been marked with recordings from writers such as the afore-mentioned [Tom T.] Hall, Mel Tillis ('Detroit City') and the late Shel Silverstein ('Marie Laveau,' among many from the late tunesmith), Bare has always had a knack for finding a great song." - Chuck Dauphin, Billboard Magazine

"Bobby Bare has been one of country music's most consistent - and most respected - singer/songwriters for over 50 years." - Adrian Peel, Digital Journal

Country Music Hall of Famer, Bobby Bare is one of the most iconic country artists of our time, with chart-topping songs like "Detroit City," "500 Miles," "Shame On Me" and many more. Artists from Little Jimmy Dickens and Hank Williams to big band acts like Phil Harris and the Dominoes all influenced his unique style leading to nearly five dozen top 40 hits from 1962 to 1983. The often referred to "Bruce Springsteen of Country" went on to earn multiple Grammy nominations and wins along with induction into the Country Music Hall of Fame in 2013 among many other awards and accolades. In 2017, Rolling Stone named him one of the 100 Greatest Country Artists of All Time.

Look who's on the Diner this week!
On RFD-TV
All shows subject to change

CRAIG CAMPBELL
Thursday, Aug. 3
7 p.m. Central
Saturday, Aug. 5
10 p.m. Central
PREVIOUSLY AIRED

DEAN MILLER
Thursday, Aug. 10
7 p.m. Central
Saturday, Aug. 12
10 p.m. Central
PREVIOUSLY AIRED

THE STEELDRIVERS
Thursday, Aug. 17
7 p.m. Central
Saturday, Aug. 19
10 p.m. Central
PREVIOUSLY AIRED

BAILLIE & THE BOYS
Thursday, Aug. 24
7 p.m. Central
Saturday, Aug. 26
10 p.m. Central
PREVIOUSLY AIRED

VINCE GILL & PAUL FRANKLIN
Thursday, Aug. 31
7 p.m. Central
Saturday, Sept. 2
10 p.m. Central
PREVIOUSLY AIRED

August 2017

Crystal Gayle celebrates 40th anniversary of song

Rarely do first takes on a song become the master tracks for an artist, but that's how chart-topping history began for Crystal Gayle's "Don't It Make My Brown Eyes Blue." Now, four decades later, Gayle's signature hit marks its 40th anniversary since its release on June 24, 1977.

"I did not re-sing it. It just fell into place beginning with Pig Robbins' opening work on the piano. It was magic in the studio that day," Gayle said with a smile. "Don't It Make My Brown Eyes Blue" opened the world's eyes to Gayle. The crossover smash earned her a Grammy® Award for Best Female Country Vocal Performance and also made her album We Must Believe In Magic the first by a female country artist to go platinum.

She was awarded CMA Female Vocalist of the Year in 1977 and 1978, and the Academy of Country Music honored her with the same award in 1976, 1977 and 1979.

"It opened up so many doors that I couldn't do everything that was offered for me to do. I was offered so many television specials. I hated turning anything down. It was only me, and I couldn't do it all. To be in California one night, and they would want you the next night in New York -- I couldn't do that constantly. But I did as much as I could," she told Billboard in 2014.

"Don't It Make My Brown Eyes Blue," became an iconic staple and solidified her as one of the top female vocalists during the 1970s and 1980s. Gayle is currently putting the finishing touches on a new album that will include some of her favorite classic country songs of all time.

Follow Crystal Gayle on Twitter and Facebook or visit crystalgayle.com.

CRYSTAL GAYLE ON TOUR:

Aug. 5 Spencer Theater – Alto, N.M.
Aug. 31 Oxford Performing Arts Center – Oxford, Ala.
Sept. 2 Loretta Lynn Ranch – Hurricane Mills, Tenn
Sept. 8 Tulalip Resort Casino – Maryville, Wash.
Sept. 22 Cactus Pete's – Jackpot, Nev.
Sept. 23 Cactus Pete's – Jackpot, Nev.
Sept. 29 South Point Hotel & Casino – Las Vegas, Nev.
Sept. 30 South Point Hotel & Casino – Las Vegas, Nev.
Oct. 1 South Point Hotel & Casino – Las Vegas, Nev.
Oct. 11 Northern Quest Resort & Casino – Airway Heights, Wash.
Oct. 13 Fort Hall Casino – Fort Hall, Idaho
Oct. 20 Dosey Doe – The Woodlands, Texas

Loretta Lynn postpones new album; recovering at home

Country music legend Loretta Lynn has postponed her album and canceled her tour after suffering a stroke earlier this year. Lynn, 85, has been advised by her doctors to stay home while she is recuperating.

The star was originally supposed to release her new album in August. She says she will release it next year instead.

The singer released this statement on her website:

Thank you so much for all of your prayers, love, and support. I'm happy to say that I'm at home with my family and getting better by the day! My main focus now is making a full recovery so that I can get back to putting all of me into what I love, sharing my music with all of you. My new album, Wouldn't It Be Great, was originally scheduled to come in August this year. I now want to wait to release it next year because this record is so special for me. It deserves me at my best and I can't wait to share it. I want to thank everyone for hanging in there with me. I am getting stronger every day and can't wait to get back out there with all of you. I'm just letting everybody know that Willie ain't dead yet and neither am I, and I can't wait to see all of you on the road!"

August 2017

COUNTRY LEGENDS OF THE PAST & PRESENT
BY TOM WOOD

Leroy Van Dyke

We moved to Nashville for the first time in 1960, and I can remember riding in the back seat of our blue-and-white Ford Fairlane, listening to my dad singing along with the radio.

I've laid around and played around this old town too long Summer's almost gone, yes winter's coming on I've laid around and played around this old town too long. And I feel like I gotta travel on.

Those lyrics by David Lazar, Larry Ehrlich, Paul Clayton and Tom Six didn't make much sense to a five-year-old, but I remember liking the booming, melodic country voice that my dad tried his best to imitate.

The voice belonged to Billy Grammer, and his 1959 version of "Gotta Travel On" sold more than a million singles and peaked at No. 5 on the U.S. country charts and No. 4 on pop charts.

That signature hit earned the Illinois native an invite to join the Grand Ole Opry. He also had seven other songs in the Top 100, the highest among those being "I Wanna Go Home" (1963) at No. 18. You may recall that song as its better-known name "Detroit City" and made famous by Bobby Bare. His last hit was in 1969, but that was far from the greatness or highlight of his musical career.

Billy's off-stage accomplishments and presence at key events in history tell a remarkable story about both the man and his music.

The son of an accomplished musician (violin, trumpet), Billy achieved far greater fame than his father or 12 siblings ever imagined. The young Grammer learned to play the guitar with such proficiency that he founded his own acoustic guitar company.

The Grammer Guitar quickly became the go-to guitar for many country stars and earned a place in the Country Music Hall of Fame in 1969. Grammer owned the company from 1965-68, then sold it after a fire destroyed the factory. The new owner stopped making Grammer Guitars in 1970, and they are considered collector's items today, selling for thousands.

Billy's most famous song "Gotta Travel On" provided the base-name for his band, the Travel On Boys. It was recorded by numerous artists, including Buddy Holley, who opened his 1959 shows with the song until his death in a plane crash that February.

On May 15, 1972, Billy and the band were performing at a George Wallace rally in Maryland when the Alabama governor was running for president. Following Wallace's speech, he was shot and paralyzed by Arthur Bremmer in an attack that stunned the nation. Billy wept that day.

Other career highlights for Billy include delivering the invocation at the glittering opening of the Grand Ole Opry House on March 16, 1974, and his 1990 induction into the Illinois Country Music Hall of Fame. Others honorees that day were Tex Williams, Patsy Montana and Lulu Belle and Scotty.

Finally, in 2009 the Grand Ole Opry paid tribute to Billy for recognition of his 50 years of membership in the world's most exclusive country club, where only the cream of the crop of artists are invited to join.

Billy — who had gone blind from a degenerative eye disease — died two years later on Aug. 10, 2011, just 18 days before what would have been his 86th birthday. He suffered a heart attack seven months prior to his death.

Sources: Wikipedia, www.grammer guitar.net

Author Tom Wood, who writes thrillers and Westerns, is a regular contributor to Country Family Reunion News. Reach him at tomwoodauthor.com

It's A Family Tradition

By Claudia Johnson

Aubry Rodriguez: Ambition and Talent Keeps Legacy Alive

There's a stunning young performer singing her heart out around St. Louis this summer in anticipation of heading back to Nashville to pursue her future. Her name's Aubry Rodriguez and, yes, she is the daughter of THAT Rodriguez – Johnny, of course – making her Country Music aristocracy.

However, at 19 Aubrey is not a woman to rest on anyone else's laurels, not even a dad who's charted 45 singles, taking 15 to the top 10 and six to No. 1 in his 40-plus years as an entertainer. But, that's not to say Aubrey is not aware of her father's place in country music history.

"I am so incredibly blessed to be around the people he knows and have him to open doors for me," she said appreciatively.

Since Aubrey knows how to walk through those doors, she began performing with her father's band around four years ago, giving her valuable professional experience and enabling her, she said, to see first-hand "the impact he's had on so many people."

"I've always been conscious of it, and it makes me just tear up sometimes," she confessed.

Born in 1998 in San Marcos, Texas, Aubrey is Johnny's only child. Her parents divorced when she was small, and she and her mother, Debbie, subsequently moved to Missouri to be near and care for her material grandparents, both of whom she's recently lost. After completing her first year as a Belmont University student in Nashville, she returned to

Missouri this summer to a jampacked schedule of performing solo at small venues and clubs.

"I do three-hour sets," she explained, saying that she performs "mostly covers with some original songs." Yep. She's a songwriter, too.

"Music just came naturally to me," she said, noting that from her childhood she's saved "random little notepads of songs I wrote." She said she was making up tunes as early as four and has continued to write throughout her life. "Sometimes I can write a song in five minutes, and then sometimes I may write a little melody or a few lyrics, and it may take weeks for it to come together," she said.

Songwriting talent, 12-years of piano lessons and mastery of the guitar combined with a powerful voice and a strong work ethic have enabled her to remain employed as an entertainer to support her dream of becoming a music entertainment attorney. That's why she's majoring in both Music and Music Business at Belmont, a college known internationally for its music education offerings, which Aubry praised for creating an environment for people with her aspirations and background. Since there are other students there from comparable backgrounds, Aubry said it's not unusual to meet children or grandchildren of renowned performers.

Some people recognize her name, but it makes little difference as she studies and works toward achieving her goals – and doing it as independently as she can.

"I have dreamed of attending Belmont since my freshman year of high school and feel right at

August 2017

home on campus," she wrote in her GoFundMe.com campaign narrative last fall when she asked for public help in raising funds for college, adding, humbly, "I would be thankful for any amount of donation and am extremely grateful for all the love and support :)."

What she did not state in her backstory is that she's Johnny's daughter. That same independent spirit has her performing solo around Nashville during the academic year, and she's been on the lineup at numerous Nashville venues, including The George Jones and Manuel American Designs. Earlier this year her name was right there along with last names like Twitty, Miller, Hamilton, Hawkins, Carter, Reed and more at the 2017 Next Generation, Sons and Daughters of Country Legends at the Nashville Palace.

Aubry envisions a career in which she's not only an attorney but also a successful performer, confessing that she hopes to someday "sell out Madison Square Garden." She's under no delusion that it will be easy, regardless of her last name. "You have to be a good advocate for yourself and be assertive," she observed. Testimony to her belief in taking control of ones destiny is her Facebook page, www.facebook.com/AubryRMusic, which lists her upcoming schedule for dozens of solo gigs and provides links to her music, including a stirring original called "Pray."

Aubry is taking her legacy and translating it into a future where she writes her own history in the annals of Country music.

About Aubry's Dad...

By Sasha Dunavant

Recording 15 Top 10 and six No. 1 hits, including "You Always Come Back (To Hurting Me)," "That's the Way Love Goes" and ""I Just Can't Get Her Out of My Mind," Johnny Rodriquez is by far County Music's most successful recording artist of Hispanic descent. Discovered by Tom T. Hall and Bobby Bare while singing at a Texas attraction, Rodriguez moved to Nashville in 1971 where he soon began recording and writing songs.

His debut album, "Introducing Johnny Rodriguez," went to #1 on all three major trade charts and by 1973, he was nominated by the Country Music Association for "Male Vocalist of the Year" and won the Billboard Trend Setter Award for first Mexican-American to capture a national audience.

Since 1974, when Rodriguez had his first TV appearances, a role on "Adam 12" and a contestant on "The Dating Game" among them, he has been a favorite on national talk shows and performance format shows. In the past 40 years, Johnny has released 35 albums and charted 45 singles.

He has beat the pavement touring in every state in the U.S. and enjoys an enormous response when touring overseas.

Rodriguez has been honored for his contributions and place in music's traditions and history. This artist brings the Hispanic communities and Country Music together with his bilingual songs. Rodriguez was inducted into the Texas Country Music Hall of Fame in Carthage, Texas in 2007 for his contribution to Country Music. In 2010, Rodriguez received the Pioneer Award from the Institute of Hispanic Culture.

Aubry and Johnny performing at the Next Generation: Sons & Daughters of Country Legends show held each June in Nashville.

August 2017

Madame Tussauds is now open in Nashville

Madame Tussauds, the world-famous wax attraction, is now open at Opry Mills in Nashville! This is Madame Tussauds' first music themed attraction and the only location in Tennessee. This group & family-friendly attraction will provide an interactive experience, where you will be able to touch, see, feel and photograph the figures.

Step into immersive iconic scenes and musical performances that are unique to Madame Tussauds Nashville. Take a musical journey from past to present, in this one-of-a-kind, music themed Madame Tussauds.

Celebrate your favorite country, rock, jazz, and blues artists in brilliantly themed interactive settings and some of those 50 figures are brand-new creations for Nashville.

Tickets are $19 in advance ($24 day of visit) for ages 13+, and $14 in advance ($19 day of visit) for ages 3-12. For more information visit

www.madametussauds.com/nashville.

STORE HOURS

Monday to Saturday 10AM–9PM

Sunday 11AM–7PM

BEST ENTRANCE

Entry 5 near Romano's Macaroni Grill

LOCATION IN MALL

Located right next to the entrance

across from Macaroni Grill

PHONE

(866) 841-3263

Hank Williams, Patsy Cline and Johnny Cash strike a pose!

Minnie Pearl's wax figure is joined by her great niece Barbara Sanders, great-great niece Sarah Steinlein and great great great niece Sarah Grace Steinlein.

Brad Paisley (the real one) takes the stage with Little Jimmy Dickens.

August 2017

Texas native Mark Chesnutt 2017 tour schedule

A native of Beaumont, Texas, traditional-minded country singer Mark Chesnutt began his run up the charts in 1990 with "Too Cold At Home," and followed that initial hit up with blockbuster 90s favorites such as "Brother Jukebox," "I'll Think Of Something," "Gonna Get A Life" and "I Don't Want To Miss A Thing." Along the way, he has earned one Gold album and four Platinum albums. He has been nominated for several industry awards, and has a couple CMA trophies to his credit – including the 1993 Vocal Event of the Year prize for "I Don't Need Your Rockin' Chair," a hit for The Possum, George Jones. Chesnutt continues to be a touring favorite, with close to 175 dates on his calendar – which is booked throughout the remainder of 2017.

Increasing the excitement of summer 2017, Chesnutt is crisscrossing the country on tour, bringing timeless hits and new music to his loyal fan base. In addition to shows in the states, his schedule includes stops in Canada and the U.K. Tickets and VIP passes are available at MarkChesnutt.com.

MARK CHESNUTT ON TOUR

June 30 Frontier Park - Hays, KS
July 2 Donna City Park - Donna, TX
July 7 Country Concert at Hickory Hills - Fort Loramie, OH
July 8 Lawless Harley Davidson - Scott City, MO
July 14 The Country Club-GA - Augusta, GA
July 15 Jamboree In The Hills - Morristown, OH
July 21 Northern Edge Navajo Casino - Fruitland, NM
July 22 Chaffee County Fair - Salida, CO
July 28 Billy Bob's Texas – Fort Worth, TeX
July 29 Delta Downs Racetrack Casino - Vinton, LA
Aug. 2 Yamhill County Fair - Mcminnville, OR
Aug. 4 Clearwater River Casino - Lewiston, ID
Aug. 9 Jackson County Fair - Jackson, MI
Aug. 11 Goodhue County Fair - Zumbrota, MN
Aug. 18 Havelock Country Jamboree - Ennismore, CAN
Aug. 26 Sangamon River Music Festival - Mahomet, IL
Sept. 3 Millport Country Music Festival - Millport, U.K.
Sept. 22 Cabarrus Arena - Concord, NC
Sept. 23 U.S. Cellular Center - Asheville, N.C
Sept. 24 Dorton Arena - Raleigh, NC
Sept. 30 Central Washington State Fair - Yakima, WA
Oct. 06 Medina Entertainment Center - Medina, MN
Oct. 07 Q & Z Expo Center - Ringle, WI
Oct. 14 Municipal Auditorium - Nashville, TN
Oct. 15 Showplace Music Hall - Memphis, TN
Oct. 20 Arlington Music Hall - Arlington, TX
Oct. 28 Coastal Carolina Fair - Ladson, SC
Nov. 8 Dick Clark's American Bandstand Theater - Branson, MO
Nov. 10 The Center for the Performing Arts- The Palladium - Carmel, IN
Nov. 11 Meyer Theatre - Green Bay, WI
Dec. 1 Memorial Auditorium - Chattanooga, TN
Dec. 2 Freedom Hall Civic Center - Johnson City, TN
Dec. 3 Knoxville Coliseum - Knoxville, TN
Dec. 8 Coach's & Cowboy's - Tyler, TX
Dec. 9 Dosey Doe - Conroe, TX

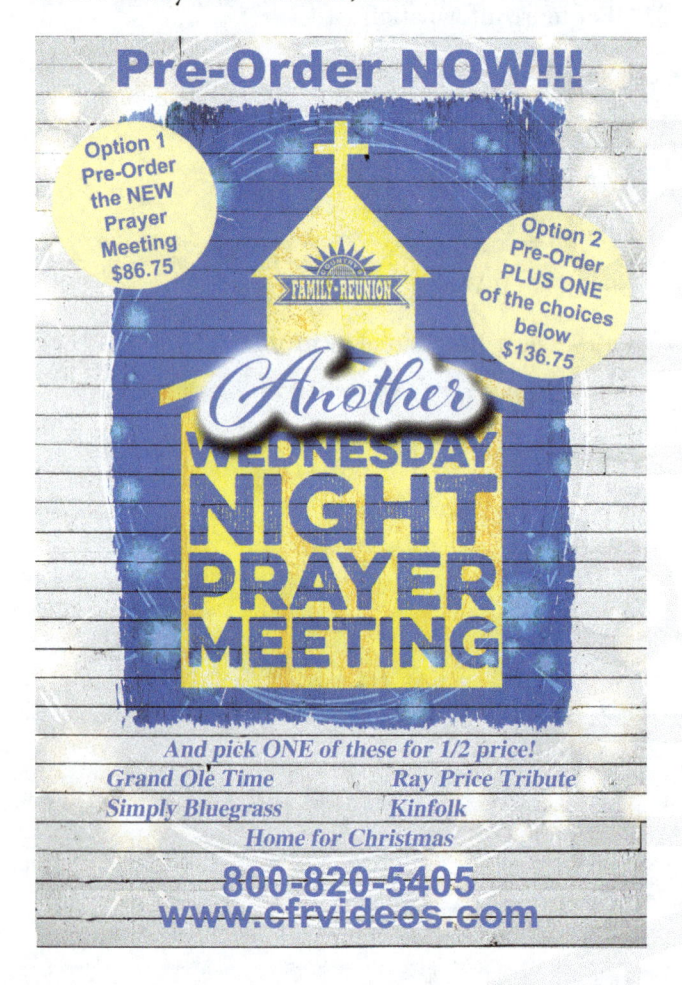

148 CFR NEWS

August 2017

Pride Accepts Grammy Lifetime Achievement Award

Country icon Charley Pride is back with his brand new album, Music In My Heart, which is available now. The project serves as Pride's first album in more than six years, and is released via Music City Records. The highly anticipated project features 13 new studio recordings that were produced by acclaimed singer/songwriter Billy Yates. Fans can purchase Music In My Heart on Amazon, iTunes and wherever music is sold.

Pride has continued to turn heads with the new collection. In addition to a recent feature by Billboard, Pride has been included in spotlight feature interviews with the Associated Press, Huffington Post, Goldmine Magazine and more. Media is raving, with Billboard saying "Charley Pride's vocals are just as soothing to the soul as a glass of Granny's tea and those pair of shoes that you always find yourself drawn to.....just like returning to the well."

The trailblazing singer celebrated street week by traveling to New York City to accept the Lifetime Achievement Award from The Recording Academy® at their 2017 Special Merit Awards. The awards ceremony and live tribute concert were held on Tuesday, July 11, at The Beacon Theatre, where Pride also performed.

While in the area, Pride also stopped by CBS Evening News, ABC News' 'Live From The Couch', Access Hollywood, Fox News Radio, SiriusXM, CNBC SquawkBox and more.

Pride also appeared at the Summer NAMM Show in Nashville July 15. The multi-Grammy® award winner performed songs from his brand new album, along with many of the 36 chart-topping hits that propelled him to superstardom and an induction into the Country Music Hall of Fame.

Music In My Heart Track Listing:

1. New Patches
2. Make Me One More Memory
3. Natural Feeling For You
4. All By My Lonesome
5. It Wasn't That Funny
6. The Same Eyes That Always Drove Me Crazy
7. I Learned A Lot
8. You're Still In These Crazy Arms Of Mine
9. The Way It Was In '51
10. I Just Can't Stop Missing You
11. You Lied To Me
12. Standing In My Way
13. Music In My Heart

Charley Pride On Tour:

Aug. 26 – Enniskillen Airport, Northern Ireland – Harvest Country Music Festival

Aug. 27 – Westport House, County Mayo, Ireland – Harvest Country Music Festival

Sept. 10 – Lancaster, Pa. – American Music Theatre

Sept. 22 – Arlington, Texas – Arlington Music Hall

Sept. 23 – Crockett, Texas – Crockett Civic Center

Sept. 29 – Branson, Mo. – The Welk Resort Theatre

Oct. 21 – Shipshewana, Ind. – Blue Gate Theater

Oct. 28 – Wendover, Nev. – Peppermill Concert Hall

Nov. 03-04 – Lincoln City, Ore. – Chinook Winds Casino

Nov. 11 – Mescalero, N.M. – Inn of the Mountain Gods

August 2017

Summer

Summer has kept me busy with a lot of family activities. As many of you know my son-in-law, Elliott, has been in the academy for the last 6 months training as a Trooper with the Tennessee Highway Patrol. He graduated on June 30th and is now home to begin a new chapter in his life. I have to tell you just seeing a police car in my driveway gives me the woolies !! Of course Larry and the guys here at the company think it's cool. Larry thinks he's going to get a pass now on his speeding!!!

Elliott was a very important part of our company and he is sorely missed, but I am very proud of the decision he made, even though I told him absolutely, positively "NO". lol.

Please remember him in your prayers.

Birthday

It's time for another BIRTHDAY...... where does the time go? Last year Rio wanted a Shopkins birthday party. This year she is FOUR and wants a swim party with Princess Sofia theme. I am not sure why she didn't pick a Mermaid theme but Princess it is. Rio just had her second dance recital and is now teaching Sedona dance moves!! Look for them both on the "Diner show soon.

DINER CHAT

Don't miss Diner Chat every THURSDAY at 2:00 Central Time. Jason, from customer service, is with me every week as we talk about what is happening in country music or what is just happening.

AND.....our guests these last few weeks have been awesome. Chicken Man himself, Gus, has joined us along with the legend Stonewall Jackson. Sharon Wilburn whose father is Doyle Wilburn of the Wilburn Brothers was my guest and country singer Shane Owens. If you don't like computers then this is a great way to stay in touch. Just call the number on your cell phone and listen in.

NEWS NEWS NEWS

Yes, I have some great news......Precious Memoires Memorial Book 2 will be ready by Christmas. AND you are going to love it !!!! Not only am I including the country music legends that were not in the first book like Jean Shepard, Patsy Cline and Merle Haggard BUT ALSO.....I am adding a special section on the stars of the old family TV shows that you loved. I have just visited over 150 graves sites in California of these wonderful TV shows like Bonanza, The Donna Reed Show, I Love Lucy, The Adventures of Ozzie & Harriet, Petticoat Junction, The Three Stooges, The Honeymooners, Mash, The Beverly Hillbillies, Andy Griffith Show, The Lone Ranger, and many more. It will also include the gravesites of Marilyn Monroe, Elizabeth Taylor, George and Gracie Burns, Spencer Tracy and more. So look for a pre-order offer for a signed copy.

NASHVILLE MEMORIAL TOURS

YES...Starting in the fall I will be hosting a 2-½ hour tour in Nashville. I will be taking you to 3 Nashville cemetery's include indoor mausoleums where we will visit over 30 of the country music legend's final resting places. The tour will begin at the Music Valley Drive location where you will take a 24-passenger bus in comfort that will include a guided tour and stops for photos. Look for more information about this exciting tour. www.NashvilleMemorialTours.com or call 615-673-2846 and ask for Renae. Price: $69.00

August 2017

Up-and-coming country artist Shane Owens making music

Up-and-coming country artist Shane Owens made his debut on the hallowed Grand Ole Opry stage on April 29 in Nashville, Tennessee.

Owens released his latest single, "All The Beer In Alabama," which he co-wrote with Dan Murph and Phillip Douglas. This tune is an alternative to the party songs that are played heavily on the modern country airwaves.

As Owens explains, country music is the way he lives every day and the way he was raised. "I know nothing else," says the artist, who grew up singing in church. Owens says his family, including his wife of 20 years, has always supported him. His kids have continued to push him to be the best artist that he can be. It was with their confidence that he persisted in pursuing a career in music, despite the many hurdles placed in his way.

One of those trials happened after he lost his prior record deal. Not sure he wanted to continue in music, Owens was slotted to play a concert in Alabama that Jones headlined. As it so happened, producer James Stroud was in the audience and loved what he heard. As Owens recalls, after the show Stroud approached him and asked if he wanted to cut a record. He reluctantly agreed and soon found himself working alongside Stroud and Randy Travis, who served as executive producer on the project. That album, Where I'm Comin' From, was released in December. Owens is of course grateful to have worked with the two legends.

Veteran country star Randy Travis praised Owens for his genuineness, humility and unblemished vocal ability.

His new CD is available on his website www.shaneowenscountry.com for $12 plus s/h.

Shane was recently on Larry's Country Diner where he surprised Gus by singing the Chicken Truck song and had everyone laughing!

August 2017

There's Something about that song

by Claudia Johnson

Editor's Note: In our new series, "Something About the Song," CFR News writers Claudia Johnson and Sasha Dunavant, a mother-daughter writing duo, will explore some of Country's most enduring – and endearing – songs. Selections for the series could be perennial crowd favorites, songs with groundbreaking subject matter, one-hit wonders, career defining recordings of major stars, songs that started a trend… you get it. They'll be chosen because they've made us stop and think, "Something about that song." Visit us on social media to let our writers know the songs that made a difference in your life. #somethingaboutthatsong

Harper Valley PTA: Timeless Appeal Over Four Decades

In the four decades since its release, a simple Country song about a small town widow has become an anthem for women who dare to confront society's moral standard bearers.

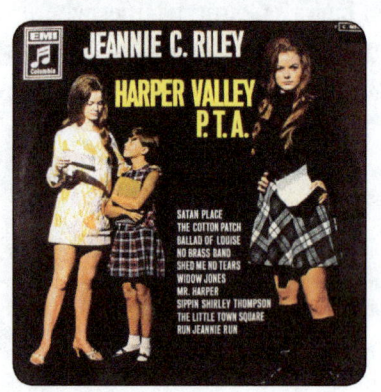

The theme and lyrics of Jeannie C. Riley's "Harper Valley PTA" not only captured popular culture of the era in which the song was written, they have become metaphors for hypocrisy and misogyny.

Who doesn't know the story? When the Harper Valley PTA issues a cowardly note suggesting that Mrs. Johnson is an unfit mother to a teenage daughter for reportedly "drinking, running 'round with men and going wild" and wearing her dresses "way too high," she shows up at the junior high clad in a miniskirt and wielding some unsavory truths about the PTA's note-issuing leaders who are assembled self-righteously at the PTA meeting.

One by one she exposes indiscretions, implying that Mr. Baker's secretary left town because of an unwanted pregnancy, that the widow Jones' is an exhibitionist and that Mrs. Taylor is a closet alcoholic because of her philandering husband, Bobby, who has prodded Mrs. Johnson herself to engage in adulterous behavior with him. Mr. Harper isn't even present because he's once again staying too long at Kelly's bar, and while Shirley Thompson is present, she's been drinking before attending the school function.

In six tightly written stanzas, songwriter Tom T. Hall creates the powerful visual of what must have been mortified hypocrites with their secrets as freshly hung out as a line full of linens flopping in the wind.

Listeners can see Mrs. Johnson walk to that blackboard for her moment of reckoning. Hall does not tell us why she is a widow, but given the fact that Mrs. Johnson's daughter is in junior high – the now defunct precursor to middle school – she quite possibly lost her husband in Vietnam as the United States was fully engaged in the war there by 1968. Mini-skirts and mini-dresses were introduced in 1964 and donned by models, celebrities and entertainers, but in a small town they would still have raised eyebrows in 1968.

When Mrs. Johnson tells them that Harper Valley is just another "Peyton Place," she was referring to a well-known book and movie that had become a television series in its fourth season when the song was released.

"Peyton Place" had already become a metaphor for the kind of moral duplicity Mrs. Johnson was experiencing. The song's storyteller is revealed when she calls the event "the day my mama socked it to the Harper Valley PTA." Sock-it-to-me was a catchphrase of the later '60s made popular by the comedy show, "Laugh In." Shirts, posters, bumper stickers and other items proclaimed "sock-it-to-me." Every mom had the recipe for a lemony Bundt cake called Sock-it-tome Cake, a favorite for reunions and funerals.

With a name inspired by the name of a real Nashville-area school, Harpeth Valley Elementary, Harper Valley is not a real place – but it could be anywhere, which explains its enduring appeal. A perennial karaoke favorite, the song was first offered to songstress Skeeter Davis, who rejected it, but when it was recorded by artists Billie Jo Spears and Margie Singleton, Plantation records rushed to release the Riley version.

The single achieved the 1960s highest climb into the charts, jumping in its second week from No. 81 to No. 7 on the U.S. Billboard Hot 100. It reached No. 12 in the United Kingdom, No. 4 on the U.S. easy listening chart and No.1 on both the country and

August 2017

pop charts in Canada and No. 1 in Australia. Selling more than six million records, Riley became the first woman to reach No.1 on U.S. pop and country charts simultaneously, holding that position until Dolly Parton's "9 to 5" in 1981.

Riley's recording netted her a Grammy award for best female country vocal performance and was nominated for Record of the Year and Song of the Year in the pop field. Country music singers like Loretta Lynn, Dolly Parton, Lynn Anderson, Jeannie Seely and Dottie West included the tune on their albums, and Billy Ray Cyrus was one of the few male performers to cover it. Melinda Schneider and Beccy Cole covered the song on their 2014 album Great Women of Country. As recently as 2015 the song was included by the British punk rock band Squeeze on their Cradle to the Gravealbum. Attesting further to the universal appeal of the message, the song has been translated and recorded in Sweden, Norway and Iceland.

Over the years the song has inspired other works. "Harper Valley P.T.A. (Later The Same Day)" was a parody written and recorded by comic country performer Sheb Wooley. The tune was used with new lyrics by Tammy Faye Bakker in a song she recorded in the 1980s to protest what she believed was unfair treatment she and her husband, Jim, endured resulting from ministry related scandals.

A 1981 single called "Return to Harper Valley" told from the viewpoint of Mrs. Johnson written by Hall and recorded by Riley failed to chart. Riley's 1980 autobiography and 1981 gospel album where called From Harper Valley to the Mountain Top.

The original song inspired a motion picture made in 1978 and a movie in 1981, both starring "I Dream of Jeannie" star Barbara Eden. Decades later the song returned to television when Martina McBride covered it for the "Desperate Housewives" soundtrack album. It was also used in the award-winning AMC series, "Mad Men," in an episode called "A Tale of Two Cities" in Season 10.

Some forty years after its release, fans can still remember every word to "Harper Valley PTA," and on any given weekend, someone, somewhere is belting it out at karaoke. It's very likely that everyone listening identifies with Mrs. Johnson and not with the PTA, hoping they'd have the guts to sock it to someone when necessary.

Country Music Questions & Answers

Q: A wonderful article and pictires of Roni Stoneman in the July issue, but what is she doing now? Is she married, any children? What is Patsy Stoneman and the rest of the kids that were in the band doing?

Verlys Marquardt Markesan, WI

A: Roni is doing well and still tours. Last year she did a tour of Ireland. Her upcoming events are: Donna Stoneman (Queen of Mandolin) will join Roni at specific events. These will be listed as and when. Events will be annotated with a *Sep.23 2017 - GalaxRexfest* 5 pm/113 East Grayson St. Galax VA Outdoor Street Event, (in the event of inclement weather Rex Theatre) Stevie Barr, Rexfest Sponser, Barrs Fiddle Shop, Galax, VA Oct. 7-8 2017 - Mineral Area Bluegrass Association RONI LIVE on stage Sat 7th? TBA - Leadwood, MO Bluegrass Festival John Hartley 573 218-8257 Oct. 13-14 2017 Hoedown on the Harpeth * - RONI LIVE on stage w. sister Donna – Sat 14th Old Time Music and Bluegrass Festival, Hayshed Farms, Kingston Springs, TN www.hoedownontheharpeth.com

Q: I would like to know if Kelly Lang's husband is T.G. Sheppard? And was Kelly's father Velton Lang who was Conway Twitty's road manager. I knew all Conway's band people. I was at Velton's home and met Kelly's mom.

Steve Strochoz, Nazareth, PA

A: Yes, Kelly and T. G. Sheppard were married in 2007. And, yes, Velton is Kelly's father and he did work for as Conway Twitty's road manager for 25 years. Velton died in 1998.

If you have questions send them to Paula, CFR News, P.O. Box 210796, Nashville, TN 37221 or email them to paula@gabrielcommunications.com.

August 2017

Salute to the KORNFiELD
Everything you always wanted to know about the cast
By Sasha Kay Dunavant

Misty Rowe, Diverse and Persevering

Mistella "Misty" Rowe is well known to Country Music fans for her 19-year stint on "Hee Haw." However, the stage, TV and film actress is also a singer, writer, producer and director who has never stopped working during the nearly five decades she's been in the entertainment industry.

Born on June 1, 1952, in Glendora, California, Rowe was discovered in her teens by veteran voice actor Noel Blank, who has continued to be a friend and project collaborator throughout her long career. In the ensuing years, she has guest starred in more than 200 television shows such as "The Dating Game," "Fantasy Island," and "The Love Boat" and had recurring roles in five TV series.

In addition to "Hee Haw" she was cast as Maid Marion in a Mel Brooks' series "When Things Were Rotten." She played a carhop named Windy on "Happy Days" and was a Country singer on "Airwolf." She continued her "Hee Haw" career playing a cheerful blonde in a sexy halter-top and Daisy Duke shorts on a 1978 "Hee Haw" spinoff show called "Hee Haw Honeys" with Kathie Lee Gifford, Lulu Roman and Kenny Price.

She's twice played Marilyn Monroe in film. "Misty Rowe plays one of Hollywood's most tragic sex symbols well enough to stand the comparison and sometimes looks almost her double," said Cosmopolitan magazine about her 1976 portrayal of Monroe in Goodbye, Norma Jean.

She portrayed Marilyn again in 1989 in the film Goodnight, Sweet Marilyn. Her other movies include The Hitchhikers in 1972, SST: Death Flight in 1977, Loose Shoes in 1980, The Man with Bogart's Face in 1980, National Lampoon's Class Reunion in 1982 and Meatballs Part 2 in 1984.

After appearing on numerous European magazine covers, she met Robin Leach of "Lifestyles of the Rich and Famous," who sent her to Canada to stay in a castle and later visited her on "Hee Haw" as a guest star.

One magazine pictorial proved lucrative and unforgettable for Rowe. Her friend and "Hee Haw" co-star, Barbi Benton, helped her land a Playboy magazine spread, which ran in the same 1976 issue with President Jimmy Carter's famous interview. A savvy businesswoman even at 23, Rowe asked for a female photographer, photo approval and double the normal fees, which she used to buy her second home. Rowe is lauded for her directing as well as her acting in stage productions.

After "Hee Haw," she began playing Louise in "Always … Patsy Cline." The performance garnered fantastic reviews, such as the one from Blowing Rock Stage Company in North Carolina, which raved, "Every single performance SOLD OUT! Not one, but multiple standing ovations. Our appreciation to Misty Rowe who is far more than a superb actress but also a very gifted and special director."

Some of the other classic plays in which she's appeared include "The Glass Menagerie," "Damn Yankees," "Pump Boys & Dinettes" and "Lil' Abner." Rowe says one of her favorite memories was starring with former football player Joe Namath in "Lil' Abner" on a national tour. The shorts she wore as Daisy Mae in the production she also wore on a poster that would sell more than a million copies.

In addition to directing 20 stage productions, at age 63, the energetic Rowe looks back over an impressive

August 2017

list of projects she's created or produced. She's written and starred in an autobiographical musical review "Blondes STILL Have More Fun." Another original, "Misty Christmas, Finally a Fruitcake You'll Like," made its debut in Atlantic City. In 2012 Rowe released a DVD "Misty's Magical Mountain Top" that encourages children to use their imagination.

2014's "Forever Doo Wop" was an eight-person cabaret at the Riviera's Le Bistro Lounge in Las Vegas. Rowe's comedic work has been performed in countless clubs, including some of New York's most coveted comedy venues. Using her sense of humor, natural beauty and determination, Rowe has overcome obstacles like an embarrassing childhood lisp and the loss of her first daughter with former husband, actor James DePaiva. Rowe has a grown daughter, Dreama, with DePaiva and is now happily married to producer Barry Singer.

Perhaps Mike Scott of Entertainment Spotlight summed up Rowe's talent when he reviewd her autobiographical dark comedy, "Just Another Blond." "Blond and beautiful Misty Rowe transcends the setting of the entertainment industry and shows us a profile of despair, courage and eventual star and the playwrite."

August 2017

Singer Songwriters
By Sasha Kay Dunavant

Mary Chapin Carpenter: Hall of FameSongwriter, Unlikely Country Star

The singer-songwriter whose background seemed unlikely to produce a Grammy Award-winning artist may well be Mary Chapin Carpenter.

Born in Princeton, New Jersey, she lived in Japan as a youth, attended some of New Jersey's most exclusive private prep schools and graduated from one of the country's most prestigious New England colleges.

Carpenter began writing songs and playing guitar and piano still in high school. After graduating from Brown University with a degree in American Civilization in 1981, she began performing around Washington D.C. where she met producer, John Jennings, who persuaded her to collaborate with him.

This collaboration resulted in the 1987 release of "Hometown Girl," an album with many of the tracks written by Carpenter, such as "A Lot Like Me," "Family Hands," "Just Because" and "Waltz." Carpenter and Jennings co-wrote the sixth track on the 1987 album called "A Road Is Just A Road." Though it produced no singles, it established Carpenter as a singer-songwriter.

In 1989 she released her album, "State of the Heart" with two of the album's four singles that made it to the Country charts, "How Do" at No. and "Something of a Dreamer" at No. 16, written by Carpenter. "Never Had It So Good," a No. 8 Country single, was co-written with Jennings.

Further commercial success came with Carpenter's third album, "Shooting Straight in the Dark." The album reached No. 11 on Billboard's Country Albums chart. Carpenter's composition "Down at the Twist and Shout" peaked at No. 2 and nabbed her an invitation to perform it at Super Bowl XXXI. The song won Carpenter a Grammy for Best Female Country Vocal Performance in 1992. For the album Carpenter also wrote "You Win Again" and co-wrote with Jennings "Going Out Tonight," both making it to the Top 20.

It was 1992's "Come On Come On" album that carved Carpenter's mark into Country songwriting history. Climbing to No. 6 on Billboard's Country Albums chart, seven of the album's singles resulted in three years of chart topping success for Carpenter. Five of the singles were written or co- written by Carpenter such as the No. 11 hit "The Hard Way," a No. 2 single "He Thinks He'll Keep Her" and "I Take My Chances." The No. 4 hit "I Feel Lucky" brought her a Grammy for Best Female Country Vocal Performance in 1993. Country super star, Joe Diffie co-wrote and recorded the No. 2 hit single, "Not Too Much To Ask" with Carpenter. Penned by Lucinda Williams, Carpenter's recording of "Passionate Kisses" garnered her the Grammy for Best Female Vocal Performance and Song of The Year in 1994. "Come On Come On" was certified platinum four times and sold more than four million copies. The album reached No. 4 on Canadian charts and made Billboard's Top 200.

Carpenter's first and only No. 1 album was 1994's "Stones in the Road." Carpenter wrote "House of Cards," "Tender When I Want to Be," which reached No. 6 as a single," and the No. 1 "Shut Up and Kiss Me."

In 1995 Carpenter won the Grammy for the Best Country Album for her work on her fifth album, "Stones in the Road." For "Shut Up and Kiss Me" she was awarded her fourth consecutive Grammy for the Best Female Country Vocal Performance in 1995.

Carpenter's sixth album, "A Place in the World," for which she wrote all 12 tracks, made it to number three on Billboard charts in 1996. She released the album "Time* Sex* Love*" in 2001, which veered from Country by addressing issues from middle-aged women's perspective, with all tracks written or co-written by Carpenter.

Her 2008 Christmas album, "Come Darkness, Come Light," contained several original songs. All tracks on the 2004 album "Between Here and Gone," 2007's No. 10 charting album the "The Calling" and 2010's "The Age of Miracles" album were written by Carpenter. Country favorites Vince Gill and Alison

Krauss sang the background vocals on a few of "The Age of Miracles" songs. The album reached No. 6 on Billboard Magazine Top Country Albums and peaked at number #28 on the Billboard's 200 albums chart. She released "Ashes and Roses" in 2012, "Songs from the Movie" in 2014 and "The Things That We Are Made Of" in 2016.

In 2012 Carpenter was inducted into the Nashville Songwriters Hall of Fame. In addition to her songwriting and ability to play multiple instruments, she was recognized for her vocals with 1990 and 1992 Top Female Vocalist awards from the Academy of Country Music as well as 1992 and 1993 Female Vocalist of the Year awards from the Country Music Association.

Throughout her career, she has actively supported various charities, including CARE and Habitat for Humanity, and has conducted fundraising concerts for such causes as the elimination of landmines. Having sold more than 14 million records, Carpenter is actively touring and continues to write and record.

Lacy J. Dalton gives inmates a seond chance with Arts In Connection

One of the biggest hits from Country singer Lacy J. Dalton was 1981's "Everybody Makes Mistakes." The singer knows that a slip-up in life shouldn't be the final straw – that true survivors know how to pick themselves back up again. Dalton is bringing that message to inmates at High Desert State Prison in Susanville, California. Each year, from September to June, Dalton – whose other hits include "16th Avenue" and "Black Coffee" - and her band leader, Dale Poune teach songwriting, beginning and advanced guitar, as well as rap to students who are serving sentences at the institution.

The program, which is titled Arts In Connections, will soon be having its' annual ceremony, which will include a private performance for select prison officials and Warden Spearman. The classes are supported by the William James Association, a national non-profit organization that was founded in Dalton's hometown of Santa Cruz, whose mission is to promote work service in the arts, environment, education, as well as community development. The WJA Prison Arts Project, in partnership with the California Lawyers for the Arts, is undertaking a $65,000 arts-in-corrections initiative testing the benefits of arts programs for incarcerated persons.

It has been launched at several state prisons with funding support from the National Endowment for the Arts, the California Arts Council, and several private foundations. "Our goal is to help our students through teaching them about copyrighting their material, as well as potentially helping them to get their work heard by music business professionals."

One might be thinking the songs that are penned reflect the musical style of a Merle Haggard, given the fact that the singer was once imprisoned at San Quentin. However, she says that the musical styles are vastly different – though no less creative.

"Much of what has been written in the past two years that we have established the program is far away from Country Music," says Dalton. "But it is no less relevant to today's times – and what they have gone through. I definitely plan on reaching out to the songwriting community in Nashville to help gain their input on the work that is being done at High Desert."

Participating in the program, Dalton says, has helped to give those imprisoned a sense of purpose – one that will help integrate them back into society when their sentences are completed.

"For these people, being able to show that they can make a positive out of a negative situation as they have done is very meaningful. It's a chance for them to work together, through composing lyrics and poetry collectively with each other. They have made their mistakes, and are paying the price for what they have done. But, it doesn't have to end there. It shouldn't end there. An act that they may have committed very young in life – as many of them have – shouldn't have to define their futures. I believe that each of them has the chance to be rehabilitated, and to make a worthwhile contribution to society, and re-establish their lives."

For more information about the William James Assoc., go to www.WilliamJamesAssociation.org.

August 2017

SEPTEMBER

Glen Campbell: A Life Multiplied by Talent, Success and Love

By Claudia Johnson

Most people want to be remembered as more than a number – not just the date they were born or the digits on an official document or even the amount of money they've amassed.

In the weeks since the death of Glen Campbell his life has been recalled through the songs he sang, the women he loved and the success he achieved. The well-deserved tributes are adding up, and the loss of a man with Campbell's talent, humor and humanity multiplies the grief.

His impactful life was far more than calculations, but numbers are important in telling the story of a life lived robustly and a death faced with courage. In honor of that life, CFR News recalls Campbell's extraordinary life by the numbers.

81. The number of years on earth from his birth in Billstown, Arkansas, on April 22, 1936, until his death from complications associated with Alzheimer's in Nashville, Tennessee, on Aug. 8, 2017.

12. His birth order in a family of 12 born to sharecroppers John Wesley and Carrie Dell (Stone) Campbell of whom he was the seventh son.

14. His age when he joined a migrant labor crew to pick tomatoes with mostly Mexican laborers.

4. The age he began to play the $5 Sears and Roebuck guitar his father bought for him. He began his career while still a teenager as a session musician, performing on recordings by artists in a cross-section of genres such as Bobby Darin, Ricky Nelson, Dean Martin, Nat King Cole, the Monkees, the Mamas and the Papas, The Righteous Brothers, Nancy Sinatra, Merle Haggard, Jan and Dean, Frank Sinatra, Ronnie Dove, Phil Spector and Elvis Presley.

22. How old he was when he formed his first band, the Western Wranglers, in 1958.

62. Highest chart position for "Turn Around, Look at Me," his first single for Crest records in 1961. This single released on a regional label, caught the attention of Capitol Records, which signed him and launched his climb up the charts.

586. Number of 1963 studio sessions in which Campbell played guitar for The Wrecking Crew, the group of studio musicians who worked with Phil Spector to create his influential Wall of Sound production style. Campbell was inducted in 2007 into the Musicians Hall of Fame for his time on The Wrecking Crew.

4. The number of months he was a member of The Beach Boys, filling in for Bryan Wilson in early 1965. He performed and played guitar on several of their hit singles as well as the groundbreaking album "Pet Sounds."

70. The collection of studio and live albums Campbell released between 1962 and 2017 that included dozens of hit singles, many of which bridged the gap between Country and Pop.

19. Hits reaching the Top 10 on the charts, including No. 1 hits like "Southern Nights," "Rhinestone Cowboy," "Wichita Lineman," "Galveston" and "I Wanna Live" along with other perennial favorites like "Country Boy (You Got Your Feet In L.A.)," "By The Time I Get To Phoenix," "Try A Little Kindness," "Dreams Of The Everyday Housewife" and "Everything A Man Could Ever

Need." His first hit song, "Gentle on my Mind," was named 1967's Single of the Year by the Academy of Country Music, which also earned Campbell the Album of the Year and Top Male Vocalist honors.

1967. The year Campbell made history by winning four Grammys in the country and pop categories. For "Gentle on My Mind" he received two awards in country and western, and "By the Time I Get to Phoenix" did the same in pop.

1968. A great year for Campbell during which he was awarded Album of the Year by the Academy of Country Music for his collaborative album, "Bobbie Gentry & Glen Campbell" and was named ACM's Top Male Vocalist. The Country Music Association named him the 1968 Entertainer of the Year and Male Vocalist of the Year.

3. Years between 1969-1972 that his television variety show the "The Glenn Campbell Goodtime Hour" brought Campbell, Jerry Reed and a host of musical and comedic guests to prime-time television in a much-watched show crafted by writers like Steve Martin and Rob Reiner. Campbell was named TV Personality of the Year in 1968 and again in 1971 by the Academy of Country Music.

1. Campbell's win of the CMA of Great Britain's Entertainer of the Year award in 1974.

2 million. Records sold of 1975's "Rhinestone Cowboy," which topped both the country and Hot 100 charts simultaneously and was the inspiration for the 1984 movie "Rhinestone" starring Sylvester Stallone and Dolly Parton. He entitled his 1994 autobiography "Rhinestone Cowboy." Campbell received three American Music Awards related to the song: the 1976 Pop/Rock Single of the Year and Country Single of the Year and the 1977 Country Album of the Year. The Academy of Country Music recognized "Rhinestone Cowboy" in 1975 with awards for Single of the Year and Song of the Year.

1977. The year "Southern Nights" was the number one track played on jukeboxes throughout the United States.

1. Celebrity romance with fellow country artist Tanya Tucker, 22 years his junior, that produced a number of duet recordings including the single "Dream Lover." They performed the national anthem together at the 1980 Republican National Convention. The volatile relationship lasted only two years but provided plenty of tabloid gossip.

13. The number of years Campbell was host of the Glen Campbell Open on the PGA Tour from 1971 to 1983. A golfer since his 20s, he sometimes wore cleated cowboy boots rather than standard golf shoes. Eight pages in his autobiography are dedicated to golfing.

1. For a single year from 1982-1983 "The Glen Campbell Music Show" was a syndicated U.S. music television series presented by Campbell.

82. His list of singles that appeared on either the Billboard Country Chart, the Billboard Hot 100 or the Adult Contemporary Chart or a combination.

11. Motion pictures in Campbell's filmography, which includes 1969's "True Grit" with John Wayne, 1970's "Norwood" with Joe Namath and "Any Which Way You Can" with Clint Eastwood in 1980. Campbell sang the theme for "True Grit," earning an Academy Award nomination for Best Song and a Golden Globe nomination for Most Promising Newcomer for his supporting role. In 1981 the title track for "Any Which Way You Can" broke into the Top 10 on the Country Singles Chart.

1. Campbell was the 2008 recipient of the Q Legend Award, the UK's annual music awards run by the music magazine Q.

4. Campbell was married four times beginning at age 17, with spouses being Diane Kirk, Billie Jean Nunley, Sarah Barg and Kimberly Woollen, to whom he had been married for 25 years when he died. These marriages produced five sons, Travis, Kane, Dillon, Cal and Shannon, and three daughters, Debby, Kelli and Ashley, many of whom are entertainers themselves. At his death he had at total of 10 grandchildren, great grandchildren and great-great grandchildren.

3. Number of prestigious GMA Dove Awards Campbell won after publicly overcoming alcohol and cocaine addiction while raising three young children with his fourth wife, Kim, who introduced him to Christianity in the early '80s and helped get him sober. In 1986 he took the award for Album By A Secular Artist for "No More Night." His 1992 tune, "Where Shadows Never Fall" won Southern Gospel Recorded Song of the Year. His "A Glen Campbell Christmas" was named Country Album of the Year in 2000.

11. Number of times Campbell was honored with awards from the Academy of Country Music (ACM) during his lifetime.

September 2017

2. Campbell received two of the Academy of Country Music's most prestigious awards, the Cliffie Stone Pioneer Award in 1998 and the Career Achievement Award in 2015, joining a very exclusive list of artists to be so honored.

23. Campbell's position on Billboard's 100 Greatest Country Artists of All Time set in 2016.

3. Campbell is included in the Country Music Hall of Fame, The Musician's Hall of Fame and the Grammy Hall of Fame.

10. Number of Grammy Awards including two in 1967, Best Country & Western Solo Vocal Performance, Male, and Best Country & Western Recording, for "Gentle On My Mind," and two more in 1967, Best Vocal Performance, Male, and Best Contemporary Male Solo Vocal Performance for "By The Time I Get To Phoenix." In 1968 he took the Album of the Year Grammy for By The Time I Get To Phoenix. Three of his singles were entered into the Grammy Hall of Fame, "Wichita Lineman" in 2002, "By The Time I Get To Phoenix" in 2004 and "Gentle On My Mind" in 2008. In 2012 he received the Grammy Lifetime Achievement Award. The Best Country Song award for 2014 went to his single "I'm Not Gonna Miss You."

6. Years he lived after his diagnosis with Alzheimer's in 2011, during which time he toured nationally, won a Grammy for his final release, "I'm Not Gonna Miss You," and garnered an Academy Award nomination.

1. Campbell is credited with being the sole writer of one song, Grammy-winning "I'm Not Gonna Miss You," dedicated to his wife, Kim. Of all the songs he brought to life that had flowed from the minds and pens of others, this one summed up his true feelings about what is important in the end.

"I'm still here, but yet I'm gone," he wrote of his ever-encroaching dementia. "I don't play guitar or sing my songs. They never defined who I am – the man that loves you 'til the end."

1. The Country Radio Broadcasters Career Achievement Award was presented to Campbell in 2012.

1. Lifetime Achievement Award presented in 2014 by Hollywood Music In Media, a fitting recognition considering the number of his own hits or his studio sessions recordings for other artists that have been used in television, movies and commercials.

151. Number sold-out shows as he navigated the Alzheimer's during "The Glen Campbell Goodbye Tour," with his children becoming key members of his band. Filmmaker James Keach crafted an Academy Award nominated documentary, "Glen Campbell: I'll Be Me," based on the tour.

50 million. Number of albums sold across a six-decades long career.

5,429%. Percentage of increase in sales of Campbell's music in the first week after his death.

Even with a recounting of the numbers, Campbell's greatest contribution can never be quantified; his ability to make people feel good, feel like his singing was about them, feel they'd be his friend if they met him and feel a personal loss when he was gone.

The sum of his life's numbers is infinity.

He will be missed.

Farewell statements from other artists on the loss of Glen Campbell

"Sorry to hear about my good friend Glen. The loss is too big to put into words. He was an incredible voice, incredible musician, incredible friend, movie star and recording artist. We had so much fun together, and sort of grew up together in our music and our careers. There were so many memories that only he and I shared. Glen and I were brothers in every sense of the word. When I hear or see his name, I see the Glen I've always known. There will never, ever be another Glen Campbell." – Roy Clark

"Well Glen Campbell was special because he was so gifted. Glen is one of the greatest voices that ever was in the business, and he was one of the greatest musicians. He was a wonderful session musician as well. A lot of people don't realize that, but he could play anything. And he could play it really well. So he was just extremely talented. I will always love you, Glen!" – Dolly Parton

"I had the pleasure of inducting Glen into the Country Music Hall of Fame. He could write it, sing it and play it. He was a triple threat. He never forgot

September 2017

his friends and made room for them on any project could. He was one of the finest musicians I've ever known and certainly the prowess of his entertainment legacy goes without saying that. He was our golden boy. We loved him and the world loved him."
– Brenda Lee

"It's always tragic when you hear of a friend passing, but he had to be miserable that last few years of his life. At least he doesn't have to deal with that anymore. We worked together a lot through the years. In fact, Glen played on almost all First Edition music. He played a dynamic riff on the guitar that was trend setting. I also shot a few of his album covers back in the day and, at the time, I never knew people were paid to do that, but a few weeks later I received a check in the mail that was unexpected and highly received. I'll never forget that. He was a good friend and it breaks my heart that he's not here to contribute to music anymore." – Kenny Rogers

"I'm sad to learn of the passing of one of my heroes and friends, Glen Campbell. I loved his singing and guitar playing but I really admired him for his down to earth and friendly personality. I spent only a week working with him in Branson and he made us all feel like old friends. Rest In Peace old buddy."
– Mark Chesnutt

"My hero... My Friend... Glen Campbell, is gone. My heart is heavy... A lot of memories...the end to a beautiful era in music. His incredible legacy is what we have now. Thank you, my friend, for always treating me as an equal, though clearly I am not. May God comfort your sweet family, and welcome you into His presence. The Heavenly Band, just got way better. I love you, Glen. Happy Trails."
– Collin Raye

"This is so sad. One of my proudest moments with Glen was when he borrowed my guitar for a TV Taping in Nashville. He is a respected talent. He was a great artist…I recently recorded one of his hit songs 'Try a Little Kindness so I take a little bit of Glen with me everywhere I go." – Janie Fricke

Nadine
The Church Lady

Lord, give me a sense of humor, Give me the grace to see a joke, To get some humor out of life, And to pass it on to other folk.

My cousin picked up this hitchhiker the other day and hadn't gone 10 miles down the road when the police stopped him. The hitchhiker had a bag with him and the policeman made him open it up and it was full of big ol' knives. He told him he worked in a circus as a juggler so the policeman told him to get out and prove to him that he was a juggler. These two drunks was going by and one looked at the other one and said, "Man, these sobriety checks are getting rougher all the time!"

Church sign

The atheist can't find God for the same reason a thief can't find a policeman.

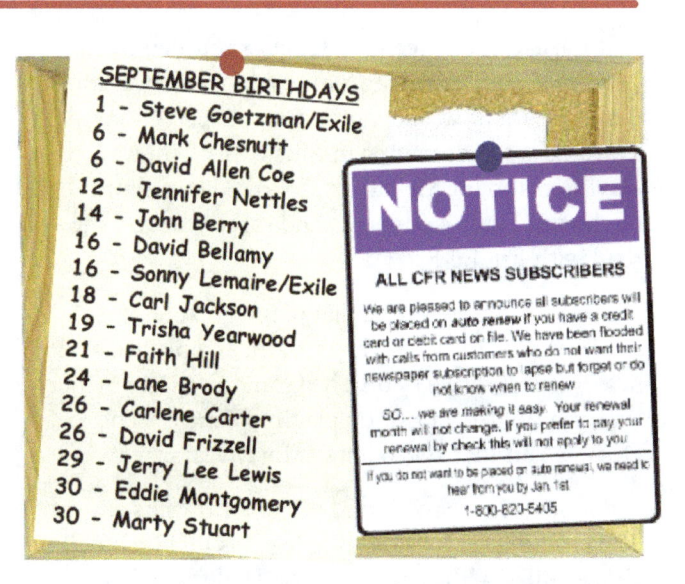

SEPTEMBER BIRTHDAYS
1 - Steve Goetzman/Exile
6 - Mark Chesnutt
6 - David Allen Coe
12 - Jennifer Nettles
14 - John Berry
16 - David Bellamy
16 - Sonny Lemaire/Exile
18 - Carl Jackson
19 - Trisha Yearwood
21 - Faith Hill
24 - Lane Brody
26 - Carlene Carter
26 - David Frizzell
29 - Jerry Lee Lewis
30 - Eddie Montgomery
30 - Marty Stuart

NOTICE

ALL CFR NEWS SUBSCRIBERS

We are pleased to announce all subscribers will be placed on auto renew if you have a credit card or debit card on file. We have been flooded with calls from customers who do not want their newspaper subscription to lapse but forget or do not know when to renew.

SO… we are making it easy. Your renewal month will not change. If you prefer to pay your renewal by check this will not apply to you.

If you do not want to be placed on auto renewal, we need to hear from you by Jan. 1st.
1-800-820-5435

September 2017

Tim Atwood, former Grand Ole Opry Band player was born to play the piano

Tim Atwood was raised in a music loving household in Peoria, Illinois. As a boy he remembers watching his Uncle Tommy Atwood sing tenor for The Florida Boys—now members of The Southern Gospel Music Hall of Fame. He knew from the first time he saw his Uncle Tommy perform that he too wanted to be an entertainer.

When Tim was thirteen years old, he started his career as a drummer for the gospel group The Harris Family. Harris Family piano man Dave Galloway taught Tim a Floyd Crammer lick on the keyboard. Tim was hooked.

At the age of eighteen, a chance encounter and a word of encouragement from Faron Young was all it took for Tim to sell his home and move to Nashville. Two weeks after arriving in Music City Tim was playing piano for Mel Street...followed by a short hitch with Lynn Anderson...and three years on the road with Jim Ed Brown.

It was during that time that piano great Jerry Whitehurst took an interest in Tim as a player...Tim began to sub for Jerry on The Grand Ole Opry which lead to a full time position playing piano on The Opry...a run that lasted almost forty years.

For 30+ years Tim played piano for music's elite at The Grand Ole Opry backing legends that included Vince Gill, Garth Brooks, Carrie Underwood, Merle Haggard, Willie Nelson, Jim Ed Brown, Jeannie Seely and Little Jimmy Dickens. Tim's versatility on keys allowed him the opportunity to play outside the country box, performing with Barry Gibb, Bob Hope, Don Ho, Keb Mo, Lisa Marie Presley and Jewel.

As a young man playing for Grand Ole Opry patriarch Roy Acuff, Mr. Acuff relinquished large portions of his Opry segments to Tim to wow the crowd. Bashful Brother Oswald, a longtime member of Roy's Smoky Mountain Boys, once joked, "Roy must really like Tim. He didn't even give Elvis an encore!"

Beyond the stage Tim continues to be a sought after studio musician recording with some of those same artists with whom he shared the spotlight's fringe—artists who include Dolly Parton, Ray Price, George Jones, Bobby Bare and Charley Pride.

Tim's TV appearances include Opry Live, Opry Backstage, Late Night with David Letterman, Nashville on The Road, Nashville Now, Pop Goes The Country, On Stage, Hee Haw, The Morning Show and features on CBS and NBC news. Tim is the reigning AWA Instrumentalist of The Year. He is the ten time musical director for The Inspirational Country Music Awards, staff player for the WSM/Durango stage during CMA Fest, and has composed theme music and musical beds for a variety of TV and radio productions, including a national campaign for Easter Seals. In November Tim will host The Midnight Jamboree for the fourth time and will conclude the year as a headliner for a series of holiday Opry shows in Texas.

As an artist, Tim has a musical arsenal at the ready that includes hundreds of selections. Tim can fire off a country song with ease, pull the trigger on a rock-n-roll favorite, reload with some back water blues, and win the day with a gospel classic.

As a showman, Tim is a high energy package with a quick wit and an unpredictable sense of humor who will engage the audience to buckle in for a roller coaster ride of laughs and emotions.

Tim Atwood will entertain you. Watch him on Larry's Country Diner Thursday, September 7 at 7 p.m. Central or Saturday, September 9 at 10 p.m. Central.

September 2017

RCA Studio B Celebrating 60th Anniversary With Special Events & Performances

Elvis Presley, Waylon Jennings, Chet Atkins and Other Legends Recorded at Historic Studio

Historic RCA Studio B in Nashville celebrates its 60th anniversary through Oct. 29 with special surprise performances during random public tours and unique after-hours programming.

Located on Music Row in Nashville, Tennessee, the studio was once the recording home of country and pop music legends such as Chet Atkins, Dolly Parton, Elvis Presley, Charley Pride, Eddy Arnold, Bobby Bare, Floyd Cramer, the Everly Brothers, Waylon Jennings, Willie Nelson, Roy Orbison and Jim Reeves, among others.

Studio B played a major role in establishing Nashville as an international recording center. The studio's heyday was from 1957 to 1977, when it was operated by RCA Records. For many years, Country Music Hall of Fame member Chet Atkins managed RCA's Nashville operation and produced hits in Studio B.

After-hours programming includes two panel discussions.

"The King at B: Top Musicians Remember Elvis," was held on August 31. Musicians David Briggs, James Burton, Charlie McCoy and Norbert Putnam talked about their extensive work with Presley at the historic studio.

"Hit-Makers Reflect on Historic RCA Studio B" takes place Sept. 21 at 7:30 p.m. with Bobby Bare, Dave Cobb, Lloyd Green and Connie Smith sharing their perspectives on working at the studio.

A studio tour will be offered 30 minutes before the program. Tickets for are on sale now and can be purchased for $25.

Surprise performances will occur during public tours during the three-month celebration. The guest performers will be contemporary artists who have been influenced by Studio B recording legends.

The studio closed its doors on Aug. 17, 1977, coincidentally, the day after its most famous client, Elvis Presley, passed away. Studio B is now operated by the Country Music Hall of Fame and Museum as a cultural attraction for visitors and a classroom for Nashville middle and high school students.

Following the Mike Curb Family Foundation's philanthropic 2002 purchase and subsequent lease in perpetuity to the non-profit Country Music Hall of Fame® and Museum, the storied studio's exterior has been renovated and the interior has been returned to its 1970s-era prime as an analog "temple of sound."

Built by Dan Maddox in 1957, RCA Studio B first became known as one of the cradles of the "Nashville Sound" in the 1960s. A sophisticated style characterized by background vocals and strings, the Nashville Sound both revived the popularity of country music and helped establish Nashville as an international recording center.

Studio B has also been home to numerous innovations in recording practices, including the development of the "Nashville number system," a musician's shorthand for notating a song's chord structure, which facilitates the creation of individual parts while retaining the integrity of the song.

First made available to Country Music Hall of Fame® and Museum visitors in 1977, RCA Studio B was donated to the Museum by the late Dan and Margaret Maddox in 1992. It was operated as an attraction until shortly before the opening of the Museum's new downtown facility in 2001.

The studio has begun a new life as a:

• Cultural attraction for visitors, who can become acquainted with the studio's place in the evolution of Nashville as the Music City.

September 2017

• Classroom for Nashville-area middle and high school students, learning the science of sound and recording technology;

The museum is grateful for the generosity of the Mike Curb Family Foundation. In 2002, the foundation philanthropically purchased Historic RCA Studio B and subsequently leased it in perpetuity to the Country Music Hall of Fame and Museum.

Historic RCA Studio B is supported, in part, by Fender Musical Instruments Corporation, the Metropolitan Nashville Arts Commission, and the Tennessee Arts Commission.

For more information, visit the Historic RCA Studio B website.

35th Anniversary of Sylvia's No. 1 Hit "Nobody"

This year marks the 35th anniversary of Sylvia's No. 1 smash crossover hit "Nobody," which dominated the country music charts, leading the acclaimed singer to win the ACM award for "Female Vocalist of the Year." The chart-topping vocalist shows no signs of slowing down anytime soon. She performed on the Grand Ole Opry recently.

"I can't imagine a better way to celebrate the 35th Anniversary of 'Nobody' topping the charts than to perform it on the Grand Ole Opry," says Sylvia. "I've been listening to the Opry my whole life. In fact, my earliest memory of listening to the Opry was during a road trip from Kokomo, Indiana to Lafayette, Tennessee on a Friday night to visit my grandparents. It makes me wonder what little child might be out there listening this Saturday night dreaming of someday standing on that stage…"

After high school graduation, Sylvia moved to Nashville to realize her dream of becoming a recording artist and in a few short years signed with RCA Records. The rest is history!

Look who's on the Diner this week!
On RFD-TV
All shows subject to change

Thursdays at 7 p.m. central   Saturdays at 10 p.m. central

TIM ATWOOD September 7 & 9

TONY JACKSON September 14 & 16

BOBBY BARE September 21 & 23

OAK RIDGE BOYS September 28 & 30

September 2017

COUNTRY LEGENDS OF THE PAST & PRESENT

BY TOM WOOD

Hoot Hester

Hoot Hester might not have been a household name for the average country music fan, but his music certainly was.

If you attended a Grand Ole Opry performance this century, you heard the bluegrass star playing. Hoot was a longtime member of the house band, performing weekly shows from 2000-2014.

You may have heard him playing as a backup band member with Alabama, Hank Williams Jr. or Conway Twitty. Perhaps with Randy Travis, Bill Monroe or Ricky Van Shelton. And he also appeared on several records with artists such as Ray Charles or Manhattan Transfer.

If not there, you may have heard Hoot playing on Nashville-based television shows such as Pop Goes The Country, Nashville Now or Nashville Alive.

And you've probably heard of the Grammy-winning Western swing band The Time Jumpers. If you jumped on their bandwagon during those early years, you certainly heard Hoot playing.

Hoot Hester, an acclaimed fiddler player who also excelled on other instruments, co-founded The Time Jumpers in 1999 with Dennis Crouch.

The Time Jumpers brought together an ever-changing lineup featuring both the famous like Vince Gill and "Ranger Doug" Green as well as extraordinary A-list sessions players and musicians and vocalists such as Paul Franklin, Joe Spivey, Larry Franklin, Kenny Sears and many others.

Born Hubert Dwane Hester near Louisville, Ky., on Aug. 13, 1951, Hoot died of cancer at age 65 on Aug. 30, 2016. He eventually left The Time Jumpers to help daughter Rachel launch her own career.

"I was disappointed when Hoot left The Time Jumpers, but looking back I realize it was the right thing for him to do," Kenny Sears said in a memoriam posted at www.thetimejumpers.com after Hoot's death. "He got to spend his last years playing music with his daughter Rachel. What a wonderful way to finish a long and meaningful career."

Other members of The Time Jumpers shared similar memories of their friend and peer.

"Besides being a great musician, Hoot was a loving father," Joe Spivey recalled. "[His departure from the group] opened the door for me to become a Time Jumper! His musicianship, humor and his unique perspective on the human condition will truly be missed!"

At the website memorial, "Ranger Doug" Green called Hoot "a lifelong friend" that he'd known since 1971. "The entire Nashville music community have lost a very special talent and a very special soul," he added. "He was one of a kind, and can never be replaced for there will never be another like him."

I never had the pleasure of meeting Hoot Hester, though I feel I know him through his music and comments like these.

He must have been a real Hoot!

Sources: Wikipedia, www.grammer guitar.net

Author Tom Wood, who writes thrillers and Westerns, is a regular contributor to Country Family Reunion News. Reach him at tomwoodauthor.com

Jimmy Capps, Larry Mahonn and Hoot Hester on Larry's Country Diner. Hoot also performed with the CFR Band on one of the Country's Family Reunion cruises.

September 2017

It's A Family Tradition

By Sasha Kay Dunavant

By Sasha Kay Dunavant

The Maddox Brothers and Rose

The role of the family is an integral theme of Country Music. Some of County's greatest songs have captured memories from family life. Family acts, including sibling duos, have long been a staple on the Country stage. Some families have produced numerous talented members, both performers and songwriters, who separately made their impact on the genre. In other families, each generation has expanded the legacy of the one before it. This series celebrates Country Music's family connections.

Fred, Cliff, Don and Cal Maddox and their sister, Rose, known professionally as "The Maddox Brothers and Rose," spent their childhood during the early years of The Great Depression as sharecroppers.

Originally from Boaz, Alabama, the Maddox family relocated to California in 1933. The children and their parents hitchhiked and rode the rails to harvest crops as far to the east as Arizona and as far north as Washington. They worked from sun up to sun down and often slept and ate on the ground where they worked.

In 1937 the children formed a musical group and soon began performing on Modesto, California's, radio station, KTRB. In 1939 the Maddox boys and 11-year-old Rose entered a hillbilly band competition at the Centennial Sacramento State Fair and were officially named, "California's Best Hillbilly Band." A year later The Maddoxs performed on radio station KFBK in Sacramento, California, exposing their talents to the entire West Coast.

Red, Cal and Don Maddox were drafted into World War II. Their little sister, Rose, missed her brothers terribly and tried to have some solo success. While their other brother's were at war, Henry and Cliff played for other bands. Rose persistently urged Bob Willis to hire her to be in his band, The Texas Playboys, but he was uninterested. Rose warned Willis that her brothers would be back from the war someday. Rose was right about that. In 1946 The Maddox Brothers and Rose were together again. The group recorded for 4 Star Record Company in 1947. They had a high intensity performance that consisted of Swing, Boogie, early Rock and Roll and Folk music. People were drawn to The Maddox Brothers and Rose's type of music, comedy and sound. Their talent and outlandish performances mesmerized many people.

Fred, Cal and Rose formed a trio and called themselves "The Alabama Outlaws." They later would gain the name, "America's Most Colorful Hillbilly Band." The band signed with Columbia Records in the 1950s. The Maddox Brothers and Rose recorded more than 40 singles with the label. They opened their show with the song, "George's Playhouse Boogie" and closed each show with their theme song, "I Want To Live and Love."

During the 1950s, the siblings performed on the Grand Ole Opry and Louisiana Hayride. They performed with several musicians, including lead guitarists Gene Breeden, Jimmie Winkle and Roy Nichols, and steel guitarist, Bud Duncan. The Maddox Brothers and Rose were popping during the Rockabilly heyday in the mid 1950s. Rose eventually signed with Capitol Records around the same time the members of The Maddox Brothers and Rose went their separate ways in 1957.

It is believed that Fred Maddox's Bass hit the first Rock and Roll note. The instrument is on display at the Experience Music Project in Seattle, Washington. Red Maddox opened a nightclub, "Fred Maddox Playhouse." The club was very successful during the late 1950s and the early 1960s. Cal assisted Rose in building a powerful solo career. She later began singing for Dave Stogner and Arky Stark. Rose had a series of solo hits, such as "Gambler's Love," "Sing A Little Song of Heartache," "The Philadelphia Lawyer," "The Tramp On The Street," and her biggest hit, "Conscience I'm Guilty."

Rose and Hee Haw tycoon, Buck Owens, also had a number of chart topping songs, including "Sweethearts In Heaven," "We're The Talk of The Town," "Loose Talk" and "Mental Cruelty." Rose began having heart attacks in the 1960s and her career suffered a great deal because of her poor health. She reportedly had the ability to sing all different styles of music, including Gospel, Hillbilly and Rockabilly. Rose told a source, "I sounded like nobody else, and I guess that's why I was so distinctive." After leaving Capitol Records in 1967, Rose recorded with Starday, Decca and King Records. Rose's brother, Henry Maddox accompanied his sister in several of her 1970s and 1980s recordings.

Rose recorded two records for Arhoolie Records, including her album, "Queen of the West." Merle Haggard and The Strangers and Emmylou Harris also sang back vocals for Rose in her early 1980s songs. Rose's son died in 1982. In 1987 she recorded the "Rockabilly Reunion" album with rockabilly sensation, Glen Glenn. Don Reno, Bill Monroe and Red Smiley aided Rose in singing backup on, "Rose Maddox Sings Bluegrass." The album is critically considered to be Rose's most successful record.

Bluegrass musician, Vern Williams backed a few of Rose's Bluegrass style recordings in the 1980s. Rose had a serious heart attack in 1987. The star had no insurance during her illness, so fund-raisers and benefits were held in her honor. Rose Maddox performed through the late 1980s. She received a Grammy nomination for her album, "$35 and a Dream" in 1994. Rose died on April 15, 1998, in Ashland, Oregon. Henry, Cliff, Cal and Fred have also passed away. Don Maddox is the only living family member.

Subscribe to our new YouTube Channel for FREE and watch great videos of your favorite country artists!

September 2017

Country's Family Reunion is coming to the BIG SCREEN for one night only!!! You don't want to miss this opportunity to take a friend and enjoy the blessings from

"Wednesday Night Prayer Meeting: REJOICE"

During our "Wednesday Night Prayer Meeting" series last year, Ricky Skaggs said we needed a way to bring this special show to the marketplace. Well, guess what? Larry Black did just that. We have joined partners with Screen Vision and KAOS Connect, who together bring movie projects to nationwide audiences and created a brand new version of the project we're calling Wednesday Night Prayer Meeting: Rejoice!

One night only on September 27th at a theater near you, this brand-new 90 minute project will play on over 225 theaters across the country. You'll see all new intimate interviews with some of the people who attended the taping and are featured in this project. Ricky Skaggs, Jimmy Fortune, Bill Anderson, The Oak Ridge Boys, Teea Goans, John Conlee, Gene Watson, T Graham Brown, The Isaacs plus clips and songs from the original project. Larry Black will be on the screen to explain why this series was so important to create. We know the stories and songs captured in this movie event are sure to lift the spirit of anyone who attends.

That's where YOU come in. As some of our most valued customers, we need YOU to invite someone you know--- maybe your church group, your neighbor, a cousin-- to join you on September 27th (which happens to be a Wednesday night!).

AND to make this really special we will send you FREE an 11 x 17 special AUTOGRAPHED POSTER when you send us your ticket stub or proof of purchase with your name, address, phone number and email address. So don't miss out on this very special event on September 27, 2017 and a free poster!

Movie Poster

PO Box 210709

Nashville, TN 37221

Where to find a theater in your area?

The theater list is constantly being updated and you can find the closest theater near you by going to our website: www.prayermeetingmovie.com for tickets and details.

If you don't see a theater in your area, then contact your local Movie Theater and request a special airing. AND if you love it……contact theater and ask for a second airing!!

Need Help?

Call Jason or Deann at our Gabriel Customer Service 1-800-820-5405 or Paula at 615-673-2846. We will also be chatting about this event on Diner Chat live every Thursday at 2:00 CT. Call in and join us at 1-425-440-5100 Pin 909005#

September 2017

Dolly Parton's "Christmas of Many Colors: Circle of Love" nominated for EMMY Award

'Dolly Parton's Christmas of Many Colors: Circle Of Love' receives Emmy nomination in the "Television Movie" category! In the two-hour movie, the Partons, a family of humble means living in the mountains of Tennessee, face a devastating event that challenges their will. But when they experience a bewildering Christmas miracle, the Partons are drawn closer together than ever — with deepened faith and love for one another. Alyvia Alyn Lind, Jennifer Nettles, Ricky Schroder, and Gerald McCraney co-starred in the holiday movie 'Dolly Parton's Christmas of Many Colors: Circle of Love,' which aired on NBC, with Dolly Parton making a special guest appearance.

"I am so very proud and excited to have "Christmas of Many Colors" be nominated for an Emmy award," says Dolly Parton. "Special thanks to my partner and executive producer Sam Haskell, a wonderful cast and crew, Steve Herek (our producer) and Pamela Long for a great script. And a special thanks to all of the many fans that watched it."

"This project for me was a celebration of the family and the beautiful story of Miss Dolly Parton. Each day I played Avie Lee Parton was a joy. For "Christmas of Many Colors" to be nominated and celebrated further by the Emmy's, thrills me," adds Jennifer Nettles.

The 69th Emmy Awards will telecast live from the Microsoft Theater in Los Angeles, Sunday, September 17 (8:00-11:00 PM ET/5:00-8:00 PM PT) on CBS. Stephen Colbert will serve as host. The 69th Emmy Awards is produced by White Cherry Entertainment.

Farewell Concert to honor Kenny Rogers adds to lineup

Music stars Reba McEntire, Chris Stapleton, Lady Antebellum and Wynonna Judd have been added to the momentous lineup for "All In For The Gambler: Kenny Rogers' Farewell Concert Celebration," an all-star concert event taping at the Bridgestone Arena in Nashville, Tennessee on Wednesday, October 25, 2017 at 7PM CT. In addition, The Judds (Wynonna and Naomi Judd) will reunite for an unforgettable performance.

The new additions to the lineup will join previously announced artists Kenny Rogers, Dolly Parton, Little Big Town, Alison Krauss, The Flaming Lips, Idina Menzel, Jamey Johnson, and Elle King.

This once-in-a-lifetime concert event will honor Kenny Rogers' historic 60-year career and will feature the final performance together by Kenny Rogers and Dolly Parton.

"It is a great honor to learn that my friends Reba, Lady Antebellum, Chris Stapleton, Wynonna, and The Judds will be performing at this show," says Kenny Rogers. "I admire each one of them for the music they create and for the integrity that is always evident in their work. Having them be a part of this once-in-a-lifetime night is going to make things even more exciting for me. I appreciate them doing this, and all of the other artists who will perform, more than they know."

September 2017

New Exhibits at the Country Music Hall of Fame

Loretta Lynn: Blue Kentucky Girl

Exhibit Dates: August 25, 2017 - August 5, 2018

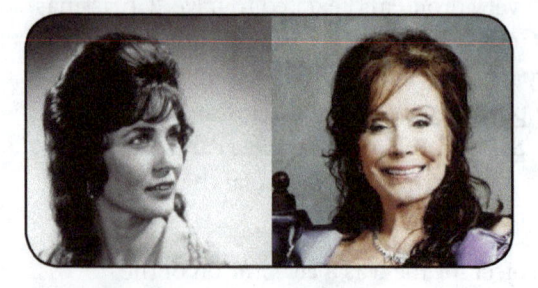

By telling her own truths, and by writing about her experiences with a perspective and voice unlike any other Southern storyteller, Loretta Lynn has become an American hero and a country music standard-bearer.

"I am so happy the Country Music Hall of Fame has asked me to be one of their main exhibits in 2017… gonna show off my 50 some odd years in country music," exclaimed Lynn on hearing news of the exhibition. "They best have a big space…I have a lot of stuff! I'm so proud to share my life, and music with the Hall of Fame. Y'all come see us!"

Her one-of-a-kind tale has been told in a feature film (with an Oscar-winning portrayal of Lynn by Sissy Spacek), two autobiographies, and a public television American Masters documentary. But her fascinating journey is worthy of further exploration. Examining the Coal Miner's Daughter through her music and her rich collection of personal artifacts will provide fresh insights into one of country music's most important artists. Inducted into the Country Music Hall of Fame in 1988, Lynn received a Grammy nomination in 2017 for Best Country Album for her latest release, Full Circle.

Lynn Anderson: Keep Me In Mind

Exhibit Dates: September 15, 2017 - June 24, 2018

The Country Music Hall of Fame® and Museum will examine the life and career of Grammy-winning country artist Lynn Anderson in an exhibition, Lynn Anderson: Keep Me in Mind, opening Sept. 15, 2017, and running through June 24, 2018.

Born in North Dakota and raised in northern California, Anderson started performing at age six, and by her teens she was appearing regularly on television. Her parents, Casey and Liz Anderson, were successful songwriters. Together, they wrote "The Fugitive," a hit for Merle Haggard. The Andersons' connections, and Lynn's talent and hard work, led to her signing with Chart Records at age nineteen, in 1966.

By the late 1960s, Anderson was a regular on television's Lawrence Welk Show, and from 1966 to early 1970 she notched five Top Ten country singles in Billboard rankings. By then, she was also an award-winning equestrian, taking home trophies and ribbons for riding show horses and cutting horses. In fact, Anderson competed in equestrian events throughout most of her life, winning sixteen national and eight world championships, as well as the top trophies at several celebrity competitions.

After marrying songwriter and producer Glenn Sutton, Anderson moved to Nashville in 1969. She signed with Columbia Records in 1970, and Sutton produced her first sixteen albums including Rose Garden, released in December 1970. The album's title track spent five weeks at #1 on the country chart and reached #3 on the Billboard Hot 100 pop chart. The album was among the first by female country singers to be certified platinum for sales of more than a million copies.

Anderson had several #1s in the 1970s ("Keep Me in Mind" among them) and numerous Top Ten hits. She won a Grammy for Best Female Country Vocal Performance in 1971. She was named the Academy of Country Music's Top Female Vocalist in 1967 and 1970, and the Country Music Association's Female Vocalist of the Year in 1971. In 1974, Anderson was the first female country singer to sell out Madison Square Garden. Anderson continued to perform and record until her death in 2015.

September 2017

Who says traditional country music isn't popular anymore!

Music buyers take a stand to show that Traditional Country Music hasn't gone anywhere. It's loved, alive, and well, as the incredible new project American Grandstand landed its first week on Billboard's Top Current Country Albums chart at No. 10. It is No. 1 on the Billboard Bluegrass Chart, and No.1 on Billboard's Heatseekers Album Chart for the week of July 29, 2017.

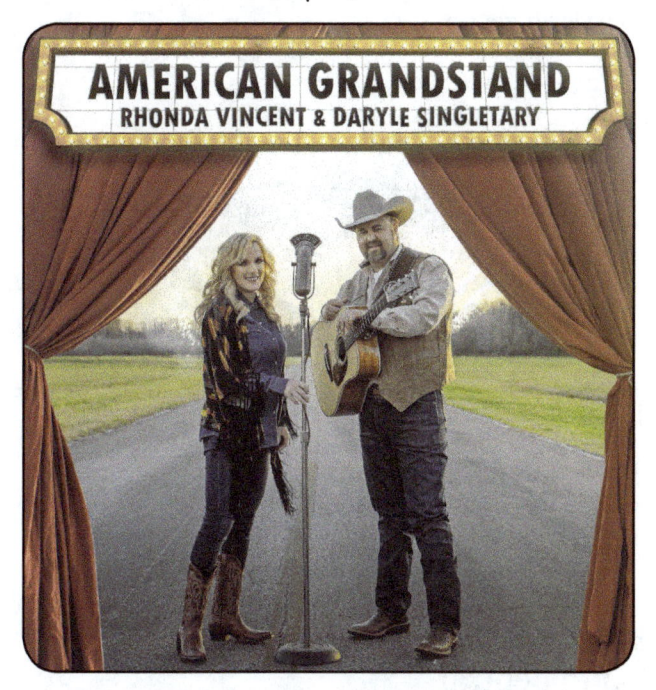

Not since George & Tammy and Conway & Loretta has there been a vocal duet performance like Rhonda Vincent & Daryle Singletary. This week marks yet another indication that buyers love the authentic, unaltered voices of two of the greatest singers in this generation of country music.

"The New Queen of Bluegrass" Rhonda Vincent and country hitmaker Daryle Singletary share their thoughts as they celebrate being at the top of the charts!

Daryle says, "I just want to say how excited Rhonda and I are on the chart debut of American Grandstand. We really didn't know what to expect, but this CD has charted way beyond our expectations and we can't say thanks enough to every single person that supported our efforts and purchased the new duet project. God Bless Country music and Country music fans. We love ya'll!!"

"This is so special! I don't know what makes me happier, #1 on the Billboard Bluegrass Charts or a Top 10 Album on the Current Country charts!" says Rhonda. "Either way, I am thrilled beyond words, and thankful to each of you who purchased and sent your love for this new music! Thank you for your incredible support of Traditional Country music, and if you don't have American Grandstand please go get it!"

This chart-topping project was released on Upper Management Music, and features 12 amazing songs; with originals like the title song written by Rhonda Vincent, along with country classics like the first single "One," that was written by hit country writer/performer Ed Bruce and originally performed by country legends George Jones and Tammy Wynette.

This dynamic duo is off to a blockbuster start, with rave reviews, and a momentum that started with their numerous Nashville performances at the CMA Music Fest, Music City Roots, and The Grand Ole Opry.

"American Grandstand" is available now at AmericanGrandstand.com and wherever music is sold.

Fans can catch "The Most Award-Winning Band in Bluegrass Music History" Rhonda Vincent & The Rage on the road throughout the remainder of the year, as the IBMA "Entertainer of the Year" and 8-time "Female Vocalist of the Year" winner makes stops at festivals and venues throughout North America, plus a return visit to Europe's Bluegrass Capital - Prague, Czech Republic www.rhondainprague.cz in September, along with a stop at Switzerland's Most Prestigious Country Music Festival in beautiful Gstaad.

American Grandstand Track Listing:

1. Above and Beyond
2. One
3. After The Fire Is Gone
4. American Grandstand
5. Slowly But Surely
6. As We Kiss Our World Goodbye
7. Can't Live Life
8. Golden Ring
9. We Must Have Been Out of Our Minds
10. Louisiana Woman Mississippi Man

September 2017

11. A Picture of Me Without You

12. Up This Hill and Down

Rhonda Vincent On Tour:

Sep 2 Fort Fairfield, ME – County Bluegrass

Sep 6 Prague, Czech Republic

Sep 8-9 Gstaad, Switzerland – Country Night Gstaad

Sep 14 Kodak, TN – Dumplin Valley Bluegrass Festival

Sep 15 Conway, MO – Starvy Creek Bluegrass Festival

Sep 16-17 Flagstaff, AZ – Pickin' in the Pines

Sep 23 Vine Grove, KY – Vine Grove Bluegrass Music Festival

Sep 30 Hartselle, AL – Hartselle High School Auditorium

Oct 19 Breman, GA – Milltown Music Hall with Daryle Singletary

September
1 & 2, 8 & 9
15 & 16 and 22 & 23

Fridays...7 p.m. central
Saturdays...11 p.m central

September
29 & 30

There's Something about that song

"The Pill" Captured Societal Changes and Made an Impact on Women

by Claudia Johnson

Editor's Note: In our series, "Something About the Song," CFR News writers Claudia Johnson and Sasha Dunavant, a mother-daughter writing duo, will explore some of Country's most enduring – and endearing – songs. Selections for the series could be perennial crowd favorites, songs with groundbreaking subject matter, one-hit wonders, career defining recordings of major stars, songs that started a trend…you get it. They'll be chosen because they've made us stop and think, "Something about that song." Visit us on social media to let our writers know the songs that made a difference in your life..

Some songs result from societal changes, and others spark changes in society. Loretta Lynn's controversial song, "The Pill," did both.

In an interview last year with songfact.com, Lynn noted that during the 1975 release of "The Pill," she experienced a "rough time." She'd recorded the song in 1972, but her label held it back three years fearing it would be rejected by Country Music listeners.

"I didn't understand that, because everybody was taking the pill," she said. "I didn't have the money to take it when they put it out, but I couldn't understand why they were raising such a fuss over taking the pill."

Lynn, born in 1932, was exactly the kind of woman the pill was intended to help. Married in 1948 at age 15 to Oliver Vanetta (Doo) Lynn, she was the mother of four by age 20, well before the pill was available. However, her twins were born in 1964, four years after oral contraceptives went on the market.

"You wined me and dined me when I was your girl," she sings in "The Pill," lamenting, "Promised if I'd be your wife, you'd show me the world. But all I've seen of this old world is a bed and a doctor bill."

As anyone who has seen the biopic "Coal Miner's Daughter" knows, her husband was anything but faithful, which makes the lyrics to "The Pill" even more poignant.

"All these years I've stayed at home, while you had all your fun," she sang. "And every year that's gone by, another baby's come."

Penned by a songwriting team that included Lorene Allen, Don McHan and T. D. Bayless, "The Pill" employs an extended "poultry" metaphor, giving it a comic edge while compounding the sobriety of a woman's perceived place and very real limitations during the days before birth control was readily available.

The song lyrics were crafted to speak directly to the philandering husband, warning him "You've set this chicken one last time" and saying that she is "tired of all your crowin' how you and your hens play."

In contrast to the bold declarations that "this incubator is overused" and "this chicken's done tore up her nest" in "The Pill," Lynn endured, remaining married to her husband 48 years until his death in 1996, though her marriage was admittedly difficult. She has written candidly about how he slept with her sister-in-law, left her when she was pregnant and was absent for the birth of their son.

expanding and enhancing Hurricane Mills, the family farm and later a tourist attraction near Nashville, Tennessee. As with most stars, rumors circulated about infidelity, but Lynn has reiterated that she was a faithful wife, even addressing longtime speculation about her relationship with duet partner, the late Conway Twitty.

"Everybody thought me and Conway had a thing going, and that's the furthest from the truth," she

September 2017

clarified in a PBS documentary about her life, adding, "I loved Conway as a friend, and my husband loved him."

In "The Pill" the offending "rooster" is told that "it's gettin' dark, it's roosting time" and that the discarded maternity clothing is being replaced with "miniskirts, hot pants and a few little fancy frills."

"Yeah I'm makin' up for all those years, since I've got the pill," Lynn sang.

Despite the song being banned from country airplay, Lynn defended it.

"If I'd had the pill back when I was havin' babies, I'd have taken 'em like popcorn," she told People magazine. "The pill is good for people. I wouldn't trade my kids for anyone's. But I wouldn't necessarily have had six, and I sure would have spaced 'em better."

In an interview with Playgirl Magazine, Lynn revealed that she had some unexpected fans in the medical community. Rural doctors thanked her with one telling her that her song had bought more attention to the availability and value of the pill than any pamphlets they'd distributed. Yet, the song almost caused her to be banned from the Grand Ole Opry.

"You know I sung it three times at the Grand Ole Opry one night, and I found out a week later that the Grand Ole Opry had a three-hour meeting, and they weren't going to let me [sing it]…" she told Playgirl, adding defiantly, "If they hadn't let me sing the song, I'd have told them to shove the Grand Ole Opry!"

A No. 1 Country hit in Canada and No. 5 County hit on U.S. charts, the song brought Lynn unprecedented publicity and earned her a No. 70 spot on the Pop charts, the highest of her career. At age 85 she is the reigning Queen of Country Music, having written more than 160 songs, released 60 albums and sold 45 million records. She remains the most awarded woman in Country Music with accolades for her singing as well as her songwriting. But in 1975, she influenced a generation of women to draw the line with their mates and take control of their bodies and their families when she sang, "I'm ready to make a deal, and ya can't afford to turn it down, 'Cause you know I've got the pill. Oh, but daddy don't you worry none, 'cause mama's got the pill."

Q: I really enjoy your newspaper. I wold love to hear more about Johnny Lee and his daughter.

Anita Hunter, Hot Springs, AR

A: Johnny Lee was born Johnny Lee Hamm on July 3, 1946 in Texas City, Texas. Lee worked 10 years with Mickey Gilley, both on tour and at Gilley's Club in Pasadena, Texas. The movie Urban Cowboy, which was largely shot at Gilley's, catapulted Lee to fame. The record spawned several hit singles, including Lee's "Lookin' for Love."

From 1982 to 1984, Lee was married to Dallas actress Charlene Tilton, with whom he had a daughter Cherish (born 1982). He later had a son with former wife Deb whom he married in 1986, named Johnny Lee Jr. (1990-2014). After Johnny Lee, Jr. died at the age of 23 of a drug overdose, Lee became active in combating the illegal drug epidemic.

His new autobiography titled, "Still Looking for Love" was released this year.

Lee performs with his daughter Cherish quite often and he is now a grandfather. Cherish's son, Wyatt was born in 2016.

Johnny Lee and daughter Cherish performing at the Next Generation: Sons & Daughters of Country Legends show in June 2016. She was pregnant with son Wyatt at the time.

If you have questions send them to Paula, CFR News, P.O. Box 210796, Nashville, TN 37221 or email them to paula@gabrielcommunications.com.

September 2017

The People Who Make Us Laugh

Johnny Counterfit

By Danny M. Nichols

Life itself is portrayed by the world of Country Music entertainment. From the depths of sorrow to the heights of jubilation, performances reach our hearts and spirit. This series takes a look at the lighter side of life and feature those artists, both past and present, who bring smiles to our faces and warmth to our hearts. It highlights those performers who exemplify the great comedic spirit of America.

When English writer Charles Colton coined the phrase "Imitation is the sincerest form of flattery" back in 1820, he surely must have foreseen the career of Johnny Counterfit. There are few entertainers of the current era who are as proficient as Counterfit in the craft of impressionism.

Indeed, he compliments those whom he imitates, while showing the greatest of respect for them as individuals. His impressions include musical entertainers as well as famous or well-known celebrities in the entertainment business and government. When they hear Counterfit's impressions of their songs, routines or voices, they often marvel at how accurately he portrays them.

"I try never to over-do an impression," he said. "I try to make them show respect and honor to the individual."

Respect and honor are qualities he also shares with his audiences. His performances are family oriented, a characteristic that he attributes to something he learned from Red Skelton.

"I watched an interview with Red Skelton once, and all those years ago he said something that always stuck with me that I remember to this day," Counterfit said. "He said if you have good material you don't have to rely on cuss words or bad language in your shows. So I've done that."

Counterfit was born in Omaha, Nebraska, but moved with his family at age three to Portland, Oregon, where he grew up and attended the public schools. His fascination with voice impersonations is rooted from his childhood when he would watch cartoon characters on television and imitate their voices. Later he developed a love and appreciation for the entertainment business as he watched and listened to prominent entertainers perform. He discovered early on that he had a gift for imitating voices.

"My first exposure as an artist came when I performed one night a week for free at a local lounge," he recalled, explaining how he made the decision to go into show business. "After about six weeks they had to open up the back room to accommodate the more than 100 people who would attend. It was then I considered making a career out of this gift."

He launched his career in January 1981.

"I played two years in various nightclubs in the Portland area and I worked jobs also in warehousing and unloading trucks," he said. "After that I began doing fairs and theaters in the area."

September 2017

Two events are credited by Counterfit as being instrumental toward propelling his career forward beyond the boundaries of Oregon. In 1986 he was contacted by CBS to provide voices for their "Claymation Christmas Celebration," which garnered a Primetime Emmy Award for Outstanding Animation. In 1987 Counterfit was invited by ABC in Hollywood to participate in their television show, "Americas Funniest People." Both were successes that brought national recognition and demand for Counterfit's talent and genius.

Diligence and determination, however, were required to grow this "gift" into the successful career he now enjoys. The entertainer likens his career to a fish swimming up-stream as often the tide of the entertainment industry flowed in opposing directions to his dream. He said he simply "rolled up his sleeves and did what was necessary" by creating the opportunities that guided his career toward becoming the successful entertainer he is today.

"I've never been one to sit back and wait for the phone to ring," Counterfit observed. "I don't have many recreational hobbies. When not performing I am writing songs, books, studying characters or rehearsing."

He travels the country entertaining, while still honing his talents to bring his audiences the best show possible. Counterfit said he tries to perform as much as possible with his band, The Time Travelers, but will accept solo engagements when a band is not required. He acts as his own business manager.

"I've had people wanting to manage me but I prefer managing myself," he said proudly explaining the choice to act as his own business manager. "That way I control my own destiny."

Counterfit moved to Nashville, Tennessee, in September 1993 after visiting the city several times to meet with agents and media personnel.

"Within six months I managed an appearance on the Grand Ole Opry, and within a year had appeared on TNN, The Nashville Network station" Counterfit recalled, adding, "Success came by hard work and determination. I've never had a recording label behind me so I've had to make my own opportunities."

When asked who his personal favorite artist is to portray, Counterfit responds "Johnny Cash, of course, but I try to let my audiences choose the characters they wish to hear." Other performers admired by Counterfit are Dell Reeves for his impressions and Roger Miller for his humorous song lyrics.

"I've enjoyed all forms of entertainers over the years, from Lawrence Welk to Fred Astaire to Red Skelton," he said. "For me, it's about entertaining my audiences and making them happy. It really only matters what the audience wants."

A great supporter of veterans, Counterfit has hopes of doing something special to honor them.

"I hope to put together a tour that would lead the Time Travelers and me, along with other artists, to Veterans Hospitals throughout the U.S. where we would perform free for the veterans and their families," he said. "I am hopeful our government will sponsor such a tour but if not, would hope private companies or individuals would help sponsor it."

Meanwhile, Counterfit stays busy promoting his shows, recordings, his published novel, advertising, national and international interviews, radio commercials and making commercial demos. He enjoys American history, and his performances bring people as close as they will ever get to some of those famous Americans personalities like John Wayne, Jimmy Stuart, Dean Martin, Frank Sinatra, Elvis Presley, Ronald Reagan, Bill Clinton, and yes, even Archie and Edith Bunker. Hearing all those voices again brings back priceless memories for Counterfit's audiences.

"People have been engaged in acting for centuries," he said. "That's what I do. When performing I take on the persona of the character and work to portray that person as accurately as possible through voice impression and mannerism."

Counterfit is blessed to love the work he does, and his audiences are blessed with the true professionalism incorporated into each and every performance.

"I get up every morning loving what I do for a living," he said. "There's no better way to live than that."

September 2017

Singer Songwriters

By Sasha Kay Dunavant

Johnny Bond: Remembered for Multiple Talents

Throughout the history of Country Music, thousands of songs have been written and performed. Many of those songs were written by famous performers. Some were written for a star's own records, while others were created to be sung by another artist. This Singer-Songwriter Series explores some of those talented individuals whose work we know and love.

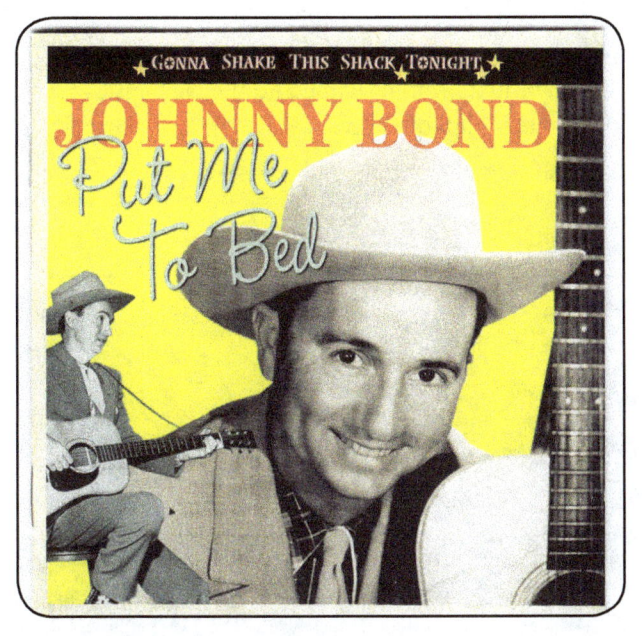

Born into poverty in 1915 in Enville, Oklahoma, Cyrus Whitfield Bond was inspired by musical legends like Milton Brown and Jimmie Rodgers. Bond learned as a child to play the trumpet, ukulele and guitar. At age 22 he changed his name to "Johnny Bond" and moved to Oklahoma City, where he formed a trio with Jimmy Wakely and Scotty Harrell that eventually became the Bell Boys.

Bond would go on to become a radio, television and movie performer, a celebrated songwriter and a successful recording artist.

In 1947 he released several top five hits, including "So Round, So Firm, So Fully Packed," "The Daughter of Jole Blon" and "Divorce Me C.O.D."

The very next year Bond produced a top ten hit, "Oklahoma Waltz." He continued on his winning streak in 1949 with the hits, "Tennessee Saturday Night" and "Till The End of The World."

After landing a spot in the Roy Rogers movie, "Saga of Death Valley," the trio appeared on Gene Autry's radio show, Melody Ranch, until it was cancelled in 1956. Later in the '50s he was a regular on the Los Angeles-based country music television series Town Hall Party. A versatile talent, Bond also appeared in 38 movies, such as David O. Selznick's "Duel in the Sun," "Six Lessons from Madame La Zonga," " Wilson" and "Song of the Wasteland."

In the mid 1940s, Bond had begun releasing his own written material like "I'm A Pris'ner of War," "Der Fuhrer's Face," "You Let Me Down" and "Love Gone Cold."

He soon established himself as a songwriter as solidly as an entertainer, and by 1957 he had written 123 songs, among them some major hits for various artists across the following decades.

Artists such as Bob Willis, Jimmie Dean, Sons of the Pioneers and Foy Willing, covered, "Cimarron," a song Bond wrote after seeing the movie of the same name.

"Cimarron roll on to my lonely song, carry me away from these skies of gray," the lyrics speak to the Cimarron River, promising, "Though I'm feeling blue, I'll roll on with you."

Bond's song, "I Wonder What You Are Doing Tonight," with lyrics universally understood by anyone with a broken heart, was recorded by numerous artists, including Johnny Rodriguez, Porter Waggoner, Bobby Bare, Flatt & Scruggs, Roy Clark, Bill Monroe, The Louvin Brothers, Hank

September 2017

Snow, Red Allen & The Kentuckians, Jerry Lee Lewis, Chet Atkins, Johnny Cash, Les Paul and Mary Ford and Arthur Alexander.

"Tonight I'm sad my heart is weary wondering if I'm wrong or right to dream about you though you've left me; I wonder where you are tonight." Bond wrote.

Bond's "Tomorrow Never Comes" laments, "Many weeks have I waited, many long nights have I cried, just to see that happy morning when I'd have you right by my side."

A hit for Glen Campbell, it was also recorded by Elvis Presley, Little Jimmie Dickens, the Statler Brothers, Ernest Tubb, Lynn Anderson and Loretta Lynn.

Hank Thompson, Ernest Tubb and Marty Robbins recorded "I'll Step Aside," which Bond himself had written and recorded earlier in his career.

Tex Ritter, Walter Brennan and Marty Robbins recorded their own renditions of "Conversations With A Gun," Bond's poem set to music in which the performer reminds the gun of its part in the history of the wild West.

Jim Reeves recorded Bond's haunting "Your Old Love Letters."

Today I burned your old love letters, I burned them gently one by one, Before I'd light the flame I'd read it, To try and find the wrong I've done," Bond penned.

Bond's light-hearted and humorous personality showed through his original work. In 1957 Columbia Records did not renew Bond's songwriter's contract, so he signed with Starday, where he remained for more than a decade. Bond was encouraged to write "drinking songs" that had become popular in the 1960s. Though he was not enamored with the subject matter, he was successful.

He continued to record, releasing 14 albums between 1960 and 1971. The only number one hit was 1964's spoken-word recording of "Ten Little Bottles," which he wrote about a man forced by his wife to empty his bottles of homebrew, and by the time he's tasted each one and is so intoxicated that he cannot tell his story.

Bond died of a stroke in 1978 and was posthumously honored with election into both the Country Music Hall of Fame and the Nashville Songwriters Hall of Fame.

THE JIMMY WAKELY TRIO, CIRCA 1940
L TO R: JOHNNY BOND, JIMMY WAKELY, DICK REINHART

September 2017

Singer Tony Jackson is ready to fill their shoes!

Tony Jackson is the son of a Navy man. He led a base-to-base existence, at one point living with his family in Rota, Spain for three years. His early musical background was sketchy at best. "I sang 'White Christmas' in the Christmas play in the sixth grade," he recalls. 'Everybody seemed to love it, but I was a wreck. My mother forced me to sing in the church choir, but I was kind of buried in the voices along with everybody else."

Two weeks after graduating from high school, Jackson joined the Marines. "I told my dad I was joining because I was sick of taking orders," he says with a wry grin. "I was a computer and electronics geek as a teenager," he says. "When I talked to the recruiter, he told me the Marine Corps had just started a computer science school in Quantico, Virginia. Fortunately, I scored high enough on the entrance exam to go to that school." It was a smart move.

It was while in the Marines that he first started paying serious attention to country music. "My mother listened only to gospel," he says. "My dad was into jazz, hip hop, R&B, new jack swing—stuff like that. But Armed Forces Radio played everything. When I was living in Spain—when I was 10 to 13—Randy Travis came over there on a USO tour. Some friends and I were out there early when they were setting up the stage, and we actually got to talk to him before we realized he was the guy who'd be performing later. He was really cool to us. In the Marine Corps, when my friends and I played music for each other, we were all homesick. So when you'd listen to these country songs that talked about family and home and heartbreak, it would really grab you."

When he finished service, a prominent bank in Richmond snapped him up to work in its Information Technology division, initially assigning him the lowly chore of re-setting passwords. "I was way overqualified," he says, "so I got promoted fast. I was a senior vice president by my early 30s."

He continued listening to country music and one song that particularly appealed to Jackson was George Jones' heartbreaking 1974 hit, "The Grand Tour." When Jones died, Jackson and some friends went into a Richmond studio and recorded it. In the process, they also made a performance video that eventually wound up on YouTube. By sheer accident, singer Donna Dean Stevens saw the video and instantly decided Jackson should do "The Grand Tour" on the Old Dominion Barn Dance, which she had just resurrected. After she witnessed Jackson's standing ovation—an honor that hadn't yet been accorded to any of the show's headliners—she offered to co-manage and co-produce him with noted talent manager Jim Della Croce. A commanding performer in her own right, Dean Stevens recorded for Mercury Records in Nashville as Donna Meade. She is also the widow of Country Music Hall of Fame member Jimmy Dean and a zealous guardian of his vast musical legacy.

Dean Stevens and Della Croce then whisked Jackson to Nashville, where he recorded most of Tony Jackson at the hallowed RCA Records Studios. In one of his best-loved songs, George Jones considered the dwindling ranks of country superstars and asked plaintively "Who's Gonna Fill Their Shoes."

Is it premature to see Hall of Fame material in a guy who's just releasing his first album? To put it plainly, Jackson is one of the most gifted singers ever to grace country music. His video "The Grand Tour" ignited an unprecedented 20 million Facebook views!

The respect Jackson has already earned within the music community is evident throughout Tony Jackson, as the new album is titled. It features songs and/or performances by Rock and Roll Hall of Fame members John Sebastian, Steve Cropper

September 2017

and Dr. John "Mac" Rebennack, Country Music Hall of Famers Vince Gill, Bill Anderson and Conway Twitty and Nashville Songwriters Hall of Fame luminary Norro Wilson.

But it is ease with which Jackson makes every song—even the familiar ones—distinctly his own that sets him apart. Who else would dare to try and then succeed in bringing a fresh layer of emotional urgency to such a classic as George Jones' "The Grand Tour" or Conway Twitty's eternal "It's Only Make Believe"?

Jackson recruited John Sebastian and Vince Gill in revivifying (after 50 years) the Lovin' Spoonful's 1966 romp, "Nashville Cats." "When asked if we should recut the song," Sebastian begins, "I said absolutely but we have to get Vince Gill, Paul Franklin and today's real Nashville Cats in on the session and fortunately it was preserved on video," he beams.

After capturing perfectly, the excitement of new love in Bill Anderson's "I Didn't Wake Up This Morning," he moves on to a memory-stirring homage to Merle Haggard, Hank Williams Jr. and Willie Nelson in "They Lived It Up," a lyrical scrapbook from Anderson and Bobby Tomberlin.

Jackson shines as a keen-eyed songwriter in his own right with such memorable excursions as "Drink By Drink," "Old Porch Swing" and "She's Taking Me Home."

From start to finish, Tony Jackson stands out as a "discovery" album, the kind you listen to with such delight that you have to recommend it to friends

Jackson is currently a headliner on the Old Dominion Barn Dance in Richmond, Virginia, and is almost certainly the only major bank executive ever to abandon a prominent IT job in finance at a Fortune 500 company to embark on a career in country music. He didn't grow up a country fan, but country fans are going to love him!

Catch him on Larry's Country Diner Thursday, September 14 at 7 p.m. or Saturday, September 16 at 10 p.m. Central Time.

September 2017

OCTOBER

Giant Talent, Gentle Soul – Don Williams Dead at 78

By Claudia Johnson

Don Williams was known as Country Music's Gentle Giant, in part because of his imposing 6'1" frame but mostly because of his genial demeanor and massive talent.

The singer and songwriter, who died last month at age 78 following a brief illness, began performing as a child, winning his first talent competition as a three-year-old. The alarm clock he took home as a prize was virtually worthless to a toddler, but it may have foreshadowed what became one of his most memorable recordings in a lauded 50-year career. "Tulsa Time," released in 1978 as the first single from Williams' album, "Expressions," became his eighth number one country chart hit. While the song's narrator reveals his failure due to his inability to make necessary adjustments in pursuit of his dreams, the opposite was true of Williams.

As a teenager growing up on the Texas Gulf Coast in Portland, a small town near Corpus Christi, Williams played guitar in local bands. His first paying gig came in 1957, when he and some friends played and sang for the opening of Billups Service Station in Taft, Texas, for the hefty fee of $25.

In 1960, two years after high school graduation and following an honorable discharge from the U.S. Army, Williams married Joy Bucher, with whom he had two sons, Gary and Timmy, and to whom he remained married until his death on Sept. 8, 2017. To support his family he took a variety of jobs. At various times he was a bill collector, a bread truck driver and a furniture salesman. He also worked in a smelting plant and spent time in the Texas oil fields, but his music remained important.

While living in Corpus Christi in 1964, he formed the Pozo Seco Singers with Lofton Cline and Susan Taylor. The trio sang a variety of music from folk to pop and country. Their first single, "Time," became a Top 10 hit and other hits climbed the charts before they disbanded in 1969.

By 1971 the Williams family had moved to Nashville where Don had a songwriting contract. A recording contract soon followed, and he debuted on the charts in 1973 with "The Shelter of Your Eyes." His mellow vocal style and choice of love songs and ballads set him apart from other artists of the time, resulting in 17 number one Country hits during his career.

In 1973 Williams became the first country music artist to make a concept music video in support of his single "Come Early Morning." Consistently nominated for male vocalist and other awards throughout the '70s, he was voted Male Vocalist of the Year by the Country Music Association in 1978. "Tulsa Time" was named Record of the Year by Academy of Country Music in 1979. Only four of the 46 singles he released during his career didn't make it to the Top Ten.

His popularity abroad grew, and he earned a devoted following in England, Ireland and New Zealand. At the height of the UK country and western boom in 1976 he had Top 40 pop chart hits with "You're My Best Friend" and "I Recall a Gypsy Woman" and in 1978 a No. 2 album, "Images." In 1975 the CMA of Great Britain voted Williams both Male Singer and Performer of the Year and voted "You're My Best Friend" Album of the Year. He even became a superstar in South Africa and Kenya.

During the 1970s Williams appeared with Burt Reynolds in two films, "W. W & The Dixie Dance Kings" and "Smokey & The Bandit II." In each he played and sang. He also headlined a variety of prestigious venues, from the Sporting Club in Monte Carlo to the Roxy in Los Angeles, from a sold-out Carnegie Hall in New York to London's Royal Albert Hall.

October 2017

In 1980 his 11th No. 1 Country hit, "I Believe in You," became his only Top 40 chart hit.

"I like to think of God as love, he's down below he's up above," Williams sang in what is perhaps his most enduring song. "He's watchin' people everywhere; he knows who does and doesn't care. And I'm an ordinary man – sometimes I wonder who I am, but I believe in love, I believe in music, I believe in magic and I believe in you."

He and his wife owned a 100-acre farm near Nashville and another home in Hawaii. Williams relaxed by fishing and tinkering with his prized '56 Chevy, but he continued performing worldwide through his final performance in 2016.

"It's time to hang my hat up and enjoy some quiet time at home," he said when announcing his retirement last year. "I'm so thankful for my fans, my friends and my family for their everlasting love and support."

In 2010 the Country Music Association inducted Williams into the Country Music Hall of Fame, which is Country Music's greatest recognition. Another type of honor was bestowed upon him earlier this year when he was the subject of a tribute album, "Gentle Giants: The Songs of Don Williams," that included performances of his hits by artists such as Lady Antebellum, Trisha Yearwood, Allison Krauss, Dierks Bentley, Christ Stapleton and others.

In his song, "Handful of Dust," Williams noted that in the end "a handful of dust sums up the richest and poorest of us." But that is not the end of the verse any more than it was the measure of his long life and career.

"True love makes priceless the worthless, whenever it is added to these handfuls of dust."

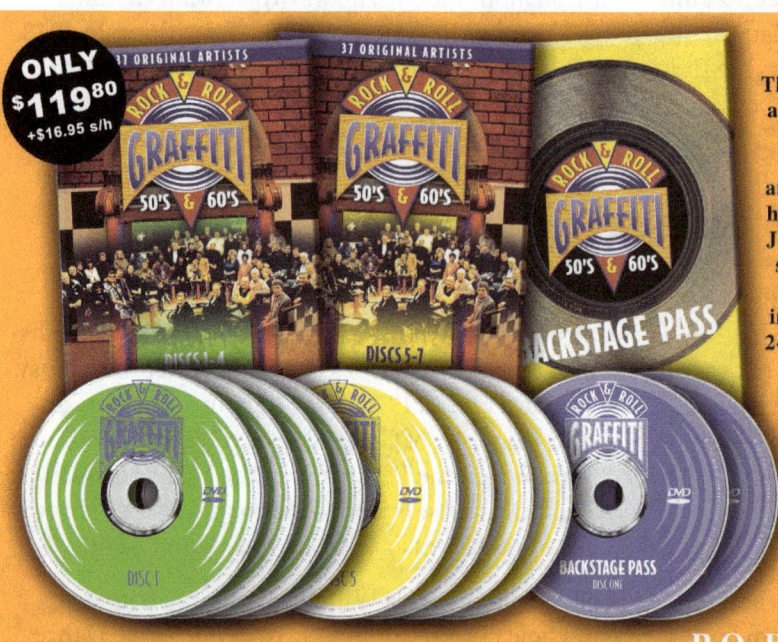

Are you a Rock & Roll Fan?

This collection features the hit-makers from the 50's and 60's. 37 performers who created the music of a lifetime. It is the music you listened to when you were dating, the songs you heard while falling in and out of love, and the hits they played at the sock hop. This is the music of an era! It is YOUR music. Join us for the Rock and Roll Graffiti Collection to see and hear the stories behind the music and the songs of the 50's and 60's. The 9 dvd collection includes the free bonus series, "Backstage Pass," a 2-hour look behind the scenes at the taping of Rock and Roll Graffiti.

This is a once in a lifetime gathering. Enjoy!

1,2, 3
Everlasting Love
She Shot A Hole in My Soul
Then You Can Tell Me Goodbye
Down in the Boondocks
Sugar Shack

Tequila
Dizzy
Sea Cruise
Moody Blues
Be My Baby
Lots More!

ONLY $119.80 +$16.95 s/h

800-820-5405
P.O. Box 210796, Nashville, TN 37221

October 2017

Troy Gentry – Lucky to Have Been Here

One of Country Music's most successful collaborations ended with the recent death of Troy Gentry, who along with Eddie Montgomery was half of the award-winning duo Montgomery Gentry.

Eddie Montogmery (left) and Troy Gentry (right).

On Sept. 8, 2017, Gentry went up for a 'spur of the moment' helicopter ride just before 1 p.m. at the Flying W Airport and Resort in Medford, N.J., where Montgomery Gentry was scheduled to play later that evening, when the pilot of the Schweitzer 269 helicopter, James Robinson, made a distress call to the airport.

"Initial reports were the helicopter was going to attempt to crash land," Medford police said in a statement regarding the deaths of Gentry and Robinson. "Emergency crews arrived at the airport, and shortly thereafter the helicopter suddenly crashed in a field just south of the airport runway."

Kentucky natives, Gentry and Montgomery began performing together around 1990 when the friends formed a band, Early Tymz, that also included Montgomery's younger brother, John Michael Montgomery. The trio later entertained as Young Country, but John Michael Montgomery left to pursue a solo career, and Gentry went on to win the Jim Beam National Talent Contest in 1994, touring as a solo artist and opening for Patty Loveless, Tracy Byrd and others. When Gentry reunited with Eddie Montgomery in the late 1990s, both entertainers soon achieved their well-deserved success.

"It's the chemistry that's worked for years," Gentry stated on the duo's official website. "We have two separate singing styles that when they come together, they're very identifiable."

Explaining how they remained popular across two decades, Gentry said their sound didn't "get old or get sterile."

"The back and forth between our vocals definitely keeps you listening and keeps you interested in the song," he observed.

Montgomery Gentry released their debut album, the platinum-seller "Tattoos & Scars," in 1999, which earned them recognition as American Music Awards Favorite New Country Artist that year.

The duo was nominated for Country Music Association and/or Academy of Country Music top duo or group awards each year between 1999-2009, winning the CMA for Vocal Duo of the Year and the ACM Top New Vocal Duo or Group in 2000. They were inducted into the Grand Ole Opry in 2009 and into the Kentucky Music Hall of Fame in 2015.

Montgomery Gentry was a representative of the workingman, releasing blue-collar Country anthems with a Southern rock edge and a universal theme of God, country, family and community.

"We're going to continue to do the same music that we always have, and if that puts us in that leadership role, then so be it," Gentry assured their fans when their seventh studio album, "Folks Like Us," was released in 2015. "I definitely want to be the one on the front end and not trying to copy something else that's already been done."

Montgomery Gentry's albums produced more than 20 singles on the Billboard Hot Country Songs charts, including the No. 1 hits "If You Ever Stop Loving Me," "Something to Be Proud Of," "Lucky Man," "Back When I Knew It All" and "Roll with Me." Ten more of their songs reached the Top 10 on the country charts, including the No. 3 hit "Gone," the most played country song by a duo in 2005. Their albums "Tattoos & Scars," "My Town" and "You Do Your Thing" are all certified platinum by the Recording Industry Association of America.

"I reckon we're like a married couple, sort of," Eddie Montgomery said in a 2013 interview with The Des Moines Register. "You hear horror stories all the time about duos, but we've always just been friends having fun and making music."

October 2017

The friends had survived recent challenges in their personal lives. Gentry's wife of 18 years has been undergoing treatment for breast cancer, and Montgomery is still mourning the 2015 death of his 19-year-old son.

A 2001 song, "Lucky to be Here," co-written by Gentry and Montgomery, encapsulates the hope-filled attitude that defined their music and foreshadows the strength Gentry's wife, Angie, daughters, Kaylee and Taylor, friends and fans will need as they mourn his passing.

"I'm not one to whine or cry or wallow in self-pity," the lyrics state. "I take life in stride and smell the roses when I can. I am one of those lucky guys who's happy just to be here, doin' what I love and thankful that I am. When I die I'll thank the good Lord face to face for his patience and grace."

Troy and Angie Gentry

KICKIN' BACK
COUNTRY'S FAMILY REUNION
A SPECIAL GATHERING OF GOOD FRIENDS

$79.80
+$6.95 s/h

Kick Back with Bill Anderson, Ricky Skaggs, Jimmy Fortune, T. Graham Brown, Rhonda Vincent, Mark Wills, David Ball, Jeannie Seely, Larry Gatlin, Gene Watson and more. And NEW to CFR Ashley Campbell, Randy Travis, Phil Vassar, Lorrie Morgan, John Rich and several others kick back with the veterans for a great new series!

1-800-820-5405
www.cfrvideos.com

John Conlee receives "Legend Award" from Kentucky Country Music Association

Country legend and Kentucky native John Conlee was recently awarded the first ever Legends Award by the Kentucky Country Music Association during his performance at the Kentucky Opry. The award was created to honor an artist who is not only from Kentucky, but has also promoted Kentucky throughout their career in both music and interviews.

"It is always gratifying to be recognized by those from my home state of Kentucky. My profound thanks to the Kentucky Country Music Association and Kentucky Governor Matt Bevin for their very kind honors," said Conlee.

Along with his award, Conlee received a letter from Kentucky Governor Matthew Bevin recognizing not only his successful career but his dedication to country music, the "Common Man" and the state of Kentucky as well. Bevin noted that this award was a "perfectly fitting tribute."

"John Conlee is a perfect fit for our first Legend Award," said Kenneth Reynold, President and Founder of the Kentucky Country Music Association.

"He has never forgotten where he came from and has been a great promoter of not only country music but of Kentucky."

For more information visit johnconlee.com.

JOHN CONLEE ON TOUR:

Oct. 5 – The Historic State Theatre – Elizabethtown, Ky.

Oct. 6 – Mitchell Opera House – Mitchell, Ind.

Oct. 7 – Sesser Opera House – Sesser, Ill.

Oct. 8 – Historic Rodgers Theatre – Poplar Bluff, Mo.

Oct. 19 – Sunset Theatre – Asheboro, N.C.

Oct. 20 – Carteret Theatre – Morehead City, N.C.

Oct. 21 – Red Barn Convention Center – Winchester, Ohio

Oct. 22 – Harvest Performance Center – Rocky Mount, Va.

Nov. 16 – Main Street Crossing – Tomball, Texas

Nov. 17 – Route 92 – Youngsville, La.

Feb. 01 – The Palace Theater – Corsicana, Texas

Feb. 02 – Stampede Houston – Houston, Texas

Feb. 22 – Wadsworth Auditorium – Newnan, Ga.

Feb. 23 – Tallassee High School Auditorium – Tallassee, Ala.

Feb. 24 – Theatre Dublin – Dublin, Ga.

Feb. 25 – Mars Theatre – Springfield, Ga.

President/Founder of Kentucky Country Music Association Kenneth Reynolds Presents John Conlee with Legend Award.

October 2017

Nadine
The Church Lady

Lord, give me a sense of humor,
Give me the grace to see a joke,
To get some humor out of life,
And to pass it on to other folk.

If I believed in reincarnation, I'd come back as a bear. When you're a bear, you get to hibernate. You do nothing but sleep for six months. I could deal with that. Before you hibernate, you're supposed to eat yourself stupid. I could deal with that, too. When you're a girl bear, you birth your children (who are the size of a walnut) while you sleep and wake up to partially grown, cute, cuddly cubs. I could definitely deal with that. If you're a moma bear, everyone knows you mean business, you swat anyone who bothers your cubs, if your cubs get out of line, you swat them, too! I could deal with that. If you're a bear, your mate expects you to wake up growling. He expects that you will have hairy legs (and chin) and excess body fat.

Yep, I would come back as a bear!

Church sign

Some of the people who say "our Father' on Sundays go around the rest of the week acting as if they were orphans.

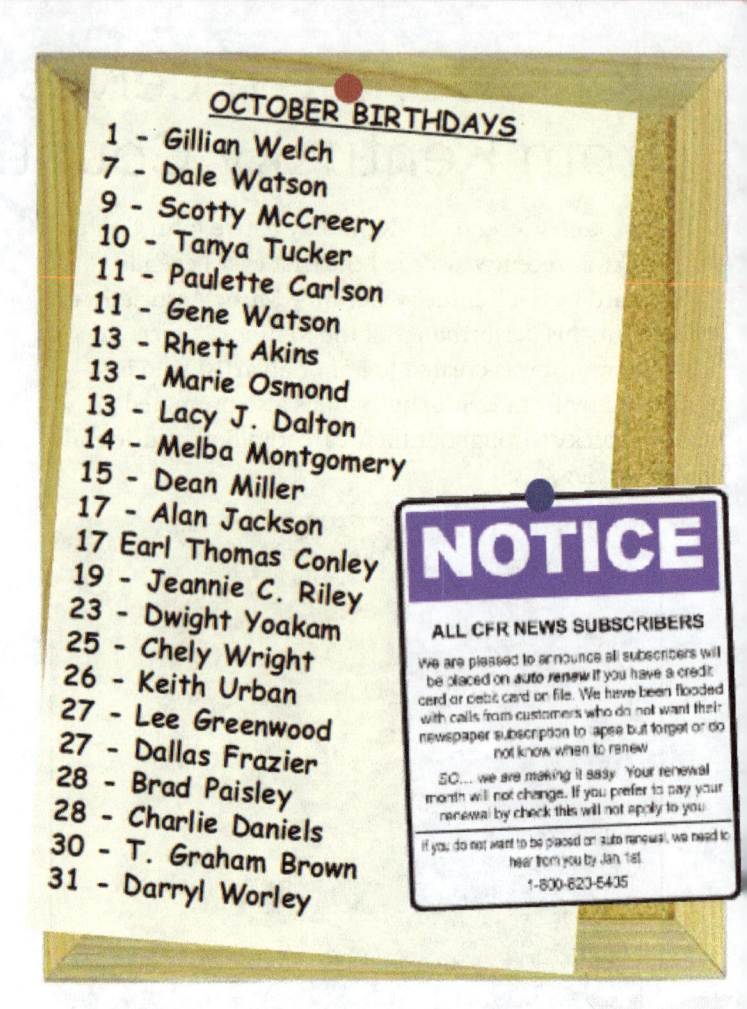

OCTOBER BIRTHDAYS
- 1 - Gillian Welch
- 7 - Dale Watson
- 9 - Scotty McCreery
- 10 - Tanya Tucker
- 11 - Paulette Carlson
- 11 - Gene Watson
- 13 - Rhett Akins
- 13 - Marie Osmond
- 13 - Lacy J. Dalton
- 14 - Melba Montgomery
- 15 - Dean Miller
- 17 - Alan Jackson
- 17 - Earl Thomas Conley
- 19 - Jeannie C. Riley
- 23 - Dwight Yoakam
- 25 - Chely Wright
- 26 - Keith Urban
- 27 - Lee Greenwood
- 27 - Dallas Frazier
- 28 - Brad Paisley
- 28 - Charlie Daniels
- 30 - T. Graham Brown
- 31 - Darryl Worley

NOTICE
ALL CFR NEWS SUBSCRIBERS

We are pleased to announce all subscribers will be placed on *auto renew* if you have a credit card or debit card on file. We have been flooded with calls from customers who do not want their newspaper subscription to lapse but forget or do not know when to renew.

SO... we are making it easy. Your renewal month will not change. If you prefer to pay your renewal by check this will not apply to you.

If you do not want to be placed on auto renewal, we need to hear from you by Jan 1st.

1-800-823-5405

John Anderson back on the road after medical procedure

Country music hit-maker John Anderson is set to return to the stage on September 3, 2017, after rescheduling a few weekend of shows in August to undergo some medical procedures.

"I am thankful for the outpouring of prayers from friends and fans. All medical procedures went great and we'll plan on seeing you all real soon," says John Anderson.

2017 marks the 35th anniversary of Anderson's iconic hit "Swingin'" from his acclaimed album Wild & Blue.

Be sure to follow Anderson on Instagram, Twitter and Facebook or visit johnanderson.com.

JOHN ANDERSON ON TOUR:

Oct. 5 Dosey Doe - Woodlands, Texas

Oct. 7 Sugar Creek Casino - Hinton, Okla.

Oct. 14 Lake Of The Torches Resort Casino - Lac Du Flambeau, Wis.

Oct. 24 State Theatre - Eau Claire, Wis.

Oct. 25 Barrymore Theatre - Madison, Wis.

Oct. 26 Meyer Theatre - Green Bay, Wis.

Oct. 27 Sondheim Center for the Performing Arts - Fairfield, Iowa

Oct. 28 Meramec Music Theatre - Steelville, Mo.

Dec. 01 Harvester Performance Center - Rocky Mountain, Va.

Dec. 02 The Beacon Theatre - Hopewell, Va.

The Josie Music Awards Celebrate Independent Music Artists

The spirit of independence and the joy of music were celebrated in Nashville in September when independent multi-genre musicians and songwriters were recognized during an awards show at the Nissan Stadium attended by thousands of fans and industry professionals from around the globe.

Josie Passantino (left) and Casie Mason (right) at the 2016 Josie Awards Show.

The Josie Music Awards, now in its third year, is a brand of The Josie Network, LLC owned by the partnership team of Josie Passantino and her mother, Tina Passantino, who created and have broadcast an award-winning radio program, The Josie Show, since October 2009 when Josie was still a teenager. More than 2,000 interviews have been conducted with Josie's guests, who include recording artists, Grammy Legends, Platinum Recording Artists, composers, County Music Hall of Fame Legends, writers, movie stars and also upcoming independent artists.

It's the independent artists that The Josie Music Awards honor.

"Winners are selected on their talent, skill, material, professionalism and more and NOT by button pressing voting," Josie says on her official website, josiemusicawards.com, explaining that nominees are reviewed and selected by a respected team of industry professionals who are not associated with any of the nominees.

Josie's career is an example of how independence can drive success. Josie has always dreamed of owning her licensed radio station, and in 2013 when she turned 18, her station, Country Blast Radio, launched. It plays country music from both signed and independent artists. For two consecutive years the station was named Favorite Radio Station of the Year from New Music Weekly Magazine. Country Blast Radio can be heard at countryblastradio.com and on the Country Blast Radio mobile apps 24 hours per day, seven days per week.

"A highlight of each and every week's programming is our live Friday evening show, during which listeners may call in with their questions for the guests or participate online in the real-time chat room where they post questions that I ask the guests for them," Josie explained.

Among her thousands of guests have been Aaron Tippin, Billy Dean, Mickey Gilley, Richard Sterban (Oak Ridge Boys), Craig Wayne Boyd and the late Ray Price. The Josie Show covers live events on location and hosts events through its Josie Show Concert Series. The Josie Show was presented with the "Most Indie Friendly Radio Show" honor through the Independent Country Music Association" in 2014.

In addition to her talents as a radio host and awards show producer, Josie is a musician who plays cello, tuba and baritone, a singer and songwriter who has released a single, the founder of the Confidently Ready cosmetics line and the author of a 2016 book The Artist Collection: Every Music Artist Has a Story with each participant in the book as co-authors. She is a voting member of the Country Music Association, Canadian Country Music Association and the Manitoba Country Music Association. At only 22 years old, she serves on a national advisory panel that rates commercial country radio music. The inspiring young woman was included as one of 50 women featured in the book Ari'el Rising that profiles empowered women in the 21st Century who are making a difference with their passion, experiences and calling.

October 2017

In 2015 she established The Josie Music Awards, an all genre music award show ceremony that includes a lavish red carpet and many performances and is the largest independent artist award show globally. All three years the show has been held in Nashville, attracting a global slate of guests including independent artists, songwriters, record labels, talent agencies, promotion companies, producers, engineers, management companies and the media.

"The event was created solely to celebrate those in the independent music industry that work so hard every day and deserve to have a night of their own," Josie said.

She noted that it is not only a celebration, it is also an outstanding way for independent artists to connect with industry professionals.

In addition to their near 80 awards the show also includes performances and the Lifetime Achievement Awards are presented annually with Razzy Bailey and Vern Gosden being past winners. Since The Josie Network acquired the Independent Country Music Hall of Fame, this year will also include HOF Inductees during the ceremony.

"Sometimes you have to make the hard decision and turn your world upside down to achieve your dreams," Josie muses, advising, "Go after what you want, make great friends along the way, and love the whole journey."

Look who's on the Diner this week!
On RFD-TV
All shows subject to change

Thursdays at 7 p.m. central Saturdays at 10 p.m. central
Previously Aired

DARYLE SINGLETARY & RHONDA VINCENT
October 5 & 7

SHANE OWEN
October 12 & 14

MOE BANDY
October 19 & 21

ASHLEY CAMPBELL
October 26 & 28

October 6/7, 13/14, 20/21

Fridays...7 p.m. central
Saturdays...11 p.m central

October 27/28

October 2017

COUNTRY LEGENDS OF THE PAST & PRESENT
BY TOM WOOD

Marion Worth

Lady Marion was a sultry siren with a milky voice. And from what I've read and heard, seeing one of her shows was well Worth the price of admission.

We're talking about Marion Worth, of course.

Marion spent nearly two decades as a regular cast member of the Grand Ole Opry from the early 1960s until her final appearance in 1980 when health issues forced her to step away.

Growing up in Birmingham, Alabama, the health field was her dream job. She wanted to become a nurse long before considering a move to the entertainment industry.

But entertaining was in Marion's blood first as he railroad-working father taught her to play the piano and guitar. She won her first talent show at the ripe age of 10 — and for the next four weeks after that.

Still, she began training for a medical career before landing a bookkeeping job with a local record company. That drew back into talent shows with her sister—and she won again. That time, it was enough to convince Marion that the music industry was where she belonged.

Saying and doing are two different things, of course, and she was up to the arduous challenge before her.

In the late 1940s, she made a number of radio appearances and worked at several radio and television stations. Those connections led her to back to Birmingham where she met entertainer and producer Happy Wilson.

They eventually got married and began recording singles that didn't go very far in the early 1950s. They moved to Nashville around 1955 and shuttled from Nashville to Birmingham and other parts of the South for weekend shows during this time.

Marion's career finally took off in 1959 with her first hit "Are You Willing, Willie," which reached No. 12 on the U.S. Country charts. Her next two releases, "That's My Kind of Love" and "I Think I Know" reached Nos. 5 and 7 on the 1960 charts, making them her two biggest hits.

The next year, she connected with fans with "There's Always Be Sadness" (No. 21), followed by a pair of Top 20 sings in 1963, "Shake Me I Rattle (Squeeze Me I Cry" at No. 14 and "Crazy Arms: at No. 18. That was the same year she joined the Grand Ole Opry.

She placed six more songs in the Top 50 from 1963-68, and never charted after that. But she remained as popular as ever at the Grand Ole Opry and across the country and in Canada.

Marion is cited as one of the first country music stars to play Carnegie Hall in New York City and in Las Vegas. She became an ambassador the country industry.

Her husband, Happy Wilson, died in 1977 and Marion's final Opry performance was on March 22, 1980. She died on Dec. 19, 1999, in Nashville, suffering from emphysema. She was 69.

Sources: Wikipedia, bham.wiki.com, and fayfare.blogspot.com operated by nationally recognized independent Grand Ole Opry historian Byron Fay.

Author Tom Wood, who writes thrillers and Westerns, is a regular contributor to Country Family Reunion News. Reach him at tomwoodauthor.com

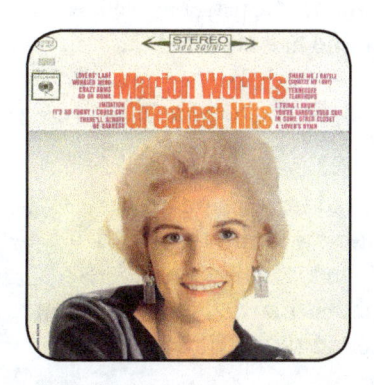

October 2017

Joe Bonsall undergoes hand surgery to correct genetic issue

Joe Bonsall of The Oak Ridge Boys, has taken some time out of his busy schedule to undergo a much-needed surgery. On Monday (August 28), Bonsall announced that he would be undergoing surgery on his right hand on August 29.

Bonsall shared that the reason for his surgery is a rare genetic condition called Dupuytren's contracture. According to the Mayo Clinic, Dupuytren's contracture is described as follows:

"A hand deformity that...affects a layer of tissue that lies under the skin of your palm. Knots of tissue form under the skin — eventually creating a thick cord that can pull one or more fingers into a bent position."

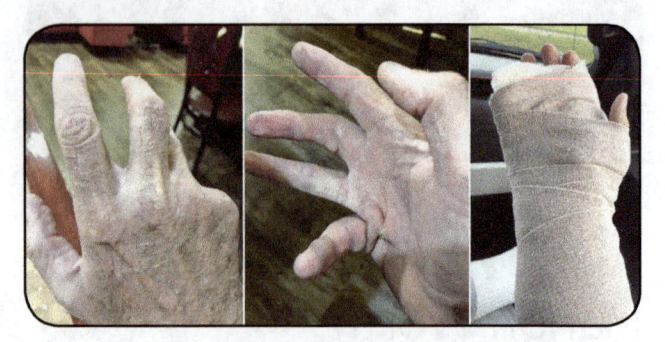

The photos that Bonsall included with his surgery announcement show how his fingers have become bent due to the condition. It looks quite painful and we wish him a speedy recovery.

Country Artists of a Bygone Era

Theron Hale and His Daughters Brought Contrasting Sound to 1920s Opry

By Claudia Johnson

Of the Grand Ole Opry's early performers, Theron Hale and His Daughters were distinctively different. Hale, born in Pikeville, Tennessee, in 1883 was a gifted banjo and fiddle player as well as a successful salesman who had attended Carson Newman College as a young man. His band mates and daughters, Elizabeth Jean and Mamie Ruth, were trained musicians who played several instruments.

While still in his teens and working on his parents' farm, Theron gained notoriety for his talent and began teaching the banjo in his native southeastern area of Tennessee. He married Laura Vaughn in Tennessee around 1905. The couple along with two-year-old Elizabeth Jean and six-month-old Mamie Ruth were renting a home in Creston, Iowa, where Hale was an agent for a sewing machine company, according to the 1910 U.S. Census. Hale's parents, his sister and other family members also moved to Iowa. His mother, Sarah Elizabeth, lived with his sister in Iowa until her death in 1929. His father, Thomas Franklin Hale, a Baptist Minister, died in Iowa in 1925.

Theron moved his family back to Tennessee to what is now known as East Nashville in 1915. The 1920 Census shows him to be a self-employed cattle trader. The 1926 Nashville City Directory lists Theron as a salesman, but by then he was also a performer on the WSM Barn Dance, which was soon to be known as the Grand Ole Opry. He played fiddle, daughter Mamie Ruth, 16, played second fiddle or mandolin and Elizabeth, 18, accompanied them on the piano. Photos of the family trio showed them to be well dressed and refined. They were inducted into the Opry, where they played regularly into the 1930s,

October 2017

having been among the first group of performers to record albums in Nashville for the Victor label. Among their best-known recordings are "Hale's Rag," "Jolly Blacksmith," "Turkey Gobbler," "Red Wing" and "Over The Waves."

Their music featured slow, twin fiddle melodies in stark contrast to the more raucous hillbilly music usually associated with the era. Because their sound was more akin to chamber music, the group was not among the acts often invited to play at the popular barn or square dances. All their performances were in conjunction with WSM, and they did not tour as Theron maintained a sales career in Nashville while his daughters pursued formal education.

Mamie Ruth graduated from Trevecca College, then a Nazarene institution, in Nashville and later studied at the Nashville Conservatory of Music. The 1930 Census lists her occupation as a violin teacher, and for a time she taught at Vanderbilt University. She married Rev. Edward Kelly Hardy, a Nazarene minister whose father was president of Trevecca, in 1931 and served as the orchestra director at the church in Nashville where her husband was associate pastor. The couple moved to Atlanta, Georgia, where he was a pastor, and became parents to two daughters, Barbara Anne and Faye Ruth, who were ages 4 and 5 respectively when their mother died from surgery complications in 1939, according to Mamie Ruth's obituary.

In the 1940 Census Ruth is living with her grandmother, Laura. Barbara is also living in Nashville with her aunt, Elizabeth, who is married to Samuel Briggs Burkhalter and is a public school elementary teacher, having graduated from Trevecca and Peabody universities. Elizabeth died in 2004 at the age of 95. Rev. Hardy had a long and distinguished career as a pastor until his death in 1981. Barbara died in 1988, and Faye, a college professor, died in 2014.

After his daughters left his Grand Ole Opry act, Theron continued playing and recording until the late 1940s, often accompanied by Opry guitarist Sam McGee. One memorable recording from this time was "Fire in the Mountains." The pair made several recordings sponsored by the Tennessee State Extension Project to promote traditional square dancing music.

In the 1940 Census both Theron and his wife, Laura, list their marital status as "married," but they reside in two different households. He lives in a boarding house in East Nashville and is employed as a door-to-door salesman. Laura is listed as head of household and proprietor of a boarding house that she is shown as renting.

An odd note for which no explanation can be found in public records is a new marriage certificate for Theron Evan Hale and Mrs. Laura Hale, both in their 50s, dated Jan. 10, 1940, and filed in Williamson County, Tennessee. The couple had reported their status as married and living together in every census since 1910. In Nashville City Directories published throughout the 1940s Theron and Laura reside together at a home on Gallatin Pike, and he is occupied as a salesman for a floor wax manufacturer.

Theron died of a heart attack on Jan. 29, 1954. His obituary in the Nashville Tennessean recalled that he played with Uncle Dave Macon, The Dixie Dewdrops, Burt Hutchinson and Oscar Stone. He is credited with popularizing the songs "Down Yonder" and "Listen to the Mockingbird" in which he used his fingers to produce the sound of bird whistles on the fiddle strings. Laura lived for 16 more years after his death.

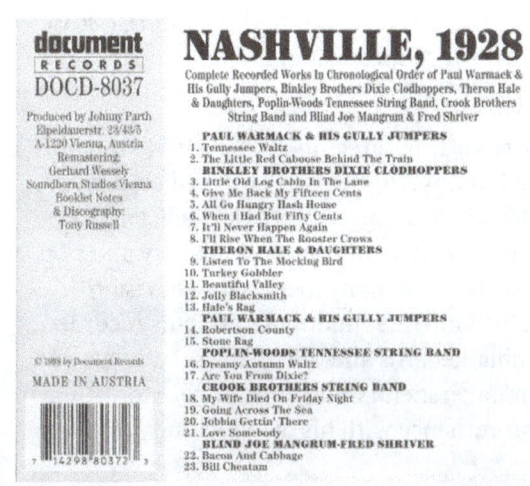

document RECORDS
DOCD-8037

Produced by Johnny Parth
Elpeidauerstr. 23/45/5
A-1220 Vienna, Austria
Remastering:
Gerhard Wessely
Soundborn Studios Vienna
Booklet Notes
& Discography:
Tony Russell

© 1998 by Document Records

MADE IN AUSTRIA

NASHVILLE, 1928
Complete Recorded Works In Chronological Order of Paul Warmack & His Gully Jumpers, Binkley Brothers Dixie Clodhoppers, Theron Hale & Daughters, Poplin-Woods Tennessee String Band, Crook Brothers String Band and Blind Joe Mangrum & Fred Shriver

PAUL WARMACK & HIS GULLY JUMPERS
1. Tennessee Waltz
2. The Little Red Caboose Behind The Train
BINKLEY BROTHERS DIXIE CLODHOPPERS
3. Little Old Log Cabin In The Lane
4. Give Me Back My Fifteen Cents
5. All Go Hungry Hash House
6. When I Had But Fifty Cents
7. It'll Never Happen Again
8. I'll Rise When The Rooster Crows
THERON HALE & DAUGHTERS
9. Listen To The Mocking Bird
10. Turkey Gobbler
11. Beautiful Valley
12. Jolly Blacksmith
13. Hale's Rag
PAUL WARMACK & HIS GULLY JUMPERS
14. Robertson County
15. Stone Rag
POPLIN-WOODS TENNESSEE STRING BAND
16. Dreamy Autumn Waltz
17. Are You From Dixie?
CROOK BROTHERS STRING BAND
18. My Wife Died On Friday Night
19. Going Across The Sea
20. Jobbin Gettin' There
21. Love Somebody
BLIND JOE MANGRUM-FRED SHRIVER
22. Bacon And Cabbage
23. Bill Cheatam

October 2017

Rose Lee and Joe Maphis impact country music still today

Joe Maphis was born Otis W. Maphis on May 12, 1921 in Suffolk, Virginia. One of the flashiest country guitarists of the 1950s and 1960s, Joe Maphis was known as The King of the Strings, playing many stringed instruments with ease.

Joe's family moved to Cumberland, Maryland in 1926 when his father Robert Maphis landed a job with the B&O Railroad. Joe's first band was called the Maryland Rail Splitters. He also played in the local (Cumberland) Foggy Mountain Boys as well as The Sonnateers before Maphis hit the road in 1939. He played across Virginia until he became a regular featured performer on the "Old Dominion Barn Dance," broadcast live on radio WRVA-AM and aired in 38 states.

In 1944, Joe went into the U.S. Army. His musical skills landed him a gig entertaining the troops around the world. Maphis was discharged from the Army in 1946. On his return to the states, he began playing on WLS radio in Chicago. In the late 1940s he returned to Richmond, Va. and the Old Dominion Barn Dance until the early 1950s. During this period Maphis met many country music stars of the day who played the same circuit including Merle Travis. While in Virginia, he also met the musically talented Rose Lee (Doris) Schetrompf, his future wife. Maphis and Schetrompf, of Clear Spring, Md., were married in 1953. A talented vocalist and rhythm guitarist, Rose backed Joe onstage throughout the remainder of his career.

Maphis' recording career took off in 1951 when he was invited to Los Angeles by Travis and country music entertainer Johnny Bond . He made two LPs with Travis, recorded for countless country and pop stars and worked on many themes for television programs and movie soundtracks. Maphis recorded for Columbia Records and other labels. Later based in Bakersfield, California, he rose to prominence with his own hits such as "Dim Lights, Thick Smoke (And Loud, Loud Music)" as well as playing with acts like Johnny Burnette, Doyle Holly, The Collins Kids, Wanda Jackson, Rose Maddox and Ricky Nelson. "Dim Lights" has become a honky-tonk standard with numerous artists recording versions of the tune including Flatt and Scruggs, Vern Gosdin, Daryle Singletary and Dwight Yoakam.

Maphis was a band member and featured soloist on the Town Hall Party radio (and later television) program broadcast throughout the 1950s. Emanating from the Los Angeles area, Maphis was a regular on the program which including many recording stars of the day including Tex Ritter, Johnny Cash, Gene Autry, Bob Wills and the Texas Playboys and many others. "Town Hall Party," was later syndicated under the name "Ranch Party," and seen in most parts of the country. He was also a regular guest on the Jimmy Dean television show in the 1960s. Joe and Rose performed on the PBS television broadcast "Austin City Limits," in 1984 as part of the programs, "Legends Series." Fellow music industry insiders and fans had begun calling Joe and Rose, "Mr. and Mrs. Country Music."

Maphis was diagnosed with lung cancer in 1985. He died on June 27, 1986. His guitar hero was Mother Maybelle Carter, matriarch of the Carter Family. Maybelle's daughter June Carter Cash and June's husband Johnny Cash so admired Maphis that he was laid to rest in the Cash and Carter family Hendersonville, Tennessee burial plot next to Maybelle, her husband, Ezra Carter, and her daughter, Anita Carter.

After Joe passed away in 1986, Rose started working as a seamstress in the Opryland theme park costume department.

In "Finding Her Voice: the Saga of Women in Country Music," Rose reflected on her years in show business. "I don't miss singing," she said. "The only thing I miss is the traveling. I probably wouldn't

October 2017

have gone on with it as long as I did, except it was in Joe's blood. We were a couple."

Rose Lee's time in the sequin and fringe-laden world of the Opryland theme park reconnected her to the entertainment world she'd been a part of for 30 years. That feeling was what drew Maphis to the Country Music Hall of Fame and Museum. There, she was surrounded by treasured country artifacts and the spirit of her beloved Joe. Rose's own guitar strap was even featured in the long-running Bakersfield sound exhibit.

Maphis remains an integral part of music history and the Nashville community. In 2013, a YouTube video was posted from Rose's 90th birthday party. The event featured many classic country stars and industry legends sharing their appreciation for her life and career. Rose and Joe's son Jody is an active Music City musician, having played drums for Earl Scruggs, Johnny Cash and Marty Stuart.

Joe and Rose Lee had three children: Dale, Lorrie and Jody. Dale died in an automobile accident in 1989. Jody Maphis is an active musician carrying on the family tradition. He has played drums or guitar for Earl Scruggs, Johnny Rodriguez, Johnny Cash, Gary Allan, Marty Stuart and many others.

Oak Ridge Boys announce new CD release

Country Music Hall of Fame members and five-time GRAMMY winning group, The Oak Ridge Boys, announced they will release a project with acclaimed producer Dave Cobb in the first quarter of 2018.

At a listening event during Americana Music Association AmericanaFest at Nashville's historic RCA Studio A, where the album was recorded, the Oaks performed songs from the yet-untitled project recorded with multi-award winning producer Dave Cobb. This is the group's second project with Cobb, who produced the Oaks' acclaimed The Boys Are Back album released in 2009.

For the new project, Cobb's vision for the Oaks was to dig way back into their roots of gospel music. But a different kind of gospel. One that took a hard look at the early days of rock and roll, which was influenced by spiritual, or black gospel.

The album will be released by Lightning Rod Records and distributed by Thirty Tigers.

According to Logan Rogers, founder of Lightning Rod Records, "Everyone has heard the Boys sing gospel, but nobody has heard it quite like this. Under Dave Cobb's direction, they touch on unchartered territory—and for a long-tenured act like The Oak Ridge Boys, that's saying something."

The event was hosted by Peter Cooper, Senior Director, Producer and Writer at the Country Music Hall of Fame and Museum.

For more information, visit oakridgeboys.com

Precious Memories MEMORIAL
A journey of Country Music greats, their celebration of life and sacred resting places

$24.95 + $6.95 s/h

Available at
www.renaethewaitress.com
or send check to:
Renae Johnson
P.O. Box 210796
Nashville, TN 37221

October 2017

7th Annual NATD honors many in the entertainment industry

The Nashville Association of Talent Directors (NATD) have announced seven highly-respected individuals who will be recognized at the 7th Annual NATD Honors Gala scheduled for November 14, 2017 at the Hermitage Hotel and presented by the Grand Ole Opry and Springer Mountain Farms.

Honorees being awarded for their accomplishments and service to the Nashville entertainment industry include; music industry vet David Corlew, Nashville Predators' CEO Sean Henry, respected promoter and talent buyer Barbara Hubbard, Country Music Hall of Famer and Grand Ole Opry star Charley Pride, veteran music agent Bobby Roberts, Grand Ole Opry star and Grammy-winner Jeannie Seely and head of the Nashville Convention and Visitors Corp. Butch Spyridon.

The 7th Annual Honors Gala will feature surprise appearances and performances from well-known celebrities, special moments and splendid company. It has truly become one of the most anticipated evenings for the Nashville entertainment industry and business community.

The Nashville Association of Talent Directors (NATD) was founded in 1958 and professionally represents, directs, and promotes the entertainment industry through its members.

About Jeannie Seely

"Miss Country Soul" Jeannie Seely is a GRAMMY® award-winning artist who has been recording and performing for more than six decades. A Pennsylvania native, Seely moved to LA where she met many songwriters including Dottie West who ultimately encouraged her to move to Nashville. Within a month, Porter Wagoner hired her as the female singer for his road and television series. On September 16, 1967, Seely's biggest dream came true when she became the first Pennsylvania native to become a member of the world famous Grand Ole Opry. Seely subsequently became the first female to regularly host segments of the weekly Opry shows. She's also credited for changing the image of female country performers by being the first to wear a mini-skirt on the Opry stage. On March 2, 1967, the National Academy of Recording Arts & Sciences honored Jeannie with the 1966 GRAMMY® Award for the "Best Country Vocal Performance by a Female." A BMI-awarded songwriter, Seely's songs have been recorded by Country Music Hall of Fame members Faron Young, Merle Haggard, Connie Smith, Ray Price, Willie Nelson, Ernest Tubb and Little Jimmy Dickens, as well as by many other artists including Doyle Lawson, Lorrie Morgan and Irma Thomas. Along with placing records on the Billboard country singles chart for 13 consecutive years, Seely also served as a radio disc jockey on her own Armed Forces Network Show. For more information, visit jeannieseely.com.

About David Corlew

David Corlew has worked with The Charlie Daniels Band for 44 years, serving as Daniels' personal manager for the last 28 years. Corlew also holds the title of President/Co-Owner of Blue Hat Records which recently celebrated their 20th year of releasing albums and DVD projects. Even winning a GRAMMY Award for Amazing Grace Vol. II (A Country Salute to Gospel) in 1998. In 1999, The Corlew Music Group was formed, producing over 150 cuts to date, from artists such as Reba, Kenny Chesney, Brad Paisley, Jason Aldean, and many other country superstars. In 2005, Corlew formed d corlew films which has filmed several projects for Charlie Daniels' Band, including their 2005 tour of Iraq and Southwest Asia as well as developing projects for CMT, GAC, and other networks. Corlew and Daniels also co-founded the not-for-profit organization The Journey Home Project which sees it's mission to assist veterans with military organizations who do the most good. David is a former President of the Academy of Country Music Board of Directors and Governor to the Nashville Chapter Board for NARAS. He is currently a member of the Vanderbilt-Ingram Cancer Center Board of Directors and President of the Stars For Stripes Board of Directors.

About Sean Henry

When he's not interacting with fans, marketing partners or community leaders, promoting Predators activities through his

October 2017

popular @PREDSident twitter account, Sean Henry, as President and CEO of Bridgestone Arena and the Nashville Predators, is leading the organization's staff towards achieving One Goal: to be the No. 1 Sports and Entertainment venue in the world with a Stanley Cup Champion Nashville Predators as the centerpiece.

About Barbara Hubbard

A spit fire with an Arkansas twang came to Las Cruces, New Mexico in the early 50's and has since left a legacy in the community and an impression on the entertainment businesses. Barbara Hubbard started as a biology teacher where she met her husband and later explored careers as a Campus Activities Program advisor and cheer-leading coach for New Mexico State University. She was named Director of Special Events in 1977 which quickly lead her to her current title as Executive Director of the American Collegiate Showcase. Although ACTS has changed over the years, their mission remains the same: providing educational scholarships and experience for students wishing to display their talents in the performing arts field.

About Charley Pride

Charley Pride is celebrating more than 50 years as a recording artist. He has enjoyed one of the most successful careers in the history of country music and is credited with helping to break color barriers by becoming the first black superstar within the genre. A true living legend, he has sold tens of millions of records worldwide with his large repertoire of hits. A three-time GRAMMY(r) award winner and GRAMMY(r) Lifetime Achievement recipient, Pride has garnered no less than 36 chart-topping country hits, including "Kiss An Angel Good Morning," a massive #1 crossover hit that sold over a million singles and helped Pride land the Country Music Association's "Entertainer of the Year" award in 1971 and the "Top Male Vocalist" awards of 1971 and 1972. A proud member of the Grand Ole Opry and Country Music Hall of Fame, Pride continues to perform concerts worldwide and has toured the United States, Canada, Ireland, The United Kingdom, Australia and New Zealand over the last several years. For more information, visit CharleyPride.com.

About Bobby Roberts

Bobby Roberts began his music career singing with his father, famed country music entertainer and "America's King of the Yodelers," Kenny Roberts. In school, he formed his own band performing with his brothers. As he progressed through college he was asked by other bands to assist them in getting bookings and so he started his first agency in the basement of his home in Lansing, Michigan. As the agency grew, Bobby decided to develop a full-time regional booking agency and gave up the performing side of the business, soon opening a branch office in Orlando, FL. During his 4 years in Florida Bobby built a successful southern office for his agency and began booking "national" acts in venues that he represented such as rock legend Leon Russell. In 1981, Leon asked Bobby if he would move to Nashville, TN area and oversee his various interests and book, as well as manage, his career. Making the move to Nashville, and after 4 years with Leon, Bobby decided to open an agency chasing his dream of representing national recording artists. From 1986 – 2014 he quietly built one of the most successful, independently owned booking agencies from the Nashville suburb of Goodlettsville, TN. During this time the Bobby Roberts Company represented Aaron Tippin, Pam Tillis, John Anderson, Ray Price, Bobby Bare, Eddie Rabbitt, B.J. Thomas, Merle Haggard, Waylon Jennings, Don Williams, Tammy Wynette and many more.

About Butch Spyridon

Butch Spyridon has served as the head of the Nashville Convention & Visitors Corp (NCVC) since 1991. Over the last 25 years the NCVC has led the strategic development of Nashville's hospitality industry. During that time, Nashville has evolved into a global, year-round destination. Visitor spending in Davidson County exceeded $5.7 billion and accounts for one third of the visitor spending in the entire state.

October 2017

Charley Pride and Jimmie Rodgers honored as Music Legends

In collaboration with the Recording Academy™, "Great Performances" presents "GRAMMY Salute To Music Legends℠", the second annual all-star concert offering a primetime spotlight for the Academy's 2017 Special Merit Awards recipients. The celebration and tribute concert feature rare performances by honorees and renditions by those they've inspired.

The celebration, led by GRAMMY®-winning industry icon Paul Shaffer as musical director, was recorded in July at New York's Beacon Theatre, and will air Friday, Oct. 13 from 9–11 p.m. on PBS. (Check local listings.) Historically held during GRAMMY® Week, this is the second time the Recording Academy has celebrated the Special Merit Awards with a stand-alone event and musical tribute.

This year's Lifetime Achievement Award honorees are Charley Pride, Shirley Caesar, Ahmad Jamal, Jimmie Rodgers, Nina Simone, Sly Stone, and the Velvet Underground.

Additional Special Merit Awards honorees celebrated include Trustees Awards recipients producer, arranger, and songwriter Thom Bell; record executive Mo Ostin; and recording executive, A&R man, and music publisher Ralph S. Peer; and audio inventor Alan Dower Blumlein, who is the Technical GRAMMY Award recipient. Also honored is Keith Hancock, this year's recipient of the Recording Academy and GRAMMY Museum®'s Music Educator Award™.

Along with never-before-seen video packages celebrating each of the honorees' contributions to the music industry and our cultural heritage and heartfelt testimonials from the presenters, the star-studded event features performances by Lifetime Achievement Award honorees John Cale and Maureen "Moe" Tucker of the Velvet Underground, Lifetime Achievement Award honoree Shirley Caesar, jazz pianist Stanley Cowell, past GRAMMY nominee Andra Day, 12-time GRAMMY winner Kirk Franklin, GRAMMY Winner Le'Andria Johnson, past GRAMMY nominee Neal McCoy, six-time GRAMMY winner Randy Newman, GRAMMY-winning Living Colour founder and songwriter Vernon Reid, past GRAMMY nominee Catherine Russell, Lifetime Achievement Award honoree Charley Pride, past GRAMMY nominee Valerie Simpson, past GRAMMY nominee Russell Thompkins Jr. of the Stylistics, five-time GRAMMY winner Dionne Warwick, past GRAMMY nominee Charlie Wilson, and two-time GRAMMY winner Dwight Yoakam. There is also a special appearance by GRAMMY winner Whoopi Goldberg, who accepts for the late Nina Simone.

The musical program follows (the honorees in bold type; performers in parentheses):

Jimmie Rodgers •"Hobo Bill's Last Ride" / "Mule Skinner Blues" / "T For Texas" (Dwight Yoakam)

Charley Pride •"Is Anybody Goin' To San Antone" (Neal McCoy)

•"Kiss An Angel Good Morning" (Charley Pride)

The Lifetime Achievement Award honors performers who have made contributions of outstanding artistic significance to the field of recording, while the Trustees Award recognizes such contributions in areas other than performance. Both awards are determined by a vote of the Recording Academy's National Board of Trustees. Technical GRAMMY Award recipients are determined by vote of the Academy's Producers & Engineers Wing® Advisory Council and Chapter Committees and ratified by the National Board of Trustees, and presented to individuals and companies who have made contributions of outstanding technical significance to the recording field. Visit www.grammy.org/recording-academy/awards for complete lists of previous recipients.

October 2017

Jeanne Pruett and family; prayers asked for son, Jack

Jeanne Pruett, born Norma Jean Bowman in Pell City, AL, in 1937, enjoyed success in the '70s and early '80s with hits in country and pop genres.

One of 10 children, she used to listen to the Grand Ole Opry with her parents and harmonized with her brothers and sisters. Jeanne moved to Nashville in 1956 with her husband Jack Pruett, who went on to become Marty Robbins' guitarist. Pruett herself began writing songs while raising the family, and Robbins signed her to his publishing company in 1963 and recorded several of her songs (1966's "Count Me Out" being the biggest). In the meantime, Pruett also tried her hand at recording, cutting a few singles for RCA beginning in 1963 and giving it another shot with Decca in 1969. Her first record came out the day Grand Ole Opry stars Patsy Cline, Cowboy Copas and Hawkshaw Hawkins died in a tragic plane crash.

Jeanne still counts those Saturday night shows sharing the stage with Marty among the most memorable of her Opry career.

Tammy Wynette, Conway Twitty and others also covered Jeanne's songs. "It is easier to be accepted in the music business by your peers as a performer after you have proven yourself as a writer," she says. "The acceptance of fans is another thing. You sell them after you have gone into the studio and come up with the best you have." She first won their acceptance in 1971 with the single, "Hold to My Unchanging Love." Her own version of "Love Me" reached the Top 40, but those records just set the stage for what was to come.

"Satin Sheets" hit country radio in March 1973, aided by 1,600 pieces of pink satin fabric that Jeanne cut by hand and sent to radio programmers and music executives across the nation. The international hit topped the country charts that May. A few weeks later, Jeanne became an official Opry member – the last vocalist to join the show before it moved from the Ryman to the Grand Ole Opry House.

Jeanne's other hits included "I'm Your Woman," "You Don't Need to Move a Mountain," and "Welcome to the Sunshine (Sweet Baby Jane)." In 1983 alone, she had three Top 10 hits: "Back to Back," "Temporarily Yours," and "It's Too Late."

In 2006 Jeanne announced her retirement from performing. Now she's become almost as renowned for her skills in the kitchen as for her work on the stage. She's the author, editor, and publisher of the best-selling "Feedin' Friends" cookbook series. "I still do a lot of home canning, such as tomatoes and preserves," she says. "And I love it."

The girl from Alabama is now back on the farm. She and husband Eddie Fulton have a 160-acre ranch and farm outside Nashville. On sunny days, you might find Jeanne on nearby Center Hill Lake aboard her 65-foot houseboat — dubbed, like its owner, "Miss Satin Sheets."

Jeanne's son, Jack Jr. suffered a heart attack in September and had heart surgery, but is healing. In his younger years Jeck Jr. was bass player with The Winters Brothers Band. Donnie and Dennis Winters are the sons of Don Winters who also sang with Marty Robbins, where the boys became friends and bandmates. Later Jack and his sister Jael, played and sang with their mom.

October 2017

Country Music Questions & Answers

Q: I've been told Penny Gilley is Mickey Gilley's daughter and I don't think she is. Is she?

A: Mickey Gilley has four children Kathy, Michael and Keith Ray with his first wife, Geraldine (1953-1961) and Gregory with 2nd wife, Vivian (1962 - present).

"I'm a second cousin," Penny says. "I married into the family years ago. All my daughters are Gilleys and when I started my recording career, they wanted me to keep the name. We have a lot of fun with it. Mickey always says I'm his daughter."

Q: How many times has Lorrie Morgan been married?

A: Lorrie Morgan's first husband, Ron Gaddis, was a musician in George Jones' band. They were married in 1979 and divorced 2 years later. In 1986, Morgan married Keith Whitley. He died in 1989 of alcohol poisoning. Morgan then wed Brad Thompson, a bus driver for Clint Black, from 1991 to 1993. Later marriages were to singer/songwriter Jon Randall from 1996 to 1999 and Sammy Kershaw, who married in 2001 but divorced 6 years later. She married Randy White on Sept. 15, 2010. This is the sixth marriage for Morgan, who has been married to three different country singers.

Q: Did Trace Adkins and his wife get a divorce?

Gwen Baker, Springdale, AR

A: After filing for divorce in 2014, Trace Adkins wife voluntarily pulled out of the divorce after 15 months of negotiating, so he and Rhonda are still married.

Trace Adkins and wife, Rhonda

If you have questions send them to Paula, CFR News, P.O. Box 210796, Nashville, TN 37221 or email them to paula@gabrielcommunications.com.

Coming Soon!

Nadine's Comedy MEMORIAL TOUR
Precious Memories MEMORIAL TOURS

VISIT THE SITES WHERE SOME OF COUNTRY MUSIC'S LEGENDS HAVE BEEN LAID TO REST!

Nashville Memorial Tours
615-593-1430
NashvilleMemorialTours.com

October 2017

There's Something about that song

"El Paso" – Timeless Ballad Tells Unforgettable Tale of Love and Death

By Claudia Johnson

The ballad is an ancient form of poetic storytelling. With elements like unrequited love, ill-fated heroes and untimely death, the ballad was established early in Country Music's history as a popular sub-genre.

Perhaps the most well known of the thousands of ballads recorded in modern times is Marty Robbins' "El Paso." Since its release on Robbins' 1959 album "Gunfighter Ballads and Trail Songs" the song has become the standard-bearer for Country-Western storytelling. "El Paso" deviated from the typical storytelling method by having the protagonist tell the story as opposed to the listener hearing a third-party rendition.

This method allowed Robbins, who penned the song as well as singing it, to disclose the feelings and thoughts of the narrator and not just describe his actions as an observer. The uncut, original recording of the song was almost five minutes long — far longer than the typical radio-play release. Though the length was unusual for a commercial single, it was in keeping with the ballad storytelling tradition.

The song's length, however, was a concern for the record company, so before the release radio stations were provided the full-length version and an edited three-minute version. They preferred the longer version.

Within months the song topped both the pop and country charts, and in 1961 it took the Grammy Award for Best Country & Western Recording. In the mesmerizing ballad a gunslinger tells the story of his love for a Mexican maiden, Feleena, who caught his attention with her beauty and lively dancing in Rosa's Cantina in the West Texas town of El Paso.

"I was in love, but in vain I could tell," he admits, making the reader question if Feleena even knew of his interest in her. The gunslinger casts Feleena as wicked and evil, even accusing her of casting a spell on him. The listener can visualize the scene. Music is playing and patrons are laughing while the gunslinger watches Feleena from across the cantina as she drinks with a cowboy.

He describes the man as "young," "handsome" and "dashing and daring," perhaps comparing himself unfavorably and adding to his jealousy, thusprompting a deadly challenge.

No match for the gunslinger, the cowboy's response was insufficient, and he was killed instantly. In a sobering moment of remorse, the gunslinger "stood there in silence, shocked by the foul evil deed." The murder left him few choices but to attempt escape, and the theft of a horse from outside the cantina became his second capital offense of the evening. As he found himself in the badlands of New Mexico, he realized that he could not return to El Paso without being killed, but his love was stronger than his fear of death. "Maybe tomorrow a bullet may find me; tonight nothing's worse than this pain in my heart," he agonizes.

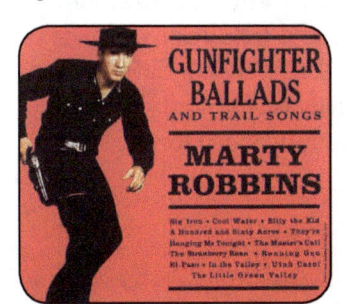

Returning to El Paso, he has paused on a hill overlooking Rosa's Cantina when he spots mounted cowboys to his left and right "shouting and shooting."

"I can't let them catch me," he resolves. "I have to make it to Rosa's back door."

He grasps that he's been shot when he feels "a deep burning pain" in his side that renders him unable to continue riding. He falls from his saddle, but his "love for Feleena is strong" so he rises and continues.

"Though I am weary, I can't stop to rest," he determines. "I see the white puff of smoke from the rifle. I feel the bullet go deep in my chest."

The only hint that Feleena may have actually returned his feelings is in the final moments of his life when she finds him.

"Kissing my cheek as she kneels by my side," the gunslinger sings. "Cradled by two loving arms that I'll die for. One little kiss, then Feleena, good-bye."

October 2017

Robbins' beautiful, clear voice along with the harmonies of vocalists Bobby Sykes and Jim Glaser of the Glaser Brothers and an inspired Spanish guitar accompaniment by Grady Martin, who later recorded an instrumental version for his own album, create a haunting performance of a timeless tale that has not stopped captivating listeners across six decades.

The song became a regular on the Grateful Dead's concert playlist, with the band performing their most requested song a total of 389 times over 25 years of touring.

Chosen by the Western Writers of America as one of the Top 100 Western songs of all time, "El Paso" has been recorded by numerous artists. An alternative country band, Old 97s, version was included on the "King of the Hill" original TV soundtrack. The singer Lolita recorded a German version that became an international hit. A modified version of "El Paso" called "Miners Fight" became the official fight song of the University of Texas at El Paso in the 1980s.

Parody versions were released by H. B. Barnum, whose 1960 "El Pizza" set in a California pizza joint became a radio hit. Homer and Jethro parodied the ballad in a novelty tune called "Velvita's Cafe." For his 1979 TV special "Comedy is Not Pretty!" Steve Martin created a comedic music video for the song.

"El Paso" has claimed its place in popular culture as well. In 2001 Old ElPaso used a version of the song in a Super Bowl commercial for its taco kit. The song has been identified by the writers of The Beach Boys' "Heroes and Villains" album as a primary influence.

The 2015 film "Dumb and Dumber To" featured the song. The USS El Paso, which sailed from 1970-1994, used the song as its breakaway salute.

Introducing the song to a new generation in the 2013 series finale of AMC's "Breaking Bad," protagonist Walter White steals a car in which there is a cassette containing "El Paso." The finale's title, "Finlina," was a play on the word finale as well as symbolic of what a man will do in pursuit of his desires.

And what of his object of desire?

Who was she? In 1966 Robbins wrote "Feleena From El Paso," an eightminute track on his album, "The Drifter." The song reveals more of Feleena's story, both before the pivotal evening at Rosa's Cantina and in the future when she is courted by the ghost of the dead cowboy. Ten years later he revisited the ballad with a hit called "El Paso City" that finds an airplane passenger speculating about whether he has a mystical connection with the gunslinger.

"Somewhere in my deepest thoughts, familiar scenes and memories unfold," he sings. "These wild and unexplained emotions…I get the feeling sometime, in another world I lived in El Paso."

Tim Atwood featured on several shows & releasing new CD

During his career, Tim Atwood has played behind some of the greatest Country Music performers of all time. But, in 2017, Atwood's star as a vocalist is shining brighter than ever as a solo artist on his own – with several shows, television appearances, and a new album project by year's end.

Atwood, who played in the staff band at the world-famous Grand Ole Opry for thirty-eight years, has developed a reputation as one of the most polished and energetic stage shows in the entertainment business, performing for audiences of all ages. Fans of his traditional style will have several opportunities to enjoy his music and story-telling abilities in the coming weeks.

On Thursday, September 7, Atwood shined in the spotlight as a featured guest on Larry's Country Diner on RFD-TV. The singer was featured on RFD's The Penny Gilley Show on Friday, September 8 in a performance filmed at the iconic Fort Worth Stockyards at Lil' Red's Longhorn Saloon. Also, Atwood will be a performer on an upcoming airing of Wednesday Night Prayer Meeting on RFD, sharing music and testimony with artists such as Country Music Hall of Famers The Oak Ridge Boys and Randy Travis, Linda Davis, and Mark Wills.

After a long career shining while playing at the Opry behind artists such as Garth Brooks and Carrie Underwood, 2017 has been a banner year for Tim Atwood on many levels as a performer in his own right. The Peoria, Illinois native – a recent winner of the Musician of the Year award from the Academy of Western Music – is also nominated for Musician of the

October 2017

Year as well as Entertainer of the Year at the upcoming ROPE (Reunion of Professional Entertainers) Awards set for October 5 in Music City. He's included with some of the most beloved artists in the format, such as Gene Watson and Jeannie Seely.

And, as a recording artist, his star is shining as never before. Atwood, signed to i2i Records has been touring non-stop around the United States to promote his faith-based album That Old Time Religion, which includes the break-out track "Let's All Go Down To The River," a performance with the sensational Mandy Barnett, which has earned a Top-5 ranking on the Cash Box Country / Gospel charts.

And, there's more music coming from Atwood – who earned his wings in the business playing for three years in the band of Jim Ed Brown. The singer is in the midst of completing his third Country disc, with the lead single and title cut "I'll Stand Up And Say So" primed for a Fall 2017 release. Needless to say, it's a busy time for Tim Atwood – and he's grateful for every bit of it.

"I am a blessed man, and I know it" Atwood humbly states. "I'm not sure where this journey will take me, but one thing is for sure. I am enjoying the ride.

Tim's CD "Buy This Piano A Drink" is $12.95, his gospel CD "That Old Time Religion" is $15.00. Add $5.00 shipping and handling for each order and send check to Tim Atwood, PO Box 1442, Nashville, TN 37077. He will be happy to sign them if customers will send a note with what they would like it to say.

Also, "Mom" and "I'll Stand Up and Say SO" will be on his upcoming CD. If anyone would like to pre-order it they will receive a discounted price of $15.00 plus $5 s/h. It should be released in a few months. That CD is titled "I'll Stand Up and Say So." Please indicate which CD you are ordering when you send your check.

Learn more at timatwood.com.

Jo Dee Messina cancels tour after cancer diagnosis

Jo Dee Messina has been diagnosed with cancer and has cancelled all tour dates after October 7. Jo Dee will begin treatment this fall.

The news was shared via a post by "Team JDM" on Jo Dee's website. Included in the post was a lyric video for Jo Dee's new song, "Here," which she penned and recorded after learning of her diagnosis.

Read the full statement by Team JDM below.

"Over the years, Jo Dee has built a close relationship with her fans, so those of us at Team JDM wanted to be the first to let you know that she was recently diagnosed with cancer. It has been a trying summer, but her heart has been filled with gratitude for the many opportunities she has had to see God's hand at work.

"As many of you know, Jo Dee is a believer who feels blessed to be surrounded by the love of God — a love that has brought her the inner peace. On her lowest of low days, she has been able to see God's hand at work and feel His love as she continues her walk. It is because of our Father's love that she has been able to find the beauty in the days that could have brought her the most fear, gratitude in moments that most would call unfair, and companionship during times she might feel the loneliest.

"We don't know anything specific regarding the treatment plan at this point, but Jo Dee is working closely with a team to explore all options. She has taken the semester off from classes at The King's University, and her last tour date for the year will be October 7 (all other 2017 dates are being postponed), as she will begin cancer treatment this Fall.

"Jo Dee has been working with producer Seth Mosley, and in a recent writing session wrote the song 'Here' with Seth and Mia Fieldes. Seth was deeply moved to see her faith following her diagnosis while the two worked in the studio together. 'It was one of the most powerful moments I've had in my entire studio career,' Seth told Team JDM. 'To see Jo Dee singing "there's no pain, there's no fear, here" through the cancer and the chaos that she is walking through . . . God is going to use her and her story to intercept people in their pain and remind them that He is near.'

"We will continue to keep fans updated on Jo Dee's journey and appreciate the outpouring of love, prayers, and support she has already received."

—Team JDM

October 2017

The People Who Make Us Laugh

Life itself is portrayed by the world of Country Music entertainment. From the depths of sorrow to the heights of jubilation, performances reach our hearts and spirit. This series takes a look at the lighter side of life and feature those artists, both past and present, who bring smiles to our faces and warmth to our hearts. It highlights those performers who exemplify the great comedic spirit of America. Jeanne Pruett, born Norma Jean Bowman in Pell City, AL, in 1937, enjoyed success in the '70s and early '80s with hits in country and pop genres.

Homer and Jethro – Lives Well Writ

By Danny M. Nichols

There's little that can written about Homer and Jethro that hasn't already been said. Therefore, this story is most appropriately called "Lives Well Writ" as it contained observations and remembrances about two talented musicians who lived and practiced their craft far ahead of their time. They entertained and kept their audience laughing across four decades.

Homer and Jethro were the stage names of American country music duo Henry D. "Homer" Haynes (1920–1971) and Kenneth C. "Jethro" Burns (1920–1989). Most sources agree the two were first paired in 1936 when WNOX-AM program director Lowell Blanchard pulled the youngsters from two separate bands auditioning for his Mid-Day Merry-Go-Round on WNOX-Knoxville. Destiny would then place the boys together in Blanchard's newly created band, the String Dusters. Here they performed with the stage names "Junior" and "Dude" until one night in 1936 when Blanchard literally forgot their nicknames while introducing them on air and referred to them as "Homer and Jethro." Haynes and Burns apparently liked the new names and opted to keep and continue with them for the rest of their careers.

Haynes was an accomplished guitarist, while Burns was a much-lauded mandolinist. They salted their musical performances with satire and fun, letting their pure musical talents speak for the quality of their craft. Their popularity carried them from Knoxville, Tennessee, to Renfro Valley, Kentucky, where in 1939 they became regulars on the Renfro Valley Barn Dance. Next they traveled to Chicago where they would broadcast on the Plantation House Party radio program hosted by Whitey Ford as the "Duke of Paducah." The outbreak of WWII pulled the performers apart when each was drafted into the U.S. Army with Burns serving in Europe while Haynes served in the Pacific. Following the war, Burns and Haynes reunited in 1945 and continued their careers in Knoxville and by 1947 had moved to Cincinnati, Ohio, where they played on the WLW radio station's Midwestern Hayride. They recorded singles on King Records and worked as session musicians backing other artists for two years before signing with RCA Records. During a management turmoil episode at WLW in 1948, the pair left and toured for a while before moving to Springfield, Missouri, where they performed on KWTO-AM with Chet Atkins, the Carter Family and Slim Wilson.

Known as the "Thinking Man's Hillbillies," Burns and Haynes enjoyed creating music that poked fun at the popular songs of the day. They would sing exaggerated hillbilly-styled versions of pop standards in which their audiences found great delight. Their voices and music were honed to perfection, and they could flawlessly replicate the sound of the idolized artists of their day. Burns, who was the humorist of the pair, wrote most of the parodies they performed. Their first hit became a parody of "Baby It's Cold Outside," which they recorded with June Carter in 1949. They were soon invited to perform on the National Barn Dance on WLS-AM in Chicago in 1950. Burns and Haynes also performed on several recordings by Chet Atkins and on other artists' sessions in Chicago and Nashville. It was while performing on WLS that Burns met and married Lois Johnson, twin sister of Leona Johnson, Chet Atkins' wife. Atkins would become the production genius for most of the music the duo recorded during their career together.

Burns and Haynes took their music seriously but much enjoyed their time walking on the lighter side. Although lending their voices and instruments to poke fun at contemporary pop and country hits, they would inject their own variety of humor into their performances. Always using themselves as the brunt of a joke, Burns and Haynes kept their audiences laughing while tuning up for the next song.

From 1949 until 1959, Burns and Haynes toured and recorded, releasing singles entitled "Baby It's Cold Outside," "Tennessee Border – No. 2," "(How Much Is) That Hound Dog in the Window," "Hernando's Hideaway," "Sifting, Whimpering Sands"/"They Laid Him in the Ground" and "The Battle of Kookamonga."

They won a Grammy for Best Country Comedy Performance in 1959 for "The Battle of Kookamonga," a parody of Johnny Horton's popular "Battle of New Orleans." In 1960 they released the single, "Please Help Me, I'm Falling" and in 1964 the Beatle parodies of "I Want to Hold Your Hand" and "She Loves You."

Such popularity brought opportunities to appear on national network television and appearances with other famous country stars of the day. In 1960 they appeared with Johnny Cash on NBC. The duo was hired by Kellogg's Corn Flakes to appear as commercial personalities promoting their product. The Kellogg's gig was highly successful, bringing them into homes and giving them far more exposure than their country music performances could provide. It was also during the 1960s that a country humor revival exploded in television with shows like "The Beverly Hillbillies," "Petticoat Junction" and "Green Acres." Riding on the wave of these commercial successes, Homer and Jethro stepped up their recording efforts, releasing eight albums of new material on RCA Victor between 1966 and 1967.

As Homer and Jethro they performed and created albums for three and a half decades before the famous duo was separated by the death of Haynes from a sudden heart attack on Aug. 7, 1971. After a short semiretirement by Burns, he was lured back into show business by folksinger Steve Goodman, who promoted him on tours for his excellent mandolin talents. Burns died Feb. 4, 1989, in Evanston, Illinois.

Haynes and Burns were inducted into the Country Music Hall of Fame in 2001.

NOVEMBER

Jeannie Seely Celebrates 50th Grand Ole Opry Anniversary

Contributed by Ron Harman

Grammy-winning country singer Jeannie Seely recently celebrated her milestone 50th anniversary as a member of the world-famous Grand Ole Opry. "It's been an amazing ride for a small town girl leaving Pennsylvania in a MGA Roadster, not really knowing where she was going," Jeannie recently reflected. "I was just following a dream!"

Jeannie and Bill on 50th Anniversary

Jeannie Seely was inducted into the Grand Ole Opry on September, 16, 1967, at the Ryman Auditorium in Nashville. Earlier that same year, Jeannie's hit "Don't Touch Me" garnered her a Grammy Award for Best Country Vocal Performance by a Female. She became the third female artist to receive a Grammy in country music.

"Don't Touch Me, which reached No. 1 on the Record World and Cashbox charts, resulted in Jeannie receiving several awards for "Most Promising New Artist." Jeannie's recording of "Don't Touch Me" was ranked at No. 97 in Heartaches by the Number: Country Music's 500 Greatest Singles published by the Country Music Foundation Press and Vanderbilt University Press.

When Jeannie fulfilled her lifelong dream by becoming a Grand Ole Opry member, she became the first Pennsylvania native to join the hallowed institution. She remembers her Opry induction, attended by her parents Leo and Irene from tiny Townville, as a very emotional night.

"The night I joined the Opry I was so excited that my parents had flown to Nashville to be there with me," Jeannie recently recalled.

Jeannie Seely Old and New Opry

"I had it all in my mind how I was going to acknowledge them and thank them for always helping me follow my dreams. However, when they introduced me, I was so nervous, excited, and emotional that when the band hit the A chord I just started singing! Fortunately that wonderful audience gave me an encore so I was able to have a second chance to introduce my parents!"

Membership in the Grand Ole Opry is coveted among country artists, and comes only upon invitation by the Opry management. Several factors go into that decision, including career accomplishment and commitment. During a recent interview Jeannie stated, "Becoming a member of the Opry is certainly one of the greatest honors that can be bestowed upon you. It is very, very special."

50 years to the day of her induction, Jeannie stood on the Opry stage as Country Music Hall of Fame member Bill Anderson and Opry General Manager Sally Williams marked the occasion with gifts, presentations, and accolades. "Jeannie Seely lives and breathes the Grand Ole Opry," noted Sally. "It is an honor for all of us to celebrate such a talented, dedicated, trailblazing member of our Opry family. Watching her perform tonight, I think we can all agree she's just getting started."

During its 92-year history, the Opry has had around 300 members. Only eight of the current 63 Opry members joined prior to Jeannie Seely, and she becomes only the sixth female in country music history to attain 50-year membership. The other women are Jean Shepard, Minnie Pearl, Wilma Lee Cooper (all deceased), Loretta Lynn, and Connie

November 2017

Smith. On October 17th, Chris Young will become the 64th and newest Opry member. Earlier this year Crystal Gayle and Dailey & Vincent also joined the cast.

"The Grand Ole Opry actually has been a part of my life since I first listened to it when I was only four years old in Townville," Jeannie recalls. "For many years it seemed like an impossible dream to even attend it, let alone be on it. After I started seriously pursuing my career, I made it my goal to, someday, somehow, become a member of the Opry."

Jeannie says she was thrilled when "Don't Touch Me" topped the charts in July of 1966, and that she immediately started lobbying to be invited as an Opry guest – with membership in the back of her mind. "Nothing in my career means more than being a part of that wonderful 'family,'" she explains. "To me, next to the Hall of Fame, your name on that membership wall signifies, more than anything else, your place in Country Music History."

"Celebrating my 50th Anniversary reminds me how fast time flies when you're having a wonderful time," Jeannie notes. "I feel my role now is to carry on the tradition as best I can with a helpful eye on the new talent I'm privileged to introduce who will carry this marvelous American treasure into the future for many more generations to enjoy."

While discussing her recent Opry anniversary, Jeannie also took time to reflect on her Pennsylvania roots. At age 11 she performed on radio station WMGW in Meadville, and by 16 she had sung on TV station WICU in Erie. "Some of my favorite memories during those years are attending country music shows at Hillbilly Park near Franklin," she recalls. "I saw greats there like Bill Monroe, Jean Shepard, Little Jimmy Dickens, Ralph Stanley, and Wilma Lee & Stoney Cooper, all of whom became popular Opry stars."

After graduating from Townville High School and working for three years at a bank in Titusville, the town where she was born, Jeannie moved to California where she honed her songwriting skills. She became a regular act, along with an unknown Glen Campbell, on the "Hollywood Jamboree" television series.

Upon the encouragement of Dottie West who recorded one of her songs, Jeannie moved to Nashville in the fall of 1965. "It's true that when I got here I only had $50 and a Ford Falcon to my name," she chuckles. Although every record label in town initially turned Jeannie down, Porter Wagoner hired her as the female singer for his road show and television series.

Aptly nicknamed "Miss Country Soul" and still referred to by that title today, Jeannie placed records on Billboard's country singles chart for 13 consecutive years. For over a decade she toured and recorded with duet partner Jack Greene.

Jeannie Seely released over two dozen albums on the Monument, Decca, and MCA labels. Her recent projects have been self-produced and issued on her own label. A BMI-awarded songwriter, Jeannie's most recent album, Written in Song, was released in January, It contains songs she wrote which were previously recorded by artists like Willie Nelson, Dottie West, Merle Haggard, Connie Smith, Ray Price, Faron Young, Ernest Tubb, Irma Thomas, and several others.

During her career Jeannie has made numerous appearances on national television shows, performed in concert around the world including military tours in Europe and Asia, published her own book of witticisms, appeared in two motion pictures, and starred in numerous musicals and stage productions.

Known throughout her career as an individualist as well as for her infectious humor, Jeannie is widely recognized for changing the image of female country performers. She's credited for wearing the first mini-skirt on the Grand Ole Opry stage – and she was the first female to regularly host segments of the Opry.

Jeannie continues to make frequent concert appearances, but any weekend she's not out of town she can be found performing on the Grand Ole Opry. During the course of her 50 year membership, Jeannie has performed on over 5,000 Opry shows. "I think that one of the most unique things about the Grand Ole Opry to me is that there are always three generations represented on the stage and three generations in the audience, and you don't find those two things are true at other venues or events you go to," she explains.

Jeannie has no plans to slow down anytime in the near future. The same night that she celebrated her 50th anniversary on the Opry stage and at a reception backstage in the Opry House, she hosted the Ernest Tubb Midnite Jamboree at the nearby Texas Troubadour Theatre. At the end of September she performed, per the request of fellow Opry member Blake Shelton, at the grand opening for Blake's "Ole Red" restaurant and live music venue in Tishomingo, Oklahoma.

In October Jeannie will be traveling for performances in the Texas cities of Arlington, Corsicana, and Seguin, as well as in Sisseton, South Dakota. She'll also host a birthday celebration show in Nashville for her close friend Dottie West. In November she's slated to be honored by the Nashville Association of Talent Directors at their annual honors gala, and in December she's booked for a New Year's Eve show at The Welk Theater in Branson, Missouri.

In February 2018 Jeannie Seely will be one of the featured performers on the week-long "Country Music Cruise" on Holland America's Nieuw Amsterdam. Other performers will include Opry members Larry Gatlin and the Gatlin Brothers. Lorrie Morgan, and Dailey & Vincent, along with several other artists including Hall of Famers Alabama and Bobby Bare.

Jeannie's most recent performance in her hometown area was at the Crawford County Fair in August of 2015. "The folks back in Pennsylvania have been so good to me over the past 50 years," Jeannie is quick to point out. Her most recent trip to the Keystone State was in April when she traveled to Harrisburg and was recognized by the Pennsylvania House of Representatives for her 50 years at the Opry. A resolution honoring Jeannie was sponsored by Rep. Kathy Rapp (R-Warren/Crawford/Forest).

"I am so thankful to have been raised in that area. Looking back, I can see how my upbringing encouraged me to seek the heights of my dreams, but also kept me grounded. I'm so fortunate for the longevity of my career which I owe to the country music fans in places all around the country and all around the world. I appreciate each and every one of them. I've been very blessed, and I'm very grateful."

Ron Harman works at the Country Music Hall of Fame, and he maintains Jeannie's Website at www.JeannieSeely.com and her Artist Facebook Page at www.Facebook.com/JeannieSeely.

Tim Atwood played and sang with Jeannie as the keyboard player on the Opry for many years until he was let go in 2014.

Join me the first four Thursdays & Saturdays in November as we watch a special Larry's Country Diner IN REVIEW!

then watch...

TIM ATWOOD
Nov. 30 & Dec. 2
Encore Performance

Thursdays 7 p.m. & Saturdays 10 p.m. Central

On RFD-TV
All shows subject to change

November 2017

Nadine
The Church Lady

Lord, give me a sense of humor,
Give me the grace to see a joke,
To get some humor out of life,
And to pass it on to other folk.

A senior couple in our Sunday school class went to Holland for two weeks. They took a bus tour with a bunch of fellow Americans out to visit a cheese farm. A young guide led them through the process of cheese making, explaining that goat's milk was used. He showed the group this lovely hillside where a lot of goats were grazing. He explained that these were the older goats put out to pasture when they no longer produced. He then asked the group, what do you do in America with your old goats? Our friend responded, they send us on bus tours!

Church sign

Thanksgiving is here!

What if we woke up today with only what we had thanked the good Lord for yesterday?

Hello?! I think we better get busy thanking Him!

John Carter Cash Welcomes Baby Girl, Grace June

John Carter Cash and his wife Ana Cristina have announced the arrival of their baby girl, Grace June Cash.

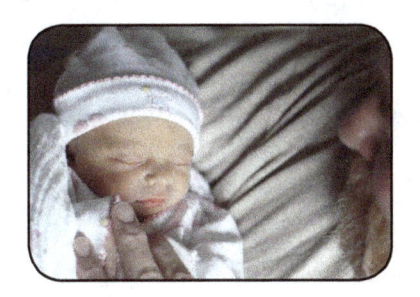

The newest member of the Carter-Cash family arrived on Sept. 11 at 5:44 pm. Grace June, is the granddaughter of country music royalty—Johnny Cash and June Carter Cash. She is the first child for happy couple and believed to be named after her late grandmother.

"My husband John Carter and I are proud to announce the birth of our daughter, Grace June Cash," Ana posted on Instagram. "She was born on September 11th, 2017 at 5:44 pm. Welcome to the world sweet little angel."

Cash has three other children from his previous marriages—Jack Ezra, Joseph John and Anna Maybelle. The couple married in 2016 and announced they were having a girl this past April.

November

Country's Family Reunion presents....

Kickin' Back
A Special Gathering of Good Friends

Fridays...7 p.m. central
Saturdays...11 p.m central

November 2017

Mark Chesnutt presented first ever Trailblazer Award at the 2017 Texas Country Music Awards

On Thursday, September 28th, multi- platinum selling country artist and Texas native, Mark Chesnutt, was presented the first ever Trailblazer Award along with a Thank You Plaque for serving as a Spoken-person for the Texas Country Music Association (TCMA) at their 2017 awards ceremony. Though Chesnutt was unable to attend due to an unexpected illness, his good friend and co-writer Roger Springer accepted the award in his honor.

"It was unfortunate that Mark got ill and could not make it to the Awards show. "said Linda Wilson, founder of the TCMA. "He was missed, but the Finalists and Award Recipients along with amazing performances made the 2017 Texas Country Music Awards show an evening that will go down in history."

Mark was heavy hearted that he could not attend the event, but was thrilled that Roger Springer, co-writer of the #1 singles "It's a Little Too Late" and "Thank God For Believers" was there to accept it in his place.

"I am very sorry to have missed such a special event," Chesnutt said. "Receiving the Trail Blazer award from my home state is such an honor, and I am thankful for my friend Roger Springer for accepting it in my absence."

The TCMA is an organization dedicated to the promotion and support of both established and new artists, songwriters and musicians from Texas, as well as those who perform in the state. Chesnutt doubles as spokesperson for Texas Country Cares, the TCMA's charity, which will show the support of the music community in times of need throughout the state.

The Texas Country Music Association, Inc. is a non-profit charitable organization with 501c3 status and donations are tax deductible. To join, donate or for more information visit www.texascountrymusic.org.

For more information on Mark Chesnutt, please visit www.markchesnutt.com.

Just in time for Christmas!

We gathered a ton of country music legends to share their favorite Christmas stories and songs with each other and YOU. All on 3 DVD's plus an Audio CD with all the songs from the show.

Songs Include:
It's Christmastime Again - Getting Ready for a Baby
Christmas Time At Home
New Star Shining
Jingle Bells
They Saw A King
Hangin' Around the Mistletoe
Mary Had a Little Lamb
Tennessee Christmas
Still Believing In Christmas
Remember Me
Winter Wonderland
Thank God For Kids
Away In A Manger
O Holy Night

$79.80 plus $6.95 s/h

Artists Include:
The Isaacs - Duane Allen
Rhonda Vincent - Ricky Skaggs
Teea Goans - The Whites
T-Graham Brown - Joey + Rory
Mandy Barnett - William Lee Golden
Jimmy Fortune
Linda Davis, Rylee Scott and Lang Scott

800-820-5405
www.cfrvideos.com
P.O. Box 210709, Nashville, TN 37221

COUNTRY LEGENDS OF THE PAST & PRESENT

BY TOM WOOD

Jimmy Dean

I was watching Ferris Bueller's Day Off the other day, and the 1986 comedy got me thinking about country music star Jimmy Dean.

Huh?

Surely, you remember the scene. Ferris and his pals walk into a four-star restaurant without reservations. The "snooty" Maitre D' ultimately seats them after Ferris is hilariously identified as Abe Froman. You know … The Sausage King of Chicago.

"Sausage King" is a title befitting Jimmy Dean, the Country Music Hall of Famer who in 1969 established his namesake Jimmy Dean Sausage company with his brother, Don, and others. The company was sold to Sara Lee in 1984 for a reported $80 million, and Dean remained as company pitchman until 2003. The brand is now owned by Tyson Foods.

Enough about sausage; let's recall Jimmy Dean, who rose from tough, humble beginnings in Texas to become a talented singer, songwriter and actor who entertained generations of fans in all mediums.

His signature hit was 1961's "Big Bad John" — a crossover which quickly shot to No. 1 on various charts and sold some five million singles. It earned Dean a 1962 Grammy for best Country and Western Recording, and also earned nominations for Song and Record of the Year.

"Big Bad John" wasn't Dean's only chart-topping single.

He reached No. 1 again in 1965 with "The First Thing Ev'ry Morning (And the Last Thing Ev'ry Night)", and had Top 10 hits with "P.T. 109" (No. 3, 1962, an ode to President John F. Kennedy), "Bumming Around" (No. 5, 1952), "I.O.U" (No. 9, 1976, an ode to his mother), "Dear Ivan" (No. 10, 1961) and "Stand Beside Me" (No. 10, 1966).

In all, Dean recorded more than 30 albums.

Beyond the records and the business success, Dean also appeared in a James Bond movie (Diamonds Are Forever, 1971) and Big Bad John (1990).

Television works included recurring roles on Daniel Boone (1968-70) and J.J. Starbuck (1987-88), as well as appearances on Murder, She Wrote and several other shows and TV movies.

In addition, he also hosted or appeared on several TV talk shows or game shows, most notably The Jimmy Dean Show (1963-66). The variety show featured his Nashville buddies on a regular basis, but is notably credited with helping launch the career of puppeteer Jim Henson and his dog Rowlf, who was later featured on Sesame Street. You can watch The Jimmy Dean Show on RFD-TV.

Jimmy died at age 81 in 2010 at his Virginia home.

Author Tom Wood, who writes thrillers and Westerns, is a regular contributor to Country Family Reunion News. Reach him at tomwoodauthor.com

November 2017

Country Artists of a Bygone Era

Foley Achieved Stardom Across Entertainment Platforms

By Claudia Johnson

It only seems fitting that the man known as Mr. Country Music would have been tapped to host the first network television show exclusively for the country audience.

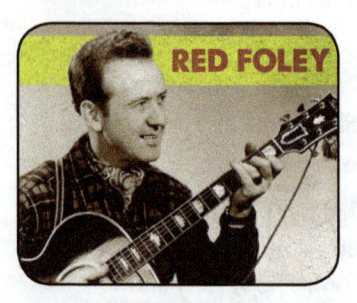

Clyde Julian Foley, nicknamed "Red" for his ginger-colored hair, was already an experienced host of radio and live stage productions, when Ozark Jubilee premiered on ABC TV in 1955 for its six-year run. In fact, he had already become the first country music performer to host a network radio program when he cohosted NBC's "Avalon Time" in 1939 with Red Skelton.

While growing up in Berea, Kentucky, he was joining his musical family for impromptu concerts by age nine, and in 1917 he took first place at a statewide talent competition. Not only was he a gifted singer, he played French harp, piano, banjo, trombone, harmonica and guitar.

Foley's professional break came in 1930 when he was only 20 years old. A talent scout chose him to sing with the house band, Cumberland Ridge Runners, on National Barn Dance, a WLS-AM radio show broadcast from Chicago. In 1939 he joined the band's producer, John Lair, in establishing the Renfro Valley Barn Dance at Mt. Vernon, Kentucky, where he spent seven years as host. He appeared as himself in Tex Ritter's movie, "The Pioneers," and co-wrote and released one of the most memorable songs ever written about a dog – "Old Shep."

During World War II he recorded his first song to hit No. 1 on the Folk Records charts, spending 13 weeks at the top and becoming a No. 5 country hit. "Smoke On The Water" was about the war's outcome, predicting, "There'll be no time for pity when the Screamin' Eagle flies. That will be the end of Foley's ballad recordings often drew upon historical or current events for inspiration, like "There's a Blue Star Shining Bright (In a Window Tonight)," "The Sinking of the Titanic" and "The Death of Floyd Collins," the tale of a Kentucky explorer trapped in a cave for more than two weeks 55 feet below ground, dying just days before rescuers reached him. The 1925 tragedy became one of the first major news stories to be reported using the new technology of broadcast radio, which five years later had catapulted Foley himself into recognition.

One of the first Country artists to record in Nashville, he released seven top five hits with his group, Cumberland Valley Boys, between 1947 and 1949, including a No. 1 singles, "New Jolie Blonde (New Pretty Blonde)" and "Tennessee Saturday Night." "Just a Closer Walk with Thee," "Steal Away" and "Chattanoogie Shoe Shine Boy" each became million sellers in 1950.

Other No. 1 hits during his long career were "Shame on You" with Lawrence Welk, "Birmingham Bounce," "Mississippi" (with The Dixie Dons), "Goodnight Irene" (with Ernest Tubb), "Midnight," and "One by One" with Kitty Wells.

For eight years beginning in 1946, the year he moved to Nashville, he hosted The Prince Albert Show, the segment of the Grand Ole Opry, during which he also sang and played straight man to country comedians. He and performers like Roy Acuff, Minnie Pearl, Little Jimmy Dickens, Hank Williams and others were part of the Opry's first European tour, where they entertained at military bases. Starting in 1951, he hosted "The Red Foley Show" on Saturday afternoons on NBC Radio from Nashville moving to ABC Radio and Springfield, Missouri, from 1956 to 1961.

In 1953 he was one of the first eight performers named to Billboard magazine's Honor Roll of Country and Western artists.

Handsome and charismatic, television was a positive medium for his versatile talents. He appeared as a guest or semi-regular on numerous 1950s

November 2017

and '60s shows like "Masquerade Party," "Strike it Rich," "The Pat Boone Chevy Showroom," "Tonight Starring Jack Paar," "Five Star Jubilee" and "The Joey Bishop Show." He even moved to California in the early '60s to play Fess Parker's Uncle Cooter on the ABC-TV sitcom, "Mr. Smith Goes to Washington." He appeared in the 1966 film musical, "Sing a Song, for Heaven's Sake."

In 1963, he returned to Nashville and performed and toured as a member of the Grand Ole Opry, which he had been credited with establishing as America's top country music radio show.

Foley never sought a pop music career, but many of his recordings topped the pop charts, including his own recordings as well as collaborations with artists like the Andrews Sisters and the Lawrence Welk Orchestra. He recorded gospel songs that have become classics, like his 1951 hit, "Peace in the Valley" backed by the Sunshine Boys, which was one of the first gospel records to sell one million copies. In 2006, the recording was honored with entry into the Library of Congress' National Recording Registry.

The last song Foley performed was "Peace in the Valley" on Sept. 19, 1968 while on tour in Fort Wayne, Indiana, with 19-year-old Hank Williams, Jr. and singer Billy Walker.

"He came over to the side of the stage and said, 'Billy – I've never sung that song and feel the way I do tonight,'" Walker said, recalling that earlier in the evening he and Foley had prayed in the dressing room. "Two hours later Red Foley had passed from this life."

Foley has two stars on the Hollywood Walk of Fame – one for television and one for his recordings. The State of Kentucky honored him with an historical marker at his boyhood home. In 2002, he was inducted into the Kentucky Music Hall of Fame. Foley was the first Kentuckian elected to the Country Music Hall of Fame. During his 1967 induction he was called "one of the most versatile and moving performers of all time" and "a giant influence during the formative years of contemporary Country music and today a timeless legend."

Q: I would like some information about Vern Gosdin. I haven't heard anything about him, is he still living. I love his music. He has a beautiful voice.

Rose Small, Macon, MO

A: Vernon (Vern) Gosdin passed away April 28, 2009. He has his first stroke in 1998, but came back and continued intertaining until he suffered anohter stroke in early April 2009. He died at a Nashville hospital the evening of April 28, 2009, at the age of 74. His remains were buried at Mount Olivet Cemetery in Nashville, Tennessee.

Known as "The Voice" he had 19 top-10 solo hits on the country music charts from 1977 through 1990. Three of these hits went to Number One: "I Can Tell By the Way You Dance (You're Gonna Love Me Tonight)", "Set 'Em Up Joe", and "I'm Still Crazy".

Q: I'd like to know how many wives Randy from the Western Store has? We enjoy your show and look forward to it every week. LOVE NADINE!

Jean Snook, Kimberling City, MO

A: This is a question that gets asked every so often. Randy has one wife, Johnelle. Sometimes people think Ann Tarter is also his wife, however, she is not. She and her husband live in Kentucky where the Tarter company is located.

Q: I would like to know if "Cumberland Highlanders" are coming back. Also, how about more up to date shows on Saturday night. The only up to date is Vincent & Dailey.

Nancy Gibson, Nacogdoches, TX

A: While Country's Family Reunion and Larry's Country Diner both are shown on RFD-TV, we do not have anything to do with the network other than paying to air our shows there. If you would like to contact them, their information is: Rural Media Group, Inc.

49 Music Square West, Ste 301, Nashville, TN 37203 (402) 289-2085. We hope this helps.

If you have questions send them to Paula, CFR News, P.O. Box 210796, Nashville, TN 37221 or email them to paula@gabrielcommunications.com.

November 2017

Larry's Country Diner Shines in Branson!

The cast of Larry's Country Diner welcomes T. Graham Brown to the opening night in Branson.

The Sheriff (Jimmy Capps) and T. Graham Brown joking around.

Rhonda Vincent receives recognition.

Rhonda teams up with Billy Yates, who head up the show "Raiding the Country Vault" in Branson.

Gene Watson and Nadine dance the night away.

Gene Watson and Billy Yates.

November 2017

Jimmy Fortune always 'wows' the crowd during his sell out shows!

Larry is honored with a resolution from the state of Missouri for all he has done to promote Country Music and Branson.

A group of 'church ladies' following Nadine's fashion sense.

The Isaacs bring their 'A' game to Branson to entertain the audience.

Another successful week in Branson ends with Larry and Luann Black, Randy Little, the cast and fans who gave Larry a miniature set of the Diner on stage for one last photo!

November 2017

Winners of annual R.O.P.E. Golden Awards

R.O.P.E., which stands for Reunion Of Professional Entertainers, held their 30th Annual Golden Awards Banquet and Show on October 5 in Nashville. The highlight of the night was a Tribute to Living Legend, "The Voice With A Heart," Mac Wiseman.

The room was filled with country legends as well as friends and family to honor Mac and the winners of each of the categories. The catagories included: Entertainer, Musician, Songwriter, Media, Business and D.J. Each were voted on by members of R.O.P.E. which was formed in 1983.

Winners in each category were:

Entertainer: tie - Jeannie Seely and Gene Watson

Musician: Tim Atwood

Songwriter: Dallas Frazier

Media: Roxane Atwood

Business: Gus Arrendale

D.J. : Keith Bilbrey

Congratulations are due all around for these wonderful folks who support traditional Country Music and Country's Family Reunion.

Jeannie Seely and Gene Watson tied for R.O.P.E.'s 2017 "Entertainer of the Year" honors, are pictured with Living Legend Honoree

Gus Arrendale, Business winner, Cory Birchfield, Jan Howard, Hawkshaw Hawkins Jr., Cyndae Arrendale and D.J. winner, Keith Bilbrey.

Husband and wife, Roxane and Tim Atwood won for Media and Musician.

Leona Williams, who was nominated for Entertainer, with Mac Wiseman.

November 2017

There's Something about that song

It was 10-4 to "Convoy" During CB Obsessed '70s

By Claudia Johnson

It's difficult to explain the obsession with Citizens Band (CB) radio in the mid-1970s in light of today's text messaging, social media and video chatting. With the decline of railroad shipping, the trucking industry exploded. Just as the railroad had provided material for music and movies, trucking was embraced by popular culture.

"Keep on Truckin'" could be found on everything from bumper stickers to T-shirts. Movies like "Smokey and the Bandit," "Steel Cowboy" and "Breaker Breaker" elevated the hardworking truck driver to hero status. CB radios were used by truckers to communicate on the long hauls, especially about locations of troopers who were enforcing the new 55 miles per hour speed limit imposed to offset the oil crisis. When CB radios became affordable to consumers, hundreds of thousands were sold for private vehicles. Suddenly, it wasn't just truck drivers who had their own "handle," phrases like "catch you on the flip flop," "Smokey" and "10-4 good buddy" were splattered throughout normal conversation.

Timing was perfect for a song to encapsulate the phenomenon. "Convoy" was that song.

Co-written by Chip Davis and C.W. McCall, who performed the novelty song on its 1975 single release, "Convoy" spent six weeks at No. 1 on country charts and crossed over for a week at No. 1 on the pop charts in the U.S., and hit No. 1 in Canada, Australia and New Zealand and No. 2 in the United Kingdom. It is listed 98th among Rolling Stone magazine's 100 Greatest Country Songs of All Time. Without an understanding of CB lingo, the song is difficult to follow, but at the time of its release it was more easily understood.

The song chronicles a cross-country trucking rebellion led by a fictional trucker with a handle of "Rubber Duck." In addition to a chorus, which is actually sung, McCall provided story narration and voiced the CB chatter among truckers Rubber Duck, Pig Pen and Sodbuster.

The story begins en route from Shakeytown (Los Angles) to Flagtown"(Flagstaff, Arizona) when Rubber Duck notices a convoy is forming.

"We got a little convoy rockin' through the night," Rubber Duck says to the other truckers listening. "Come on and join our convoy, ain't nothin' gonna get in our way."

Rubber Duck tells them he is going to "put the hammer down." Other truckers and travelers join in, and the convoy is emboldened enough to break the speed limit and disregard the mandated rest that was supposed to be logged on "swindle sheets" for review by federal authorities.

When they reach Tulsa, Oklahoma, they encounter a roadblock with bears (state troopers) on the ground and in the air.

"Them bears was wall-to-wall. Yeah, them smokies is thick as bugs on a bumper; They even had a bear in the air!"

At Chi-town (Chicago) the National Guard is called in for air and ground trooper reinforcement.

"Well, we shot the line and we went for broke with a thousand screamin' trucks, an' eleven long-haired Friends a' Jesus in a chartreuse micro-bus," Rubber Duck says.

Heading for the New Jersey shore, and thus onto a toll road, Rubber Duck sees the bridge lined with troopers and realizes he does not have the money required to open the toll gate.

That's when he tells the convoy, "We just ain't a-gonna pay no toll, which leads to the most memorable line of the song, "So we crashed the gate doing ninety-eight…Let them truckers roll, 10-4."

November 2017

The song sold more than two million copies, earning its Gold Record status in 1975.

"Convoy," a 1978 movie based on the song and for which a new, custom version was written, starred Kris Kristofferson, Ali McGraw and Ernest Borgnine.

The song has been used in several commercials, including one for Priceline with William Shatner of "Star Trek" fame singing the lyrics. Over the past 40 years it has been covered by artists from all genres of music, from country to pop to rap. Several parodies have been released, and there's even a Christmas version!

C.W McCall, whose real name is William Dale Fries, Jr. released other music, but he is most remembered for "Convoy." The 89-year-old lives in Ouray, Colorado, where he served as mayor for two terms and was very active in the environmental movement. His last solo album released in 1990 called "The Real McCall: An American Storyteller," could not be more aptly named, as "Convoy" captured a distinctive era in American culture.

Josie Awards honors Indie country

The Josie Music Awards was started by Josie Passantino and Tina Passantino. This team set out and successfully created an award show where winners are selected on their talent, skill, material, professionalism. Nominee suggestions go through a lengthy review process.

The 2017 Josie Music Awards was held in Nashville on September 23, 2017. While it honor all genres of music, much of its focus is on country music. As such, many of the winners are people you may recognize from all over the United States. Winners include:

Lifetime Career Achievement:LuLu Roman

Lifetime Musical Achievement: Anderson Family(Lynn Anderson, Liz Anderson, & Casey Anderson)

2017 Independent Country Music Hall of Fame Inductees:
Margie Singleton
Bobby Flores
James T. Walden Sr.

The Josie Show Humanitarian Award: Dean Holmen (Music City Hayride)

Country Blast Radio Charting Award: Jimmy Parker

Web Series of the Year:
Kenny Lee - Hicksville Junction

Soaring Career: Brenda Best

Stage Performance of the Year: Dee Rock

Fans Choice: Rebecca Mae & Jack Lawless (Duo)

Junior Category (ages 6-12)

Artist of the Year: Taylon Hope

Vocalist of the Year: Ava Paige

Young Adult Category (ages 13-17)

Artist of the Year: Tommy Brandt II

Vocalist of the Year: Kadin Hernandez

Rising Star of the Year: Macy Tabor

Entertainer of the Year: Maggie Baugh

Duo/Group of the Year: Hanah & Hailee

Song of the Year: "Lost Boy" Landon Wall

Rising Star of the Year: Linda Lee

Duo/Group of the Year: 2Country4Nashville

Song of the Year: The Way It Used To Be (Donna Ray, Mike Jones, Jerry Howard)

Album of the Year: Cody Wickline (Son of a Working Man)

Independent Country Gospel Bluegrass Music Association Inducted: Col. Carolina Rose, Allen Frizzell

A complete list of winners can be found at: http://www.josiemusicawards.com/

November 2017

Dolly's new "I Belive In You" CD to help Imagination Library

Dolly Parton has joined forces with PledgeMusic to launch an order campaign in support of her first-ever children's album, I Believe In You. Comprised of original tunes penned by Dolly, including a reading of her famed "Coat Of Many Colors", the album is available digitally now, with the physical release Friday, October 13.

Fans can order the album in digital and CD form now on Parton's campaign page. The leaders in direct-to-fan platforms, PledgeMusic allows artists to get more personal with their fans, offering pledgers behind-the-scenes content and items not available anywhere else.

Inspired by her passion for fostering a love of reading amongst children and their families, as well as her beloved organization Imagination Library, I Believe In You is the star's first album written specifically for kids and those young at heart. This year marks 50 years since Dolly released her first album, and 20 years since Imagination Library was established; making the forthcoming album a special contribution to the singer/songwriter's legendary career and the cause so close to her heart.

Since its inception in 1996, the Imagination Library has expanded into four countries serving more than one-million children by providing a brand new, age-appropriate book each month.

With her PledgeMusic campaign, Dolly is inviting fans to join her in her dedication to promoting literacy and joy through music throughout America's promising youth.

Fans who pre-order the album via PledgeMusic will get the AccessPass, which will give them special access to exclusive items straight from Dolly. These include: an early digital download of the album; a custom outgoing voicemail recorded by Dolly herself, plus a CD and digital download; a Recording King RD-T16 guitar autographed by Dolly, and specially crafted to produce a vintage tone, deluxe hard case included; a signed tour laminate; and much more.

The track listing is as follows:
1. I Believe in You
2. Coat of Many Colors (new recording)
3. Together Forever
4. I Am a Rainbow
5. I'm Here
6. A Friend Like You
7. Imagination
8. You Can Do It
9. Responsibility
10. You Gotta Be
11. Makin' Fun Ain't Funny
12. Chemo Hero
13. Brave Little Soldier
14. Bonus track spoken audio: Coat of Many Colors (book read by Dolly Parton)

To order I Believe In You, please visit: www.pledgemusic.com/projects/dollyparton

Looking for a great stocking stuffer?

Phil Johnson
JUST LIKE YOU

CD now available
Includes *The Day He Wore My Crown*

To Order call: 1-800-820-5405 or send a check for $14.95 plus $6.95 s/h to CFR, P.O. Box 210796, Nashville, TN 37221
www.renaethewaitress.com

November 2017

The People Who Make Us Laugh

As his alter ego, "Cousin Jody" and his real-life personal James Clell.

Life itself is portrayed by the world of Country Music entertainment. From the depths of sorrow to the heights of jubilation, performances reach our hearts and spirit. This series takes a look at the lighter side of life and features those artists, both past and present, who bring smiles to our faces and warmth to our hearts. Entitled "Country Comedians," this series highlights those performers who exemplify the great spirit of America.

Cousin Jody – More than Just a Funny Face

By Danny Nichols

Rural comedy coupled with considerable musical talent transported James Clell Summey from Possum Hollow, Tennessee, where he was born in during the World War I era, to the Grand Ole Opry, where he performed as Cousin Jody.

Summey's parents were musical, so he grew up learning to play several instruments, including the guitar and steel guitar, which he called a "biscuit board." He first appeared publically on a radio variety show he established in Knoxville, Tennessee, that aired daily and became an instant success.

Summey first played with a group in 1933 that called themselves the Tennessee Crackerjacks. A young Roy Acuff joined the band, eventually luring Summey from the mountains of East Tennessee to Nashville for an Opry performance in 1937. The dobro had been developed in the 1920s, and Summey was an accomplished player who was the first artist to feature the instrument at the Opry. Acuff used Summey's dobro talent to back up most of his early recordings. Listen to Acuff's original recordings of "The Great Speckled Bird" and "Wabash Cannonball." That's Summey on the dobro.

Creative differences with Acuff promoted his exit from the band. Summey worked with artists like with Pee Wee King and Lonzo and Oscar and even played steel guitar for Eddie Arnold before carving his own niche in the comedy genre with Oral Rhodes as half the Odie and Jody duo. As "Our Cousin Jody," the multi-talented performer became a star in his own right and was an Opry regular for more than 30 years. Once asked why he had chosen the stage name Cousin Jody, he replied, "Don't I look like your Cousin Jody?"

He made appearances on "Ed Sullivan's Toast of the Town," "The Kate Smith Show," "The Dave Garroway Show" and "Steve Allen's Tonight." Newspapers covering his brand of entertainment often noted that he was a "pantomime artist" in addition to a singer and musician. He was also featured actor in several cowboy movies with Roy Rogers and Johnny Mack Brown.

During musical performances with his group, the Country Cousins, he would open the number by telling funny stories in an exaggerated hillbilly voice. His stage persona wore a tattered hat, had no teeth and dressed in flamboyant shirts and baggy, garish pants. In reality he was a distinguished 6'5" man who served in the U.S. Army Air Corps during World War II.

Cousin Jody and the Country Cousins traveled throughout Europe entertaining the troops during the early 1960s and became a popular act beyond the Opry, appearing at festivals and small concert venues and releasing recordings like "Lady Cop" and "Television Set."

In 1966 Summey became involved in a lengthy federal lawsuit he filed against The National Informer Publishing Co. and its Chicago owners, Vincent and Josephine Sorren. The Informer, a tabloid paper, had run a professional publicity photo of Summey dressed as Cousin Jody with a caption that suggested he was a sexual deviant. Summey's suit argued that the article was "false, libelous and malicious" and was published to willfully "injure, disgrace and defame" him. He asserted that his personality had been invaded along with his right

November 2017

to privacy and his natural copyright to his own features had been violated. He stated that the attack had permanently damaged his good name. In 1968 Summey was finally granted a default judgment for $200,000.

Summey made additional headlines in 1968 when he married his third wife, Marie Hill, after meeting her in a Nashville laundry mat a few months prior.

The comic died in 1975 at age 61 following an extended illness, leaving behind his wife, Marie, a son, Clell Vernon Summey, whose mother was Summey's first wife, Dorothy, and a daughter, Jodena Summey, whose mother was his second wife, Sarah.

He also left behind a favorite sing-along song, "On Top of Old Smokey," that families on long car trips and school children on buses were singing for decades after Summey's recording sealed its popularity.

Loretta Lynn's first performance after stroke

Loretta Lynn's Ranch posted on their Facebook page on October 2 about her return to performing with this announcement:

Yesterday was a special day here at the Ranch, it marked the end of our first Tennessee Motorcycles and Music Revival.

Thank you to everyone who came out. Most of y'all probably know that we ended the event with the Loretta Lynn's Ride for Mission 22, which dedicated a whole day of the event to raising money for Mission 22, an organization that brings awareness and is committed to helping stop veteran suicide.

The last performance of the day was Ms Loretta Lynn herself, taking the stage for the first time since her stroke in May. Singing "They Don't Make 'em Like My Daddy Anymore" - "Dear Uncle Sam"- "You Ain't Woman Enough" and finally "Coal Miner's Daughter".

During interludes she entertained with anecdotes and jokes and heartfelt messages to her fans and to our vets.

She took the stage to a standing ovation, and left the stage to one as well. Many tears were shared and the outpouring of fan support was incredible and humbling.

November 2017

Entertainers love of food & restauarants

Music and food make perfect duo. It's no wonder, then, that so many stars have tried their hand or lent their name to eating establishments. This series looks at some of the greatest hits as well as some eateries that failed to climb the charts with diners.

Roy Rogers Restaurants – half a century in and still a favorite

By Sasha Kay Dunavant

In the latter part of the 1960s, the Marriot Cooperation hatched a very marketable idea that associated all-American singing cowboy Roy Rogers with all-time favorite American foods.

The Roy Rogers Restaurant creators wished to please distinctly American taste buds by featuring what they called "The Big Three" on the menu – hamburgers, roast beef sandwiches and fried chicken. In 1968 with Roy Rogers' blessing, Marriot opened the doors to its first Roy Rogers Restaurant in Falls Church, Virginia.

Early television commercials for Roy Rogers Restaurant were created near the Rogers family home in Apple Valley, California. The beloved cowboy along with close friends Mel Marion and Earl Bascom were filmed in various locations like historic Las Flores Ranch in Summit Valley and the Campbell Ranch in Victorville.

When Marriot bought the Gino's restaurant chain in 1982, 180 of the 313 Gino's were converted into a Roy Rogers, expanding the chain into the Baltimore-Washington area. At its peak there were 650 Roy Rogers locations.

In 1990 Hardees bought the Roy Rogers chain for $365 million. The Hardee's Corporation eventually sold the remaining Roy Rogers locations to McDonald's, Wendy's and Boston Market between 1994- 1996. In fact, the original Falls Church location is now a McDonald's. Even the location across from Marriott's headquarters in Bethesda, Maryland, has been converted into a McDonald's.

Peter Plamondon Sr. was the head of the restaurant division at Marriot Corporation when the brand was created and held a longtime special interest in the Roy Rogers chain. In the late 1990s Plamondon formed Plamondon Companies with a goal of restoring the Roy Rogers chain to its wholesome atmosphere through new and improved ideas. His plan was expanded further when he sold the chain to sons Peter Plamondon Jr. and Jim Plamondon in 1998.

Even though CKE Restaurants, known for Carl's Jr., had taken over Hardee's from Imasco, its previous owner, Imasco would not release the Roy Rogers chain trademark and franchise very easily. It was only after three years of negotiation that Plamondon Companies finally reached a private purchase agreement in 2002.

The first Plamondon-owned Roy Rogers restaurant was opened in Fredrick, Maryland, with more than 50 locations now dotting the Mid-Atlantic region. The company also oversees around 30 franchises. The owners say their staff follows "The Code of Roy," which is "Hard work. Character. Honesty."

Modern updates by the Plamondon brothers at various locations include special summer events, a Brews & Blues Festival with the choice of more than 50 international beers, country music concerts and weekly family nights. The salad bar has evolved into the "Fixin' Bar" with 18 different fixings to go with any meal from horseradish to Pico de Gallo. Some locations serve food cafeteria style, and catering is available for events. The Big Three continues to be served along with a variety of side items.

Regardless of the changes, the Plamondons prioritize taking an active role in the communities where they operate with a primary philanthropic focus on education. A successful fundraising program is offered to the organizations that wish to partner with their local restaurant.

The Plamondons continue to adhere to "Roy's Promise," which states, "There's no reason in the world you can't get good food even if you are in a hurry."

"As we look to the future, we see that the values Roy stood for are more relevant than ever," they observe, adding, "That's why we work everyday to live up to Roy's Promise."

November 2017

DECEMBER

Moe Bandy Receives a Special Gift As Former First Lady Barbara Bush Writes Foreword For His Autobiography

Fans who have been wanting Moe Bandy to tell his life story are now in luck!

Moe's autobiography 'Lucky Me' will be released this Christmas.

Moe with President and Mrs. Bush at their home in Kennebunkport, Maine

"The main reason I did this book was for my great grandchildren," says Moe. "I wanted to give them a true record of the life that their grandpa Moe lived."

Moe Bandy's life story is an amazing one. He started his recording career while he was a sheet metal worker in San Antonio, Texas. But after a decade of hard work, Moe traded his sheet metal for Gold albums.

"'Lucky Me' was also the title of my latest album. But it really sums up my life. I was lucky in so many ways in my life and my career. And I am blessed in so many ways with the life I have today. So I think 'Lucky Me' is a very appropriate title for my life story."

Moe Bandy's country music accomplishments are many, including 10 #1 songs, 40 Top Ten hits, 5 Gold Records and numerous ACM and CMA awards. In the 1980s, Moe performed to one sold out crowd after another at his Americana Theatre in Branson Missouri.

"The book is all in my own words. I told my life story to Scot England over the past year. And he put it all together. We also interviewed many of my family members, my band members and a bunch of the country artists I have worked with over the years."

Gene Watson, Janie Fricke, Joe Stampley, Jimmy Capps and Becky Hobbs are among those who share their memories of working with Moe. 'Lucky Me' also includes Moe's backstage stories about many other country music legends ranging from George Jones and Tammy Wynette to Marty Robbins to Mel Tillis.

"There is a lot about Gene Watson and me. And of course we tell the entire story of Moe and Joe. I also set the record straight about my career as a rodeo clown. There are a lot of stories about my love of rodeo. And I share many memories of my thirty year friendship with President George Bush and his wife Barbara."

And the former First Lady Barbara Bush surprised Moe when she agreed to write the foreword for the book.

"We sent an advance copy to Mrs. Bush. And I was so honored when she said she would like to write the foreword for it. She wrote it all herself, with no help from anyone. And I am so touched that she would take the time to do that for me. It was one more very special gift from Mr. and Mrs. Bush."

Bandy also shares some of his toughest life struggles.

"I cover my heart attack and open heart surgery in the book. But the toughest thing to talk about was my alcoholism. I was a horrible alcoholic for many years. But at the age of 40, I took my last drink. I have not had a sip of alcohol for 33 years. And I tell exactly what happened and who helped me stop drinking, I tell all of that in the book."

December 2017

The deluxe, hardback 294 page 'Lucky Me' includes 250 rare photos from Moe's personal collection.

"I wanted the book to be entertaining. And I wanted it to be honest. And I think we accomplished both of those things. I am very proud of it. I hope my fans will be proud of it. And I hope my great grandkids will be proud of their ol' grandpa."

To order Moe Bandy's 'Lucky Me', you can phone (615) 804-0361 for credit card orders.

Personal checks can be mailed to: England Media 102 Rachels Ct. Hendersonville TN.

"We also wanted to keep the price very affordable for everyone. The book costs $25.99, including postage, and signed copies are $28.99."

You can also place an order or get more info at www.moebandybook.com

Things to do in Nashville over Christmas holidays

Outdoor Nativity Display at Gaylord Opryland Hotel features special lighting effects and an audio rendition of the biblical story of the birth of Christ. November 10, 2017 – January 1, 2018, Magnolia Lawn, Free from 4 pm – Midnight | Daily

Delight in the joy of the holiday season during Holiday LIGHTS at Cheekwood. November 24 – December 31, 5:00 – 10:00 PM (closed Mondays). $22 adults, $17 children advance sales. Tickets purchased at the gate are subject to a $5 per ticket processing

Outdoor Nativity Display at Gaylord Opryland Hotel.

Holiday Lights at Cheekwood.

December 2017

Nadine
The Church Lady

*Lord, give me a sense of humor,
Give me the grace to see a joke,
To get some humor out of life,
And to pass it on to other folk.*

Our son was helping this preacher get his Christmas Cantata ready and they were heading out of the church and the preacher said he was going to the hospital to see his wife who had just had a baby. My son went with him and they got in her room and she had another woman that she shared the room with.

The preacher walked over to his wife's bed and said, "Well Sister Davis, how in the world are you?" and then he leaned over and hugged her and kissed her for a while and she said, "I'm doing fine preacher man, they're gonna bring the baby back in here in two hours, why don't you came back then?" And he said, "I wouldn't miss it, gonna make some rounds and I'll be back." And he leaned over and gave her a big ol' kiss and said, "I'll see you in a little bit." And they left and the lady in the other bed looked at Mrs. Davis and said, "Lordy, honey, your preacher sure is a lot more friendlier than mine!"

Church sign

The devil doesn't come dressed in a red cape and pointy horns, he comes as everything you've ever wished for. Pray for wisdom and discernment.

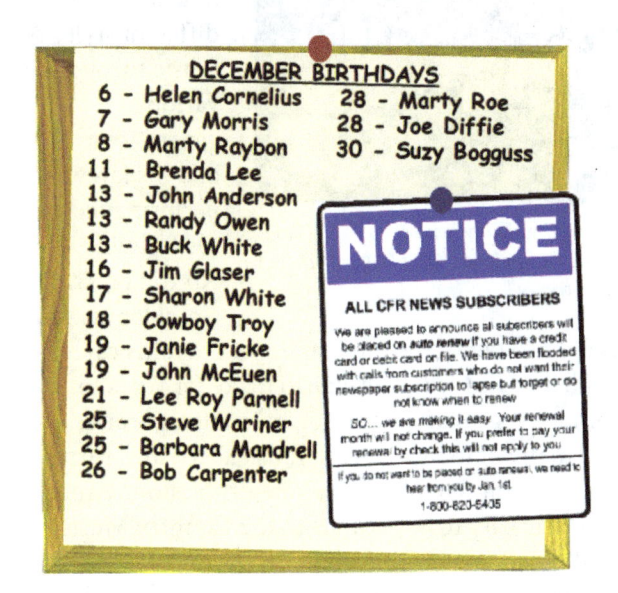

DECEMBER BIRTHDAYS
- 6 - Helen Cornelius
- 7 - Gary Morris
- 8 - Marty Raybon
- 11 - Brenda Lee
- 13 - John Anderson
- 13 - Randy Owen
- 13 - Buck White
- 16 - Jim Glaser
- 17 - Sharon White
- 18 - Cowboy Troy
- 19 - Janie Fricke
- 19 - John McEuen
- 21 - Lee Roy Parnell
- 25 - Steve Wariner
- 25 - Barbara Mandrell
- 26 - Bob Carpenter
- 28 - Marty Roe
- 28 - Joe Diffie
- 30 - Suzy Bogguss

NOTICE — ALL CFR NEWS SUBSCRIBERS

We are pleased to announce all subscribers will be placed on auto renew if you have a credit card or debit card on file. We have been flooded with calls from customers who do not want their newspaper subscription to lapse but forget or do not know when to renew.

SO... we are making it easy. Your renewal month will not change. If you prefer to pay your renewal by check this will not apply to you.

If you do not want to be placed on auto renewal, we need to hear from you by Jan 1st.
1-800-820-5435

Smash Hit-Single 'The Auctioneer' featured in New Subway Commercial

Leroy Van Dyke first gained notoriety in 1956 with his breakout, smash-hit "Auctioneer." The self-penned record went a million-plus a week after its release, and is still popping up in places 61 years later. An excerpted version of the recording is the track to Subway's latest television ad campaign. Go to Youtube.com to catch the commercial proudly boasting the fast-talking tune.

"I was totally surprised to learn that Subway was using Auctioneer in their television ad campaign. Our thanks to Subway... we're having a lot of fun with it!"

Van Dyke went to auction school between his junior and senior year of college after being inspired by his cousin, Ray Simms. The track was written while he was serving as a Special Agent, US Army Counterintelligence Corps in Korea in 1953 and is a tribute to Sims.

The song rose to fame when Van Dyke entered a talent contest simulcast on WGN radio and TV in Chicago while working in the advertising department for a chain of livestock newspapers. He placed third, ironically enough, but the phones were ringing before he even left the studio. Within two weeks he had the track recorded and had sold one million records in just three months.

Van Dyke recently celebrated the 55th Anniversary since his induction into the world-renowned Grand Ole Opry with a performance at Opry's Country Classics at Ryman Auditorium on October 19.

December 2017

All In For The Gambler: Kenny Rogers Farewell Celebration' Full of Surprises and Emotional Moments

Kenny and Dolly, who sang "You Can't Make Old Friends" and "Islands In The Stream"

Kenny Rogers' musical career has touched many different styles of music throughout various generations, and his farewell performance to Nashville, All In For The Gambler, served as a reminder of the musical impact that his career has had – and will continue to make for years to come. An all-star cast of Rogers' contemporaries – and many of today's hottest musical artists – turned up last night (October 25) at the Bridgestone Arena in Music City to pay tribute to the Country Music Hall of Fame member, who is in the midst of his farewell tour, "The Gambler's Last Deal." Perhaps the most emotional moment of the night belonged to Dolly Parton, who teamed with Rogers one last time on their 1983 hit "Islands In The Stream" after surprising both Rogers – and the audience – with a heartfelt performance of "I Will Always Love You" to her friend and collaborator. The two also reminisced about their lengthy friendship – which dates back to a Rogers appearance on her syndicated TV show from the mid 1970s – almost a decade before they first teamed up. The two also closed out their performing career together with the Grammy-nominated "You Can't Make Old Friends," a single from 2013.

Reba singing "Reuben James"

The evening was a mixture of song performances that balanced many of the singer's iconic hits – as well as many of the early days of Rogers' career as the lead vocalist of The First Edition. Jamey Johnson paid tribute to the singer's versatility with a raucous take on Mickey Newbury's "Just Dropped In (To See What Condition My Condition Was In)," a First Edition hit from five decades ago. The Flaming Lips shined the light on "Ruby, Don't Take Your Love To Town," with Reba McEntire tipping the hat to the group's "Reuben James." Elle King gave a jaw-dropping performance of "Tulsa Turnaround," one of the First Edition's lesser-known tracks – that Rogers himself recorded for his 1979 album Kenny. Rogers' fellow Texan Kris Kristofferson paid tribute to the band's cover of "Me and Bobby McGee," which he wrote.

Chris Stapleton singing "The Gambler"

Of course, the main focus of the evening was on the record-setting solo career Rogers embarked on in the mid-1970s, and those hits were on full display during the evening. Justin Moore nodded to the beginning of the singer's hit making era with "Lucille," with spellbinding performances taking place from Aaron Lewis ("Coward Of The County", The Oak Ridge Boys ("Love Or Something Like It"), Chris Stapleton ("The Gambler"), Little Big Town ("Through The Years"), and Lady Antebellum ("She Believes In Me"). A special moment took place with the appearance of Don Henley – who once lived with Rogers and his family - to perform the classic "Desperado," which Rogers cut in 1977 for his Daytime Friends album.

Many of the 80s and 90s hits of the singer were featured during The Gambler's Last Deal as well. Billy Currington delivered a sensual take on "Morning Desire," with Lady Antebellum's Charles Kelley and Idina Menzel teaming up for "We've Got Tonight," a 1983 Rogers hit with Sheena Easton. Two of the singers' most frequent collaborators figured prominently in this era with appearances with Lionel Richie giving a beautiful take on "'Lady," a number one Pop and Country hit that he wrote for Kenny's Greatest Hits album in 1980, and Alison Krauss saluted the singer with a pristine version of his romantic ballad "Love The World Away."

Another incredible performance came from Lady Antebellum's Hillary Scott and mother Linda Davis – who has toured extensively with Rogers over the years – uniting on stage for the singer's 1987 chart-topper "Twenty Years Ago."

There were several other great musical moments during All In For The Gambler, with Naomi and Wynonna Judd reuniting for "Back To The Well," and an all-star group of Rogers' former opening acts paying tribute to the icon with a sing-along performance of his 1982 hit "Blaze Of Glory," including Travis Tritt, The Gatlin Brothers, Kim Forester, T.G. Sheppard, Crystal Gayle, Lee Greenwood, T. Graham Brown, and Billy Dean.

Blackbird Presents' Keith Wortman, creator and executive producer of Nashville's recent highly acclaimed "Sing Me Back Home: The Music of Merle Haggard," is the creator and executive producer of "All In For The Gambler." GRAMMY® Award Winner Don Was served as music director, and presided over a stellar house band backing the performers at this historic concert event taping. Kenny Rogers' manager, Ken Levitan, also served as executive producer. The event was filmed and recorded for multi-platform distribution throughout traditional media (worldwide broadcast, music, and digital).

Linda Davis and daughter Hillary Scott singing "Twenty Years Ago"

The Judds singing "Back To The Well"

Group Singing "Blaze Of Glory" - Billy Dean, Kim Forester, T. Graham Brown, Lee Greenwood, T.G. Sheppard, Travis Tritt, Crystal Gayle, Steve Gatlin, and Rudy Gatlin

Photos by Ron Harman

December 2017

Justin Roman, son of Lulu, dies of heart attack

On Sunday night, October 29th, LuLu Roman, Country and Gospel singer and star of television's Hee Haw received the devastating news that her son, Justin, was being rushed to Summit Medical after suffering a massive heart attack. LuLu and her assistant Kim were enroute back home from an engagement in Branson, Missouri. She arrived at the hospital where she was told by staff that all had been done to revive her son but that he had died.

LuLu now finds herself facing the costs of a funeral which can be both exorbitant and overwhelming. Because the loss of her son was so very unexpected and came during a time of particular financial difficulty, stress has been added to grief. I am starting this GoFundMe page so that anyone who is able to assist her in defraying these costs can do so. LuLu has not asked me to do this, but I just left her home and can see that the prospect of all that lies ahead is already taking its toll on her. Her remaining son, Damon, flew in and helped make the plans for the memorial service which was held on Friday, November 3rd.

Merle Haggard Museum new Nashville attraction

A new Nashville attraction will be devoted to the music and memory of Merle Haggard.

Bill and Shannon Miller will open the Merle Haggard Museum and Merle's Meat + Three Saloon in summer 2018. The Shannons have co-founded museums for Johnny Cash and Patsy Cline in recent years.

The Tennessean reports the museum will feature instruments, clothing, memorabilia, awards and other artifacts that belonged to Haggard, who died last year.

Haggard's parents moved from Oklahoma to Bakersfield, California, where the singer was born. Haggard was an architect of country music's "Bakersfield Sound."

Bill Miller paid just over $7 million for the 15,447-square-foot building last fall. The Merle Haggard Museum will be located on an upper floor and the saloon will be on the ground level.

Country's Family Reunion presents....

December 1, 2
8, 9
15, 16
and
23, 24

Another Wednesday Night Prayer Meeting

Country's Family Reunion at the Ryman
December 29 & 30

Fridays...7 p.m. central
Saturdays...11 p.m central

December 2017

Gene Watson gets back to his 'Gospel Roots' with album release December 8

Gene Watson continues to stay true to his traditional country style with the release of his new record with New Day Christian Distribution, My Gospel Roots, available December 8. At the recent R.O.P.E. Awards, Watson celebrated his win for the 2017 Entertainer of the Year, an honor he shared with one of his best friends in the music business, Jeannie Seely.

"New Day Christian has a storied legacy of distributing quality Christian products," said Dottie Leonard Miller, President New Day Christian. "We're excited to add Gene Watson to that list. Gene's voice is synonymous with Country music, and we couldn't be more thrilled to partner with him as he returns to his 'roots.'"

Despite a busy few months in the studio, Watson, who is often known as "The Singer's Singer," shows no sign of slowing down his touring schedule. Fans can expect to hear his powerhouse vocals on classics like "Love in the Hot Afternoon," "Farewell Party" and "Fourteen Carat Mind," alongside Watson's gospel renditions.

---

7 HOURS for ONLY $79.80 plus $6.95 s/h

ANOTHER WEDNESDAY NIGHT PRAYER MEETING
Wouldn't it be great to walk into a Wednesday night prayer meeting and as you're walking in you see *The Gatlins, The Oaks, The Issacs, Jimmy Fortune, Gene Watson, Rhonda Vincent, John Conlee* – just like the last Wednesday Night Prayer Meeting, but wait, there are some new faces, *Randy Travis, The Malpass Brothers, Jason Crabb, The Martins* and other old and new faces. All ready to sing and share.

Seven hours of content on each series, as opposed to less than 3 hours of content on TV.

800-820-5405
www.cfrvideos.com

Look who's on the Diner this week!
ON RFD-TV
All shows subject to change

Thursdays 7 p.m. & Saturdays 10 p.m. Central

TIM ATWOOD Nov. 30 & Dec. 2
TONY JACKSON Dec. 7 & 9
BOBBY BARE Dec. 16 & 18
OAK RIDGE BOYS Dec. 21 & 23
Best Of... favorite moments from years past Dec. 28 & 30

December 2017

COUNTRY LEGENDS OF THE PAST & PRESENT

BY TOM WOOD

Crook and Chase

There have been more mountains than valleys in the storied broadcasting careers of Lorianne Crook and Charlie Chase, but the duo reached a pinnacle when they were called to the stage of the Grand Ole Opry on February 20, 2017.

That star-studded night, Crook and Chase were presented with the fourth annual Bob Kingsley Living Legend Award — which recognizes deserving members from radio, media and record labels who help promote the country music industry.

High praise came from the likes of Garth Brooks and Trisha Yearwood, the co-hosts, and they were joined in the celebration by Trace Adkins, Tanya Tucker, T.G. Sheppard, Jeannie Seely, John Michael Montgomery, Moe Bandy, Ricky Skaggs and The Whites, among many others.

They were all there to pay tribute to Crook and Chase, who as Garth noted, like the Opry stage itself, "made country music famous."

Established as a benefit for the Opry Trust Fund, Kingsley was the first recipient of the Living Legend Award, followed by Joe Galante and Jim Ed Norman. It was the second such major honor for Crook and Chase, who in 2013 were inducted into the Country Radio Hall of Fame.

Crook and Chase saw their solo careers take off in the early 1980s on competing stations in the Nashville television market, both doing entertainment reports. Each had built solid and loyal audiences, and local producer Jim Owens felt they could achieve even greater followings if teamed together.

Owens was right. The clever name, pairing the velvet voice of Crook with the baritone of Chase, two good-looking and likable personalities — it all combined to an instant hit with fans.

They began with This Week in Country Music and were so successful that the show soon morphed into The Crook & Chase Show, one of the anchor shows on The Nashville Network.

Crook and Chase not only highlighted past and present country music stars, but also introduced fans to up-and-comers like Garth Brooks, who would become a megastar in his own right.

The show became so popular that their meet-and-greet lines at Fan Fair were as long as those of the entertainers they covered. All of this heady success led to publishing a 1995 memoir titled Crook and Chase: Our Lives, The Music, And The Stars.

The show names Crook & Chase Tonight, Music City Tonight With Crook & Chase, Crook & Chase Show, Crook & Chase Show, Funny Business, Today's Country, The Crook and Chase Countdown, and a few others), the medium (radio, TV, syndication, internet) and the affiliates (TNN, RFD, iHeart Radio) have all changed over the years — but the personalities and their mission haven't.

The stories they tell, the music they play and the connection to fans all comes through loud and clear on their current show The Crook and Chase Countdown, which can be heard on various iHeart Radio affiliates across the nation or online.

Indeed, the hallmark of success for Crook and Chase may be that their fans feel like they know each on a first-name basis.

Lorianne and Charlie doesn't have the same ring as Crook and Chase, but fans continue to welcome each into their living rooms on a weekly basis.

Author Tom Wood, who writes thrillers and Westerns, is a regular contributor to Country Family Reunion News. Reach him at tomwoodauthor.com

December 2017

Dottie West birthday celebration

A celebration for Dottie West's birthday was held at 3rd & Lindsley in Nashville on October 18 as a fundraiser for the Nashville Musicians Emergency Relief Fund.

Hosted by Jeannie Seely and packed with performances by artists and family members who turned out to support the cause and keep Dottie West's name in the public.

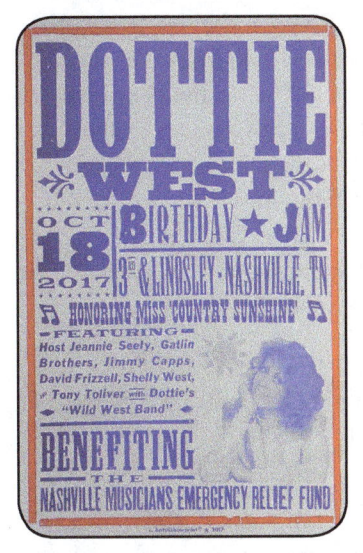

Photos by Ron Harman & Charlotte Sneed

Steve, Larry and Rudy Gatlin perform at the Dottie West Birthday Jam.

Kerry West (Dottie's son) and Jeannie Seely sing together as a tribute to his mom.

John Schneider plays and sings to show his love and share his memories.

David Frizzell and Dottie's daughter, Shelly West perform.

December 2017

Country Artists of a Bygone Era

Smathers Family Brought National Recognition to Clogging as Country Art Form

By Claudia Johnson

An Appalachian style of dance known as clogging brought Ben Smathers and the Stoney Mountain Cloggers from the mountains of North Carolina to the television, movies, concert stages and the Grand Ole Opry.

[Photo: BEN SMATHERS AND THE STONEY MOUNTAIN CLOGGERS — GRAND OLE OPRY, Door Knob Records]

Smathers claimed he learned clogging from an old man named Sam Green, who had mastered the traditional dance brought to American by the early Irish, Dutch and German settlers. According to Smathers, Green was able to clog with a teacup of water on his head and never spill a drop since all his motion and action was from the waist down.

Smathers was devoted to the dance form, explaining in a 1986 interview that the key to doing it well was the emotional grasp of its spirit.

"If you can't feel it in your heart, it has no meaning," he told the Associated Press.

Though Smathers was employed by the Southern Railway, eventually working enough years to draw a pension for his service, he founded the Stoney Mountain Cloggers in Hendersonville, N.C., where they danced locally and soon became regulars on a country music television show out of Greenville, S.C.

Smathers credited his wife, Margaret, who along with four of their children who would be members of the group over the years, with bringing them and their craft before a national audience. In a 1981 interview he recalled how Margaret had saved enough money for a bus ticket to Nashville so she could deliver a tape of their performances to the manager of the Grand Ole Opry. Two weeks later they were booked on the show, and the eight-member group continued to be part of the Opry beginning in 1958 until their last performance there in 1993, which was three years after Ben Smathers' death.

For many years they continued to live in North Carolina and drove the 624-mile round trip each weekend to Nashville, but eventually they moved to Middle Tennessee.

Smathers' shows consisted of vocal performances by some of the dancers, recitations by Smathers, back up by a five-piece band and, of course, clogging. When troupe members were replaced over the years, it was always with Smathers' own family members or dancers from his native North Carolina.

In the 1960s they performed live at various venues with the Roy Rogers and Dale Evans Show, and in the early 1980s they found themselves at Carnegie Hall alongside Roy Acuff, Tammy Wynette and Merle Haggard. That wasn't their first appearance there, either. They are credited with introducing clogging to the prestigious hall as well as the Chicago Hilton, various Las Vegas casinos and dozens of state fairs. The group appeared on nationally televised shows on all three networks, including appearances on "Dolly," the variety show hosted by Dolly Parton. In 1966 Smathers played a clogger in the feature film starring Randy Boone and Sheb Wooley called "Country Boy" about a young man who hopes to become an Opry star.

The group's career took an exciting turn when Charlie Daniels remembered being impressed with one of their performances and in the late 1970s invited them to tour with him, which they did for several years translating an ancient form of dance into performances that country rock fans could appreciate. The climax of each show was their spirited dance to the high-powered fiddle classic "Orange Blossom Special."

A true departure from Smathers' normal performances was a spoken word novelty song called "I Spent a Year with Her Last Night," which tells the story of a blind date that went very, very wrong.

When in 1979 Smathers suffered a heart attack, he was told he would never dance again. He dedicated himself to heart-healthy habits to expedite a return to the stage, which he accomplished in six months.

In September 1990 at age 61 Smathers died as the result of complications from open-heart surgery at Vanderbilt Hospital in Nashville. In addition to his wife and his mother, three daughters, Candy, Sally and Debbie survived, as did sons Hal, Mickey and Tommy.

Perhaps in honor of the mountains that had inspired his art, his remains were cremated and sprinkled over the Great Smokey Mountains.

Friends show up at Opry to celebrate Bill Anderson's 80th Birthday

The Grand Ole Opry brought on the stars at the show on Saturday, October 28 to celebrate Bill Anderson's 80th birthday (Nov. 1).

The artists performing on the Opry Saturday night who were in attendance to wish Bill Anderson a Happy Birthday were John Conlee, Mo Pitney, Mike Snider, Steve Wariner, Riders In The Sky, Jeannie Seely, Ricky Skaggs, The Whites, Connie Smith, Mark Wills, Don Schlitz, and the Opry Square Dancers.

www.countryroad.tv
Subscribe and watch OVER 500+ HOURS OF ENTERTAINMENT!
FULL EPISODES!! Country's Family Reunion, Larry's Country Diner, Gene & Moe, Sports Reunions, Marty Robbins Spotlight, Wednesday Night Prayer Meeting Rejoice movie and more!
Available on your computer, ROKU, Apple TV (4 or newer), & Amazon Fire.
Only $9.99 per month

December 2017

Country Pioneer Margie Singleton Releases New Video

Legendary country singer-songwriter, Margie Singleton was a pioneer at the forefront of country music in the 1950s and '60s. During her career, Margie recorded a total of 9 Top 40 Billboard country singles, including her biggest hit, "Keeping Up With the Joneses," a Top 5 hit with Faron Young. Margie's hit, "Old Records" was a Top 10 smash on Cashbox and Record World, two of the most influential charts of the day. She was the first female artist to record a full album with George Jones, 14 tracks in all, including two of Margie's original songs, and she was a backup singer for The Jordanaires.

In 1967, Margie's husband, Leon Ashley had a #1 Billboard Country hit, "Laura," a song they penned together. Margie's songs have been covered by fellow legends like Charley Pride, Tom Jones, Kenny Rogers, Tammy Wynette, and many others. It's been quite a career for Ms. Singleton…but she's far from done!

Now, at the age of 82 years young, Margie Singleton has released a hip new single and video, for a song she first wrote and recorded during her 1960s heydey…

"Jesus Is My Pusher" is Margie's most ambitious track and video to date, and it shows that Margie is nowhere near slowing down. The single is being released to Christian and country radio stations, while the video is available on her Youtube channel. Watch "Jesus Is My Pusher" on YouTube.

Video production for the video is by Kenny Harrison/Shadow Wave Production, Director : Kenny Harrison /Margie Singleton, Video shot on location in Hendersonville, Tennessee, on Old Hickory Lake, Hendersonville Pentecostal Church and Buck's Place Recording Studio.

"Jesus Is My Pusher" is taken from her upcoming album release, scheduled for early 2018. The single was recorded at D&D Recording Studio in Shreveport, LA with Dexter Mathis.

Margie Singleton was born Margaret Louise Ebey in 1935 in Coushatta, Louisiana. As a young child, she was influenced by country, blues and gospel music. In 1949,at the age of 13, she married Shelby Singleton. In 1958, she made her radio and professional debut on the Louisiana Hayride. In 1960 she moved to the "Jubilee USA," which was the first Country Music Program to be televised nationally and was carried on the ABC Network. Singleton left "Jubilee USA," to go to the stage of the Grand Ole Opry. In 2017, Margie Singleton was inducted to the Independent Country Music Hall of Fame during the Josie Music Awards. Margie lives in Nashville, TN. For more information, please

visit http://margiesingletonmusic.com/

https://www.facebook.com/margie singleton35/ or find her on the wikipedia website.

December 2017

Party continues after Country Music Hall of Fame Inductions

Those attending the Hall of Fame reception after the induction of Jerry Reed, Don Schlitz, and Alan Jackson, included Hall of Fame members such as Bill Anderson, Charlie McCoy, Kris Kristofferson, Randy Travis, Bobby Bare, Bobby Braddock, and Jimmy Fortune (shown in the photo), as well as the family members of deceased Hall of Members.

During the Medallion Ceremony, the audience observed a moment of silence in memory of Hall of Fame members lost in 2017: Glen Campbell, Jo Walker-Meador, and Don Williams.

Jimmy Capps, Michele Capps, Keith Bilbrey, Jan Howard, Emy Joe Bilbrey, Jimmy Fortune, Nina Fortune - Photos by Ron Harman.

Alan Jackson and Jan Howard (inset of them together years ago).

Favorite Christmas CDs

All of these great country Christmas CDs are available online through amazon.com or the artists' websites with the exception of Marty Robbins which is available through CFR. Marty Robbins Christmas CD is $14.95 plus $6.95 shipping and handling and can be ordered by sending a check to P.O. Box 210709, Nashville, TN 37221 (while supplies last).

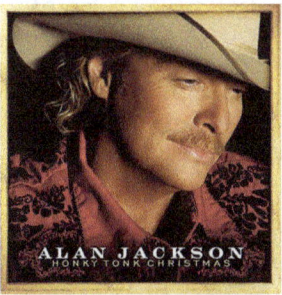

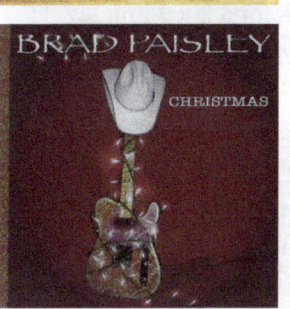

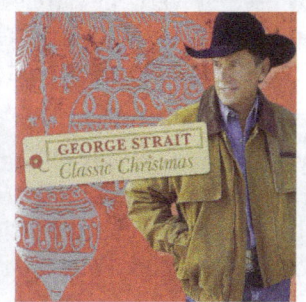

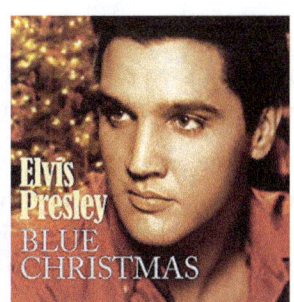

December 2017

There's Something about that song

Color of Christmas is Blue for Country Music Lovers

By Claudia Johnson

Editor's Note: Our series "Something About the Song" explores some of Country's most enduring – and endearing – songs from perennial crowd favorites to career defining recordings to trendsetting tunes.

Many musical genres claim "Blue Christmas" as their own, but the holiday classic was first catapulted to No. 1 by Ernest Tubb during the 1949 Christmas season, solidifying its place as a Country Christmas song.

Despite Tubb's success with the song, it is impossible to think about "Blue Christmas" without hearing those passionate and sad lyrics delivered in the velvet voice of a young Elvis Presley, who was only 22 when he recorded it for his 1957 Christmas album.

"I'll have a blue Christmas without you," the lyrics say, adding, "I'll be so blue thinking about you," followed by the colorful word play that within one sentence takes the gleeful greens and reds of the holidays and forever turns them blue.

"Decorations of red on a green Christmas tree, won't be the same, dear, if you're not here with me."

And that is the crux of the matter. For whatever reason, the singer will not be with the object of his or her affection on Christmas. The song has been called one of unrequited love, but there's evidence it is love known and lost that is being lamented. A verse included on Tubb's original recording but omitted by Presley hints at the loss of a far deeper relationship than the abbreviated song suggests.

"When you say your prayers on this Christmas Eve, will you feel the same dear as when you prayed with me?" the singer asks.

A Christmas classic of another hue, "White Christmas," became a colossal hit for Bing Crosby in the early 1940s, some half a dozen years before "Blue Christmas" was written. "White Christmas" recalls magical Christmas memories of glistening snow, joyful children and sleigh bells, while it wishes listeners equally "merry and bright" holiday experiences. In contrast, with acknowledgement that love is perhaps lost forever, everything in "Blue Christmas" is tinted blue, capturing the depth of sadness the singer is feeling and striking a melancholy cord with anyone whose sense of loss is augmented during the holidays.

"When those blue snowflakes start falling, that's when those blue memories start calling."

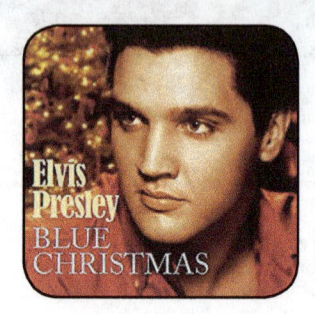

In "Blue Christmas" the singer doesn't wish the former lover a "white Christmas" but simply says, "You'll be doing alright with your Christmas of white, but I'll have a blue, blue, blue Christmas."

Presley's album version was released as a new single in 1964 and became a hit on the British singles chart. At the same time, The Beach Boys recorded a version featuring Brian Wilson on vocals. It reached No. 3 on the U.S. Christmas charts.

In 1974 the song was featured in a children's holiday special called "The Year Without a Santa Claus." The Dean Martin version can be heard in the background as Jim Carrey dresses for a Christmas party in the 2007 movie, "The Number 23," and is also featured in the 2015 film "Wild Card." The Presley version was used by Verizon Wireless for a 2009 holiday commercial. Hit TV show "Glee" showcased the song in its 2011 Christmas episode and included it in the cast's Christmas album.

Written by radio script and commercial jingle writer Jay W. Johnson and set to music by composer Billy Hayes in 1948, "Blue Christmas" was initially recorded by two separate big band leaders, Russ

December 2017

Morgan and Hugo Winterhalter. In addition to Tubb's hit, the song has been recorded dozens of times by a variety of artists representing a plethora of genres. However, it's long been and continues to be a favorite for inclusion on Christmas albums by Country artists and is a staple for Christmas shows and concerts. Some Country singers that have recorded the song include The Browns, Tammy Wynette, Martina McBride, Loretta Lynne, Jim Reeves, Johnny Cash with (and without) the Statler Brothers, Willie Nelson, Marie Osmond, Merle Haggard, Ray Stevens, Wynonna, Brooks and Dunn, Asleep At The Wheel, Anne Murray, Willie Nelson, Jimmy Dean, Vince Gill, Clay Walker and Brenda Lee – just to name a few.

According to the book The Stories Behind Country Music's All-Time Greatest 100 Songs, there was an initial verse penned by the lyricist that was scrapped as the final version took shape.

"I expect to have a colorful Christmas tinged with every kind of holiday hue, and though I know I'll find every shade in the rainbow, this design of mine will be mostly blue."

Though it is beautiful in word and sentiment, the song would have been quite different had the verse remained. The final song is timeless, and the simplicity of its 10 lines that are known by heart by generations of listeners coupled with the intensity of the empty feeling of being without one's beloved at Christmas has made the song as relevant for Christmas 2017 as it was in 1949. That's why it still ranks as the all-time No. 1 Christmas single on Billboard's Country Singles chart.

Visit us on Facebook to tell us about the songs that made a difference in your life.

Q: What are the lyrics to This Old House?

Linda Gerde, Iowa

A: This ole house once knew his children
This ole house once knew his wife
This ole house was home and comfort
As they fought the storms of life
This old house once rang with laughter
This old house heard many shouts
Now he trembles in the darkness
When the lightnin' walks about

[Chorus:]

Ain't a-gonna need this house no longer
Ain't a-gonna need this house no more
Ain't got time to fix the shingles
Ain't got time to fix the floor
Ain't got time to oil the hinges
Nor to mend the windowpane
Ain't a-gonna need this house no longer
He's a-gettin' ready to meet the saints
This ole house is a-gettin' shaky
This ole house is a-gettin' old
This ole house lets in the rain
This ole house lets in the cold
On his knees I'm gettin' chilly
But he feel no fear nor pain

'Cause he see an angel peekin'
Through a broken windowpane

[Chorus]

This ole house is afraid of thunder
This ole house is afraid of storms
This ole house just groans and trembles
When the night wind flings its arms
This ole house is gettin' feeble
This old house is needin' paint
Just like him it's tuckered out
But he's a-gettin' ready to meet the saints

[Chorus]

This ole house dog lies a-sleepin'
He don't know I'm gonna leave
Else he'd wake up by the fireplace
And he'd sit there and howl and grieve
But my huntin' days are over
Ain't gonna hunt the coon no more
Gabriel done brought in my chariot
When the wind blew down the door

[Chorus]

Songwriters: Stuart Hamblen - This Ole House lyrics © Hamblen Music Company

If you have questions send them to Paula, CFR News, P.O. Box 210796, Nashville, TN 37221 or email them to paula@gabrielcommunications.com.

December 2017

The People Who Make Us Laugh

Everyone's Grandpa was Comedic and Musical Entertainer

By Danny Nichols

Known as "Grandpa Jones" to most of the world and remembered for his comedic role on the successful and long-running Hee Haw television series, Louis Marshall Jones was far more than a Country comedian and musician. Television was in its embryotic stage when in 1931 Jones launched his professional career by joining the Pine Ridge String Band that provided musical accompaniment for the popular Lum & Abner nationally syndicated radio show.

By the time "Hee Haw" made the airways in 1969, Jones was 56 years old and had 38 years of entertainment experience behind him. He'd had been a member and regular performer of the Grand Old Opry for 23 years by the time the comedy TV series launched. His career encompassed all 25 years of "Hee Haw" and continued until his 1998 death, with his only professional break being during his WWII military service.

Comedy was ever present with Jones but equaled only by the seriousness of his professionalism.

"When on stage, he owned it," said wife Ramona in an interview with the Tennessean newspaper, adding, "He didn't want any confusion, whispering or talking in the background."

His sense of humor included not only the novelty songs for that he became known for but also for the jokes, poems and stories he loved to tell. Humor was a component of his stage acts but presenting a great musical delivery brought his greatest sense of satisfaction.

The persona and stage name of Grandpa Jones is credited to musician/songwriter Bradley Kincaid, who in 1935 gave Jones the nickname "Grandpa." Legend recounts it came about as a result of listeners writing into the radio station wishing to know the name of the singer with the "old voice." It was Kincaid who was to have responded with the name "Grandpa Jones." Kincaid, however, recalled the name was given to Jones, then 22, because of his off-stage grumpiness at early-morning radio shows. Whichever the case, Jones liked the name and kept it for the remainder of his career.

Roy Clark and Grandpa Jones crack each other up!

Jones learned to play both the guitar and banjo. Yodeling was incorporated into his songs and performances and is likely attributed to Jones' admiration of Jimmie Rodgers whom he idolized. Jones soon learned the entertainment business was highly competitive and that being an entertainer required more than being a performer. He honed the character of Grandpa Jones to include foot stomping and leg kicks while always wearing his pants tucked inside his boots. His approach incorporated a two-pronged approach in winning over his audiences. Just the looks of Grandpa Jones, dressed in his flat round hat, spectacles, white hair and moustache endeared one to this grandfather looking figure. To put the seal on the deal, however, Grandpa delivered with his wit, professionalism and his musical and comedic talents.

December 2017

In 1937, Jones had worked his way to West Virginia where he met entertainer Cousin Emmy (Cynthia May Carver) who taught Jones the clawhammer style of banjo playing. This style fit more readily with the concept of Grandpa Jones as it presented a "rough backwoods flavor" to his performances. Jones preferred the simpler, old time country and gospel songs. In November 1938, Jones married Eulalia Marie Lasher and they became the parents of one child, Marsha Marie born in December 1939. The marriage ended in divorce in 1942.

Jones recorded his first hit song, "It's Raining Here This Morning," in 1944 for King Records. Putting his entertainer career on hold, Jones enlisted in the U.S. Army during World War II and resumed it again in 1946 after his discharge from service. During his career, Jones would record on labels for King Records, RCA, Decca and Monument.

1946 was to have been a pivotal year for Jones with having moved to Nashville, Tennessee in March where he started performing on stage at the Grand Ole Opry. On October 14 of that year he married Ramona Riggins who was also an accomplished performer in her own right. Jones had met Ramona while both worked for WLW Radio in Cincinnati, Ohio. Ramona would perform on stage with Jones for more than 50 years. They became the parents of three children, Mark, Eloise, and Alisa.

Grandpa Jones became a household name in 1969 when he became one of the original cast members of the greatly successful television show "Hee Haw." Featured by himself or with his wife, Ramona, or fellow banjo picker and friend, David "Stringbean" Akeman, Jones enjoyed bringing his brand of entertainment into the homes of millions of Americans. One of his favorite skits involved Buck Owens, Roy Clark, Kenny Price and Jones singing together in the Hee Haw Gospel Quartet. Jones was a serious fan of southern gospel music.

Jones recorded many songs during his career, but he is best remembered for "T For Texas," "Are You From Dixie," "Night Train To Memphis," "Mountain Dew" and "Eight More Miles To Louisville"

Grandpa Jones was inducted into the Country Music Hall of Fame in 1978 and the Kentucky Music Hall of Fame in 2002.

The Country Music Hall of Fame commemorated Grandpa Jones for his "exuberant banjo playing," "infectious verbal comedy" and "one of country music's most dedicated champions of old-time music."

"Jones not only helped keep banjo playing alive during times when it had fallen into disfavor with most professional musicians, but he also helped to keep alive the songs of pioneers like Jimmie Rodgers, Bradley Kincaid, Lulu Belle & Scotty and the Delmore Brothers," the Hall of Fame website observed.

Jones published his autobiography in 1984 and chose for its title, Everybody's Grandpa: Fifty Years Behind The Mike. Jones worked continuously for another 14 years on the Grand Ole Opry. In January 1998, after having giving two show performances at the Opry, Jones suffered two strokes. He passed away on Feb. 19, 1998 in Hermitage, Tennessee at the age of 84.

Grandpa Jones worked diligently throughout his career to bring humor and old-time country music to his fans and audiences. He entertained the world for more than six decades. He will forever be remembered as "Everybody's Grandpa."

ALL the 'Nadine' songs you've watched us perform on 'Larry's Country Diner' now on DVD!

Just $15.00 + $3.00 s/h

Perfect for Christmas gifts!

THREE WAYS TO ORDER!
- Call (307) 578-7909
- Email your request to dansnadinedvd@gmail.com
- Mail check or money order to: Dan Miller, P.O. Box 2288, Cody, WY 82414

December 2017

New Children's Book 'Santa Doesn't Believe In The Tooth Fairy' Available for Christmas

It happened when Ian Black heard a small voice from the back of the minivan say, "Dad, what if I lost my tooth on Christmas Eve and both Santa and the Tooth Fairy came to my house at the same time?"

Ian responded with, "Nathan, that's a great idea for a Christmas book!" From there, an idea was born! He quickly came up with the rest of the story and with the help of his mom, Luann, they came up with what this delightful tale.

Santa resembles Larry Black and the Tooth Fairy resembles Nadine, but that is said to just be coincidence, or maybe not! You decide.

Priced at only $19.95, this 32 page book will have you and your children laughing with every page turn. So buy your copy today and see what really happens when Santa meets the Tooth Fairy for the first time!

Go to https://santatoothfairy.com/ to find out more about this book.

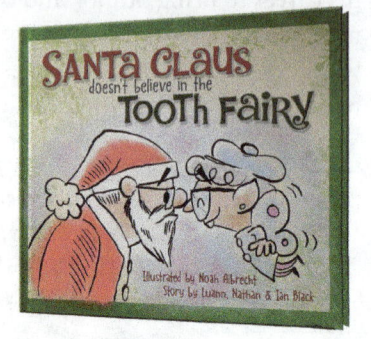

Larry's grandkids LOVE this new book and think Santa and the Tooth Fairy look suspiciously like Larry and Nadine!

LOOKING FOR A GREAT CHRISTMAS GIFT?

Have you ever wondered what would happen if Santa Claus and the Tooth Fairy both showed up at your house at the same time? Well, that's exactly what happened to little Joey who lost his tooth on Christmas Eve. You can't imagine what happens next...

Priced at only $19.95, this 32 page book will have you and your children laughing with every page turn. So buy your copy today and see what really happens when Santa meets the Tooth Fairy for the first time!

To buy your copy go to www.santatoothfairy.com or call 1.800.628.3318

GREAT STOCKING STUFFER!
$19.95 PLUS S/H

December 2017

CountryRoad.TV a new way to watch shows

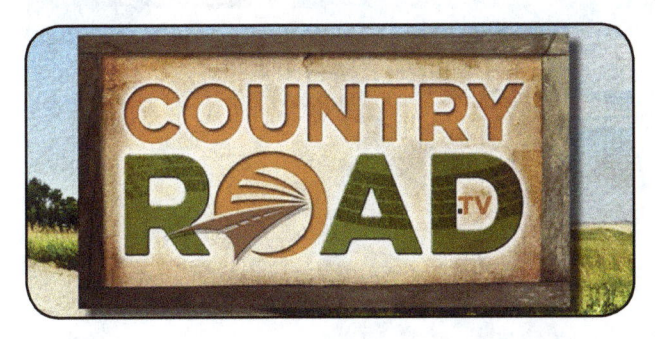

We have officially launched our own online streaming network, www.CountryRoad.TV!!

Imagine having anytime access to ALL of the content you've enjoyed from us over the years... Everything we've ever produced. Full volumes and episodes! If you were to purchase all the DVD series we've created over the past 20 years, it would cost more than $4000... And you can get it all, right now, for $9.99 per month.

Your $9.99 monthly subscription gives you immediate access to over 500+ hours of content to watch whenever you want on your computer, laptop, smartphone, tablet-- even link it to your TV with Roku, Apple TV or Amazon Fire!

Located at www.CountryRoad. TV on the internet, this is an online TV service like no other, not available anywhere else except Country Road TV. We have all the seasons of "Larry's Country Diner," over 20 Years of "Country's Family Reunion," all of Marty Robbin's television specials (including never-before-available content), "The Gene and Moe Show," sports entertainment, special events, and we'll be adding NEW CONTENT all the time! This is a project we've spent the past year getting ready so you can enjoy EVERYTHING we've ever created for one low monthly price.

Now, don't worry if you DON'T have good internet in your area, because you can still subscribe to our Double-Disc-A-Month Club, which provides almost 4 hours of content every month delivered via DVD right to your door. But if you DO have good internet, Country Road TV is the way to go.

We just added our feature movie "Wednesday Night Prayer Meeting Rejoice." Over the next few months, we plan to add more and more unique content that you're sure to love... like the "Roast and Toast of Larry Black," and brand new shows featuring your favorite artists.

Entertainers Love of Food & Restauarants

Dolly Parton's Restaurants Offer More than Food

By Sasha Kay Dunavant

Back in the 1980s, Dolly Parton wanted to create a place where someone could be entertained while they also enjoyed a relaxing and fulfilling meal. Through The Dollywood Company she partnered with Fred Hardwick and the Herschend Family Entertainment Corporation in 1988 to open the doors of the first Dixie Stampede near Parton's home in Pigeon Forge, Tennessee. The entertainment proved to be impeccable, and in 1992 the second location was opened in Myrtle Beach, South Carolina, with a Civil War theme. The original Tennessee location and a second one in Branson, Missouri, that opened in 1995 continue to thrive.

In June of 2003 the forth location of the Dixie Stampede was opened in family friendly Orlando, Florida. A few years later in 2008 the location was purchased and bulldozed by Orlando Premium Outlets to make way for a new strip mall.

The South Carolina location was re-themed by Dollywood Corp. in 2011 as Pirates Voyage Dinner & Show. A four-course BBQ feast is served while Crimson and Sapphire pirates perform epic battle sequences set to Parton's music.

The crowd-interactive production begins with a pre-show about an hour before the colorful extravaganza begins. In Pigeon Forge the pre-show begins with entering into a non-alcohol-serving saloon. Patrons gear up for the show with help from the Americana, Southern Gospel, and Country music played by humorous but skilled musicians during a live performance. The songs include Dixie inspired melodies and a mix of Dolly's top songs.

December 2017

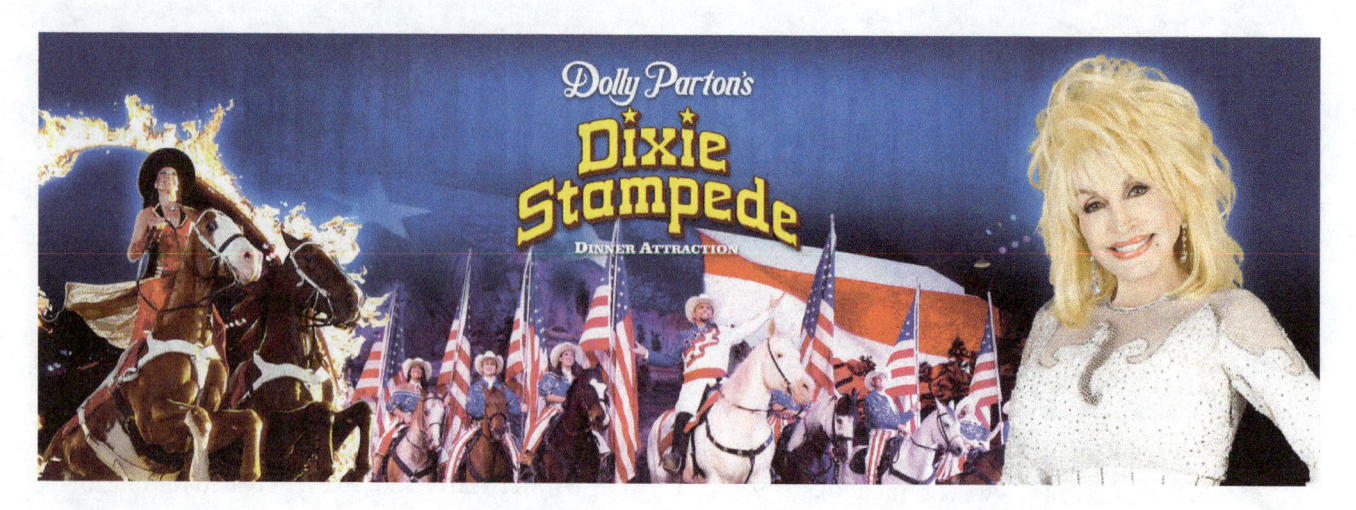

In Branson the pre-show includes music from the White River Wranglers inside the Dixie Stampede's carriage room. The music is similar to that heard at the Pigeon Forge location with wonderful acoustics and early Country music sounds. Before the show customers are asked if they would like to be seated on the North's Union side or the South's Confederate side of the stadium-styled arena. As the show begins cheerful servers dressed in the blue of the Union or Confederate gray begin serving a four-coarse meal. Everyone receives hefty portions including a small rotisserie chicken, hickory smoked pork loin, corn on the cob, a half baked potato or herb roasted potato, vegetable soup, a biscuit and to top it all off, a scrumptious pastry. There are also vegetarian options available at both locations. The show includes two hours of music, sounds, lights, pyrotechnics, intricate costuming, humorous skits, powerful sets, well-trained animals and amazing trick riders. The show has a theatrical quality yet it also displays showmanship and professionalism with a down-home feel

On the official Dixie Stampede website Dolly Parton describes a Christmas experience from when she was a young girl in the Smoky Mountains. She recalls hunting for Christmas trees with her father and hanging stockings by the chimney with her brothers and sisters. There is no doubt that Dolly's vision for her restaurants was to recreate that same festive, family feeling with the special Christmas productions at the Dixie Stampede attractions in Pigeon Forge and Branson, Missouri, which is done each year November 1 through January 1. The pre-show is fun–filled. It offers live music medleys and a chance to purchase holiday non- alcoholic beverages served in a souvenir boot. Nachos and popcorn are readily available for purchase as well. The main event includes a sugar plum fairy that turns toys into life. Santa makes an appearance, and a spectacular living nativity scene is a must-see during the holiday season.

The holiday adventure starts in the Pirates Village with a cast of pirates presenting an entertaining and interactive experience that includes a pirate holiday sing-a-long. Visitors experience the 12 Days of Christmas with a pirate twist – everything from ten crewmen leaping and six Jolly Rogers to a parrot in a palm tree. Kids can be "transformed" in a pirate or mermaid makeover at the Village's Join the Crew area. Finally, guests enter the arena for the main holiday show, a swashbuckling spin on "A Christmas Carol" with Captain Scrooge and his faithful first mate Bob.

Not only has Parton's beautiful voice and lyrics entertained for decades, her family-friendly restaurants create lifetime memories for their visitors.

December 2017